THE COMPLETE BOOK OF
ASIAN
COOKING

THE COMPLETE BOOK OF
ASIAN
COOKING

Edited by
LYDIA DARBYSHIRE

NEW BURLINGTON BOOKS

A QUINTET BOOK

First published by New Burlington Books in
2002
6 Blundell Street
London N7 9BH

ISBN 1-86155-387-0

This book was designed and produced by
Quintet Publishing Limited
6 Blundell Street
London N7 9BH

Designer: Ian Hunt
Art Director: Clare Reynolds
Senior Editor: Anna Briffa
Editor: Lydia Darbyshire

Creative Director: Richard Dewing
Publisher: Oliver Salzmann

Typeset in Great Britain by
Central Southern Typesetters, Eastbourne
Manufactured in China by
Regent Publishing Services Ltd
Printed in China by
Leefung-Asco Printers Ltd

The material in this publication previously
appeared in: *Korean Cooking; Stir Fry Cooking;
The Soy Sauce Cookbook; Vietnamese Cooking;
Japanese Cooking for Two; The Noodle Cookbook;
Chinese Vegetarian Cooking;* and *Thai Cooking.*

Contents

Introduction

The cuisine of southeast Asia has enjoyed a boom in popularity over the past few years, and the sheer diversity of the cooking styles from this enormous geographical area has meant that it is now common to find books on Thai and Indonesian cooking on the shelves in every bookshop along with titles on regional Chinese food as well as books on Korean and Vietnamese cooking.

Japanese cooking has, perhaps, been less well served, and apart from the famous dishes, like tempura and sushi, there are few well-known foods. People invariably think that Japanese cookery and its preparation is an esoteric art, requiring years of training and experience to master. This misunderstanding is a great pity, because Japanese cookery not only encompasses as great a range of flavors and textures as any other country in Asia, but also, for the most part, is easily and quickly prepared.

Thai food has become one of the most popular exotic cuisine in the world. The distinctive flavors, with hints of fresh herbs, coconut, fish sauce, and lemon grass, are the result of a special national talent for blending a great variety of herbs and spices. While remaining identifiably Thai, the cuisine is a synthesis of many Asian influences, incorporating as it does dishes and ideas from India, China, Burma, and the southern countries of Malaysia and Indonesia.

Laos, Cambodia, and Thailand have influenced Vietnamese cuisine, especially in the use of herbs. No Vietnamese meal is complete without there being at least two or three fresh herbs present, either as a garnish or in their own right as part of the meal. The Vietnamese love to wrap up their food in fresh lettuce leaves, and to include one or two herbs in the parcels, especially cilantro, mint, basil, dill, and fennel. Indian and Portuguese travelers brought spices, which developed the combinations that came to be known as curries. The French, who colonized Vietnam, forced the Vietnamese to be inventive, and it is ironic that dishes, such as steamed or stewed chicken feet, which the peasants were forced to devise from leftovers, are now so highly regarded.

The recipes in this book illustrate this diversity of cooking styles. At the same time, they show how the same basic ingredients can be used in subtly different ways to reflect a particular national preference. Many of the recipes, for example, include noodles in one form or another. Noodles are served all over southeastern Asia: you will find them served from stalls by the roadside in the wastes of northern China, in crowded ramen shops in the heart of Tokyo, on the beach in the sandy resorts of Thailand and in villages on the sub-tropical islands of Indonesia. In south and east Asia the noodle is ubiquitous, challenging rice in many areas as the main staple. Prepared in as little as five minutes, the noodle could even stake a claim to the title of the world's first and fastest fast food, although real noodle dishes bear no resemblance to the bland, anemic-looking strands lurking in pot noodle tubs on supermarket shelves.

The recipes that follow take advantage of the enormous variety of ingredients available from all over the world—exotic fruits and vegetables, fragrant spices, herbs, and preserves; contrasting grains and cereals; and quick-to-cook seafood, meat, and poultry. There are suggestions throughout for combining dishes and for substituting better known or more widely available ingredients—also listed in the glossary. Throughout, the emphasis is on authentic-tasting, easily prepared dishes.

Equipment and Techniques

EQUIPMENT

The key piece of equipment is, of course, the cooking pan, and the most important feature is size: a good stir-fry pan must hold a large volume of ingredients, at the same time allowing sufficient room for stirring and turning them during cooking.

WOKS

A wok is the most suitable pan for the majority of stir-fry dishes, but there is a choice of types, from traditional wok pans to electric models.

CARBON STEEL WOK The traditional wok is made from thin, uncoated carbon steel. It is deeply curved, with a stout wooden handle, which is designed for lifting, tilting, and shaking the pan in one hand, leaving the other hand free for using a scoop or spatula to stir the ingredients. The domed pan fits over a flaming brazier in Chinese restaurants, but at home a rack may be used to stabilize a wok on an electric hob or, if necessary, over a gas burner. However, depending on the pan stands on a gas hob, the rack may be redundant.

This type of wok conducts heat well, provides a large surface area for cooking, and is highly responsive to changes in heat. However, a carbon steel wok must be used regularly and kept oiled to prevent rusting between use. A new pan should be washed in hot soapy water to remove any protective coating, then tempered or seasoned. This is done by heating a small amount of oil in the wok, and rubbing it over the surface of the pan, until smoking hot but not burning. The pan should be wiped out with absorbent kitchen paper. The outside and any exposed metal around the edge of the handle must be oiled. Wipe with clean absorbent kitchen paper before storage and use. After each use, the pan must be wiped out and oiled before it is stored.

Depending on the food cooked, there are two ways of cleaning the pan. For most oil-based cooking, wipe it out with absorbent kitchen paper, then sprinkle in some salt and pour in a little oil. Heat this and remove the pan from the heat. Use a pad of absorbent kitchen paper to clean the wok—the salt acts as a scouring agent and removes food residues. Wipe out all the oil and salt, then heat the wok again with a little fresh oil before wiping it clean. If the food has left a cooked-on coating of sauce, the pan must be washed, dried, and tempered.

Keep this kind of wok for vegetable stir-frys and dishes containing small amounts of meat and grains. The carbon steel pan is not suitable for stir-frying fruit.

STAINLESS STEEL AND NONSTICK PANS These pans are far easier to look after than the carbon steel versions. They can be washed in hot soapy water, dried, and stored according to the manufacturer's instructions.

The quality of pans varies widely. In general, they are all slightly less responsive to changes in heat than carbon steel. Unlike carbon steel woks—when the cheapest can be excellent—price is often a good guide of quality in this group.

Consider the shape of the pan. Many are smaller than expected of a traditional wok, and they may have very flat bases, putting them more on a par with a skillet than a wok. A pan with a small, quite flat base may not be the best buy, and a large, conventional skillet with a deep sides may provide more surface area for cooking. Before you buy, check

Two designs of wok. The brush can be used to oil woks, and the strainers are useful accessories.

Metal stirring utensils.

the instructions that go with the pan, because some nonstick finishes are not ideal for the majority of stir-frying. Inexpensive nonstick finishes can deteriorate rapidly when used over a high heat and when the food is stirred constantly, even when the correct utensils are used.

SKILLETS

A wok is not essential for stir-frying. If you use a skillet it must be large, with deep sides. Ideally, choose a pan with slightly sloping sides and a curved edge around the base, which allows the food to be turned more easily.

A sauté pan is usually large with deep sides and, since sautéing is similar to stir-frying in that the food is cooked over high heat and stirred during cooking, this type of pan is suitable for stir-frying.

Heavy, nonstick, coated cast iron pans can be used for stir-frying, but they usually have to be heated slowly and kept over a medium rather than a high heat. The manufacturer may state that the pan should not be heated empty; therefore a coating of oil or fat should be added. The pan may be used for stir-frying once hot, but the heat is not as fierce and the pan is not as responsive, taking a long time to react to changes in temperature. These pans are suitable for stir-frying fruit or other ingredients that are not necessarily cooked over fierce heat.

CHOPPING BOARDS

Have a very large chopping board that can be scrubbed in hot soapy water. For the sake of food safety and hygiene, remember that wood is absorbent and easily damaged, allowing food particles to be trapped and bacteria to grow. If you do have a wooden board, scrub it in very hot water, using a mild solution of bleach or an abrasive cleaner. Rinse and

dry thoroughly after every use. Plastic-coated boards are non-absorbent and therefore less likely to be a food safety risk. However, these too must be scrubbed after each use to clean them.

KNIVES

Preparing much Asian food involves time-consuming chopping and slicing, so good-quality, sharp knives are important. Never buy a knife by looks and technical information alone. Pick it up and feel it; hold it as if you were going to cut with it to feel if it is comfortable in your hand and if it is balanced.

A food processor, mandolin slicer, or grater can be used and, for wafer-thin slices, a potato peeler is useful. A sharp knife is also needed for slicing and scoring meat and poultry.

CLEAVERS

These usually have wooden handles and come in three weights: light, medium, and heavy. They are made of either tempered carbon steel or stainless steel. The former is preferable since it is harder and maintains a sharper cutting edge for longer. For all cutting and chopping, the sharper the cutting edge the better your results.

BAMBOO STEAMERS

The advantage of having bamboo steamers is that they can be stacked one on top of the other so that several dishes can be cooked at the same time. They are particularly useful for warming up leftovers.

RICE COOKER

Because of the amount of rice that is consumed in many Asian households, city dwellers now often use electric rice cookers to cook the rice perfectly every time and to keep it hot.

SHINSOLLO

In Korean cooking, a special bronze or brass pot is used for preparing the dish of the same name. The pot has a central funnel in which hot charcoal is placed to keep the food hot.

TABLE-TOP COOKER

Small table-top burners, fueled by small butane gas canisters, are often used for both cooking and keeping dishes warm. Metal grids are used for cooking the food directly over the flame.

TECHNIQUES

The secret of success with most Asian dishes is in careful preparation, especially cutting and slicing the ingredients. Before you begin, make sure that all vegetables are clean before cutting and cooking. Drain them in a colander or sieve, and mop them on absorbent paper to prevent splitting.

PREPARATION AND CUTTING

Because most of the dishes are quickly cooked, all ingredients should be cut to cook evenly.

Slicing.

SLICES Whether the slices are thick or thin, which will depend on how much cooking is required and the finished texture, they must be even.

DIAGONAL SLICES Cut slices at an angle. For example, scallions and celery stalks should have the end cut off at an angle, then all the slices should be cut at an angle to give evenly thick, slanting slices.

Diagonal slices.

Matchstick strips.

FINGERS OR STICKS Cut fairly thick slices, then cut these into fingers or sticks. Cucumbers and zucchini should be cut into lengths, then quartered lengthwise.

THIN STICKS Finer than fingers, but not as delicate as matchstick strips, these are about ¼ inch thick.

MATCHSTICK STRIPS Literally the size of matchsticks, these should be fine and even. They cook very quickly and are useful for a garnish.

SHREDDED Cut into thin slices, then across into fine pieces. Firm cabbage and similar leaves can be shredded by cutting into chunks, then thinly slicing.

GRATED Use the coarse blade on a grater and discard the last, small chunk, which cannot be processed.

Shredding.

Chopping.

CHOPPED Cut slices, thin sticks, then cut across to chop the ingredient. Halve and slice an onion, then cut across the slices so that they fall into small, reasonably even pieces. This is not as even as dicing. The pieces should be small, unless roughly chopped, when they can be slightly larger and less even. Chop herbs by using a large, sharp knife and a guillotine action.

DICED Cut into small, even cubes, about ¼ inch or slightly larger.

CUBED Cut larger cubes than are required for dice, between ½ and 1 inch, but even in size.

CHUNKS Slightly larger than cubes and less even. There is no need to trim the food into neat squares.

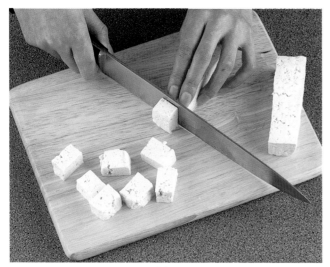

Dicing.

EATING ASIAN STYLE

In most Far Eastern countries, including China, Thailand, Korea, and Japan, people sit around a low table to eat. Every person has their own rice bowl—in Korea this is traditionally made of brass and lidded—and chopsticks are used for eating.

All the dishes for a meal are served at once, and often, particularly for dinner, which is the main meal of the day, there will be quite a few. In Korea, for example, a simply family dinner might include about twenty side dishes (*panchan*), containing a tempting array of seasoned raw or lightly cooked vegetables (*namuls*), dishes containing dried vegetables or shrimp, salted fish, and roast seaweed (*nibles*), and dipping sauces and *kimchi*, of which there will be at least one and probably four or more. Soup is an essential element of every meal, and there will also probably be some flour- and egg-coated fried vegetables (*jon*). More substantial fish, meat, and poultry dishes are served in what would be considered small amounts in the West, but with such variety on offer, large portions of any one dish are unnecessary.

Lunch is a lighter meal of noodles or rice mixed with vegetables, or another grain or beans for protein. Breakfast is traditionally almost as large a meal as dinner, although these days it tends to be lighter.

A similar arrangement occurs in Japan, where the concept of serving a succession of dishes, as happens in the West, is alien to traditional. All the dishes are served as a "set," with the exception of the dessert, which is not regarded as an integral part of the meal, although fresh fruits are often provided at the end, together with green tea. A true Japanese meal always includes rice, a soup, and a small dish of Japanese pickles, which are accompanied by a main dish of fish or meat together with a small side dish. A dinner party would be achieved by adding a second side dish and, perhaps, a second main dish. A thoughtful host will attempt to vary each of the dishes, so that the meal will combine as many different flavors, textures, and types of preparation as possible.

If you are wondering how the cook manages to juggle the preparation and serving of so many dishes, remember that Japanese cooks make most of the dishes well in advance and re-heat them as necessary. Some are served warm rather than hot. Some dishes, such as *sukiyaki*, soups, and noodles, are cooked at the table and should always be fresh and hot.

USING CHOPSTICKS

Using chopsticks is no more difficult than using a knife and fork, as long as they are held correctly. Think of your chopsticks as jaws that have been turned upside down. The lower chopstick, clamped between the tip of your ring finger, inner joint of your thumb, and the knuckle of your index finger, remains fixed in the same position during eating. The upper chopstick is held in the tips of the middle and index fingers and thumb, so that it can be opened and closed in relation to the lower chopstick.

There are several principles of etiquette that should be observed when eating with chopsticks, such as not passing food between chopsticks, and not using your chopsticks to pull a dish toward you or to push it away from you.

Position of lower chopstick.

Position of upper chopstick.

Using chopsticks.

LEFT Chopsticks and their accessories are always ornamental and decorative.

Appetizers

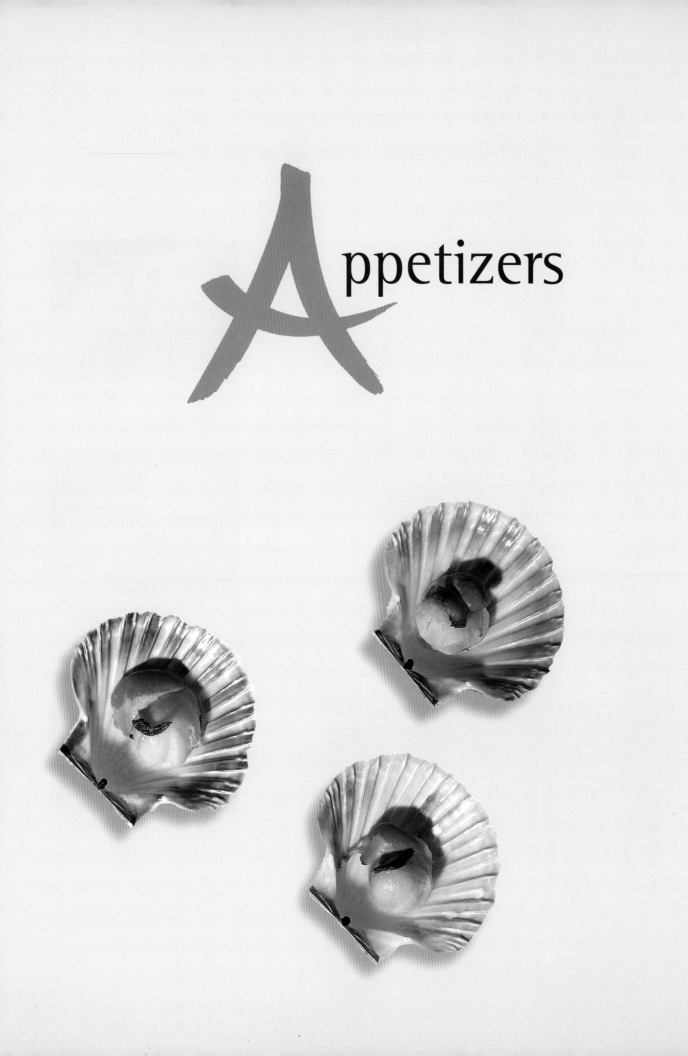

Asian cuisine as a whole includes an immense variety of dishes that can be served in small portions at the start of a meal as appetizers or as part of a buffet-style meal. Spring rolls, for example, are a perfect starter, or they can be served as part of a main meal or as a buffet dish. The great advantage of many of these dishes is that they are served cold, which means that they can be prepared and cooked in advance, leaving the cook free to concentrate on the other courses of the meal. They can also be served as snacks, to accompany drinks, in place of peanuts, or potato chips.

Fresh Spring Rolls

SERVES 4–6

Although they are rather time-consuming to prepare, the results are a nice change from the popular, fried spring rolls.

2 Chinese sweet sausages (combined weight 4 oz)

7 oz firm bean curd

1 packed cup crabmeat

2 Tbsp peanut or corn oil

2 eggs, beaten lightly

4 oz cucumber

8–12 spring roll wrappers (or crêpes; add 1 Tbsp cornstarch to a standard recipe)

6 cups bean sprouts, blanched lightly

7 oz scallions

FOR THE SPRING ROLL SAUCE

1 cup chicken broth

⅓ cup palm sugar

¼ cup tamarind juice

1 Tbsp cornstarch

● Steam the Chinese sausages for about 8 minutes and then the bean curd for about 3 minutes. Remove and cut both into long pieces, about the width of a pencil and about 4 inches long. Steam the crabmeat for 5 minutes and set aside.

● Heat a non-stick, shallow pan over medium heat, add a drop of oil and just enough egg to cover the bottom—it should resemble a thin pancake. Cook for a minute on each side. Make 8–12 thin omelets in the same way. Roll them up and slice them into lengths the same size as the sausage and bean curd. Cut the cucumber and scallions into similar lengths too.

● Take each spring roll wrapper or crêpe, lay it flat and place on a piece of bean curd, sausage, cucumber, and scallions. Add 1 teaspoon of crab, several strips of egg, and some bean sprouts. Roll up carefully and cut each into 3 lengths.

● Place all the sauce ingredients, except the cornstarch, in a pan, and boil for 5 minutes. Add the cornstarch mixed with a drop of water, boil for 1 minute and take off the heat.

● Serve cold or steamed for 1–2 minutes. Sprinkle with more crab to serve, a teaspoon of spring roll sauce, and extra chopped scallion if liked. Serve the sauce alongside.

Vegetarian Spring Rolls

SERVES 4

These spring rolls are ideal for a buffet-style meal or as cocktail snacks.

1 pack of 20 frozen spring roll skins

8 oz fresh bean sprouts

8 oz young tender leeks or scallions

4 oz carrots

4 oz white mushrooms

oil for deep-frying

1½ tsp salt

1 tsp sugar

1 Tbsp light soy sauce

● Take the spring roll skins out of the packet and leave them to defrost thoroughly under a damp cloth.

● Wash and rinse the bean sprouts in a bowl of cold water and discard the husks and other bits and pieces that float to the surface. Drain.

● Cut the leeks or scallions, carrots, and mushrooms into thin shreds.

● Heat 3–4 tablespoons of oil in a preheated wok or skillet and stir-fry all the vegetables for a few seconds. Add the salt, sugar, and soy sauce and continue stirring for about 1–1½ minutes. Remove and leave to cool a little.

● Heat about 6⅓ cups oil in a wok or deep fryer until it smokes. Reduce the heat or even turn it off for a few minutes to cool the oil a little before adding the spring rolls.

● Deep-fry 6–8 at a time for 3–4 minutes or until golden and crispy. Increase the heat to high again before frying each batch. As each batch is cooked, remove and drain it on absorbent paper.

● Serve hot with a dip sauce such as soy sauce, vinegar, chili sauce, or mustard.

Shrimp Crystal Spring Rolls

SERVES 4

6 oz cooked crispy roast pork or 4 fresh boneless pork streaky rashers

3 Tbsp clear honey

2 Tbsp dry sherry

1 tsp chili powder

8 oz rice vermicelli

1 lb fresh shrimp, cooked and halved

6 oz cooked chicken, finely chopped

3 pickled onions, cut into fine strips

3 pickled cucumbers, cut into fine strips

1 carrot, grated

1 packet of round *Banh Trang* rice paper

FOR THE DIPPING SAUCE

½ cup fish sauce

1 red chile pepper, finely chopped

1 clove garlic, finely chopped

2–3 tbsp lemon juice

2 tsp wine vinegar

2 tsp ginger wine

1 tsp sugar

TO SERVE

1 Iceberg lettuce

sprigs of cilantro

sprigs of mint

● To make the cold crispy pork, take the fresh pork. Mix the honey, dry sherry, and chili powder. Spread the mixture over the pork. Allow to rest for 1 hour. Grill the pork slices until really crisp. Turn often so that they are evenly cooked. Allow to cool and cut into thin strips.

● Make the dipping sauce by combining all the ingredients and mixing thoroughly.

● Soak the rice vermicelli in boiled water, slightly cooled. When soft, drain thoroughly and leave to cool.

● Place a clean dish towel on your working surface. Dip single sheets of *Banh Trang* into warm water and place on the dish towel. They should be pliable and soft. Place some cold vermicelli, some shrimp, chicken, pork, pickled onion, pickled cucumber, and carrot near the center of the *Banh Trang* but toward the bottom edge. Spread out the filling to a sausage shape. Roll up the bottom edge of the *Banh Trang* and tuck tightly under the mixture. Fold the left and right sides into the center and continue rolling away from you. This roll will be transparent and allow you to see the mixture inside. Repeat for the remaining mixture.

● Place the cold, rolled, transparent spring rolls on a platter. Guests help themselves to lettuce leaves, one at a time. The roll is placed on the leaf and some mint and cilantro are added. The whole is rolled up and dipped in the dipping sauce.

Shrimp Fried with Garlic and Pepper

SERVES 4

approx ½ cup peanut or corn oil for frying

11 oz large shrimp, shelled

½ Tbsp garlic, lightly chopped

2 Tbsp ground white pepper

1 tsp salt

● Heat the oil in a pan or wok, add the shrimp, and brown lightly for about 2 minutes.

● Remove all but a quarter of the oil and add the garlic, pepper, and salt to the shrimp in the pan. Fry lightly for 2 more minutes until brown.

● Drain off most of the remaining oil and serve immediately, accompanied by rice and sliced cucumber.

Shrimp Crystal
Spring Rolls

Beef Crystal Spring Rolls

SERVES 4

FOR THE MARINADE

1 tsp lemon grass, finely minced

1 tsp garlic, finely minced

1 Tbsp ginger wine

8 oz steak, cut against the grain into pieces ⅛ in thick and 2 in long

6 oz rice vermicelli

2 pickled onions, finely cut

2 pickled cucumbers, finely cut

1 carrot, grated

1 packet round *Banh Trang* rice paper

warmed water in a bowl on the table

FOR THE DIPPING SAUCE

4 Tbsp fish sauce

1 red chile pepper, finely chopped

1 clove garlic, finely chopped

1 Tbsp lime or lemon juice

1 tsp wine vinegar

1 tsp sugar

2 tsp dry sherry

TO SERVE

1 Iceberg or round lettuce

sprigs of cilantro

● Combine the marinade ingredients together and marinate the beef slices. Leave for 2–3 hours. Soak the rice vermicelli. When soft, drain thoroughly. Toss the cold rice vermicelli, pickled onion, pickled cucumber, and carrot together and place on the table in a dish.

● Prepare the dipping sauce by mixing all the sauce ingredients together and stir well. Put the lettuce leaves in a dish, the cilantro and mint on a flat plate, and place on the table. Put the *Banh Trang* on a plate and place on the table.

● Put warm water in a bowl that is large enough for the *Banh Trang* to be dipped in on the table. Put either a table-top barbecue or a fondue on the table and bring the marinated meat to the table. Guests should help themselves by dipping a *Banh Trang* into the warm water until it becomes soft and pliable. They then place some of the vermicelli and pickle, mint and cilantro, and the cooked pieces of beef on the *Banh Trang*. The mixture is then rolled up and placed on a fresh piece of lettuce. The lettuce leaf is rolled around it and then dipped in the sauce.

Beef Satay

SERVES 4

2 cloves garlic, crushed and sliced

1 tsp fresh basil

1 red chile pepper, sliced

1 Tbsp lime juice

1 Tbsp sesame oil

1 Tbsp fish sauce (optional)

½ lb steak, cubed

FOR THE DIPPING SAUCE

3 Tbsp fish sauce

1 Tbsp lime or lemon juice

1 pickled onion, thinly sliced

1 clove garlic, finely chopped

1 Tbsp peanuts, finely chopped

● Mix the garlic, basil, chile, lime juice, sesame oil, and fish sauce, if using, together. Marinate the cubes of beef in this for at least 4 hours, turning frequently.

● Make the dipping sauce by mixing all the ingredients thoroughly. Place it in a bowl on the table.

● When the beef is ready, thread onto four skewers and place on the barbecue or under a preheated high broiler until cooked, turning frequently. Baste equally frequently with the marinade.

Golden Baskets

SERVES 4–6

A classy opening dish, these crisp, deep-fried batter cases can also be offered as a delicate snack. The only problem can be finding a suitable metal mold; a tiny ladle might do, but the dimensions should be no more than a couple of inches across. The Thai molds are made from brass. You can make these cases in advance; sealed in an airtight jar, they will keep for a long time.

FOR THE BATTER

½ cup rice flour

6 Tbsp all-purpose flour

4 Tbsp thin coconut milk

2 Tbsp tapioca flour

1 egg yolk

¼ tsp sugar

¼ tsp salt

¼ tsp baking soda

approx. 4 cups peanut or corn oil for deep-frying

FOR THE FILLING

2 Tbsp peanut or corn oil

4 Tbsp onion, finely diced

1 cup pork or chicken, finely chopped

¼ cup corn kernels

2 tsp raw potato, finely diced

2 Tbsp carrot, finely diced

2 Tbsp sugar

¼ tsp black soy sauce

½ tsp salt

½ tsp ground white pepper

FOR THE GARNISH

sprigs of cilantro

1 fresh small red chile, sliced finely into circles

● Mix all the batter ingredients together well in a bowl. Heat the oil in a pan or wok to about 180°F. Dip the molds in the oil to heat up, remove and pat lightly with paper towel. Dip the outside of the molds into the batter and quickly into the hot oil again. Fry until light brown, about 5–8 minutes, remove the cups from the molds and place on paper towels to dry. Repeat to make 20–25 cups.

● Now make the filling. Put the 2 tablespoons oil in a hot wok or pan, add the onion and pork, and stir-fry for 2 minutes. Add the rest of the ingredients and fry until the vegetables are fairly soft, about 3 minutes. Take off the heat and allow to cool.

● Divide the filling among the batter cups. Garnish with cilantro leaves and small pieces of fresh red chile. Serve as an hors d'oeuvre or with cocktails.

Shrimp and Ground Pork on Sugar Cane

SERVES 4

1 Tbsp dried shrimp (optional)

1⅓ cups peeled shrimp

¾ cup ground pork

1 small onion, finely chopped

2 Tbsp cilantro leaves, finely chopped

salt and pepper

1 Tbsp fish sauce

1 egg, beaten

4 x 6 in lengths of sugar cane or bamboo skewers

all-purpose flour or cornstarch (optional)

vegetable oil for deep-frying (optional)

butterhead lettuce

● If using dried shrimp, soak for about 1 hour in warm water. Squeeze out excess water and chop finely. Wash the fresh shrimp and chop finely.

● Put the ground pork into a large bowl. Add the onion, cilantro, fresh and dried shrimp, salt and pepper, and fish sauce.

● Pour the egg into the pork and shrimp mixture, and mix well with your hand. The mixture should come together so that it can be molded around the lengths of sugar cane or around bamboo skewers. If it is too runny, sift a little all-purpose flour or cornstarch into the mixture.

● Peel the sugar cane, leaving 1 inch of the green covering on at each end, or 2 inches at one end. Mold the mixture on to the peeled part of the sugar cane.

● Broil the sticks under a moderately hot broiler, turning to ensure evenness in the cooking. Make sure that the sugar cane does not burn. Alternatively, deep-fry in hot oil for 4–5 minutes.

● Serve on a bed of lettuce. The sugar cane should be chewed or sucked as you eat the shrimp and pork.

Shrimp with Sesame Seeds on Toast

SERVES 4

4 Tbsp white sesame seeds

½ tbsp dried shrimp (optional)

1 cup peeled shrimp, finely chopped

2 cloves garlic, crushed and chopped

½ tsp fresh gingerroot, grated

1 small onion, grated

1 small egg, beaten

salt and black pepper

cornstarch for dusting

1 thin French stick or 8 slices bread, crusts cut off

vegetable oil for deep-frying

● Toast the sesame seeds in a dry wok or skillet until they begin to brown, shaking frequently to prevent them from burning.

● If using dried shrimp, soak in warm water until soft. Drain thoroughly and squeeze out excess water. Chop them finely.

● Combine the dried and fresh shrimp, garlic, ginger, grated onion, egg, salt, and black pepper, and knead together with your hands. The mixture should be stiff but not too stiff to spread. If it is too runny, dust with the cornstarch.

● Cut the French bread into ½ in slices or cut the slices of bread into triangles or shape using pastry cutters. Press the sesame seeds firmly into the shrimp mixture, using the back of a wooden spoon so that the shrimp mixture is also pressed firmly onto the bread. Refrigerate for 2 hours or longer if possible.

● Heat just enough oil to deep-fry the rounds, shrimp side down, for 1 minute. Using a pancake turner, turn carefully and fry the other side for a further minute. Drain on paper towels and serve hot.

Thai Hors d'oeuvre

SERVES 6–8

A hard-to-find treat in Thailand, but always enjoyed. The Thais use fresh tree and vine leaves, but lettuce does just as well.

5 Tbsp unsweetened grated coconut, roasted in a 350°F oven until light brown

3 Tbsp shallots, finely diced

3 Tbsp lime, finely diced

3 Tbsp gingerroot, diced

3 Tbsp dried shrimp, chopped

3 Tbsp unsalted roasted peanuts

2 tsp fresh small green chiles, chopped

1 lettuce or bunch of edible vegetable leaves

FOR THE SAUCE

2 Tbsp unsweetened grated coconut

½ Tbsp shrimp paste

½ tsp galangal, sliced

½ tsp shallot, sliced

3 Tbsp unsalted peanuts, chopped

2 Tbsp dried shrimp, chopped

1 tsp ginger, sliced

1 cup palm sugar

2½ cups water

● Make the sauce. Roast the coconut, shrimp paste, galangal, and shallot in a 350°F oven for 5 minutes until fragrant, and cool. Place with the peanuts, shrimp, and ginger in a blender or food processor and finely chop.

● Transfer the mixture to a heavy-bottomed pan with the sugar and water, mix well and bring to a boil. Simmer until it is reduced to about 1¼ cups. Remove from the heat and leave to cool.

● To serve, pour the sauce into a serving bowl and arrange all the ingredients in separate piles on a platter or in small bowls.

● To eat, take a lettuce leaf, place a small amount of each of the garnishes in the middle, top with a spoonful of sauce and fold up into a little package.

Scallops Broiled in Pork Fat with Fish Sauce

SERVES 4

4 scallops, cleaned

½ tsp salt

juice of 1 lime or lemon

1 piece fresh pork fat or rind of 8 bacon slices

4 Tbsp fish sauce

● Cover the scallops with water and add the salt and lime or lemon juice. Simmer for 1–2 minutes (do not overcook). Remove the scallops from the liquid and drain them.

● Place each scallop in a shell or heatproof dish, place some pork or bacon rind on the scallops and put under a preheated high broiler for at most 4 minutes. The pork fat should drip down on to the scallops, giving them a smoky pork flavor.

● Remove and serve with the fish sauce.

Crispy Anchovies

SERVES 4

The dried anchovies for this dish are about the size of European whitebait and are deep-fried in the same way. They can be found in most Japanese stores. If the anchovies are very salty, rub or rinse off excess salt before frying. Deep-fried anchovies mixed with a sweet/hot sauce which contrasts with their saltiness, are extremely moreish.

1 garlic clove, finely chopped

1 small onion, chopped

1 fresh red chile, seeded

¾ tsp salt

1½ tsp sugar

2 Tbsp vegetable oil, plus extra for deep-frying

about 4 oz dried anchovies, heads removed if liked, rinsed if necessary

FOR THE GARNISH

fresh cilantro leaves

● Grind the garlic, onion, and chile to a paste with the salt. Mix in the sugar. Set aside.

● Heat the vegetable oil in a skillet. Add the onion paste and cook, stirring occasionally, for 3–4 minutes.

● Meanwhile, half fill a deep-fat fryer with vegetable oil and heat to 350°F. Add the anchovies so the pan is not crowded (in batches if necessary), and fry for 20–30 seconds until very crisp and lightly colored.

● Transfer the anchovies to paper towels to drain, then tip into the skillet and heat through, shaking the pan. Pour into a serving bowl and garnish with cilantro leaves.

Deep-fried Chicken Nuggets

SERVES 2

The mixture of garlic, ginger, and soy sauce enhances the taste of the chicken, with the sliced lemon giving refreshing "bite" to these delicious nuggets.

2 boneless chicken breasts, cut into bite-sized cubes

FOR THE MARINADE

3 Tbsp soy sauce

1 oz gingerroot, peeled and grated

2 large garlic cloves, peeled and grated

salt and freshly ground black pepper

FOR THE COATING

2 Tbsp cornstarch

2 Tbsp all-purpose flour

vegetable oil, for deep frying

FOR THE GARNISH

2 slices lemon

● Marinate the chicken with the soy sauce, ginger, garlic, salt, and pepper for 30 minutes.

● Mix the cornstarch with the flour. Take each piece of chicken from the marinade and roll in the flour mixture until completely coated.

● Heat the oil to 350°F and deep-fry the chicken pieces for 4–5 minutes or until golden brown.

● Garnish with the sliced lemon and serve on a bed of salad leaves.

Chicken Satay

SERVES 4

2 Tbsp coconut cream or plain yogurt

1 clove garlic, crushed

1 tsp chili powder

1 tsp ground cumin

1 tsp ground coriander

1 Tbsp lemon juice

½ lb fresh chicken, cubed

FOR THE DIPPING SAUCE

2 Tbsp coconut cream or plain yogurt

1 clove garlic, crushed

½ tsp ground cumin

1 tsp ground ginger

1 tsp ground coriander

1 Tbsp lemon juice

1 Tbsp chopped fresh mint

● Combine the coconut cream or yogurt with the garlic, chili powder, cumin, coriander, and lemon juice. Marinate the chicken pieces in the mixture for at least 4 hours, turning frequently.

● Make the dipping sauce by mixing together all the ingredients except the mint. Leave to blend in a cool place.

● When the chicken is ready, thread it onto four skewers. Place on the barbecue or under a preheated high broiler and cook until well done, basting frequently with the marinade and turning.

● Heat the dipping sauce and toss in the mint leaves. Serve separately.

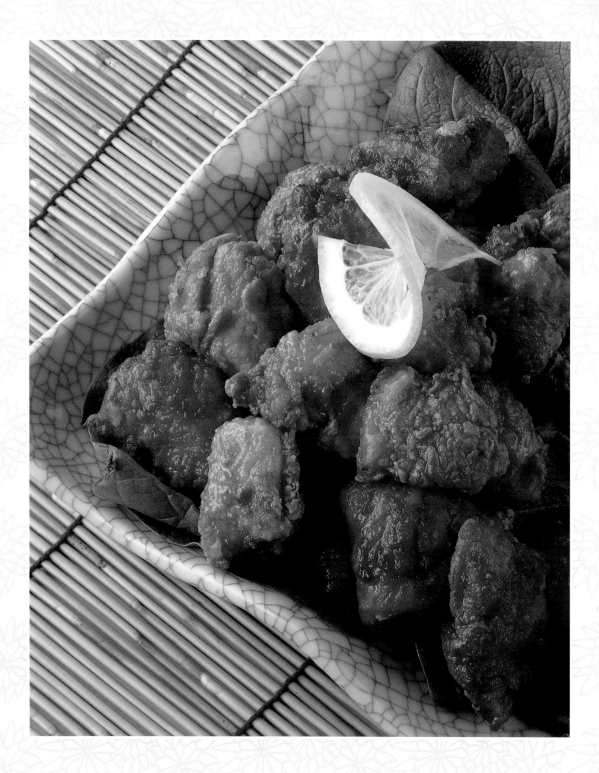

Deep-fried Chicken Nuggets

Shrimp and Scallop Satay

SERVES 4

Satay was probably introduced into Vietnam by traders from India. Bite-sized pieces of succulent meat, seafood, poultry, or vegetables are seasoned and cooked over charcoal. A dipping sauce is always presented with the satay.

⅔ cup dry sherry or dry white wine

1 Tbsp wine vinegar

1 Tbsp dill, chopped

salt to taste

12 large scallops, washed

12 large shrimp in their shells

1 cucumber, cut into ½ in slices

FOR THE DIPPING SAUCE

1 large onion, finely chopped

2 Tbsp vegetable oil

2 cloves garlic, chopped and crushed

2 fresh red chile peppers, finely chopped

6 tomatoes, skinned

1 Tbsp sweet basil, chopped

● Place the sherry, vinegar, dill, and salt in a pan and bring to a boil. Reduce the heat to a simmer and add the scallops. Allow to simmer for 2 minutes. Remove the scallops and keep the liquid to use as the baste when barbecuing.

● Skewer the shrimp, cucumber, and scallops alternately so that each skewer has three shrimp, three scallops, and three pieces of cucumber. Leave, covered, in a refrigerator.

● Gently fry the onions in the oil for 3 minutes. Add the garlic and fry for a further minute. Add the chile and tomatoes and fry for another 5 minutes. Add the basil leaves and stir. Remove from the heat and leave to cool.

● Place the satay on the barbecue or under a preheated high broiler and cook for 3–4 minutes on each side. Baste with the reserved cooking liquid.

Mushroom Satay

SERVES 4

1 clove garlic, crushed

1 tsp fresh ginger, ground

1 tsp fresh lemon grass, ground, or grated lemon peel

1 Tbsp fresh cilantro, chopped

2 Tbsp fish sauce (optional)

1 Tbsp sesame oil

16 firm white mushrooms

FOR THE DIPPING SAUCE

3 Tbsp roasted peanuts or 3 tbsp crunchy peanut butter

1 red chile pepper, finely chopped

1 clove garlic, minced

1 Tbsp mint, finely chopped

1 Tbsp lime or lemon juice

3 Tbsp fish sauce or 3 Tbsp light soy sauce mixed with 1 tsp anchovy extract

2 Tbsp sesame oil

½ cup thin coconut milk

● Mix the garlic, ginger, lemon grass, cilantro, fish sauce, if used, and sesame oil. Marinate the mushrooms in the mixture for 3–4 hours, turning frequently during this time.

● Make the dipping sauce by mixing together and pounding all the dipping sauce ingredients, except for the coconut milk, to make a rough paste. Stir in the coconut milk.

● Thread the mushrooms onto four skewers. Place on the barbecue or under a preheated high broiler for about 3 minutes on either side, basting with the marinade. Serve hot with the dipping sauce.

Deep-fried Mackerel

SERVES 2

*The mackerel is one of the mainstays of the Japanese diet and can be prepared in numerous ways. **Age-mono**, or deep-frying, locks in the mackerel's oils, and this gives its flesh a meat-like quality.*

1 lb mackerel, head removed and gutted

1 Tbsp soy sauce

½ Tbsp *sake*

½ fresh chile, seeded and finely chopped

½ in cube gingerroot, crushed

2–3 Tbsp cornstarch

vegetable oil, for deep-frying

● Cut the mackerel in half, slicing close to one side of the back bone. Repeat on the other side to give two fillets separated from the back bone. Remove as many bones from the fillets as possible without spoiling the flesh (a pair of tweezers is helpful). Cut each fillet into three pieces.

● Put the soy sauce, *sake*, chile, and ginger into a dish and marinate the fish for 20 minutes.

● Dry the fish, using paper towels, then coat in the cornstarch. Heat the oil to 350°F, then deep-fry the fish for about 4 minutes.

● Serve with stir-fried vegetables and sprinkle with soy sauce.

Spicy Squid

SERVES 4

When the pieces of squid are stir-fried they curl to expose the diamond cuts. The tentacles may be used or not as preferred. The choice of cooking oil is important in order to achieve a high temperature and satisfactorily crisp results.

12 squid, cleaned	2 tsp sesame oil
juice of 1 lemon	⅓ cup peanut oil
1 green chile, seeded and chopped	1 red bell pepper, diced
¼ tsp five-spice powder	4 scallions, thinly sliced
2 garlic cloves, crushed	⅓ cup soy sauce

● Slit the squid body sacs lengthwise, then cut each into 2–3 pieces. Using a small, sharp pointed knife, score a zigzag pattern on the inside of the pieces of squid. Do not cut right through the squid since this will not achieve the desired effect—simply mark a trellis pattern in the flesh.

● Place the squid pieces in a basin. Add the lemon juice, chile, five-spice powder, garlic, and sesame oil, and mix well to coat all the pieces in seasoning. Cover and leave to marinate for at least an hour—if possible leave the squid for 3–4 hours.

● Heat the peanut oil until shimmering, then stir-fry the squid until browned. The pieces should curl to expose the attractive diamond cuts. Use a slotted spoon to remove the pieces from the pan and divide them between serving plates.

● Pour off any excess oil from the pan, if necessary, leaving just enough to cook the vegetables. Stir fry the bell pepper and scallions for 1–2 minutes, then sprinkle in the soy sauce and stir for a few seconds.

● Spoon the vegetable mixture and juices over the squid and serve at once.

Nine-section Appetizer

SERVES 4–6

Traditionally in Korea, small pancakes are served in a pile surrounded by a ring of eight fillings, all in their own lacquered dish. Each person takes a pancake and fills it with whichever filling they like, then rolls it up with their fingers. The fillings should all look different and provide a variety of tastes and textures. This recipe may look complicated, but each of the fillings is very quick and easy to prepare.

1 cup all-purpose flour

salt and freshly ground black pepper

vegetable oil for frying

CUCUMBER FILLING

½ cucumber, sliced into thin strips

salt

2 tsp sesame oil

MUSHROOM FILLING

6 shiitake mushrooms, sliced

2–3 tsp sesame oil

1 tsp soy sauce

freshly ground black pepper

MEAT FILLING

4 oz sirloin or rump steak, cut into very fine strips

1 small garlic clove, crushed and finely chopped

1 scallion, white part and a little green part, finely chopped

1 Tbsp soy sauce

1 tsp toasted sesame seeds

freshly ground black pepper

1½–2 tsp sesame oil

BAMBOO SHOOT FILLING

4 oz bamboo shoots, cut into fine strips

½ in piece of fresh ginger, cut into very fine strips

1½ tsp soy sauce

1 tsp sesame oil

EGG FILLING

2 eggs

salt and freshly ground black pepper

vegetable oil for frying

CARROT FILLING

1 carrot, cut into very fine strips

1 tsp rice vinegar

1 tsp sugar

SHRIMP FILLING

1 cup shrimp, chopped

1½ tsp rice vinegar

pinch of Korean chili powder, or cayenne pepper mixed with paprika

salt

- To make the pancakes, sift the flour and seasoning into a bowl, then slowly pour in about ¾ cup water to make a smooth batter. Leave for 30 minutes.

- Heat a very shallow layer of oil in a skillet. Add spoonfuls of the batter and spread out to form 3-inch diameter rounds. Fry until lightly browned on both sides. Stack in piles in a small, shallow serving dish.

- To make the cucumber filling, put the cucumber in a colander. Sprinkle with salt and leave for 30 minutes. Rinse well and squeeze out as much water as possible. Heat the sesame oil in a skillet and fry the cucumber for 2–3 minutes. Transfer to a small, shallow serving dish.

- To make the mushroom filling, heat the oil in a skillet. Add the mushrooms and stir-fry for 3–4 minutes. Toss with the soy sauce and transfer to a small serving dish.

- To make the meat filling, mix the beef with the garlic, scallion, soy sauce, sesame seeds, and pepper. Heat the sesame oil in a skillet. Add the beef mixture and stir-fry for 4–5 minutes. Transfer to a small serving dish.

- To make the bamboo shoot filling, mix the bamboo shoots with the ginger and soy sauce. Heat the sesame oil in a skillet and stir-fry the bamboo shoots for 2–3 minutes. Transfer to a small serving dish.

- To make the egg filling, lightly beat the yolks and the whites with the seasoning. Heat the oil in a skillet. Fry the egg to make an "omelet" and cut into strips. Transfer to a small serving dish.

- To make the carrot filling, mix all the ingredients together. Transfer to a small serving dish.

- To make the shrimp filling, mix all the ingredients together. Transfer to a small serving dish.

- To assemble the appetizer, put the dish of pancakes in the center and arrange the other dishes in a ring around it.

Banh Xeo Stuffed with Ground Pork
and Bean Sprouts

SERVES 4

2 Tbsp vegetable oil

1 clove garlic, finely chopped

1 small onion, finely chopped

¾ cup ground pork

1 handful bean sprouts, washed and drained

3 eggs

1–2 tsp fish sauce (optional)

● Heat half the vegetable oil in an omelet pan or a wok. Quickly fry the garlic and onion until the aromas are released. Add the pork and stir-fry until brown.

● Toss in the bean sprouts and stir-fry for 2–3 minutes. Remove from the heat and keep warm.

● Beat the eggs with the fish sauce until light and fluffy. In an omelet pan, heat the remaining oil over a medium heat and pour in the egg and fish sauce. When the omelet begins to set, put the pork and bean sprout mixture into the center and fold over the sides to form a square.

● To finish off the top and obtain a successful rise, finish off under a preheated high broiler.

Eggstrip Bundles

SERVES 4–6

Egg strips are tied in bundles with "strings" of blanched scallion. In Korea the eggs are cooked in rectangular pans, but you can use an ordinary round crêpe pan or skillet and trim the curves of the "omelets." Serve with whichever dipping sauce you like, or even a selection of them.

5 eggs

salt and freshly ground black
    pepper

12 scallions, trimmed

vegetable oil for frying

dipping sauce of choice

● Lightly beat the eggs with the seasoning.

● Heat a very fine layer of oil in a 6-inch skillet, preferably nonstick. Pour in half of the eggs. Cover and cook over a low heat for 5–6 minutes until the bottom of the "omelet" is firm. Using a spatula, turn the "omelet" over and cook for 2–3 minutes more until the second side is firm. Remove and let cool. Cook the remaining egg in the same way.

● Lower the scallions, bulbs first, into a saucepan of boiling water, easing in the green parts as they soften. Cover and quickly return to a boil. Boil for 2 minutes, then drain and rinse under running cold water. Dry on paper towels. Split each scallion lengthwise into two or more strands by cutting through the bulb, then tearing upward.

● Trim the curves of the "omelets," then cut the "omelets" into strips about 2½ x ¼ inch.

● Make bundles of eight to ten egg strips each. Wrap a strip of scallion around the center of each bundle and tuck the end of the scallion under the binding. Arrange the bundles on a serving plate and serve with a dipping sauce.

Scallops Stuffed with Shrimp Paste

SERVES 4

12 scallops, cleaned

vegetable oil for frying

FOR THE SHRIMP PASTE

1 Tbsp dried shrimp, soaked in water until soft, drained and finely chopped or 20 defrosted frozen shrimp, finely chopped

2 small pieces of black wood ear fungus, soaked in warm water until soft, drained and finely chopped

4 oz sweet potato, boiled and mashed

1 Tbsp fish sauce or 1 Tbsp light soy sauce

● Make the shrimp paste stuffing by combining all the stuffing ingredients together.

● Steam the scallops until cooked—about 5 minutes in a bamboo steamer. Remove and leave to cool.

● Slit the scallops in their thickest part and spoon in the stuffing. Heat the oil until very hot. Gently lower the stuffed scallops in a basket and fry for 2 minutes.

Mung Bean Pancakes

MAKES ABOUT 8 PANCAKES

These pancakes are a popular street snack, but they are also made in restaurants and homes for celebratory occasions such as birthdays, weddings, and New Years. The street versions are usually a thick round, approximately 7 inches across, but those cooked in restaurants or homes are thinner and smaller.

1 cup less 2 Tbsp whole mung beans, soaked for 10 hours

2 Tbsp short-grain rice, washed and soaked

½ cup red bell pepper, diced

1 garlic clove, crushed and finely chopped

½ onion, diced

2 scallions, white and some green parts sliced

1 Tbsp crushed toasted sesame seeds

2 tsp sesame oil

1 Tbsp soy sauce

6 oz mung bean sprouts

vegetable oil for frying

● Rub the beans, without draining them, between your palms to detach the skin. Pour off the water, which will take a lot of the skins with it. Repeat the process until all the skins have been removed. Put the beans into a blender or food processor.

● Drain the rice and add to the blender or food processor with 4 tablespoons water. Mix to a paste, then, with the motor running, slowly pour in ½ cup water. Pour into a bowl and stir in the red bell pepper, garlic, onion, scallions, sesame seeds, sesame oil, and soy sauce.

● Add the mung bean sprouts to a saucepan of boiling water. Cover and quickly return to a boil. Boil for 2 minutes, then drain and squeeze out as much water as possible. Separate the bean sprouts and stir into the batter.

● Heat a little oil in a skillet, preferably nonstick. Stir the batter and add a ladleful to the pan, spreading it out evenly with the back of the ladle. Trickle one teaspoon vegetable oil over the top of the pancake. Cover the pan and cook the pancake until brown, 2½–3 minutes.

● Turn the pancake over and cook, uncovered, for 2½–3 minutes more.

● Slide the pancake onto a warmed plate and cook the remaining batter in the same way.

Scallops Stuffed
with Shrimp Paste

Fried Mussel Pancakes

MAKES 8 PANCAKES

Mussels and pancakes may seem an unlikely combination, but here the batter is made from tapioca flour. This is market food—if you stroll through the night market of any provincial town in Thailand you can hear, and smell, the sizzling of this dish.

1 cup peanut or corn oil for frying

2 cups raw mussel or oyster meat

8 eggs

11 oz large bean sprouts

3 Tbsp scallions, finely sliced

2 tsp ground white pepper

FOR THE BATTER

2 cups water

½ cup all-purpose flour

1 cup tapioca flour or cornstarch

2 Tbsp baking powder

2 Tbsp sugar

2 eggs, beaten

2 tsp salt

● Mix all the batter ingredients together thoroughly (alternatively, use store-bought tempura batter). Heat a large, heavy skillet, preferably cast iron, and add about ½ inch oil.

● Mix ¼ cup of the mussel meat and ¼ cup of the batter together and pour into the pan. Cook over medium heat for about 5 minutes until brown on the bottom, then break one egg on top of the mussel cake. Flip over carefully and fry until the egg is lightly browned, 3–5 minutes. Remove the mussel cake from the pan and drain well on paper towel. Repeat with the rest of the mussel and batter to make eight cakes.

● Add the bean sprouts to the pan and fry lightly. Place on a serving plate, and arrange the mussel cakes on top. Sprinkle with the scallion and white pepper before serving.

● Serve accompanied by Siricha chili sauce or other thick chili or hot sauce.

Scallion and Shrimp Pancakes

SERVES 4–6

This is a more elaborate version of the previous recipe. Break and lightly beat the eggs as you need them.

1 cup all-purpose flour

1 cup rice flour

salt and freshly ground black pepper

2 eggs

2 tsp sesame oil

dash of soy sauce

vegetable oil for frying

10 large scallions, white and some green parts split lengthwise and cut into strips

1 red bell pepper, cut into strips

1 zucchini, cut into strips

1 cup cooked, shelled shrimp

● Season the flours, then stir in the two eggs, the sesame oil, and the soy sauce. Slowly pour in about ⅔ cup water, stirring, to make a medium-thick batter. Leave for 30 minutes.

● Heat a very fine layer of vegetable oil in a large skillet, preferably nonstick. Pour in one-third of the batter. Scatter over one-third of the scallions, pepper, zucchini, and shrimp. Cook over a medium-hot heat for 5–7 minutes until set and browned underneath. Carefully turn over the pancake and cook for 5–7 minutes more.

Vegetable Snow Pancakes

SERVES 4

Light pancakes made from egg whites and flavored with scallions are the ideal base on which to serve mixed vegetables. Large white radish peps up the already delicious broccoli and mushroom mixture.

2 egg whites

2 Tbsp cornstarch

salt

2 scallions, finely chopped

FOR THE STIR-FRIED VEGETABLES

2 in piece white radish, peeled

½ lb broccoli

½ lb mushrooms, thinly sliced

3 Tbsp soy sauce

1 Tbsp superfine sugar

1 Tbsp rice vinegar or cider vinegar

oil for cooking

3 Tbsp sesame seeds

● Lightly whisk the egg whites with 3 tablespoons water, adding the cornstarch a teaspoonful at a time. Whisk in a little salt, then stir in the scallions.

● Cut the white radish lengthwise into thin slices, then cut the slices into fine strips. Place these in a bowl and set aside.

● Cut the broccoli into small pieces and mix them with the radish. Place the mushroom slices in a separate bowl and add the soy sauce, sugar, and vinegar. Mix well but try not to break up the mushroom slices. Cover and set the mixture aside.

● The pancakes may be cooked individually in a wok or three to four at a time in a large skillet. Heat a little oil, then lightly whisk the batter and pour a spoonful into the pan to make a thin round pancake. Cook until set and browned underneath, then turn and cook the second side until lightly browned. Drain the pancakes on paper towels and keep them hot. Make eight small pancakes.

● Heat a little oil, then use a draining spoon to add the mushrooms. Stir-fry over high heat for about 1 minute, until the mushrooms are browned. Add the radish and broccoli and continue cooking for about

3 minutes. Stir in the sesame seeds and cook for 1 minute, then pour in the juices from marinating the mushrooms.

● Arrange the pancakes on individual plates, then top each with a portion of the stir-fried vegetables. Serve at once.

Scallion Pancakes

SERVES 3–4

These delicious pancakes are one of Korea's national dishes. They are served straight from the sizzling pan and cut into squares so they can be picked up easily with chopsticks. For variety, add strips of bell pepper.

¾ cup all-purpose flour

¾ cup rice flour

salt

1 large egg, beaten

1 tsp sesame oil

3 Tbsp vegetable oil

6 scallions, quartered lengthwise, each length cut into 3-in long strips

vinegar dipping sauce to serve

● Stir together the flours and salt. Stir in the egg, then slowly pour in 1 cup water, stirring, to make a smooth batter. Stir in the sesame oil. Leave to stand for 30 minutes.

● Heat 1 tablespoon vegetable oil in an 8-inch nonstick skillet over a medium-low heat. Sprinkle one third of the scallions evenly over the bottom, then pour over one-third of the batter. Cover and cook for 5–6 minutes. Turn the pancake, cover again and cook for 3 minutes more. Remove the lid and cook for another 2 minutes.

● Transfer to a warm plate and repeat. Cut the pancakes into 2-inch squares and serve hot with vinegar dipping sauce.

Chicken Livers with Bell Peppers in a Sweet Soy Sauce

SERVES 2

Chicken livers are widely eaten in Japan. Cooking in soy sauce and sugar disguises the smell of the liver, which some people find off-putting. It also softens the flesh.

10 oz chicken livers, cut into bite-sized pieces

1 Tbsp vegetable oil

½ green bell pepper, seeded and thinly sliced lengthwise

1½ Tbsp soy sauce

1½ Tbsp *mirin*

½ Tbsp superfine sugar

● Dip the livers into a bowl of boiling water until blanched, then drain.

● Heat the oil in a skillet and fry the green bell pepper for about 3 minutes. Remove and set aside.

● Add the livers to the pan, frying over a medium heat for about 7 minutes. Sprinkle over the soy sauce, *mirin*, and sugar and continue to cook, stirring, for about 5 minutes.

● Return the green bell pepper to the pan and stir in lightly for a few minutes.

● Serve hot with rice and a vegetable dish.

Vietnamese Pancake

SERVES 2

The Vietnamese fried pancake or omelet reflects the Indian influence in Vietnamese cuisine. This omelet can be eaten on its own as part of a mixed array of starters, or left to cool, cut into strips, and placed as a garnish on noodles, salad, or rice dishes.

3 eggs

1–2 tsp fish sauce (optional)

1 Tbsp vegetable oil

1–2 tsp dried shrimp soaked in warm water until soft and drained, or 10 shelled shrimp

1 tsp fresh mint, finely chopped

1 tsp cilantro, finely chopped

● Beat the eggs and the fish sauce together until light and fluffy.

● In an omelet pan, heat the oil over a medium heat. Add the egg and fish sauce mixture. Before it sets, stir in the shrimp, mint, and cilantro. Continue cooking until set.

● To finish off the top and obtain a successful rise, finish off under a preheated hot broiler. Ease around with a wooden spatula and fold the omelet.

Soups

In the West soups provide additional bulk to the meal and are always served at the start of proceedings. In an Asian meal, however, soups are meant either to act as a lubricant to help wash down the bulky and savory foods, in which case they are offered throughout the meal, or, on more formal occasions, a soup or soups are served between courses to refresh and cleanse the palate.

Hot and Sour Soup

SERVES 4

A little vinegar can be added to the soup if you find that the pickled vegetables do not give a sufficiently sour taste.

3 dried Chinese mushrooms, soaked in warm water for 30 minutes

2 cakes of bean curd

2 oz Szechwan preserved vegetables

2 oz pickled vegetables, such as cucumber, cabbage, or string beans

2 slices gingerroot, thinly shredded

2 scallions

3¾ cups water

1 tsp salt

2 Tbsp rice wine or sherry

1 Tbsp soy sauce

freshly ground pepper to taste

1 tsp sesame seed oil

1 tsp cornstarch with 2 tsp water

● Squeeze dry the mushrooms after soaking. Discard the hard stalks, and cut the mushrooms into thin shreds. Reserve the water for use later.

● Thinly shred the bean curd, Szechwan preserved vegetables, pickled vegetables, and ginger. Finely chop the scallions.

● In a wok or large pot, bring the water to a boil. Add all the ingredients and seasonings and simmer for 2 minutes. Add the sesame seed oil, and thicken the soup by stirring in the cornstarch and water mixture. Serve hot.

Hot and Sour Shrimp Soup

SERVES 4

3 cups chicken broth

3 stalks of lemon grass, cut into ¼ in slices

3 kaffir lime leaves

12 raw medium-sized or 6 large shrimp, shelled but not deheaded

5 oz mushrooms, halved

5 fresh small whole green chiles

¼ cup cilantro leaves and stems, sliced

3 Tbsp lime juice, or to taste

½ Tbsp fish sauce, or to taste

● Boil the broth in a pan, add the lemon grass and lime leaf, then the shrimp and mushrooms. When the shrimp are cooked, about 8–10 minutes, remove the pan from the heat and add the rest of the ingredients.

● Let stand for 5 minutes, then check the seasoning, adding more fish sauce or lime juice, or breaking up the chiles to release more heat as required—the soup should be spicy-sour and a little salty. Serve accompanied by rice.

Korean Chicken Broth

MAKES ABOUT 5 CUPS

The garlic cloves can be left whole, cut into halves, or chopped, according to how strong you want the flavor to be.

1 chicken carcass, preferably with skin, or 1½–2 lb raw or cooked chicken trimmings, bones, and skin

3 thin slices of fresh gingerroot

2 garlic cloves (optional)

2 scallions, white and some green parts split lengthwise

● Put the chicken into a large saucepan. Add 7½ cups water and bring slowly to a boil. Skim the scum from the surface. Add the garlic, ginger root, and split scallions. Cover and simmer for about 3 hours.

● Drain through a strainer lined with cheesegauze. Leave until cold, then put in the refrigerator until set. Remove the fat from the surface. Cover and keep in the refrigerator for up to 4 days; boil every other day.

Dried Bean Curd Skin and Vermicelli Soup

SERVES 4

½ oz dried bean curd skin

⅔ cup tiger lily buds

¼ oz black moss

2 oz bean thread vermicelli

3¾ cups water

1 tsp salt

2 Tbsp light soy sauce

1 Tbsp rice wine or dry sherry

1 tsp gingerroot, finely chopped

2 scallions, finely chopped

2 tsp sesame seed oil

FOR THE GARNISH

fresh cilantro

● Soak the bean curd skin in hot water for 30–35 minutes and then cut it into small pieces.

● Soak the lily buds and black moss in water separately for 20–25 minutes. Rinse the lily buds until clean. Loosen the black moss until it resembles hair.

● Cut the vermicelli into short lengths. Bring the water to a boil in a wok or large pot, and add all the ingredients, together with the seasonings. Stir until well blended.

● Cook the soup for 1–1½ minutes. Add the sesame seed oil and serve hot, garnished with cilantro leaves.

Crab and Corn Porridge

SERVES 4

Corn is grown throughout Vietnam, and crabs are caught daily and sold cheaply in the market. If you want, fresh corn and crab can be used, but the recipe here saves time by using canned products. The result is just as good.

2½ cups basic chicken broth or 1 can condensed cream of chicken soup

11 oz can corn kernels

11 oz can creamed corn

11 oz can crabmeat, drained

1 egg

2 scallions, cut into thin rings

● If using condensed soup, add 2 cans of water and milk mixed. Bring the broth or soup to just below boiling point.

● Roughly chop the corn kernels or leave whole. Add the corn kernels and the creamed corn to the broth. Add the crabmeat and stir thoroughly.

● Beat the egg quickly and, holding a fork over the broth, pour the beaten egg along the back of the fork head, moving the fork in a circular motion at the same time. Remove from the heat and cover. Allow to set for about 40 seconds.

● Sprinkle with the scallions, stir once and serve hot.

Stuffed Squid Soup

This is one of a range of clear, unspicy soups that are intended to accompany other dishes as a kind of mild counterpoint, and at the table serves as a contrast to dishes that are either spicy or have oil.

2 cups ground pork

½ tsp white soy sauce

¼ tsp ground white pepper

11 oz squid (body not tentacles), cleaned

4 cups chicken broth

½ Tbsp preserved cabbage, chopped roughly

7 white peppercorns, crushed

5 garlic cloves, crushed

1 tsp fish sauce

¼ tsp sugar

3 scallions, cut into ½ in pieces

2 Tbsp cilantro leaves and stems, cut in ½ in pieces

● Mix the pork, soy sauce, and white pepper together well and use to stuff the squid. If there is any extra pork mixture, form it into small meatballs.

● Heat the chicken broth in a pan or wok, add the preserved cabbage, crushed peppercorns, and garlic, and bring to a boil.

● Place the stuffed squid in the boiling stock, with meatballs if there are any, and then add the fish sauce and sugar. Boil until the stuffed squid is cooked, about 15 minutes or until it is no longer pink when cut into.

● Add the scallion and cilantro and remove from the heat immediately. Serve accompanied by rice.

Miso Broth

1 Tbsp sesame oil

½ in piece gingerroot, peeled and finely chopped

1 clove garlic, finely chopped

1 scallion, finely chopped

4 Tbsp Chinese rice wine or Japanese *sake*

3 Tbsp light soy sauce

2 Tbsp sugar

8 Tbsp red *miso* paste

2 tsp chili oil

6 cups chicken broth

black pepper

● Heat the oil in a pan. Add the ginger, garlic, and scallion, then fry for 30 seconds.

● Add the wine first, then soy sauce, sugar, *miso* paste, and chili oil, and mix together. Add the chicken broth and bring to a boil.

● Remove from the heat, and the broth is now ready to use.

Miso Ramen with Shredded Leek

Noodles in **miso** *broth are one of the most popular noodle dishes served in Japan. It is essential to use a good quality* **miso** *paste, as this provides the crucial sweet and salty flavoring to the dish. The shredded leek should have a firm, supple texture, so if it has been prepared beforehand, soak it in a little water to prevent it from drying out.*

½ lb fresh spinach

1 lb *ramen* noodles, or 14 oz fresh or ¾ lb dried egg noodles

6 cups *miso* broth

4 in piece of leek, cut in 4 pieces and shredded

4 Tbsp cooked dried bamboo shoots *(shinachiku)* (optional)

● Bring some water to a boil in a pan, and blanch the spinach for 1–2 minutes. Rinse, drain, and divide into four equal portions.

● Bring more water to a boil in a large saucepan. Add the noodles, and boil for 4 minutes. Drain, and place into individual serving bowls.

● Heat the *miso* broth for 2–3 minutes. Pile the leek, spinach, and bamboo shoots on top of the noodles. Add the *miso* broth, and serve immediately.

Seafood Soup

SERVES 4–6

The seafood ingredients listed here are only suggestions. Use whatever is available at the fish merchant, but try to assemble a variety of textures and flavors—the more the better.

6 cups chicken broth

5 oz sea bass or other firm fish, cleaned, gutted, and cut into 6 pieces

5 large, raw shrimp, shelled

1 blue crab, cleaned, shell removed, and chopped into 6 pieces

6 mussels in their shells, cleaned well

5 oz squid, body and tentacles, cleaned, gutted, and cut into ¾ in pieces

2 stalks of lemon grass, cut into 2 in lengths and crushed

¼ cup galangal, sliced

3 kaffir lime leaves, shredded

½ cup sweet basil leaves

8 fresh small green chiles, crushed lightly

5 dried red chiles, fried lightly

2½ Tbsp fish sauce, or to taste

¼ tsp palm sugar

1 Tbsp lime or lemon juice, or to taste

● Pour the chicken broth into a wok or pan, bring to a boil, and add all the fish and seafood.

● Add the lemon grass, galangal, and lime leaf. Boil, add all the rest of the ingredients, cook for 2 more minutes, and remove from the heat.

● Taste and add more fish sauce or lime juice as it pleases you.

● Serve in bowls accompanied by rice, fish sauce, and lime or lemon juice.

Smoked Fish Soup

SERVES 4–6

4½ cups chicken broth

½ oz galangal, sliced

2 stalks of lemon grass, cut into 1½ in pieces and crushed lightly

1 tsp shrimp paste

9 oz dried smoked fish (not salted), bones removed and broken into 3–4 pieces

1 oz shallot, crushed slightly

1½ tsp tamarind or lime juice, or to taste

½ cup sweet basil leaves

1 Tbsp fish sauce, or to taste

½ tsp salt

5 dried whole red chiles, dry-fried for 3–5 minutes

● Pour the chicken broth into a pan, bring to a boil and add the galangal, lemon grass, and shrimp paste. Boil again for 2 minutes and then add the dried fish pieces, shallot, and tamarind juice.

● Bring back to a boil, and simmer for 5 minutes, then remove from the heat and add the rest of the ingredients.

● Mix and season to taste with more tamarind, lime juice or fish sauce if you like. Stand for 10 minutes before serving, accompanied by rice.

Mussel and Pineapple Curry Soup

SERVES 4

4½ cups thin coconut milk

1 quantity chili paste

7 oz cooked mussel meat
    (steam approx 1½ lb mussels
    in their shells and remove
    meat)

½ medium-sized pineapple,
    diced finely

1 kaffir lime leaf, torn into
    small pieces

2½ Tbsp fish sauce

½ Tbsp palm sugar

● Heat a quarter of the coconut milk in a pan, add the chili paste and cook for 2 minutes.

● Add the mussels, mix well, then add the rest of the ingredients and boil for 1 minute.

● Remove from the heat and serve in bowls accompanied by rice.

Seaweed Soup

SERVES 6

Wrap the meat and put it in the freezer for about 35 minutes to make cutting it into strips easier. **Wakame is the Japanese name for a green type of seaweed, available dried in packages from healthfood and ethnic stores.**

4 oz dried *wakame*, soaked for at least 30 minutes

6¼ cups fish or beef broth

1 bunch scallions, white and some green parts chopped

1 Tbsp sesame oil

1 garlic clove, crushed and finely chopped

6 oz lean tender beef, cut into fine strips

soy sauce

FOR THE GARNISH

toasted sesame seeds

● Drain the *wakame* and cut it into strips.

● Pour the broth into a saucepan. Add the scallions and bring to a boil. Lower the heat so the broth simmers slowly.

● Heat the oil in a skillet. Add the garlic and beef and stir-fry for about 2 minutes. Add to the stock together with the *wakame*. Add soy sauce to taste and heat through.

● Serve garnished with toasted sesame seeds.

White Radish Soup

SERVES 4–6

This warming, soothing soup is usually served for breakfast in Korea.

16 dried Chinese mushrooms, soaked in hot water for 30 minutes

6¼ cups chicken broth

1 lb white radish, diced

10 oz mung bean sprouts

1 tsp soy sauce

½ tsp sugar

freshly ground black pepper

● Remove the mushrooms from the soaking water. Drain and reserve the water.

● Remove and discard the stalks from the mushrooms. Thinly slice the caps and put into a large saucepan with the stock. Bring to a boil and add the white radish. Cover the saucepan and simmer slowly for about 10 minutes until the white radish is tender.

● Add the bean sprouts, return to a boil. Cover again and simmer for 3–4 minutes more. Add the soy sauce, sugar, and pepper.

Malaysian Sour Noodle Soup

SERVES 4

This is a version of laksa lemak *from Penang. The broth is made from fish, and coconut milk is not used. The soup has a spicy, sour taste.*

1 lb cod

7 cups water

4 shallots, sliced

2 cloves garlic, sliced

2 in piece galangal or 1 in ginger, chopped

3 small red chiles, chopped

2 in stalk lemon grass

2 Tbsp vegetable oil

2 tsp ground turmeric

2 tsp dried shrimp paste (optional)

4 Tbsp tamarind pulp

2 tsp salt

2 tsp sugar

½ lb rice vermicelli

FOR THE GARNISH

1½ cups bean sprouts

2 rings canned pineapple, chopped

2 in piece cucumber, shredded

3 fresh kaffir lime leaves, sliced

mint leaves, sliced

1 large red chile, sliced

● Put the cod and water in a saucepan, bring to a boil, and simmer for 15–20 minutes. Meanwhile, blend the shallots, garlic, galangal, small red chiles, and lemon grass in a mixer or food processor.

● When the fish broth is ready, take out the fish, remove the skin, and flake the meat. Heat the oil in a saucepan, then fry the shallot mixture together with the ground turmeric and dried shrimp paste for 3–4 minutes.

● Soak the tamarind pieces in warm water for 5 minutes, then sieve to squeeze and extract the juice. Add the fish broth, fish flakes, salt, sugar, and tamarind juice to the fried spice mixture in the pan, and simmer for 3–4 minutes.

● Soak the rice vermicelli in warm water for 3 minutes, rinse, and drain. Put into four bowls. Blanch the bean sprouts in boiling water for 1 minute.

● Pour the fish soup into serving bowls. Garnish with the bean sprouts, pineapple, cucumber, lime leaves, mint leaves, and red chile. Serve at once.

White Radish Soup

Sour Curry Soup

SERVES 4

This delicious soup includes lots of vegetables. The bones are cooked with the fish for more flavor.

15 oz whole freshwater fish, cleaned and gutted

5 cups water

2 oz cucumber, quartered and sliced lengthwise

2 oz string beans, cut into 2 in pieces

2 oz swamp cabbage, cut into 2 in pieces

2 oz Chinese or *pak choi* cabbage, cut into 2 in pieces

3 tbsp tamarind juice

2 Tbsp fish sauce

2 tsp lemon juice

1 tsp palm sugar

FOR THE CHILI PASTE

8 dried red chiles, chopped

2 oz shallots, chopped

1 Tbsp chopped *krachai*

1 Tbsp salt

½ tsp shrimp paste

● Cut the fish into 1½ inch long pieces. Boil 5 ounces of it in water until cooked, then remove with a slotted spoon (discard the water) and allow to cool. Remove all the bones, but retain the skin.

● Pound all the chili paste ingredients together well with a mortar and pestle or in a blender. Mix in the cooked fish pieces and pound or process again.

● Place the fish–chili paste mixture in a pan or wok large enough to hold all the ingredients, add the 5 cups water and bring to a boil.

● Add the rest of the fish, boil again for 2 minutes, then add the cucumber, beans, cabbage, and *pak choi*. Bring back to a boil, add the rest of the ingredients and simmer for 10 minutes.

● Serve accompanied by rice, sun-dried beef, or dry salted fish, and pickled vegetables as condiments.

Shrimp Pho

SERVES 4

Shrimp Pho is a very light soup. It is simple yet delicious and unusual. As a variation, and to make it a little more substantial, you could add shrimp balls.

2 pieces black wood ear fungus or 8 button mushrooms

3¾ cups fish broth or use a good-quality vegetable, fish, or chicken bouillon cube

2 cucumber, peeled

6 oz bean thread vermicelli or spaghetti

1⅓ cups fresh shrimp, cooked and peeled

⅔ cup fish sauce

4 large, cooked, unpeeled shrimp, to garnish

● Soak the black wood ear fungus for 10 minutes or until soft in nearly boiling water. When soft, slice thinly and place in the stock. Add the mushrooms to the stock if using those instead. Put into a dish and place on the table.

● Slice the cucumber into thin rounds or cut into fine matchsticks. Place in a dish and put on the table.

● Soak the vermicelli in water that has been boiled and allowed to cool slightly (about 5 minutes). Drain and place in four bowls.

● Place the shrimp in a bowl and put on the table. Meanwhile boil and simmer the broth.

● The guests garnish their bowls with the ingredients in the dishes placed on the table, then pour the hot broth over the whole. The fish sauce is added to taste and the soup bowls are garnished with the unpeeled shrimp.

Shrimp Balls

SERVES 4

1 cup shrimp, ground

1 small hard-cooked egg, finely ground

1 small onion, finely ground

1 egg, beaten

salt and pepper

● Mix all the ingredients using your hand, then shape into small balls. Drop into the simmering broth to cook.

Spicy Vegetable Soup with Shrimp

SERVES 4–6

8 cups chicken broth

7 oz pumpkin flesh, diced

5 oz banana flower (if available)

4 oz young butternut squash, cut into wedges (with seeds)

4 oz string beans, cut into 1 in pieces

½ Tbsp fish sauce

large, raw shrimp, shelled

1 cup lemon basil leaves

FOR THE CHILI PASTE

4 oz shallots, sliced

10 white peppercorns

¼ cup dried shrimp, chopped

3 fresh small green chiles, chopped

½ Tbsp shrimp paste

● Pound the chili paste ingredients together with a mortar and pestle or in a blender.

● Place the broth in a pan, add the chili paste and bring to a boil. Add the vegetables, and boil for 10 minutes. Add the fish sauce, then add the shrimp and lemon basil. Cook for 3–5 minutes.

● Serve accompanied by rice.

Chicken Pho

SERVES 4

*Traditionally, **pho** is made only with beef, but it is now being made with chicken and shrimp.*

3 celery stalks, finely chopped

3 scallions, chopped into rings (use green tops as well)

10 oz cooked chicken, finely shredded

8 oz flour sticks or spaghetti noodles

1½ pt chicken broth

2 pieces light wood ear fungus or 8 white button mushrooms, finely sliced

● Place the celery and scallions in a bowl and put on the table. Place the cooked shredded chicken in a separate bowl and put that on the table, too.

● Follow the instructions on the flour sticks pack, or boil the spaghetti until just soft. Drain and rinse with some boiling water. Place in four bowls.

● Boil up the chicken broth until simmering, then add the light wood ear fungus or the mushrooms. Place in a bowl and put on the table.

● The guests should put a mixture of celery, scallion, and shredded chicken onto the noodles then ladle the hot chicken broth into the bowls.

Indonesian Chicken Soup with Rice Vermicelli

SERVES 4

This Indonesian soup dish has a spicy, sour, and nutty flavor. **Sambal oelek** *provides the spice in this soup. If you like a hotter taste, simply add more.*

2 Tbsp vegetable oil

4 shallots, sliced

3 cloves garlic, sliced

2 in piece galangal, or 1 in fresh ginger, sliced

1 tsp ground coriander

3 tbsp candle or macadamia nuts

6 cups light chicken broth

2 tsp salt

2 cups cooked chicken meat, shredded

½ lb rice vermicelli

FOR THE TOPPING

2 tsp salt

1½ cups bean sprouts, blanched

2 scallions, chopped

1 celery stalk, sliced

2 Tbsp ready-made crispy onions

4 lime wedges

2 tsp Indonesian chili paste (*sambal oelek*) or chili sauce

● Heat the oil in a frying pan. Fry the shallots, garlic, *galangal* or ginger, and the ground coriander, then add the nuts. Blend to a paste with 3 tablespoons chicken stock in a mixer or food processor.

● Put the paste and chicken broth in a pan, and simmer for 5 minutes. Add the chicken meat and salt, and simmer for 2–3 minutes. Meanwhile, soak the rice vermicelli in warm water for 3 minutes. Rinse, drain, and divide into four bowls.

● Put the bean sprouts, scallions, and celery on top of the noodles. Pour in the soup and sprinkle with the crispy onions. Garnish with lime wedges and ½ teaspoon of chili sauce to each bowl. Serve immediately while still hot.

Pork and Spinach Curry Soup

SERVES 4–6

3 cups water

1 lb pork spare ribs, cut into 1¼ in pieces

½ Tbsp tamarind juice

½ Tbsp fish sauce

2 tsp chopped anchovies or dried salted fish

11 oz fresh spinach leaves

2 tsp garlic, sliced

2 tsp shallot, sliced

2 Tbsp peanut or corn oil

4 whole dried red chiles

● Boil the water in a pan, add the pork, and bring back to a boil. Cook until the pork is tender, about 20–25 minutes.

● Add the tamarind juice, fish sauce, and anchovy. Bring back to a boil, simmer for 5 minutes, add the spinach and remove from the heat after 1 minute. Transfer to a bowl.

● Fry the garlic, shallot, and chiles in the oil in a skillet until tan-colored. Sprinkle over the soup with the oil. Serve accompanied by rice.

Chicken Porridge

SERVES 4–6

⅓ cup long- or short-grained rice

5 cups water

½ lb corn-fed chicken breast, boned and slivered

FOR THE MARINADE

2 Tbsp fish sauce

1 tsp cornstarch dissolved in 2 tbsp water

2 tsp dry sherry

salt

FOR THE GARNISH

1 large scallion, finely chopped

salt and black pepper

fresh cilantro, chopped

● Rinse and drain the rice. Add the water and bring to a boil over high heat. Turn the heat to medium low, partially cover the pan and let the rice bubble for 5 minutes. This loosens the starch and blends the water and rice. Give the rice a stir and turn the heat as low as possible, cover and simmer for about 1 hour.

● Place the chicken in the marinade for 30 minutes. Add the chicken to the porridge and stir gently. Continue until all the pink in the chicken has disappeared. Turn off the heat, cover and serve in a couple of minutes.

● Garnish with cilantro for more flavor, and scallion and salt and pepper to taste.

Corn and Asparagus Soup

SERVES 4

6 oz white asparagus

1 egg white

1 Tbsp cornstarch

2 Tbsp water

2½ cups water

1 tsp salt

4 oz corn kernels

FOR THE GARNISH

1 scallion, finely chopped

● Cut the asparagus spears into small cubes.

● Beat the egg white lightly. Mix the cornstarch with the water to make a smooth paste.

● Bring the water to a rolling boil. Add the salt, corn, and asparagus. When the water starts to boil again, add the cornstarch and water mixture, stirring constantly.

● Add the egg white very slowly and stir. Serve hot, garnished with finely chopped scallion.

Dashi

MAKES ABOUT 6 CUPS

4 in piece dried kelp, wiped with a damp cloth

6 cups water

3 cups bonito flakes

● Make two or three cuts, about 1 inch long, in the kelp to help release the flavor. Put the water and kelp in a saucepan and heat on a low flame. Remove the kelp just before the water begins to boil.

● Add the bonito flakes when the liquid comes back to a boil, and turn off the heat. Leave the liquid to stand until all of the flakes have sunk to the bottom of the pan.

● Sieve the liquid through a cheesegauze or paper filter. Retain the bonito flakes and kelp to make a less strong *dashi*.

Dashi Broth

MAKES ABOUT 6 CUPS

2 Tbsp *mirin*

6 cups *dashi*

scant ½ cup Japanese soy sauce

3 Tbsp sugar

● Put the *mirin* in a saucepan and bring to a boil.

● Add the *dashi*, soy sauce, and sugar. Simmer for 3–4 minutes. It is now ready to use.

Miso Soup with Wakame Seaweed and Onion

SERVES 2

In Japan this soup is served at breakfast, lunch, or dinner, when it is accompanied by a main dish and a bowl of rice. Unlike Western soups, Japanese soup is sipped from the bowl, with any pieces of vegetable or tofu being eaten with chopsticks.

2¼ cups *dashi* stock

½ medium onion, sliced

2 tsp dried *wakame* seaweed

2 Tbsp *miso* paste

● Put the *dashi* stock and onion in a pan, bring to a boil, and simmer until the onion becomes transparent.

● Add the *wakame* and continue to simmer until it has expanded. (This takes only a couple of minutes.)

● Add the *miso* paste and stir using a small whisk, until dissolved. Heat for a few more minutes until the soup starts to boil. Do not boil for more than 1–2 minutes or the soup will be too salty. Serve immediately while still hot.

Miso Soup with Silken Bean Curd and Scallions

SERVES 2

Two types of bean curd are widely used in Japanese cookery, **kinu,** *or silken bean curd, and* **momen,** *or cotton bean curd. As the names suggest,* **kinu dofu** *has a very smooth, silky texture, whereas* **momen dofu** *is characterized by its more solid, coarser appearance and feel. It is* **kinu dofu** *that is usually used in miso soups.*

● Put the *dashi* stock and bean curd in a pan, bring to a boil and simmer for 4–5 minutes.

● Add the scallion and simmer for a further minute. Stir the *miso* paste into the soup using a mini whisk until it is completely dissolved.

● Simmer again until the soup just returns to a boil. Serve immediately.

2¼ cups *dashi* stock

4 oz silken bean curd cut into
   ½ in cubes

3 scallions, chopped

2 Tbsp *miso* paste

Chinese Cabbage Soup

SERVES 4

9 oz Chinese or *pak choi* cabbage

3–4 dried Chinese mushrooms, soaked in warm water for 30 minutes

2 Tbsp oil

2 tsp salt

1 Tbsp rice wine or dry sherry

3¾ cups water

1 tsp sesame seed oil

● Wash the cabbage and cut it into thin slices. Squeeze dry the soaked mushrooms. Discard the hard stalks and cut the mushrooms into small pieces. Reserve the water in which the mushrooms have been soaked for use later.

● Heat a wok or large pot until hot, add oil, and wait for it to smoke. Add the cabbage and mushrooms. Stir a few times and then add the salt, wine, water, and the water in which the mushrooms had been soaked. Bring to a boil, add the sesame seed oil and serve.

Egg and Leek Consommé

SERVES 2

*This clear soup is usually eaten with **sushi** dishes and has a subtle flavor. The use of shiitake mushrooms adds extra taste. Do not boil the leek for too long as it needs to retain some of its texture.*

2¼ cups *dashi* stock	½ tsp salt
1 in leek, halved and sliced very finely	dash of soy sauce
3 shiitake mushrooms, sliced	1 egg, beaten

● In a pan bring the *dashi* stock to a boil then add the leek, mushrooms, salt, and soy sauce. Simmer the liquid for 3–4 minutes.

● Gradually add the beaten egg to the pan, whisking continuously to stop it from forming into lumps. Serve immediately.

Tomato and Egg Flower Soup

SERVES 4

9 oz tomatoes, skinned	4 cups water
1 egg	2 Tbsp light soy sauce
2 scallions, finely chopped	1 tsp cornstarch mixed with 2 tsp water
1 Tbsp oil	

● Skin the tomatoes by dipping them in boiling water for a minute or so and then peel them. Cut them into thick slices.

● Beat the egg. Finely chop the scallions.

● Heat a wok or pan over a high heat. Add the oil and wait for it to smoke. Add the scallions to flavor the oil and then pour in the water.

● Drop in the tomatoes and bring to a boil. Add the soy sauce and slowly pour in the beaten egg. Add the cornstarch and water mixture. Stir and serve.

Chinese Mushroom Soup

SERVES 4

6 dried Chinese mushrooms

2 tsp cornstarch

1 Tbsp cold water

3 egg whites

2 tsp salt

2½ cups water

1 scallion, finely chopped

● Soak the dried mushrooms in warm water for 25–30 minutes. Squeeze them dry, discard the hard stalks, and cut each mushroom into thin slices. Reserve the water in which the mushrooms were soaked for use later.

● Mix the cornstarch with the water to make a smooth paste. Comb the egg whites with your fingers to loosen them.

● Mix the water and the mushroom-soaking water in a pan and bring to a boil. Add the mushrooms and cook for about 1 minute. Now add the cornstarch and water mixture, stir, and add the salt.

● Pour the egg whites very slowly into the soup, stirring constantly.

● Garnish the soup with the finely chopped scallion and serve hot.

Ramen with Stir-fried Vegetables

SERVES 4

Ramen noodles topped with a blend of fresh and flash-fried vegetables—deliciously simple and simply delicious!

1 lb *ramen* noodles or 14 oz fresh or ¾ lb dried thin egg noodles

6 cups soy sauce broth

FOR THE TOPPING

2 Tbsp vegetable oil

1 Tbsp sesame oil

1 small onion, sliced

¾ cup snow peas, cut in half diagonally

2–3 small carrots, cut into long matchsticks

2½ cups bean sprouts

½ lb Chinese cabbage, chopped

2 dried wood ear fungus or dried *shiitake* mushrooms, soaked in water, rinsed, and chopped

salt and pepper

● Make the topping. Heat the oils in a wok or skillet until very hot. Stir-fry the onion, snow peas, and carrots for 2 minutes, then add the bean sprouts, Chinese cabbage, wood ear or shiitake mushrooms, and stir-fry for another 3–4 minutes. Season.

● Boil plenty of water in a large pan, and add the noodles. Cook for 3 minutes before draining well. Put the noodles into four bowls.

● Heat the soy sauce broth. Pile the stir-fried vegetables onto the noodles, and pour the broth over the top.

Ramen with Garlic

SERVES 4

Do not be surprised at the amount of garlic used in this recipe. The key point of this dish is the strong garlic flavoring, which makes it a warming dish for a cold winter's day.

1 Tbsp sesame oil

16 cloves garlic, sliced

1 lb *ramen* noodles or 14 oz fresh or ¾ lb dried thin egg noodles

4 cloves garlic, crushed

6 cups soy sauce broth

4 Tbsp cooked dried bamboo shoots (*shinachiku*) (optional)

2 scallions, chopped

● Heat the sesame oil in a skillet. Fry the garlic for 2–3 minutes, or until turned golden-brown. Set aside.

● Boil plenty of water in a pan, and add the noodles. Cook for 3 minutes, then drain. Place the noodles in individual bowls.

● Put the crushed garlic and soy sauce broth in a pan. Bring to a boil, and simmer for 2–3 minutes.

● Put a quarter of the fried garlic, bamboo shoots, and scallions onto each serving of noodles. Pour the broth over the top, and serve immediately.

Ramen with Stir-fried Vegetables

Coconut and Galangal Soup

SERVES 4–6

This creamy soup has become one of the favorites on Thai restaurant menus, not least for the delicate aroma and flavor given by the galangal.

5 cups thin coconut milk

1 oz shallot, chopped finely

½ oz galangal, sliced thinly

2 stalks lemon grass, cut into ¾ in pieces

6 fresh small whole red chiles

3 kaffir lime leaves, torn into small pieces

1 tsp salt

11 oz boneless skinned chicken breasts, cut across into ¼ in thick slices

7 oz fresh mushrooms (oyster if available)

2 Tbsp lime or lemon juice

½ tbsp fish sauce

3 Tbsp cilantro leaves and stems cut into ¾ in pieces

● Pour the coconut milk into a pan and bring to a boil. Add the shallot, galangal, lemon grass, chile, lime leaf, and salt.

● Boil, add the chicken and bring to a boil again, then add the mushrooms and bring back to a boil for 2 minutes.

● Remove from the heat and stir in the lime juice, fish sauce, and cilantro.

● Serve in bowls accompanied by rice, lime quarters, and fish sauce with chiles.

Soy Sauce Broth

MAKES 6 CUPS

6 cups chicken broth

2 tsp salt

4 tsp Chinese rice wine or Japanese *sake*

2 tsp shortening

4 Tbsp light soy sauce

4 tsp dark soy sauce

black pepper

● Put the stock, salt, wine, and shortening in a pan. Bring to a boil, and simmer for 2–3 minutes.

● Turn off the heat, add the light and dark soy sauce, pepper and stir. The broth is now ready to use.

Cucumber Soup

SERVES 4

½ cucumber

2 oz black field mushrooms

2½ cups water

1½ tsp salt

1 tsp sesame seed oil

1 scallion, finely chopped

● Split the cucumber in half lengthwise, and slice it thinly, but do not peel.

● Wash and slice the mushrooms, but do not peel.

● Bring the water to a boil in a wok or large pot. Add the cucumber and mushroom slices and salt. Boil for about 1 minute.

● Add the sesame seed oil and finely chopped scallion. Stir and serve hot.

Deep-fried Bean Curd and Wood Ear Soup

SERVES 4

2 oz deep-fried bean curd, or 1
  cake fresh bean curd

½ oz wood ear fungus

2½ cups water

1 tsp salt

1 Tbsp light soy sauce

FOR THE GARNISH

1 scallion, finely chopped

1 tsp sesame seed oil

● Use either two packets of ready-made deep-fried bean curd (there are about 10 to each 1 oz packet), or cut a cake of fresh bean curd into about 20 small cubes and deep-fry them in very hot vegetable oil until they are puffed up and golden. Cut them in half.

● Soak the wood ears in water until soft (this will take 20–25 minutes) and rinse until clean.

● Bring the water to a boil in a wok or large pot. Add the bean curd, wood ears, and the salt.

● When the soup starts to boil again, add the soy sauce and cook for about 1 minute. Garnish with finely chopped scallion and sesame seed oil. Serve hot.

Ramen with Pork and Bean Curd

SERVES 4

Pork and bean curd, called **Ma Po's Tofu** *in China, is a popular family dish throughout east Asia. It is commonly served with rice. However, this spicy sauce with pork and bean curd really goes down just as well piled onto a bowl of hot noodles.*

1 lb *ramen* noodles, or 14 oz fresh or ¾ lb dried medium egg noodles

6 cups soy sauce broth

2 scallions, chopped

FOR THE TOPPING

1 Tbsp vegetable oil

1 clove garlic, finely chopped

½ in piece ginger, peeled, and finely chopped

6 oz ground pork

½ leek, finely sliced

1¼ cups chicken broth

1 Tbsp chile bean sauce *(toban djan)*

2 tsp sugar

1 tsp light soy sauce

1 Tbsp Chinese rice wine or dry sherry

1 tsp tomato paste

14 oz bean curd, diced

2 Tbsp cornstarch mixed with 2 Tbsp water

● To make the pork with bean curd, heat the oil in a wok or skillet until very hot. Fry the garlic and ginger for 1 minute. Then add the pork, and stir-fry for 3–4 minutes.

● Add the leek, and stir-fry for another minute. Then add the chicken broth, chile bean sauce, sugar, soy sauce, wine, and tomato paste, and bring to a boil.

● Add the bean curd, and simmer for about 5–7 minutes. Next, add the cornstarch paste, and stir to thicken.

● Boil plenty of water in a pan and add the noodles. Cook for 3 minutes, then drain. Place the noodles in individual bowls. Heat the soy broth.

● Put a quarter of the bean curd mixture and scallions onto each serving of noodles. Gently pour the soy broth over the top, and serve at once.

Northern Thai Soup

SERVES 4–6

4 cups water

6 oz boneless skinned chicken breasts

1½ cups ground pork

1 Tbsp preserved cabbage

½ cup onion, sliced

2 Tbsp fish sauce

½ oz dried large shrimp, soaked in cold water for 5 minutes

½ oz spinach leaf

2 Tbsp tamarind juice

● Boil the water in a pan, add the chicken and cook for 7–10 minutes until well cooked. Remove and cut across into thin slices.

● Using the same cooking water, add the pork, preserved cabbage, onion, and fish sauce. Boil and then add the rest of the ingredients.

● Boil again before pouring into bowls. Serve accompanied by rice.

Chicken Soup with Clams and Spinach

SERVES 4

Shellfish and poultry have a natural affinity. Here, chicken and clams are combined with great success, and the union is enhanced by spinach.

16 clams

1 Tbsp vegetable oil

2 garlic cloves, crushed and finely chopped

1½–2 tsp fresh ginger, finely chopped

3 scallions, white and some green parts, chopped

1 chicken breast, cut into very fine strips

3¾ cups chicken broth

12 oz fresh spinach, chopped

1½ tsp sesame oil

salt and freshly ground black pepper

● Scrub the clams and rinse them under running cold water.

● Heat the vegetable oil in a saucepan. Add the garlic, ginger, scallions, and chicken, and stir-fry for 30 seconds. Add the chicken broth and bring to a boil. Simmer for 5 minutes.

● Add the clams. Return to a boil and simmer for 3–5 minutes until the clam shells open; discard any that remain closed.

● Stir in the spinach. Simmer for 1–2 minutes, then remove the pan from the heat. Add the sesame oil and season to taste.

Boiled Rice Soup with Chicken

SERVES 4

This tasty and nourishing soup is the traditional and universal Thai breakfast. It is also made with ground pork, and an optional extra is an egg cracked straight into the dish just before serving; it partly poaches in the hot broth.

6 cups chicken broth

11 oz boneless skinned chicken breasts, cut across into thin slices

4 cups cooked rice

1 Tbsp chopped pickled cabbage

1 tsp salt

1 tsp ground white pepper

1 cup celery, finely sliced

2 scallions, sliced

⅓ cup garlic cloves, unpeeled and fried until soft

½ cup *phrik dong* (sliced red chile with vinegar)

2 Tbsp fish sauce

● Boil the chicken broth in a pan. Add the chicken, rice, cabbage, salt and pepper. Boil the chicken until cooked, about 8–10 minutes.

● Add the celery and scallion and remove from the heat immediately.

● Pour into bowls and sprinkle with the fried garlic. Serve the soup with the *phrik dong* and fish sauce in separate bowls.

Ramen with Wakame

SERVES 4

Wakame *seaweed is sold either dried or salted. The dried variety is more easily preserved and handled.* **Wakame** *is very nutritious, full of minerals and trace elements, and virtually calorie-free! It makes a healthy hot noodle soup dish.*

1 lb *ramen* noodles or 14 oz fresh or ¾ lb dried medium egg noodles

6 cups soy sauce broth

FOR THE TOPPING

2½ Tbsp dried *wakame* seaweed, soaked in hot water and then drained

4 Tbsp cooked dried bamboo shoots *(shinachiku)* (optional)

2 scallions, chopped

2 hard-cooked eggs, cut in half

● Boil plenty of water in a pan. Add the noodles, and cook for 4 minutes. Drain, and put into four bowls.

● Heat the soy sauce broth. Place the *wakame*, bamboo shoots (if used), scallions, and eggs on the noodles. Pour the soy sauce broth gently into the bowls. Serve immediately.

Ramen Noodles in Miso Soup

SERVES 2

Ramen *is Japanese fast-food. In this variation, the flavor of fried garlic and sesame oil complements the* **miso** *and chili. It is difficult not to make a noise when you eat Japanese noodles. In fact, the more you slurp, the better you will enjoy the meal, or so it is said!*

9 oz fresh *ramen* noodles

2 cups *ramen* broth

½ tsp salt

pinch of freshly ground black pepper

2 tsp sesame oil

2 tsp toasted sesame seeds

3 Tbsp *miso* paste

FOR THE COATING

1 Tbsp sesame oil

6 oz bean sprouts

1 large garlic clove, sliced

½ red bell pepper, thinly sliced

pinch of chili powder

pinch of salt

● Cook the noodles for about 2–2½ minutes in boiling water. Drain and put into the individual bowls.

● Heat the broth with the salt and pepper in a pan. When it boils, add the sesame oil and sesame seeds and stir in the *miso* paste until it has dissolved.

● Meanwhile, heat the oil in a skillet. Stir-fry the bean sprouts, garlic, and red bell pepper. Sprinkle in the pinch of chili powder and salt. Place the vegetables on top of the noodles. Pour over the *miso* soup, serve and eat immediately.

Bamboo Shoot Soup

SERVES 4

2½ cups water

3 tbsp dried salted mackerel or anchovies, chopped

1 stalk of lemon grass, cut into ¾ in pieces and crushed lightly

3 kaffir lime leaves, torn into small pieces

2½ oz pumpkin flesh, cut into ¾ in pieces

2½ oz bamboo shoots, sliced

1 oz string beans, cut into ¾ in pieces

3 small white eggplant, quartered

3 fresh small green chiles, minced lightly

3 fresh large green chiles, cut into thirds

1 Tbsp fish sauce

½ cup lemon basil leaves

● Boil the water in a pan or wok and add the dried fish, lemon grass and lime leaf. Boil for 1 minute.

● Add the rest of the ingredients, except the lemon basil, and simmer for 7–10 minutes or until the pumpkin is soft.

● Stir in the basil and remove from the heat immediately. Serve accompanied by rice.

Creamy Coconut Noodle Soup

SERVES 4

This famous Malaysian dish **laksa lemak,** *reflects the multicultural nature of that country and its people. It has a smooth texture and silky hot taste!*

8 shallots, sliced

3 cloves garlic, sliced

2 in piece galangal or 1 in ginger, peeled and sliced

4 small red chiles, sliced

1 Tbsp fresh lemon grass, chopped

5 Tbsp vegetable oil

2 tsp ground turmeric

1 tsp ground coriander

2 tsp dried shrimp paste (optional)

¼ lb bean curd, diced

2½ cups light chicken broth

2 cups coconut milk

2 tsp sugar

2 tsp salt

2 fish balls or 2 golfball-sized chunks imitation crabmeat, sliced

½ lb rice vermicelli

12 tiger or large shrimp, peeled and deveined

FOR THE GARNISH

cooked chicken from the light chicken broth, shredded

1½ cups bean sprouts

2 in piece cucumber, shredded

1 large red chile, sliced

2 scallions, chopped

● Blend the shallots, garlic, galangal, red chile, and lemon grass in a food processor. Heat 3 tablespoons of the oil in a saucepan, and stir-fry the shallot mixture with the turmeric, coriander seeds, and dried shrimp paste over a low heat for 3–4 minutes.

● Heat the remaining oil in a skillet and fry the bean curd until lightly browned. Add the chicken broth, coconut milk, sugar, salt, and fish balls or imitation crabmeat, bring to a boil, and simmer for 2–3 minutes.

● Meanwhile, blanch the bean sprouts in boiling water for 1 minute.

● Soak the vermicelli in warm water for 3 minutes, rinse, and drain well. Divide the vermicelli equally into four bowls.

● Add the shrimp to the soup, and simmer for 2 minutes. Pour the soup into the bowls; garnish with shredded chicken, bean sprouts, cucumber, sliced chili, and scallions. Serve immediately.

Noodles in Soy Sauce Soup

SERVES 2

FOR THE BASIC *RAMEN* BROTH

MAKES 5 CUPS

10 oz chicken carcass, roughly chopped

2 pork bones

½ leek

1 in piece gingerroot, peeled and cut in half

1 large garlic clove, cut in half

8 cups water

FOR THE *SHOYU RAMEN*

9 oz fresh *ramen* noodles

2 cups *ramen* broth

3 Tbsp soy sauce

½ tsp salt

pinch of freshly ground black pepper

FOR THE TOPPING

8 Tbsp corn kernels

3 scallions, chopped

¾ oz butter, cut in half

● To make the *ramen* broth, blanch the chicken and pork bones. Then put the water, bones, leek, ginger, and garlic into a large pan. Bring to a boil and simmer for 1 hour, occasionally skimming off the scum. Strain the broth through a cheesecloth. Adjust the heat to prevent the broth from boiling again (this will make the liquid cloudy).

● Boil the noodles for about 2–2½ minutes. Drain and put them in individual bowls.

● Heat the 2 cups of broth, soy sauce, salt, and pepper in a pan. When it boils, pour the soup into the bowls.

● Put the corn kernels on top of the noodles, sprinkle with the chopped scallion, then top with the butter. Eat as soon as possible or the noodles will absorb the soup and become soggy.

Cold Buckwheat Noodle Soup

SERVES 4

This soup is almost a meal in itself. Because of the number of elements that have to be prepared separately, it may appear to be a complicated recipe, but, in fact, each vegetable is simple to prepare and all of them can be done ahead.

8 oz buckwheat noodles

5 cups chicken broth

1 tsp sesame oil

½ long cucumber, thinly sliced

salt

1½ tsp rice vinegar

pinch of sugar

pinch of Korean chili powder or cayenne pepper mixed with paprika

2 hard-cooked eggs, shelled and thinly sliced

8 pieces of white radish, cut into thin strips

½ Korean pear, peeled, cored, and thinly sliced

1 cup liquid from white radish

selection of dipping sauces to serve

● Cook the noodles according to the instructions on the package. Drain and rinse under running cold water. Drain well, then put into a bowl and toss with ½ cup of the broth, and the sesame oil.

● Put the cucumber slices in a colander and toss with salt. Leave for 1 hour. Rinse the cucumber well, drain and dry thoroughly on paper towels. Mix with the rice vinegar, sugar, and chili powder or cayenne pepper mixed with paprika.

● Divide the noodles among four dishes. Pour one-quarter of the remaining broth into each dish. Arrange a few neatly overlapping slices of egg around the top of each pile of noodles. Surround with slightly overlapping vegetable and pear slices.

Hot and Sour Noodle Soup with Shrimp

SERVES 4

This is one of the representative dishes of Thai cuisine. The broth is a myriad of flavors: the sour element of lime leaves and lemon grass combined with the hot chile pepper and fish sauce, with its strong aroma.

1 Tbsp vegetable oil

2 cloves garlic, grated

2 shallots, grated

1 in piece galangal or ½ in fresh ginger, thinly sliced

4–5 small red chiles, chopped

6 cups light chicken broth

3 kaffir lime leaves, sliced

4 in piece lemon grass, chopped

½ lb rice vermicelli

20 peeled tiger shrimp

6 Tbsp fish sauce

6 Tbsp fresh lemon or lime juice

2 Tbsp palm or brown sugar

16 canned straw mushrooms

cilantro leaves

● Heat the oil in a saucepan, then stir-fry the garlic, shallots, galangal, and chile for about 1 minute. Put in the chicken broth, add the lime leaves and lemon grass, bring to a boil, and simmer for 5 minutes.

● Meanwhile, soak the rice vermicelli for 3 minutes, rinse, drain, and divide equally among four bowls. Add the shrimp, fish sauce, lemon or lime juice, sugar, and straw mushrooms to the soup, then simmer for 2–3 minutes.

● Pour the soup into the bowls and sprinkle with the cilantro leaves. Serve immediately.

Spinach Soup

SERVES 3–4

This is a favorite soup throughout South Korea.

5 oz chicken breast, thinly sliced and cut into 1 in cubes

3 scallions, finely chopped

2 garlic cloves, chopped

2 Tbsp soy sauce

1½ tsp sesame seeds

freshly ground black pepper

1½ Tbsp vegetable oil

5½ cups chicken broth

12 oz fresh spinach, trimmed, and shredded

sesame oil for sprinkling

● Mix the chicken with the scallions, garlic, soy sauce, sesame seeds, and plenty of pepper. Leave for 30 minutes.

● Heat the vegetable oil in a saucepan. Add the chicken mixture and fry until browned. Add the broth and heat until simmering. Simmer very slowly for about 25 minutes until the chicken is tender.

● Add the spinach and cook for 2–5 minutes more until the spinach is tender. Adjust the seasonings; if the liquid has reduced too much, add hot water.

● Serve sprinkled with sesame oil.

Hot and Sour Noodle Soup
with Shrimp

Dumpling Soup

SERVES 6

Korean dumpling soup is nothing like a European soup with dumplings. Instead, it contains small dumplings filled with water chestnuts, pork, and chicken, like Chinese **dim sum.**

1 carrot, chopped

1 onion, chopped

1 garlic clove, chopped

6 water chestnuts, chopped

4 oz lean pork

4 oz chicken

1 cup cooked, shelled shrimp

2 Tbsp soy sauce

1 Tbsp sesame oil

pinch of Korean chili powder or cayenne pepper mixed with paprika

30 wonton wrappers

7½ cups chicken broth

FOR THE GARNISH

scallions, chopped

● Put the vegetables and three-quarters of the pork, chicken, and shrimp in a food processor. Dice the remaining pork, chicken, and shrimp. Add the soy sauce, sesame oil and a pinch of Korean chili powder, or cayenne pepper mixed with paprika, to the food processor, and mix to a smooth paste.

● Spoon a little of the vegetable mixture into each wonton wrapper. Wet the edges and draw together to make a neat bundle. Pinch the edges together to seal.

● Bring the broth to a boil in a saucepan. Add the dumplings and diced pork, chicken, and shrimp. Simmer for 8–10 minutes. Garnish with scallions before serving.

Spinach and Bean Curd Soup

SERVES 4

8 oz fresh spinach

2 cakes bean curd

2 Tbsp oil

2 tsp salt

2½ cups water

2 Tbsp soy sauce

1 tsp sesame seed oil

● Wash the spinach well, discarding the tough and discolored leaves. Shake off the excess water and cut the leaves into small pieces.

● Cut the bean curd into about 14 pieces.

● In a wok or large pot, heat the oil until hot. Stir-fry the spinach until soft. Add the salt and water and bring to a boil.

● Add the bean curd and soy sauce and cook for 1½–2 minutes. Add the sesame seed oil just before serving the soup.

Issaan-style Soup

SERVES 4–6

4 oz each of beef or calf's heart, liver, lung, kidney, and small intestines (any offal may be used, depending on your preference), cleaned and prepared

5 cups water

1 oz galangal, sliced

3 stalks of lemon grass, cut into 1¼ in pieces and crushed

5 kaffir lime leaves, shredded

1½ Tbsp fish sauce

1 Tbsp lemon juice

2 dried red chiles, crushed

½ tsp salt

1 scallion, cut into ½ in pieces

● Boil all the offal together in a pan of water until tender, about 30–40 minutes. Rinse well in cold water and slice everything up fairly small.

● Place the cooked offal in a pan with the water, bring to a boil, and add all the remaining ingredients, except the scallion. Bring back to a boil for 2 minutes, add the scallion, and remove from the heat.

● Serve immediately accompanied by sticky or steamed rice.

Bean Sprout Soup

SERVES 4

8 oz fresh bean sprouts

1 small red bell pepper, cored and seeded

2 Tbsp oil

2 tsp salt

2½ cups water

1 scallion, finely chopped

● Wash the bean sprouts in cold water, discarding the husks and other bits and pieces that float to the surface. It is not necessary to trim each sprout.

● Thinly shred the red bell pepper.

● Heat a wok or large pot, add the oil and wait for it to smoke. Add the bean sprouts and red bell pepper and stir a few times. Add the salt and water.

● When the soup starts to boil, garnish with finely chopped scallion and serve hot.

Fish and Shellfish Main Dishes

Almost everything that the sea has to offer, from squid to seaweed, can be found in Eastern cuisine. The dishes in this section use all kinds of fish and seafood, most well known but a few less often found in Western stores. There are dishes for every type of meal, from simple broiled fish to stir-fried squid, and from grilled fish garnished with ginger sauce to lobster and sweet potato curry.

Steamed Fish with Lemon and Chile

SERVES 4

The combination of lemon or lime juice and fresh chiles in the topping gives this dish a refreshing spicy tartness.

1 lb 2 oz whole sea bass or sea perch, cleaned and gutted

½ cup lemon or lime juice

2 Tbsp small, fresh green chiles, lightly chopped

2 Tbsp garlic, chopped

2 Tbsp fish sauce

½ Tbsp salt

1 tsp sugar

¼ cup cilantro leaves and stems, cut into ½ in pieces

● Steam the fish whole for 15 minutes until tender but firm.

● Meanwhile, mix all the remaining ingredients, except the cilantro, together. When the fish is cooked, place it on a serving platter and spread the lemon juice mixture all over (the fish must be very hot when the sauce is poured over).

● Sprinkle with the cilantro and serve accompanied by rice.

Fish with Black Beans

SERVES 4

Serve this flavorsome fish dish with plain cooked rice. If it is included along with several other dishes as part of an extensive menu, the quantity of fish may be reduced by half.

2 lb flounder or whiting, skinned

3 Tbsp salted black beans

⅓ cup dry sherry

3 Tbsp light soy sauce

1 tsp sesame oil

¼ cup cornstarch

3 Tbsp oil

2 in piece fresh gingerroot, peeled and cut in fine strips

1 green chile, seeded and cut into rings

1 garlic clove, crushed

1 piece lemon grass or strip of lemon zest

1 bunch scallion, cut diagonally into strips

● Cut the fish across into ½ in wide strips and place these in a large shallow dish. Sprinkle the salted black beans, sherry, soy sauce, and sesame oil over the fish. Cover the dish and leave the strips to marinate for 2–3 hours.

● When you are ready to cook the fish, drain the strips well, reserving all the juices. Toss the strips in the cornstarch.

● Heat the oil, then stir fry the ginger, chile, garlic, and lemon grass or zest over medium heat for 4–5 minutes, to extract their flavor. Add the fish strips to the pan and stir fry them carefully, avoiding breaking the strips, until they are lightly browned.

● Add all the green onions and continue to stir fry for 2 minutes, until the onions are cooked. Add ⅓ cup water to the reserved marinating juices and pour them into the pan. Bring to a boil, reduce the heat and stir fry for 1 minute. Serve at once.

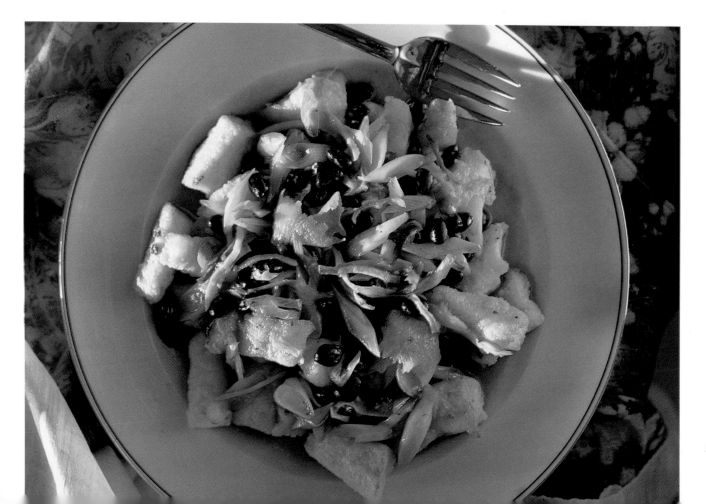

Fried Fish Strips

SERVES 3–4

*These strips are similar to French **goujons**, but they are lighter to eat as they are coated in just egg and flour, rather than batter, and then shallow- rather than deep-fried.*

1¼ lb white fish fillets, such as cod or flounder

1 plump garlic clove, halved lengthwise

seasoned all-purpose flour for coating

1–2 eggs, beaten

oil for frying

seasoned dipping sauce to serve

● Rub the fish with the cut side of the garlic halves, then thinly slice the fish diagonally.

● Coat the fish in seasoned flour, then dip in beaten egg and let the excess egg drain off.

● Heat a shallow layer of oil in a skillet. Add the fish strips, in batches if necessary so they are not crowded, and fry for about 5 minutes, depending on thickness. Transfer to paper towels to drain, then serve hot with seasoned dipping sauce.

Lemon Fish Strips with Zucchini

SERVES 4

½ lb whiting fillets or other firm white fish fillets, skinned

salt and freshly ground black pepper

¼ cup all-purpose flour

grated zest of 1 lemon

¼ cup oil

½ small onion, thinly sliced and separated into strips

1 red bell pepper cut in thin strips

½ lb small zucchini, trimmed, halved lengthwise, and cut in 2 in long sticks

⅓ cup snipped scallions

FOR THE GARNISH

lemon wedges

● Cut the fish fillets across into ½-inch wide strips. Place them in a dish, then sprinkle with the seasoning, flour, and lemon zest. Mix well to coat evenly.

● Heat the oil, then stir-fry the onion and bell pepper for 3 minutes, until lightly cooked, before adding the fish. Carefully stir-fry the fish, taking care not to break the strips, for 4–5 minutes, until lightly browned. Use a slotted spoon to transfer the fish mixture to a heated serving dish.

● Add the zucchini to the oil remaining in the pan (there should be just enough to keep the pan greased) and stir-fry them over high heat for about 2 minutes, so that they are hot and slightly tender.

● Stir in the scallions, then arrange the zucchini around the fish. Garnish with lemon wedges and serve at once. The juice from the lemon should be squeezed over the fish before the fish is eaten.

Fried Fish Topped with Chili Sauce

SERVES 4–6

The scoring makes small trenches in the flesh for the sauce, which is not intended to surround the fish, but to be poured on top at the last minute.

8 garlic cloves

5 fresh yellow chiles

2¼ lb whole perch or sea bass, cleaned and gutted

3 cups peanut or corn oil for frying

½ tsp each salt and ground white pepper

all-purpose flour for dusting

½ cup chicken broth

2 fresh red chiles, quartered lengthwise

1 Tbsp tamarind juice or vinegar

2 tsp sugar

1 tsp fish sauce

½ cup sweet basil leaves, fried in oil for 1 minute until crisp

● Pound the garlic and chile together lightly with a mortar and pestle or in a blender.

● Score the fish on both sides five or six times, sprinkle on the salt and pepper and dust with flour. Heat the oil to 350°F in a pan or wok and fry the fish well, until crisp but tender inside, about 7–10 minutes. Remove and drain the fish and put in a serving dish.

● Take out all except about ¼ cup of the oil. Then, cook the garlic and chile mixture, add the rest of the ingredients, except for the basil, and boil lightly for about 5 minutes until slightly thick. Pour on top of the fish and sprinkle over the fried basil to garnish. Serve accompanied by rice.

Broiled Salted Trout

SERVES 2

Broiling is a very simple way of cooking fish. The trout need to be fresh to make the most of this dish.

2 medium trout, gutted   soy sauce, to serve

1 tsp salt

● Make 3 cuts on each side of the fish, place them on a wire tray, and sprinkle both sides with salt.

● Broil for 5–6 minutes or until lightly browned, then turn and broil for a further 5–6 minutes. (Remember the cooking time will vary depending on the size of the fish.)

● When the fish is ready, transfer to a plate and drizzle with soy sauce. Serve with rice.

Chilled Egg Noodles with Tuna, Shrimp, Wakame, and Sesame Sauce

SERVES 4

1 lb fresh thin egg noodles

2 tsp sesame oil

FOR THE DRESSING

4 Tbsp sesame sauce

4 Tbsp sugar

4 Tbsp vinegar

4 Tbsp Japanese soy sauce

4 Tbsp chicken broth

½ in piece fresh ginger

FOR THE TOPPING

4 tsp dried *wakame* seaweed, soaked in hot water, than drained

8 oz tuna (in water)

½ cup canned corn

8 Tbsp cooked shrimp

generous handful alfalfa sprouts

● Bring a large pan of water to a boil. Cook the noodles for 3 minutes, then rinse and drain. Toss them in the sesame oil, then place onto four serving plates.

● Mix the sesame sauce, sugar, vinegar, soy sauce, and chicken broth well. Extract the juice from the ginger by grating it, then squeezing out the juice. Add it to the mixture, and mix again. Refrigerate.

● Divide the seaweed, tuna, corn, shrimp, and sprouts among each serving of the noodles.

● Pour the sesame dressing over each serving, and serve immediately.

Chilled Egg Noodles with Mackerel and Shrimp

SERVES 4

This recipe is just perfect for one of those summer's days when you are hungry but can't face the thought of eating anything hot.

1 lb fresh or ¾ lb dried thin egg noodles

FOR THE SAUCE

generous 1 cup chicken broth

½ cup light soy sauce

4 Tbsp sugar

½ cup vinegar

4 tsp sesame oil

2 Tbsp juice of squeezed ginger

FOR THE TOPPING

1½ cups bean sprouts

¼ lb snow peas

1 large fillet smoked mackerel, flaked

¼ lb cooked shrimp

handful alfalfa sprouts

1 medium-sized tomato, sliced

● Boil plenty of water in a pan, add the noodles, and cook for 3 minutes. Rinse under water, drain, and arrange on four shallow dishes.

● Heat the chicken broth, soy sauce, and sugar in a pan, and simmer for 3 minutes. Add the vinegar, sesame oil, and ginger juice, and mix well. Chill in the refrigerator.

● Blanch the bean sprouts and snow peas for 1 minute in boiling water. Remove and cut the snow peas into long matchsticks. Now arrange the mackerel flakes, shrimp, bean sprouts, snow peas, alfalfa sprouts, and tomato on the noodles. Pour the chilled sauce over and serve at once.

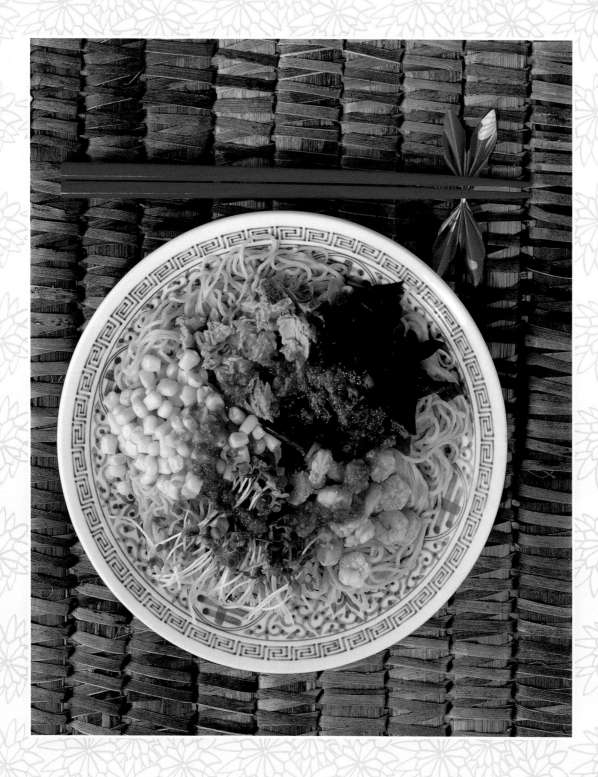

Chilled Egg Noodles with Tuna, Shrimp,
Wakame, and Sesame Sauce

Fried Fish with Pork and Ginger

SERVES 4

A relatively simple dish to prepare, the fish acquires considerable flavor from the pork fat, but is quite mild.

11 oz whole pomfret fish, cleaned and gutted

½ tsp salt

½ cup finely sliced pork belly or fresh fat back

2 salted preserved plums or 1 tbsp pickled lemon juice

¼ cup ginger, sliced

10 small garlic cloves, crushed

½ cup celery with its leaves, cut into 1 in pieces

4 scallions, cut into 1 in pieces

2 fresh red chiles, cut into lengthwise strips

● Wash and dry the fish and rub it inside and out with the salt.

● Place half the pork fat on a heatproof plate that fits a steamer, put the fish on top and cover with the rest of the pork fat. Roughly chop the salted plum and sprinkle it (or the juice) over the top together with the ginger and garlic.

● Steam for 15 minutes, then add the celery, scallion, and chile, and steam for 5 more minutes, until the fish is firm but tender.

● Serve accompanied by rice.

Steamed Fish Curry

SERVES 6–8

Although curry is the closest English description, the final mixture is quite thick and sets quite firmly in the steaming. The banana leaf wrapping not only makes the presentation attractive, but adds some flavor.

11 oz fish fillets (flounder, sole, or sea bass), skinned and cut into slices

2½ cups thin coconut milk

2 eggs, beaten

3 Tbsp fish sauce

1 cup sweet basil leaves

1 cup cabbage, finely sliced

6 squares of banana leaf (optional)

1½ Tbsp cornstarch

2 kaffir lime leaves, torn into small pieces

1 fresh red chile, seeded and cut into strips

FOR THE PASTE

10 small garlic cloves, chopped lightly

5 dried red chiles, chopped lightly

5 white peppercorns

3 shallots, chopped lightly

2 cilantro roots, sliced

1 tsp galangal, sliced

1 tsp lemon grass, chopped

½ tsp kaffir lime zest, finely chopped

½ tsp salt

● Pound together all the ingredients for the paste with a mortar and pestle or in a blender until fine. Put in a bowl and stir in the fish pieces, and 2 cups of the coconut milk. Break in the eggs and mix well. Stir in the fish sauce.

● Divide the basil and cabbage among the banana leaf squares or into six to eight ovenproof ramekins or cups. Top with the fish mixture and wrap up. Cook in a pressure cooker, or bake in a 350°F oven, covered in a pan half-filled with hot water, for 10 minutes.

● Meanwhile, boil the remaining ½ cup of coconut milk in a pan, and add the cornstarch to thicken slightly.

● After the fish mixture has cooked for 10 minutes, spoon the thickened coconut milk over the tops and sprinkle with the lime leaf and chile. Pressure-cook or bake again for 5 more minutes. Leave to stand for 5 minutes before serving, accompanied by rice.

Soba with Simmered Herring

SERVES 4

In Japan, this dish requires the use of a kind of smoked herring not usually available overseas. Kippers make an excellent substitute.

14 oz dried soba

6 cups *dashi* broth

FOR THE TOPPING

4 kipper fillets

2 Tbsp soy sauce

2 Tbsp *mirin*

2 Tbsp sugar

½ cup water

3 scallions, chopped

seven-flavor chili powder (optional)

● Rinse the kippers in hot water. Put them, together with the soy sauce, *mirin*, sugar, and water, into a pan and simmer for about 20 minutes, or until the sauce has thickened.

● Bring plenty of water to a boil in a pan, and add the *soba*. Cook for 5–6 minutes. Drain, and rinse well under cold water. Drain again. Divide into serving bowls.

● Heat the *dashi* broth.

● Place a kipper fillet onto each serving of soba, and sprinkle with chopped scallion. Pour the broth over the top, sprinkle with seven-flavor chili powder, and serve immediately.

Deep Fried Fish Cakes

SERVES 4

In Vietnam a milkfish or pomfret might be used for this recipe. Frozen cod fillets are a perfectly adequate substitute.

10 oz white fish

⅔ cup coconut milk or cow's milk

½ lb sweet potatoes, boiled and mashed

2 tomatoes, skinned and chopped

2 Tbsp fresh cilantro, chopped

2 Tbsp fish sauce or 2 Tbsp light soy sauce mixed with 1 tsp anchovy extract

2 eggs, lightly beaten

rice flour or all-purpose plain flour

vegetable oil for deep-frying

FOR THE GARNISH

lettuce leaves

sprigs of mint

● Cover the fish with the coconut milk. (If there is not sufficient, add a little water or cow's milk.) Bring the milk to a boil and simmer for 10 minutes or until the fish is tender. Remove any skin or bones and flake the fish.

● Place the fish, potato, tomatoes, and cilantro in a bowl and mix well.

● Combine the fish sauce and egg. Add half this mixture slowly to the fish mixture so that it retains its shape. Add some flour if the mixture is too runny.

● Shape the mixture into small balls. Dip each ball into the remaining egg and fish sauce mixture, and roll into the rice flour.

● Heat the oil until it is smoking and deep-fry until the balls are golden brown.

● Serve hot, garnished with the lettuce and a few sprigs of mint.

Mackerel Cooked in a Pot Lined with Pork

SERVES 4

2 large mackerel, cleaned

2 pieces bean curd

salt

salt and pepper for seasoning

3 Tbsp vegetable oil

4 oz fresh pork sides, cut into threads

4 oz black Chinese mushrooms, soaked in warm water, cut into threads

1 cup bamboo shoots, sliced

1 red chile pepper, chopped

2 slices gingerroot, chopped

1 Tbsp dark soy sauce

1 Tbsp fish sauce

½ Tbsp wine

2½ cups water

2 scallions, chopped

● Chop the mackerel into slices about 1 inch thick.

● Wash the bean curd gently with water, salt lightly to absorb the water and season. Cut the bean curd in half and then cut the pieces into cubes.

● Heat a wok and pour in 1 tablespoon oil to fry the bean curd cubes. Set aside. Heat 1 tablespoon oil and fry the mackerel until both sides turn golden brown.

● Add the remaining oil. Add the pork, black mushrooms, bamboo shoots, chile, gingerroot, soy sauce, fish sauce, wine, and sugar, and stir-fry.

● Pour the contents of the wok into an earthenware pot or heavy pan, add the water and bring to a boil over a high heat. Reduce the heat to low and braise for 20 minutes. Taste and add the green onions. Serve in the pot when cooked.

Simmered Mackerel in Miso Sauce

SERVES 2

This Japanese dish is a particular favorite in fall, when the mackerel is reputed to be at its best. The fish is cooked unboned to give extra flavor.

1 lb mackerel, head removed
and gutted

FOR THE SAUCE

½ cup water

2 Tbsp superfine sugar

1 Tbsp *sake*

2 oz *miso*

1 thin slice peeled gingerroot

2 scallions, cut in half

● Cut the mackerel in half, close to one side of the back bone, to make two pieces of fish, one with the back bone attached and one without. Cut each piece in half again.

● Put the water, sugar, *sake*, and *miso* in a pan, then heat until the liquid is simmering. Add the fish and ginger and continue to simmer, covered, for 7–8 minutes with a lid, slightly smaller than the pan and placed directly onto the fish. Use aluminum foil if you do not have a lid.

● Add the scallions and simmer for a further 5–10 minutes. Serve immediately with rice.

Golden Fish with Potatoes

SERVES 4

⅓ cup all-purpose flour

½ tsp turmeric

salt and freshly ground white pepper

zest of 1 lemon, grated

1 lb monkfish, thick cod fillet, or other firm white fish, skinned and cubed

¼ cup oil

2 celery stalks, thinly sliced

1 small onion, finely chopped

½ lb fine beans, blanched in boiling water for 1 minute and drained

1½ lb baby potatoes, scraped and cooked

● Mix the flour, turmeric, seasoning, and lemon zest, then toss the fish cubes in this mixture to coat them completely.

● Heat the oil, then stir-fry the celery and onion until slightly softened, about 7 minutes. Add the beans and potatoes, and continue to stir fry for 5–7 minutes, until all the vegetables are hot and tender.

● Push the vegetables to one side of the pan and add the fish. Stir-fry the cubes over medium to high heat, taking care not to break them, until golden-brown. Gently mix the ingredients and serve at once.

Stir-fried Rice Vermicelli with Barbecued Pork and Shrimp

SERVES 4–6

This Chinese noodle dish uses barbecued pork to provide extra flavor. If you do not have time to make **cha siu**, *you can use sliced lean pork instead.*

½ lb rice vermicelli

4 Tbsp vegetable oil

1 in piece fresh gingerroot, peeled and finely chopped

2 cloves garlic, finely chopped

½ lb Chinese barbecued pork (*cha siu*), diced

¼ lb peeled shrimp

2½ cups bean sprouts

8 water chestnuts, sliced

6 scallions, chopped

¼ lb spinach, chopped

2 Tbsp Chinese rice wine or dry sherry

4 Tbsp light soy sauce

1½ Tbsp dark soy sauce

6 Tbsp chicken broth

black pepper and salt

● Soak the vermicelli in warm water for 3 minutes, or according to the instructions on the package. Rinse under running water, and drain.

● Heat 3 tablespoons of the oil in a wok or large frying pan until very hot. Stir-fry the ginger and garlic for 30 seconds. Add the pork, shrimp, bean sprouts, water chestnuts, scallions, and spinach, and stir-fry for 2–3 minutes.

● Add the remaining tablespoon of oil and the vermicelli, stir quickly, then add the rice wine, soy sauce, and chicken stock. Keep stirring until the sauce is absorbed. Sprinkle with black pepper and salt to taste. Serve immediately.

Shrimp in Jackets

SERVES 4

When raw, tiger shrimp are dark grayish-brown with darker rings, but the shells turn rosy pink and the flesh pale pinkish-white when they are cooked. They are quite expensive, but they are large and meaty—they can range from 3 inches up to enormous specimens of 10 inches—so three tiger shrimp of about 3–4 inches are enough for one portion.

¾ cup all-purpose flour

2 tsp black sesame seeds

salt and freshly ground black pepper

1 egg, beaten

1–2 tsp sesame oil

12 raw tiger shrimp in their shells, about 3 in long

vegetable oil for deep-frying

vinegar dipping sauce to serve

● Stir together the flour, sesame seeds, and seasoning. Stir in the egg and sesame oil, then add enough water (about ½ cup) to make a light coating batter. Set aside.

● Remove the heads and fine legs from the shrimp, leaving the tails intact. With a fine knife-point, slit along the back of each shrimp and remove the dark thread.

● Half fill a deep-fat fryer with vegetable oil and heat to 350°F.

● Stir the batter, then dip the shrimp into it. Let the excess batter drain off the shrimp, then deep-fry in batches for about 3–4 minutes until crisp and brown. Transfer to paper towels to drain. Keep warm while frying the remaining shrimp. Serve hot with vinegar dipping sauce.

Shrimp with Lemon and Coconut

SERVES 4–6

The lemon, coconut, and shrimp combination is wonderful. This is a good cocktail snack, too.

1 lb 2 oz large raw shrimps, shelled

1 cup thin coconut milk

2 Tbsp lemon juice

¼ tsp fish sauce

¼ tsp sugar

¼ tsp salt

2 Tbsp shallots, sliced

5 fresh small green chiles, sliced into thin circles

● To butterfly the shrimp, cut them lengthwise almost all the way through and splay them out.

● Boil the coconut milk in a pan, add the shrimp, cook for 1 minute and remove the pan from the heat. Allow to stand for about 1 minute—until the shrimp are just cooked—then remove them with a slotted spoon and place on a serving plate.

● Add the lemon juice, fish sauce, sugar, and salt to the coconut milk in the pan, stir well for 1 minute, and then spoon this sauce over the shrimp. Sprinkle over the shallot and chile, and serve with rice.

Shrimp in Jackets

Egg-fried Rice with Shrimp

SERVES 4

Crunchy water chestnuts add a pleasing contrast in texture to this favorite rice dish. The rice should be freshly cooked.

¼ cup oil

1 tsp sesame oil

1 bunch scallions, shredded
    diagonally

7 oz can water chestnuts,
    drained and sliced

¼ lb frozen peas

¾ lb cooked shrimp, peeled

3 eggs, beaten

1 cup long-grain rice, cooked

¼ cup light soy sauce

whole cooked shrimp to garnish

● Heat the oils together, then stir-fry the onions, water chestnuts, and peas for 3–5 minutes, until the peas are thawed and hot. Add the shrimp and stir-fry for another minute.

● Lower the heat, pour the eggs into the pan and cook until they are half-set. They should be thickened, but not scrambled—if they are too thin, they coat the rice grains too freely and give the finished rice an inferior texture. If the eggs are allowed to set before the rice is added, they tend to be overcooked.

● Tip all the rice into the pan and turn it over in the egg mixture to combine all the ingredients evenly. The eggs should finish cooking almost immediately.

● Sprinkle in the soy sauce and serve at once, garnished with the whole shrimp, if liked.

Casseroled Shrimp with Cellophane Noodles

SERVES 6

The size of the shrimp is unimportant; you could use small shrimp or lobster tails, or even crab claws.

2 bacon rashers, cut into 1 in pieces

6 large shrimp, shelled

2 cilantro roots, cut in half

1 oz ginger, pounded, or chopped finely

1 oz garlic, chopped

1 Tbsp white peppercorns, crushed

5 cups cellophane noodles, soaked in cold water for 10 minutes

1 tsp butter

3 Tbsp black soy sauce

¼ cup roughly chopped cilantro leaves and stems

FOR THE BROTH

2 cups chicken broth

2 Tbsp oyster sauce

2 Tbsp black soy sauce

½ Tbsp sesame seed oil

1 tsp brandy or whiskey

½ tsp sugar

● Place all the broth ingredients in a pan, bring to a boil, and simmer for 5 minutes. Leave to cool.

● Take a heatproof casserole dish or heavy-bottomed pan and place the bacon over the base. Put in the shrimp, cilantro root, ginger, garlic, and peppercorns. Place the noodles over the top, then add the butter, soy sauce, and broth.

● Place on the heat, cover, bring to a boil, and simmer for 5 minutes. Mix well, add the cilantro, cover and cook again until the shrimp are cooked, about 5 minutes more. Remove excess broth liquid before serving.

Deep Fried Squid with Plantain Fritters

SERVES 4

1 lb fresh squid, cleaned and prepared

2 large garlic cloves, minced

2 tsp fish sauce (optional)

2 Tbsp fresh dill, chopped

black pepper

cornstarch

vegetable oil for deep-frying

NUOC CHAM SAUCE

2 small garlic cloves, crushed

1 small fresh red chile pepper, seeded, and minced

1 oz sugar

2 Tbsp fresh lime or lemon juice

¼ cup cider vinegar or wine vinegar

¼ cup fish sauce

1 Tbsp water

PLANTAIN FRITTERS

1 egg

2 Tbsp superfine sugar

1 whole ripe plantain, peeled and mashed

½ cup all-purpose flour

1 tsp baking powder

vegetable oil for frying

FOR THE BATTER

1 cup all-purpose flour

pinch of salt

pinch of ground cinnamon

1 egg, beaten

⅔ cup milk

● Make the fritters first. Make the batter by mixing the flour and salt. Stir the cinnamon, egg, and milk together and add to the flour and salt mixture. Mix thoroughly using a wire whisk. Place on a low shelf in the refrigerator for at least 30 minutes.

● Add the egg and then 2 tablespoons sugar to the plantain, beating continuously. Mix the flour and baking powder, stir into the plantain mixture and blend thoroughly. Coat the mixture, a tablespoon at a time, with the batter. Heat the oil and fry these one at a time. Set the fritters aside.

● Make the *nuoc cham* sauce. Place the garlic, chile, sugar, lime or lemon juice, vinegar, fish sauce, and water in a blender or food processor and blend for 30 seconds or until the sugar dissolves. Set aside.

● Separate the head and body of the squid by pulling it apart gently. Cut off and chop up the tentacles; discard the head. Peel off the membrane from the body. Wash the squid under cold water and cut the body into rings.

● Combine the squid, tentacles, garlic, fish sauce (if used), dill, and black pepper. Allow to marinate for 30 minutes. Coat the rings and tentacles in cornstarch, shaking off any excess.

● Heat the oil until it starts to smoke. Drop in the squid pieces a few at a time and deep-fry for about 1 minute or until golden brown. Remove and drain on paper towels.

● On a serving plate, make a ring with the plantain fritters and heap the deep-fried squid in the middle. Serve hot with the *nuoc cham* sauce in a small bowl.

Deep Fried Squid
with Plantain Fritters

Broiled Scallop Kabobs

SERVES 2–4

Rice vinegar begins to "cook" the scallops in the same way that lime juice "cooks" fish when making Mexican **ceviche,** *so the scallops need only brief cooking under the broiler if they are not to become overcooked.*

12 large scallops

1 garlic clove, crushed and
    finely chopped

1 Tbsp scallion, green part,
    finely chopped

2 Tbsp soy sauce

2 tsp rice vinegar

1 Tbsp sesame oil

½ in piece of gingerroot, grated

2 tsp crushed toasted sesame
    seeds

pinch of chili powder

● Cut each scallop in half horizontally. Thread the scallops onto skewers and lay them in a shallow, non-metallic dish.

● Mix together the remaining ingredients and pour over the scallops. Turn the skewers over and leave for 15–30 minutes, turning occasionally.

● Preheat the broiler.

● Lift the skewers from the marinade and cook under the broiler for about 4 minutes, turning occasionally and brushing with the marinade.

Simmered Squid with White Radish

SERVES 2

*The flavor of this dish comes from the subtle taste of the squid combined with the fresh white radish which is easier to cook than Japanese **daikon**, because of its higher water content.*

10 oz squid

10 oz white radish, peeled, cut in half lengthwise and cut into ½ in widths

¼ cup *sake*

2½ Tbsp soy sauce

½ cup water

● Pull the head and tentacles from the squid, then remove the transparent center bone and wash the body cavity. Take off the skin, then cut the head from the tentacles.

● Cut the body and legs of the squid into ½ in widths and blanch in boiling water. Put the radish in a pan and cover with cold water. Bring to a boil and simmer for about 6 minutes until the radish has become almost transparent, then drain.

● Heat the *sake* in a pan with the soy sauce. When it boils, add the squid and simmer for about 4 minutes. Remove the squid with a slotted spoon and set aside.

● Add the water and drained radish to the pan, simmer, covered, for about 7 minutes. Put the squid in the pan with the radish and simmer for 3–4 minutes. Serve with rice and a vegetable dish.

Stir-fried Squid with Chiles and Vegetables

SERVES 3–4

Both the hot, fermented bean paste, **kochujang,** *and Korea's excellent coarsely pounded red chili powder, are used in this spicy dish. The Korean chili powder adds a characteristic bright, carmine pink color. If necessary, you can always use cayenne pepper mixed with paprika to obtain the same result. Chile bean paste can also be substituted for the* **kochuchang.**

1¼ lb cleaned squid

3 Tbsp vegetable oil

1 onion, thinly sliced

2 garlic cloves, crushed

1 carrot, thinly sliced lengthwise

1 zucchini, thinly sliced lengthwise

2–3 long fresh red chiles, thinly sliced lengthwise

2 long, fresh green chiles, thinly sliced lengthwise

1 Tbsp *kochujang* or chile bean paste

about ½ tsp Korean chili powder, or cayenne pepper mixed with paprika

1 tsp sugar

salt and freshly ground black pepper

2 scallions, white and green parts sliced diagonally

2 tsp sesame oil

toasted sesame seeds to garnish

● Cut open each squid body so that it lies flat, then cut across into 2½ x ½-inch pieces. Cut the tentacles into 2½ inch lengths.

● Bring a large saucepan of water to a boil. Add all the squid simultaneously and remove from the heat. Stir immediately and continue to stir until the squid turns white, about 40 seconds. Drain well and discard the water.

● Heat the oil in a large skillet over a moderate heat. Add the onion, garlic, and carrot. Stir for 30–40 seconds, then add the zucchini, chiles, and 2 teaspoons *kochujang* or chili bean paste, half the chili powder or cayenne and paprika. Stir for 30 seconds. Stir in the squid, the remaining *kochujang* and chili powder or cayenne and paprika, sugar and salt and pepper. Cook slowly for 2 minutes, then add the scallions and sesame oil. Tip into a warm serving dish and garnish with toasted sesame seeds.

Thai-style Scallops

SERVES 4

A great favorite and an especially tasty alternative to normally bland treatments for this shellfish.

16 medium-sized scallops, with 4 shells if available

¼ cup butter, melted

2 Tbsp lime juice

1 Tbsp garlic, chopped

1 Tbsp shallot, chopped

1 Tbsp ginger, chopped

1 Tbsp cilantro leaf, chopped

salt and ground white pepper to taste

● Mix the scallops with all the other ingredients in a bowl, and season. If you have the scallop shells, place 4 scallops with mixture in each shell; otherwise put all in a heatproof dish.

● Bake in a 350°F oven or broil under medium heat until just cooked, about 10 minutes. Do not overcook.

● Serve with other dishes or double the recipe and serve with rice.

Stir-Fried Squid with Chiles
and Vegetables

Lobster and Sweet Potato Curry

SERVES 4–6

2 Tbsp unsalted butter

1 lb sweet potatoes, peeled and cut into 1 in cubes

1 Tbsp *sake* or dry sherry

1 whole lobster, chopped into 1 in cubes

FOR THE CURRY SAUCE

1 Tbsp vegetable oil

½ cup onion, chopped

1 Tbsp garlic, minced

2 tsp shrimp paste

1 dried chile, seeds removed, crushed

2 tsp cumin seeds

1 Tbsp coriander seeds

1 tsp dried lemon grass, sliced

1 tsp galangal, ground

2 tsp lemon peel, minced

2 Tbsp fresh cilantro, chopped

1 tsp salt

1 tsp ground turmeric

2 tsp sweet paprika

● Make the curry sauce by heating the oil over medium-high heat. Add the onion and garlic, and cook for 5 minutes or until soft. Add the shrimp paste and stir thoroughly, pressing the paste to blend it well. Cook for a further 3 or so minutes and remove from the heat.

● Grind the chile, cumin seeds, coriander seeds, and lemon grass until powdery.

● Place the onion mixture in a blender or food processor and blend until very smooth. Add the ground spices, galangal, lemon peel, fresh cilantro, salt, turmeric, and paprika. Blend until the mixture becomes a smooth paste. This makes about ¼ cup curry sauce.

● Melt the butter over medium heat and add the sweet potatoes. Cook for 15 minutes, taking care the potato does not burn.

● Stir in the curry sauce and *sake* together until the curry mixture is dissolved. Add the lobster cubes and cook for 2–3 more minutes.

Baby Clams with Chile and Basil

SERVES 4

⅓ cup peanut or corn oil for frying

1 lb 6 oz fresh baby clams in their shells, cleaned well

1½ Tbsp garlic, chopped

5 fresh red chiles, sliced lengthwise

2 Tbsp red chile paste

2 tsp white soy sauce

½ cup chicken broth

1 cup sweet basil leaves

● Heat the oil in a pan or wok until quite hot, about 375°F. Add the clams and garlic, and cook until the clams open slightly, 2–3 minutes.

● Add the fresh chiles, chile paste, and soy sauce, mix well, then pour in the chicken broth. Bring to a boil, cook for 2 minutes, stir in the basil and serve immediately accompanied by rice.

Poultry
Main Dishes

The everyday main meals in this and the following section are
suitable for family meals or for informal lunches and suppers
with friends. They are inexpensive, easy, and satisfying. Many
of the recipes in this section can be adapted to seafood- or
vegetable-based dishes and vice versa.

Stir-fried Chicken

SERVES 4

Prepare the vegetables while the chicken is marinating; then, when you start cooking, the dish is soon ready to serve.

1 lb skinned, boneless chicken breasts, cut into strips

2 Tbsp soy sauce

1 Tbsp sugar

2 scallions, white and some green parts finely chopped

1 in piece of gingerroot, finely chopped

1½ tsp crushed toasted sesame seeds

freshly ground black pepper

1 small carrot, thinly sliced diagonally

3 dried Chinese black mushrooms, soaked for 30 minutes in hot water

1½ Tbsp sesame oil

1 red bell pepper, seeded and cut into thin strips

● Put the chicken into a bowl.

● Mix together the soy sauce, sugar, scallions, ginger, sesame seeds, and plenty of pepper. Pour the mixture over the chicken. Turn the chicken over and leave for 30 minutes. Remove from the marinade; reserve the marinade.

● Meanwhile, blanch the carrot in boiling water for 5 minutes. Drain and set aside.

● Drain the mushrooms, cut out and discard any hard patches and the stalks. Slice the mushroom caps.

● Heat the sesame oil in a skillet. Add the chicken and stir-fry for 2–3 minutes. Remove from the pan and set aside. Add the mushrooms and carrots, and stir-fry for a further 2 minutes. Add the pepper and stir-fry for another minute.

● Return the chicken to the pan. Add the reserved marinade and bring to a boil. Stir and cook for 1 minute, then serve garnished with egg strips.

Boiled Chicken with Fish Sauce

SERVES 6

1 large chicken, either corn-fed or free-range

about 5 pts water

2 x 1 in sliced peeled gingerroot, about ⅛ in thick

2 Tbsp fish sauce or light soy sauce and 1 tsp anchovy extract

2 dried black Chinese mushrooms

1 Tbsp dry sherry

salt

FOR THE INDIVIDUAL DIPS

1 Tbsp light soy sauce

1 Tbsp sesame seed oil

1 Tbsp fish sauce

● Tear off the fat from the chicken cavity and discard. Cut off the tail end and rinse the chicken in cold water. Bring a large pot of water to a boil over high heat and plunge in the chicken. When the water comes to a boil again, let the chicken cook for 1 minute to firm the skin. Remove it and rinse it briefly with running warm water to get rid of any scum.

● Bring the measured amount of water to a boil with the ginger slices and fish sauce in a deep pot into which the chicken will fit snugly. Add the chicken and, when the water boils again, turn the heat down to a simmer. Cover and simmer for 1½ hours, turning the chicken from time to time to ensure that it cooks evenly all over.

● In the meantime, soak the black mushrooms in some warm water for about 20 minutes. Squeeze them dry and rinse in cold water, repeating this a couple of times. Cut off and discard the stems and add the mushrooms to the soup about 30 minutes into the cooking time. Add the sherry when the chicken is cooked and season with salt to taste.

● Serve the chicken whole in the soup and the dips in individual saucers. Guests tear off pieces of the meat with a fork or chopsticks and put it in their bowls with a little broth and mushrooms. Leftover chicken can be used for a variety of dishes.

Chicken with Broccoli and Cashew Nuts

SERVES 4

1 Tbsp cornstarch

⅓ cup dry sherry

⅓ cup soy sauce

½ cup chicken broth

1 tsp sesame oil

3 Tbsp sunflower or peanut oil

2 large boneless chicken breasts, skinned and cut into thin strips

⅓ cup unsalted cashew nuts

½ cup broccoli flowerets, broken into small pieces

7 oz can bamboo shoots, drained and sliced

6 scallions, sliced diagonally

● Blend the cornstarch to a smooth, thin paste with the sherry, soy sauce, and broth, then set the mixture aside until needed.

● Heat the sesame oil and sunflower or peanut oil, then stir-fry the chicken and cashew nuts until the chicken has become golden and cooked, and the nuts have been lightly browned.

● Add the broccoli, bamboo shoots, and scallions and continue to stir fry for 3–4 minutes, until the broccoli is lightly cooked.

● Give the cornstarch mixture a stir, then pour it into the pan and stir over medium heat, until the sauce boils. Allow the mixture to boil for a minute or so, stirring all the time, so that all the ingredients are coated in a lightly thickened sauce. Serve at once, while still hot.

Chicken with Mango

SERVES 4

1 lb corn-fed chicken, cubed

1 large carrot

½ red bell pepper

½ green bell pepper

4 oz bamboo shoots

1 large mango, just ripe and firm, cut into chunks

4 Tbsp vegetable oil

FOR THE MARINADE

½ tsp baking soda

1 Tbsp sugar

1 egg white, lightly beaten

1 Tbsp cornstarch or potato flour

salt

water

FOR THE SAUCE

1 tsp sugar

1 Tbsp light soy sauce

1 Tbsp oyster sauce

1 Tbsp sesame seed oil

1 Tbsp rice wine

½ Tbsp cornstarch or potato flour, mixed with a little water

● Mix the marinade ingredients thoroughly and combine well with the chicken pieces. Leave to marinate for 30 minutes.

● Trim and peel the carrot; cut into matchstick strips a little less than 1 inch long. Cut the peppers and bamboo shoots into strips to match the carrots. Cut the mango flesh into small, fairly thin pieces as neatly as possible.

● Heat the oil in a wok and fry the chicken pieces for about 2 minutes. Remove from the oil and drain well. Add the carrot, peppers, mango, and bamboo shoots to the hot oil and fry in batches. Remove and drain.

● Rinse and dry the wok, add the chicken and vegetables and stir in all the sauce ingredients, except the cornstarch. Stir-fry briefly and add the cornstarch to the sauce to thicken.

Chicken with Broccoli
and Cashew Nuts

Chicken Fried with Cashew Nuts

SERVES 4

A delicious dish, of Chinese origin, which is very easy to make and looks impressive.

11 oz boneless skinned chicken breasts, cut into slices

all-purpose flour for coating

1 cup peanut or corn oil

4 dried red chiles, fried and cut into ½ in pieces

1 Tbsp garlic, chopped

10 scallions, white parts, cut into 2 in pieces

⅓ cup unsalted roasted cashew nuts

3 oz onion, sliced

2 Tbsp oyster sauce

1 Tbsp light soy sauce

1 Tbsp sugar

⅛ tsp dark soy sauce

● Coat the chicken lightly with flour. Heat the oil in a skillet or wok and fry the chicken for about 5 minutes until light brown. Remove almost all of the oil from the skillet.

● Add the chile and garlic to the chicken in the pan and fry for 1 minute. Add all the remaining ingredients; fry until cooked, about 3 more minutes. Serve accompanied by rice.

Fresh Chicken with Lemon Grass and Cashew Nuts

SERVES 4

vegetable oil

2 small dried chiles

1 clove garlic, chopped

1 lb lean, corn-fed chicken, sliced

½ tsp sugar

1 Tbsp oyster sauce

1 Tbsp fish sauce or light soy sauce

3 Tbsp chicken broth or water

½ cup roasted, unsalted cashew nuts

1 Tbsp lemon grass, chopped

2 shallots, cut in quarters

● With a drop or two of oil, stir-fry the chiles until cooked evenly but not burnt. Set aside.

● Stir-fry the garlic with a few more drops of oil until golden. Add the chicken slices, sugar, and oyster and fish sauces and stir-fry until the chicken is golden in color. Lower the heat and add the stock. Cook for a few more minutes, stirring occasionally.

● When the chicken is thoroughly cooked, add the cashew nuts, lemon grass, shallots, and chiles, and stir several times, being careful not to break the chiles. Remove from the heat and serve.

Chicken and Scallion Kabobs

SERVES 4

As good as the kabobs are when broiled, they are even better when cooked on a barbecue.

about 1½ lb skinned, boneless chicken thighs

1–2 bunches plump scallions, white parts only

4 Tbsp soy sauce

1 Tbsp sesame oil

2 tsp sugar

2 garlic cloves, crushed and finely chopped

¾ in piece of gingerroot, grated

1 Tbsp crushed toasted sesame seeds

diagonally sliced pale green parts of scallion for garnish

toasted sesame seeds for garnish

● Cut each chicken thigh into three lengths. Thread pieces of chicken and scallions alternately onto short skewers. Lay the skewers in a large, shallow dish.

● Mix together the remaining ingredients, except the garnishes, and pour over the skewers. Turn to coat with the sauce, then leave for 3–4 hours, turning two or three times.

● Preheat the broiler or barbecue.

● Lift the skewers from the marinade and broil or grill for about 10–15 minutes, turning occasionally and brushing with the remaining marinade. Serve garnished with scallions and toasted sesame seeds.

Chicken Fried Rice

SERVES 4

One of the basic standard Thai dishes, this always tastes best with rice from the day before—and is easier to cook if the rice has been chilled in the fridge for a while. In place of chicken, pork or shrimps are also commonly used.

3 Tbsp peanut or corn oil

7 oz boneless skinned chicken breasts, cut lengthwise into ½ in thick slices

1 Tbsp chopped garlic

1 medium-sized onion, sliced

2 eggs

4 cups cooked rice

1 tomato, cut into 8 wedges

1 scallion, chopped

2 tsp light soy sauce

1 tsp fish sauce

1 tsp sugar

1 tsp ground white pepper

● Heat the oil in a wok or pan, add the chicken and garlic and mix well over the heat for 1 minute. Add the onion and cook for 1 minute, break in the eggs, mix very well and then stir in the rice and the rest of the ingredients. Stir well. Cook for 2 minutes and serve immediately.

● Serve accompanied by cucumber slices, whole scallions, and fish sauce with chiles.

Chicken and Egg on Rice

SERVES 2

5½ oz short-grain rice

⅔ cup *dashi* stock

1 Tbsp superfine sugar

1 Tbsp *mirin*

3 Tbsp soy sauce

2 boneless chicken breasts, diced

1 medium onion, sliced

1 egg, beaten

FOR THE GARNISH

watercress

● Rinse and boil the rice according to the instructions on the packet.

● Bring the *dashi* stock, sugar, *mirin* and soy sauce to the boil in a skillet. Add the chicken and onion. Simmer for about 8 minutes or until the chicken is cooked through.

● Pour over the egg, letting it set on top of the chicken without stirring. When the egg has set, sprinkle on some watercress as a garnish. Serve the mixture on top of the serving of rice.

Chicken Fried with Green Bell Pepper

SERVES 4

¼ cup peanut or corn oil

1 Tbsp chopped garlic

11 oz boneless skinned chicken breasts, cut lengthwise into ½ in thick slices

1 cup green bell pepper, sliced

5 fresh red chiles, sliced lengthwise

½ cup onion, thickly sliced

1 Tbsp oyster sauce

½ Tbsp light soy sauce

1 tsp fish sauce

¼ tsp dark soy sauce

½ cup sweet basil leaves

● Heat the oil in a wok or pan, add the garlic and chicken and fry well for a minute. Add the green pepper and chile, mix, then add the onion and cook for 1 minute.

● One by one stir in the rest of the ingredients, cooking for about 30 seconds after each addition. Remove from the heat immediately after stirring in the basil. Serve accompanied by rice.

Chicken Fried with Ginger

SERVES 4

⅓ cup peanut or corn oil

1 Tbsp chopped garlic

11 oz boneless skinned chicken breasts, cut into ¼ in thick slices

1 oz wood ear fungus or fresh button mushrooms, sliced

4 scallions, cut into 1 in pieces

2 oz onion, sliced

1 oz gingerroot, cut into small matchsticks

3 fresh red chiles, each sliced into 6 strips lengthwise

1 Tbsp light soy sauce

2 tsp brandy

½ tsp sugar

¼ tsp salt

● Heat the oil in a wok or pan, add the garlic and stir-fry, mixing well.

● Add the chicken, mix well for 1 minute, and then add the mushrooms. Stir for a minute and add all the rest of the ingredients. Stir-fry well until the chicken is cooked, about 8–10 minutes.

● Serve accompanied by rice and phrik nam plaa.

Thai Sweet and Sour Chicken

SERVES 4–6

A dish that is popular with most people. It is not spicy, but a spoonful of fish sauce will add zest.

4 cups peanut or corn oil

15 oz boneless skinned chicken breasts, cut across into ¼ in slices

all-purpose flour for coating

1 medium-sized onion, sliced

1 medium-sized green bell pepper, sliced

½ cup tomato katsup

½ cup tomato quarters

½ cup diced pineapple

½ cup chicken broth

2 tsp light soy sauce

1 tsp sugar

1 tsp white vinegar

● Heat the oil in a wok or pan, coat the chicken lightly with flour and fry it until it is light brown, about 5 minutes. Remove and drain on paper towel.

● Remove all the oil except for about ⅓ cup. Add the onion and bell pepper, cook for 1 minute, mix in the katsup, and then add the remaining ingredients. Stir-fry for 1 minute, add the chicken and continue to cook until the onion is tender, about 2 minutes.

● Serve accompanied by rice and fish sauce with fresh chiles.

Caramelized Chicken Wings with an Orange Sauce

SERVES 4

This dish should have a slightly nutty, burnt flavor, but be careful not to burn the sugar.

8 chicken wings

salt and pepper

2 Tbsp sesame oil

4 Tbsp clear honey

4 Tbsp vegetable oil

2 Tbsp superfine sugar

shredded peel and juice of 1 orange

● Season the chicken wings with salt and pepper. Mix the sesame oil and honey, and spread this over the wings.

● Heat the oil in a heavy-based pan and cook the chicken wings for about 4 minutes on each side or until just done. Remove the pan and keep warm. Reserve the pan juices.

● Add the sugar to the pan and heat without stirring until it caramelizes. Remove from the heat.

● Add the orange juice and reserved pan juices. Stir over a low heat until a smooth sauce forms, adding a little water or orange juice if it becomes too thick. Add half the orange peel and continue to cook over a very low heat.

● Place the chicken wings on to a warmed dish. Pour the caramel sauce over them and garnish with the leftover strips of orange.

Stuffed Chicken Wings

SERVES 4

This is a delicious and economical dish, which looks very impressive.

8 chicken wings

FOR THE STUFFING

4 oz bean thread vermicelli

3 pieces wood ear fungus

1¼ cups ground pork

1 small onion, grated finely

1 small carrot, grated finely

1 egg, beaten

1 Tbsp fish sauce or light soy sauce

salt and black pepper

● Bone the chicken wings by cutting around the bone with a sharp knife. Holding the wingtip, gently ease the bone away to leave the skin and a thin layer of chicken.

● Soak the vermicelli in warm water for 10 minutes, then drain thoroughly and cut into short strands. Soak the wood ear fungus in warm water for 10 minutes, then squeeze dry and chop into thin slices.

● Mix all the stuffing ingredients together. The mixture should be firm. Mold the stuffing into a ball and insert it into the bag of flesh and skin of the chicken wings.

● Preheat the oven to 400°F. Steam the stuffed wings for 10–15 minutes. (If you want to make a large quantity, multiply the measures accordingly and freeze after the steam stage.)

● After steaming, place in a lightly oiled roasting pan and roast in the oven for 30 minutes. Serve on a bed of lettuce as a starter or with rice and a beef stir-fried dish for a main course.

Spiced Ground Chicken

SERVES 6

One of the special characteristics of the northeastern Thai version of this meat dish is the addition of uncooked sticky rice, which is first roasted (either in an oven or in a dry wok) until golden and then pounded in a mortar. It adds a slightly nutty flavor and gives the dish more body.

1 lb finely ground chicken

¼ cup shallots, sliced

¼ cup cilantro leaves

4 Tbsp sticky rice, dry-fried for 8–10 minutes until brown and pounded finely

4 Tbsp lemon juice, or to taste

3 Tbsp fish sauce, or to taste

1 Tbsp chopped dried red chile, or to taste

½ tsp sugar

FOR THE GARNISH

fresh mint leaves

● Cook the chicken in a nonstick pan over low heat for 10 minutes—do not add water or oil. When cooked, transfer to a bowl and mix in well all the remaining ingredients except the mint.

● Check the seasoning, and add more lemon juice, fish sauce or chile if necessary. Sprinkle the mint over the top to garnish.

● Serve accompanied by raw cabbage leaves, scallions, and raw string beans.

Korean Braised Chicken Thighs

SERVES 4

Chicken thighs become richly flavored and very tender and succulent when steeped in a tasty marinade, then fried and braised in it.

8 chicken thighs

4 scallions, white parts only, very finely chopped

1 in piece of fresh gingerroot, grated

2 garlic cloves, crushed and chopped

4 Tbsp soy sauce

1 Tbsp sesame oil

1½ Tbsp crushed toasted sesame seeds

2 tsp sugar

vegetable oil for frying

1 red bell pepper, seeded and diced

2 scallions, white and pale green parts sliced diagonally

● Slash each chicken thigh three times and place in a shallow dish.

● Mix together the finely chopped scallions, ginger, garlic, soy sauce, sesame oil, sesame seeds, and sugar. Pour over the chicken. Turn to coat with the sauce and leave in a cool place for about 4 hours, turning occasionally.

● Heat a little vegetable oil in a heavy flameproof casserole. Lift the chicken thighs from the marinade, add to the casserole and brown evenly. Pour in the marinade and enough water just to cover the chicken. Bring barely to simmering point. Cover the casserole and leave to cook gently for about 30–35 minutes, turning the chicken occasionally, until very tender.

● Add the red bell pepper and sliced scallions about 5 minutes before the end of cooking.

Yellow Chicken Curry

SERVES 6

An Indian-influenced curry dish, which is very popular in Thailand.

5 cups thin coconut milk

1 lb chicken, cut into medium-sized pieces

7 oz potatoes, peeled and cut into ½ in cubes

2 tsp salt

3 Tbsp sliced shallots, fried until light brown

FOR THE YELLOW CURRY PASTE

5 dried red chiles, chopped

10 small garlic cloves, chopped

½ stalk of lemon grass, sliced

½ Tbsp shallot, sliced

2 tsp curry powder

1 tsp sliced gingerroot

1 tsp galangal, sliced

1 tsp shrimp paste

1 tsp salt

½ tsp coriander seeds

½ tsp fennel seeds

● Pound all the curry paste ingredients together with a pestle and mortar or in a blender until a fine paste is formed.

● Heat 1 cup of the coconut milk in a wok or pan and cook the curry paste for 5 minutes. Add the rest of the coconut milk, bring to a boil, add the chicken and cook until tender, about 10 minutes.

● Add the potato and salt, and cook until the potatoes are done, about 10 minutes. Pour into soup bowls and sprinkle with the fried shallots.

● Serve accompanied by ajaad salad, sliced pickled ginger and rice.

Red Chicken Curry

SERVES 6

5 cups thin coconut milk

1 quantity chile paste

10 white peppercorns, crushed

11 oz boneless skinned chicken breasts, cut across into ¼ in thick slices

3 Tbsp fish sauce

½ Tbsp palm sugar

7 small white eggplants, quartered

3 fresh red chiles, quartered lengthwise

2 kaffir lime leaves, torn into small pieces

⅓ cup sweet basil leaves

● Heat 1 cup of the coconut milk in a pan, stir in the chile paste, and white peppercorns, and cook for 2 minutes.

● Add the chicken slices, mix well and add the rest of the coconut milk. Bring to a boil, then add the fish sauce and palm sugar. Boil for 1 minute and then add the eggplant, chile, and lime leaf. Bring back to a boil, cook for 3 minutes, add the basil, remove from the heat and serve.

● Serve in bowls accompanied by rice, sun-dried beef, and salted preserved eggs.

Northern Thai Chicken Curry

SERVES 4–6

A spicy chicken curry with no curry powder—chopped red chiles add the fire to this dish.

¼ cup peanut or corn oil

1 lb chicken (with skin and bone), cut into small pieces through the bones

6 cups water

4 kaffir lime leaves, quartered

2 stalks of lemon grass, halved

1 Tbsp fish sauce

FOR THE CHILI PASTE

10 dried red chiles, roughly chopped

2 Tbsp finely sliced lemon grass

2 Tbsp sliced shallots

½ Tbsp sliced garlic

1 tsp galangal

1 tsp cilantro leaf, chopped

1 tsp shrimp paste

¼ tsp turmeric

● Pound all the chile paste ingredients to a fine paste with a mortar and pestle or in a blender.

● Heat the oil in a pan, add the chile paste and fry over medium heat for 1 minute. Add the chicken pieces, fry, then add the water and all the rest of the ingredients.

● Boil until the chicken is tender and the curry reduced to about half its original volume, about 20 minutes. Serve accompanied by rice.

Red Chicken Curry

Turkey with Chestnuts and Sprouts

SERVES 4

Chestnuts canned in brine may be substituted for the fresh ones in this recipe.

1 lb chestnuts	3 Tbsp oil
1½ lb Brussels sprouts	1 onion, chopped
1 lb skinned fillet of turkey breast, cubed	2 large sage sprigs
	1 thyme sprig
¼ cup all-purpose flour	1 cup chicken or turkey broth
salt and pepper	½ cup medium cider

● Wash the chestnuts, then use a pointed knife to make a slit in each one. Place in a saucepan, cover with water and bring to a boil. Reduce the heat and simmer for 15 minutes. Remove the shells.

● Halve any large Brussels sprouts, then blanch the vegetables in boiling water for 2 minutes. Drain.

● Toss the turkey with the flour and seasoning. Heat the oil, then stir fry the onion, sage and thyme for about 7 minutes, until the onion is softened. Add the turkey and fry until all pieces are cooked.

● Stir in the chestnuts and sprouts. Cook for 5 minutes before pouring in the stock and cider.

● Stir the mixture until it boils, then stir over medium heat for 2 minutes, until the juices are thickened. Taste for seasoning before serving.

Turkey Nests

SERVES 4

You need to have two fine metal strainers or a special frying basket to make the nests in which to serve this stir fry. If you do not want to go to all the trouble of making the nests, the stir fry may also be served in crispy baked potato shells, pastry shells, or pancakes.

6–8 oz Chinese egg noodles

oil for deep frying

¼ lb cream cheese

3 Tbsp fresh parsley, chopped

1 tsp fresh thyme, chopped

1 tsp lemon zest, grated

3 Tbsp olive oil

1 lb boneless turkey breast, finely shredded

1 red bell pepper, seeded and finely shredded

salt and freshly ground black pepper

¼ lb fine green beans, blanched in boiling water for 1 minute

¼ lb lean cooked ham, shredded

● Add the noodles to boiling water and bring back to a boil. Drain and rinse under cold water. Drain well.

● Grease two metal strainers: one measuring about 3 inches, the other 4 inches. Heat the oil for deep frying. Line the larger strainer with a layer of noodles and press the smaller one on top. Deep fry the noodles until golden, and drain on paper towels. Make eight nests.

● Mix the cream cheese, parsley, thyme, and lemon zest, then shape into eight small pats and chill them.

● Heat the oil, then stir fry the turkey and pepper, adding seasoning, until the turkey is lightly browned and the pepper tender. Stir in the beans and continue cooking for 3 minutes to heat them through. Lastly, add the ham and cook for a minute or so.

● Divide the stir-fried mixture between the nests and top each with a pat of flavored cream cheese.

Red Duck Curry

SERVES 6

7 cups thin coconut milk

1 roasted duck, boned with skin left on, cut into ½ in slices

15 cherry tomatoes

5 fresh large red chiles, sliced lengthwise

1 cup sweet basil leaves

3 kaffir lime leaves, chopped

3 Tbsp sugar

2 Tbsp fish sauce

1 tsp salt

FOR THE PASTE

3 stalks of lemon grass, sliced thinly

¼ cup galangal, chopped

7 dried red chiles, roughly chopped

3 Tbsp garlic, chopped

1 Tbsp shrimp paste

1 tsp chopped kaffir lime leaf

1 tsp cilantro root, chopped

1 tsp white peppercorns

½ tsp coriander seeds

● Pound all the curry paste ingredients together with a mortar and pestle or in a blender to a fine paste.

● Heat 2 cups of the coconut milk in a wok or pan, add the chile paste mixture and cook together for 5 minutes.

● Add the rest of the coconut milk, bring to a boil, then add the duck, cherry tomatoes, and red chile. Bring back to a boil and then add the rest of the ingredients. Boil all together for 5 minutes, and remove from the heat.

● Serve accompanied by rice, salted eggs, and sun-dried beef.

Duck with Ginger Sauce

SERVES 4

1 lb Ho Chi Minh duck (see recipe)

vegetable oil for frying

12 thin slices gingerroot, peeled and shredded

1½ Tbsp hot soy paste

1½ Tbsp sweet soy paste or hoisin sauce

1½ tsp rice wine

1½ Tbsp fish sauce (optional)

1 tsp garlic, finely chopped

1 Tbsp chili oil

1 tsp sugar

salt

1 cup chicken broth

1 scallion, shredded

1 red chile pepper (fresh, shredded, or dried, crumbled)

2 tsp cornstarch mixed with a little water

FOR THE HO CHI MINH DUCK

salt

pinch of five-spice powder

½ tsp gingerroot, finely chopped

½ tsp garlic, finely chopped

½ tsp hot soy paste

1 oven-ready duck (about 4–4½ lb)

½ cup hot water

3 Tbsp wine vinegar

¾ oz sugar

red food coloring

● Make the Ho Chi Minh duck by mixing the salt, five-spice powder, ginger, garlic, and soy paste. Put the mixture inside the duck's cavity and sew up both ends. Mix the remaining ingredients well and brush over the entire surface with a pastry brush. Leave to dry on a rack with the breast uppermost for 7 hours in a cool, dry place.

● Preheat the oven to 400°F. Put the rack together with the duck on a roasting tin and roast for 1 hour. Reduce the heat if the skin begins to burn. (Ideally, the duck should be roasted upright in the Oriental style but most household ovens cannot accommodate an upright duck.)

● Take the cooked duck meat off the bone in as large pieces as possible and cut these into neat pieces about ½ x 1 inch. Heat the oil in a wok until it starts smoking and stir-fry the duck pieces for a few minutes. Set these aside making sure to drain well.

● Empty and wipe the wok, heat some more oil in it and stir-fry the ginger very briskly; add the soy bean pastes, return the duck to the wok and stir in the rice wine, fish sauce, if used, garlic, chili oil, sugar, and salt. Stir-fry for a few more minutes.

● Add the chicken broth to the wok. As soon as it comes to a boil, reduce the heat and simmer, uncovered, for 5 minutes. Increase the heat, add the scallion and chile and cook fast for 1 minute, then stir in the cornstarch.

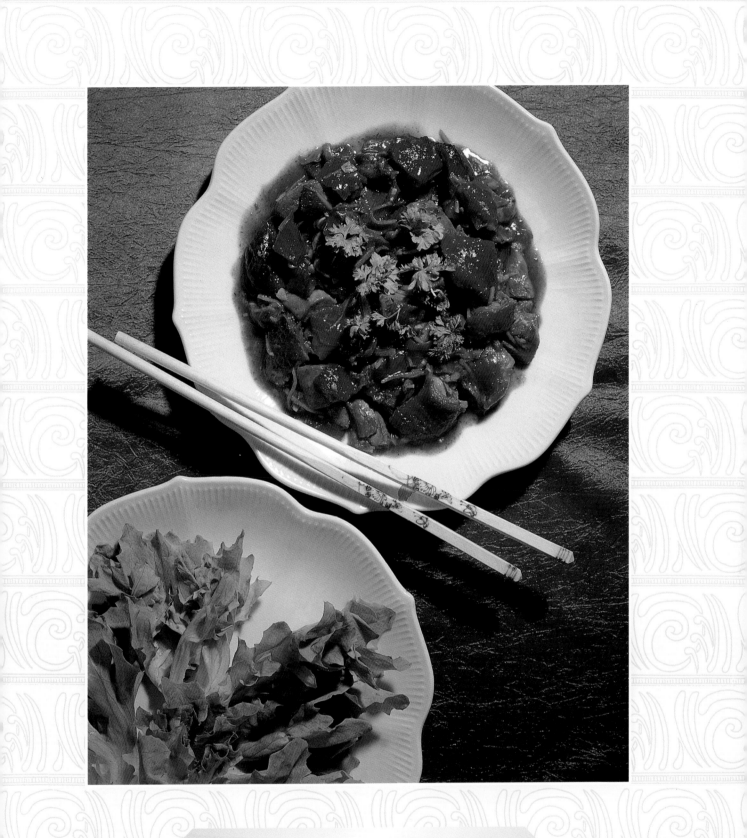

Duck with Ginger Sauce

Garlic Roasted Duck

SERVES 4

1 Tbsp fish sauce or light soy sauce

½ cup red wine vinegar

1 onion, chopped

12 juniper berries, crushed

2 tsp fennel seeds

1 clove garlic, crushed

4 duck breast and wing portions

5 oz tub unsweetened yogurt

salt and black pepper

FOR THE GARNISH

watercress

● Mix the fish sauce, vinegar, onion, juniper berries, fennel seeds, and garlic thoroughly in a large bowl and rub well into the duck portions. Cover the bowl with some plastic wrap and leave in a refrigerator for 8 hours, turning occasionally.

● Preheat the oven to 425°F. Drain and reserve the marinade. Place the duck portions, skin side down, in an ovenproof dish. Put in the oven for 30 minutes, basting at least once. Turn the duck portions over, baste, and cook for a further 30 minutes, basting at least once. Switch off the oven but leave the duck in it until ready to serve.

● Spoon 1 cup of the marinade into a hot pan, cover and allow to simmer for at least 5 minutes. Strain, whisk in the yogurt, and season with salt and black pepper to taste.

● Serve the duck on a dish garnished with the watercress. The sauce is served in a bowl. If guests are not proficient with chopsticks, the duck should be chopped into bite-sized pieces.

Duck with Rice

SERVES 4

A very popular dish, of Chinese origin, with two contrasting sauces.

1 roasted duck (rub with red food coloring before roasting), boned and cut into 2½ x ½ in slices

4 cups cooked rice

4 Tbsp thinly sliced pickled ginger

4 Tbsp thinly sliced pickled cucumber

FOR THE COOKED SAUCE

2 cups chicken broth

1 Tbsp sugar

½ Tbsp light soy sauce

¼ Tbsp dark soy sauce

1 tsp flour

FOR THE SOY CHILI SAUCE

½ cup dark soy sauce

3 fresh red chiles, sliced thinly into circles

1 Tbsp sugar

½ Tbsp vinegar

● Heat the ingredients for the cooked sauce together in a pan and boil for 1 minute. Mix the ingredients for the raw sauce in a bowl and put to one side.

● Warm the duck and rice in a 350°F oven for 5 minutes. Divide the rice between 4 serving plates, and arrange the duck meat over the top. Spoon the cooked sauce on top of each, and place ginger and pickle slices around the edges. Serve with the raw sauce.

Meat Main Dishes

The recipes in this section use pork, lamb, and beef in dishes drawn from all over the Far East. Beef, for example, is a great favorite in Korean cuisine, while many Vietnamese dishes use pork. Many of the dishes are subtly flavored with oriental spices, while others are recognizably "Eastern" by virtue only of the method of preparation. All are, however, refreshingly different.

Lamb in a Hot Garlic Sauce

SERVES 4

½ lb spinach or any green
vegetable

2 Tbsp vegetable oil

½ lb lean lamb, thinly sliced

4 cloves garlic, finely chopped

freshly ground white pepper

½ tsp sugar

1 Tbsp fish sauce or 1 Tbsp light
soy sauce and 1 tsp anchovy
extract

1 Tbsp oyster sauce

fresh sprigs of mint and/or
cilantro to garnish

● Blanch the greens in boiling water for 1 minute.
Drain and place on a serving dish.

● Heat the oil in a wok and stir-fry the lamb until
nearly cooked. This should not take more than 2
minutes. Add the garlic, pepper, sugar, fish sauce, and
oyster sauce, and stir-fry until the lamb is completely
cooked and tender.

● Pour the lamb and sauce over the greens. Garnish
with mint and/or cilantro sprigs.

Lamb Liver with Ginger and Cilantro

SERVES 4

1 lb lamb liver, cut into 1½ in wide strips and cut again crosswise into strips ⅛ in thick

2 Tbsp vegetable oil

1 large onion, cut into wedges about 1½ in wide

2 medium green bell peppers, halved

salt

1 Tbsp sesame oil

FOR THE SAUCE

2 Tbsp fish sauce or light soy sauce

2 Tbsp rice wine or dry sherry

2 tsp sugar

2 large cloves garlic, coarsely chopped

1 Tbsp fermented black beans, rinsed and coarsely chopped

2 x 1 in slices gingerroot, peeled and ground

1 Tbsp fresh cilantro, chopped

1 scallion, coarsely chopped

2 tsp cornstarch mixed with 2 Tbsp water

● Bring a large saucepan half full of water to a boil. Put in the liver slices and stir until the water begins to puff into a boil again. Drain the liver and hold under running cold water to stop the cooking. Drain.

● Combine the fish sauce, rice wine, and sugar, and stir until the sugar dissolves.

● Heat a wok over high heat and add 1 tablespoon oil. Scatter in the onion and peppers, and stir and toss vigorously until they are shining. Sprinkle in some salt and stir for about 1 minute until the onions are translucent. Transfer to a dish.

● Wipe the wok, add the remaining oil and put in the garlic, black beans, ginger, cilantro, and scallions, and stir for about 30 seconds to sear them. Add the liver and stir for a further 30 seconds.

● Add the fish sauce mixture and toss and turn the meat. Add the cooked vegetables and stir them around so they integrate with the meat. Add the cornstarch to the wok, a little at a time, stirring constantly. Sprinkle in the sesame oil, toss a couple of times, and ladle out on a hot serving dish.

Stir-fried Lamb with Mint and Chile

SERVES 4

1½ Tbsp vegetable oil

½ lb lean lamb, cut in fine strips

1 clove garlic, finely chopped

1 Tbsp oyster sauce

1 Tbsp fish sauce

pinch of sugar

1 Tbsp red fresh chile pepper, finely sliced

5 Tbsp fresh mint leaves, sliced if large

● Heat the oil in a wok and stir-fry the lamb for several minutes until almost cooked. Add the garlic, oyster sauce, fish sauce, sugar, and chile, and stir-fry for another 2 minutes or so. Taste to see if extra seasoning is necessary and adjust.

● When the meat is cooked and tender, stir the mint leaves through, remove and serve on a dish.

Sautéed Lamb with Eggplant in a Sauce

SERVES 4

2 large eggplants, ends cut off, thickly sliced

3 Tbsp olive oil

8 lamb cutlets, trimmed

2 cloves garlic, crushed

6 large tomatoes, blanched, skinned, and thickly sliced

salt and freshly ground black pepper

FOR THE SAUCE

2 Tbsp chopped fresh mint

3 cups natural yogurt

freshly ground black pepper

FOR THE GARNISH

1 lemon, sliced

sprigs of mint

● Sprinkle salt over the eggplant and leave for 20 minutes. Rinse and dry with paper towels.

● Heat 2 tablespoons olive oil in a wok over a very high heat and add the lamb cutlets. When brown, lower the heat and continue cooking until the meat is tender—about 5 minutes on each side. Remove from the wok, drain on paper towels and keep warm.

● Add the remaining oil to the wok and fry the eggplant slices with the garlic until they are lightly browned on both sides. (If the oil dries out, add a little more.) When they are cooked, push them up the side of the wok and add the tomato slices. Stir-fry for a few moments and season with salt and pepper.

● Place the vegetables on a dish and arrange the cutlets over the vegetables. Garnish with lemon slices and sprigs of mint.

● Prepare the sauce by stirring the mint into the yogurt. Grind some black pepper over it and serve in a small bowl.

Stir-fried Lamb with Ginger

SERVES 4

4 Tbsp chicken broth

1 medium carrot, diced into ½ in cubes

1 Tbsp butter

¾ cup green peas

1 Tbsp vegetable oil

2 slices gingerroot, minced

1 lb lean lamb, chopped into ½ in cubes

1 Tbsp fish sauce

1 tsp sugar

½ Tbsp hoisin sauce

salt

2 tsp cornstarch mixed with a little water

● Heat the broth in a wok over a medium heat. Add the carrot and cook until the liquid has nearly disappeared. Add the butter and peas, and leave to cook for a further 2 minutes, stirring occasionally. Scoop out and leave in a bowl.

● Heat the oil in the wok on a high heat and add the ginger and lamb. Stir quickly for about 1 minute and then add the fish sauce, sugar, hoisin sauce, and salt. Stirring for 1 minute, and then stir in the cornstarch.

● When the cornstarch thickens, it will give the lamb a beautiful gloss. At this stage add the carrots and peas. Stir and mix for 30 seconds and serve.

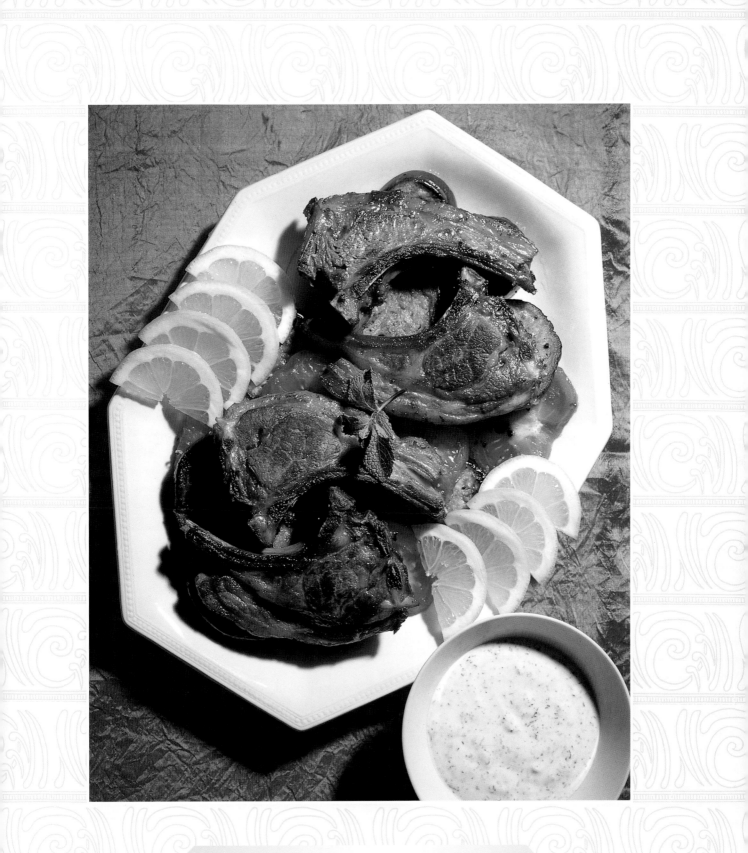

Sautéed Lamb with Eggplant
in a Sauce

Ramen with Barbecued Pork

SERVES 4

Cha siu *is a spicy Chinese marinade, and* **cha siu** *pork is widely eaten all over southeast Asia.* **Cha siu** *pork is roasted for a comparatively short time compared with roast pork dishes prepared in the West, leaving the inner part of the meat nearly rare.* **Cha siu** *sauce is available from Chinese stores.*

1 lb *ramen* noodles or 14 oz fresh or ¾ lb dried thin egg noodles

6 cups soy sauce broth

FOR THE TOPPING

12 large slices Chinese-style barbecued pork

4 Tbsp cooked dried bamboo shoots (optional)

3 scallions, chopped

● Boil plenty of water in a pan, and cook the noodles for 3 minutes. Drain and divide into four bowls. Heat the soy sauce broth.

● Put three slices of *cha siu* into each bowl of noodles. Garnish with the bamboo shoots and scallions. Pour the soy sauce broth over the top just before serving.

Pork Satay

SERVES 4–6

Now popular all over Thailand, and a specialty of market food stalls, satay arrived in the south from Indonesia, via Malaysia. The dish can be made with pork, chicken, or beef; serve all together for variety.

1 lb pork loin, cut into 3 x ¾ x ¼ in long slices

1½ cups thin coconut milk

5 kaffir lime leaves, roughly chopped

5 cilantro roots, crushed

2 stalks of lemon grass, roughly chopped

1 Tbsp curry powder

1 tsp palm sugar

½ tsp salt

FOR THE SATAY SAUCE

⅓ cup dried yellow mung beans

5 cups thin coconut milk

1 cup unsalted roasted peanuts, very finely chopped

4 oz chili paste

2 oz curry paste (see Red Duck Curry page 141)

3 Tbsp palm sugar

2 tsp tamarind juice

1 tsp salt

FOR THE AJAAD SALAD

2 cups white vinegar

⅓ cup sugar

1 tsp salt

1 small cucumber, quartered and sliced lengthwise

¼ cup shallots, sliced

2 fresh red chiles, sliced thinly into circles

● Mix the pork with all the other ingredients in a bowl and leave to marinate for 3–4 hours. Then skewer the meat onto wood or metal skewers and broil, preferably over charcoal.

● While the pork is marinating, soak the mung beans in water for 1 hour, then drain and steam them for 20 minutes or until soft. Purée in a food processor.

● Next, make the satay sauce. Mix all the ingredients together and boil in a pan or wok for 5 minutes. Remove from the heat and leave to cool.

● To make the ajaad salad, boil the vinegar, sugar, and salt together in a pan until reduced to about 1 cup. Take off the heat, cool, and mix with the cucumber, shallots, and chiles.

● Serve the kabobs with the satay sauce and ajaad salad, with pieces of toasted bread.

Satay-flavor Pork

SERVES 4

1 lb lean boneless pork, cut in thin strips

3 Tbsp lime or lemon juice

3 Tbsp ground coriander

1 tsp ground ginger

1 garlic clove, crushed

salt and freshly ground black pepper

1 tsp sesame oil

⅓ cup peanut oil

1 bunch scallions, shredded

FOR THE SAUCE

1 small onion, chopped

2 garlic cloves, crushed

juice of 1 lime or lemon

½ tsp chili powder

⅓ cup tahini

⅓ cup crunchy peanut butter

3 Tbsp soy sauce

FOR THE SALAD

½ Iceberg lettuce, shredded

½ cucumber, halved and thinly sliced

FOR THE GARNISH

scallion curls

lime or lemon wedges

● Place the pork in a bowl. Add the lime or lemon juice, coriander, ginger, garlic, seasoning, and sesame oil. Stir well so that all the pieces of meat are coated in the marinade. Cover and leave to marinate for several hours or overnight.

● To make the sauce, blend the onion, garlic, lime or lemon juice, chili and tahini to a paste in a liquidizer or food processor. Stir ¼–⅓ cup boiling water into the peanut butter to soften it to a paste, then stir in the blended mixture and the soy sauce. Add a little extra boiling water if necessary to thin the sauce.

● Arrange the lettuce and cucumber on a platter or individual plates. Add the scallion curls. Heat the peanut oil and stir-fry the pork until browned and cooked through. Add the scallions and stir-fry for another minute. Arrange the meat on the salad base.

● Spoon a little peanut sauce over the meat and scallions, then serve the rest separately. Add lime wedges to garnish and serve at once.

Stir-fried Pork Slices and Celery

SERVES 4

2 Tbsp vegetable oil

1 lb lean pork, sliced thinly and
  cut in ½ in pieces

1 tsp soy sauce

1 tsp sugar

2 cups button mushrooms

½ lb spring cabbage, cut in 2 in
  slices, with tougher stems
  discarded

4 celery stalks, sliced thinly

1 Tbsp fish sauce (optional)

3 Tbsp chicken broth

cornstarch

salt

● Heat 1 tablespoon oil in the wok, add the pork and
stir-fry over highest heat for 2½ minutes or longer if
the pork needs more cooking. Add the soy sauce and
sugar, and stir with the pork for a further 2 minutes.
Scoop into a bowl and keep in a warm oven.

● Wipe the wok and pour in the remaining oil. Add
the mushrooms, cabbage, and celery, and stir-fry for
1½ minutes. Add the fish sauce, if using, and broth
and stir-fry for another minute. Cover and leave to
cook for a further 2 minutes.

● Add the cooked sliced pork with the cornstarch and
salt to taste. Stir and mix thoroughly for a minute or
so and serve immediately with rice or noodles.

Red Pork with Rice

SERVES 6

The marinade soaks a little way into the meat from the surface. When it is sliced, the red edges of the pork makes this a decorative as well as tasty dish.

11 oz pork loin

4 cups water

¼ cup tomato paste

3 Tbsp light soy sauce

3 Tbsp sugar

3 drops of red food coloring (optional)

1½ Tbsp cornstarch

2 cups cooked rice, heated

FOR THE *NAM CHIM* SAUCE

4 Tbsp white vinegar

2 Tbsp dark soy sauce

1 fresh red chile, sliced thinly

¼ tsp sugar

● Mix together the pork, water, tomato paste, soy sauce, sugar, and food coloring in a bowl and leave to marinate for 1 hour.

● Put the pork mixture with its marinade in a pan, bring to a boil, and simmer for 30 minutes. Remove the pork and place in an ovenproof pan; roast it in a preheated 350°F oven for 10 minutes until lightly browned and glazed. Reserve the cooking liquid.

● Mix a little of the cooking liquid with the cornstarch, and then stir in 2 cups more liquid. Bring to a boil in a small pan to thicken, then remove from the heat.

● Mix together the ingredients for the *nam chim* sauce. Slice the pork and place on serving plates (on top of the hot rice). Spoon the cornstarch sauce over the top, and serve with the *nam chim* sauce.

● Serve accompanied by sliced cucumber, scallions, hard-cooked eggs, and pieces of deep-fried fresh pork fat back or pork belly.

Stir-fried Pork in Ginger with Onion

SERVES 2

The sweet, tangy flavors of the soy sauce and ginger marinade are enriched and enhanced by the pork. Like most other Japanese dishes, this is easy to prepare and can be made in no time at all.

8 oz thinly sliced pork, cut into 2 in lengths

1 Tbsp vegetable oil

1 medium sized onion, peeled and sliced

FOR THE MARINADE

1 oz gingerroot, peeled, grated, and squeezed

1½ Tbsp soy sauce

1 Tbsp *sake*

● To make the marinade, mix together the juice of the ginger, the soy sauce and the *sake* in a bowl.

● Add the pork and marinate for 30 minutes. Heat the oil in a skillet and fry the onion until it is transparent. Remove and set aside.

● Add the meat to the skillet and fry for 5 minutes or until cooked.

● Return the onion to the skillet and stir-fry for a further 1–2 minutes.

● Add the remaining marinade and stir-fry again for 1–2 minutes. Serve with a bowl of hot, plain rice.

Broiled Pork Belly

SERVES 6

These pork slices are rather like a Korean version of Spanish **tapas** *because they are served to customers in city* **suljip** *(or drinking houses) in order to increase thirst and therefore drink sales.*

1 lb belly of pork, thinly sliced

about 4 tbsp sesame oil

2 tsp sea salt

● Preheat the broiler or barbecue, or use a table-top burner. Stir together the sesame oil and salt in a small serving bowl.

● Cook the pork slices until crisp and slightly charred. Drain quickly on paper towels and serve hot with the dip. Don't forget to offer plenty of paper napkins.

Steamed Ground Pork and Eggplant

SERVES 4

1 eggplant, about 12 oz

salt and freshly ground black pepper

½ tsp vegetable oil

1 small onion, thinly sliced and then coarsely chopped

1 egg, lightly beaten

2 cups ground pork

1 Tbsp chopped pickled cucumber

1 tsp sugar

2 Tbsp fish sauce or light soy sauce

1 Tbsp cornstarch

1 Tbsp rice wine or dry sherry

● Peel the eggplant, slice it into pieces about ½ inch thick and then chop into 1 inch pieces. Sprinkle and rub with salt and pepper, and a little oil.

● Mix the onion, egg, pork, pickled cucumber, sugar, fish sauce, cornstarch, rice wine, and a little salt. Mix with a wooden spoon until the ingredients are thoroughly mixed.

● Place the eggplant pieces at the bottom of a bowl and pack the pork mixture on top of the eggplant so that no vegetable shows above the surface.

● Place the bowl in a steamer over the wok and steam vigorously for 45 minutes. If you do not have a steamer, use the largest pan you have. Turn a fair-sized bowl upside down and place it in the bottom. Put the bowl containing the pork and eggplant on top of this and add water to halfway up the bowl containing the pork and eggplant. Serve hot. A stir-fried dish is an ideal accompaniment.

Pork Fried with Garlic and Peppercorns

SERVES 4–6

3 cups peanut or corn oil for frying

11 oz pork loin, sliced into ¾ x 1 in rectangles, ¼ in thick

2 Tbsp garlic, chopped

2 tsp black peppercorns, lightly crushed

1 tsp light soy sauce

1 tsp salt

¼ cup cilantro leaves, chopped

2 fresh red chiles, cut into lengthwise strips

● Heat the oil in a wok or pan to 350°F. Fry the pork until light brown, about 8–10 minutes. Take out all but the meat and ½ cup of the oil, then add the garlic, peppercorns, soy sauce, and salt. Stir-fry for 2 minutes or until the garlic is light brown.

● Remove the pork mixture from the pan with a slotted spoon, drain well, and place on a serving plate. Sprinkle with the cilantro and chile to garnish.

● Serve accompanied by rice and sliced cucumber.

Steamed Ground Pork
and Eggplant

Spicy Broiled Pork on a Bed of Vermicelli

SERVES 4

8 oz rice vermicelli

1 lb fresh pork sides with skin, cut against the grain into ¼ in strips, about 2 in long

1 lb beef, ground

8 cloves garlic, minced

FOR THE CARAMEL SAUCE

½ cup sugar

¼ cup fish sauce

4 thinly sliced scallions

freshly ground black pepper

● Soak the vermicelli in warm water until soft. Drain and set aside.

● Make the caramel sauce by swirling the sugar gently in a wok over a hot heat. Be careful not to let the sugar blacken but ignore the smoke. Remove from the heat and add the fish sauce. Return to a low heat and gently boil until the sugar dissolves. Add the scallions and pepper and stir.

● Put 24 bamboo skewers into water and allow to soak for at least 30 minutes.

● Meanwhile, put the pork and beef into two separate bowls. Put the garlic and half of the caramel sauce onto the beef. Put the remainder of the caramel sauce onto the pork. Blend both with the hand and allow to stand for 30 minutes. Make 24 meatballs out of the beef.

● Skewer the beef balls and pork slices and cook under a hot broiler for 15–20 minutes, turning frequently. Place on the bed of vermicelli. Serve with a selection of fresh vegetables.

Deep-fried Pork Steak in Bread Crumbs

SERVES 2

This is one of the most popular dishes in modern Japanese cuisine. It is usually served with shredded cabbage and garnished with tomato katsup, brown sauce, and/or mustard.

2 x 5–7 oz boneless pork loin steaks

2 Tbsp all-purpose flour

1 egg, beaten

2–3 Tbsp dry white bread crumbs

vegetable oil, for deep-frying

● Beat the meat gently with a steak hammer or rolling pin to tenderize it. Dust with the flour, then dip into the beaten egg.

● Coat the steaks with the bread crumbs.

● Heat the oil to 330°F, and then deep fry the steaks until cooked through, about 6 minutes, depending on the thickness of the steaks.

● Serve garnished with lettuce, sliced tomato, and cucumber, adding tomato katsup, brown sauce and mustard if you wish.

Roasted Spareribs with Lemon Grass and Chile

SERVES 4

12 pork spareribs

2 Tbsp clear honey

1 tsp five-spice powder

2 cloves garlic, finely chopped and crushed

3 Tbsp dry sherry or rice wine

3 Tbsp fish sauce or 3 Tbsp light soy sauce mixed with 1 tsp anchovy extract

2 stalks fresh lemon grass, sliced thinly, or grated peel of 1 lemon

2 fresh red chile peppers, finely chopped

● Wash and dry the spareribs and place them in a large bowl.

● In another bowl, combine the honey, five-spice powder, garlic, dry sherry, fish sauce, lemon grass, and chile. Mix well. Spread the honey mixture over the spareribs and leave to marinate for 4 hours.

● The ribs can be cooked over a barbecue, turning frequently and basting with the marinade; or baked in the oven at 375°F, basting with the marinade; or broiled under a moderately hot broiler, basting with the marinade.

Beef and Bean Curd Patties

SERVES 4–6

*These light patties, **gogijon**, are served as simple everyday fare in most Korean homes. The patties are usually small so that they can be lifted with the slim Korean chopsticks.*

8 oz medium-firm bean curd

3 cups lean beef, freshly ground

2 garlic cloves, crushed and finely chopped

2 scallions, white and green parts, very finely chopped

1 Tbsp sesame oil

2 tsp soy sauce

4 tsp crushed toasted sesame seeds

all-purpose flour for coating

2 eggs, beaten

vegetable oil for frying

● Put the bean curd in a piece of cheesegauze or fine cloth and squeeze out as much water as possible. Press the bean curd through a strainer, then mix with the beef, garlic, scallions, sesame oil, soy sauce, and sesame seeds. Form into patties about 1½ inches in diameter and just under ½ inch thick.

● Toss the patties in all-purpose flour to coat evenly, then dip in beaten egg.

● Heat a thin layer of vegetable oil in a large skillet. Add some of the patties to make a single layer and fry slowly for 2½–3 minutes on each side or until golden. Using a slotted spoon, transfer the patties to paper towels to drain while frying the remaining patties.

● Serve with rice sticks and pickled cabbage.

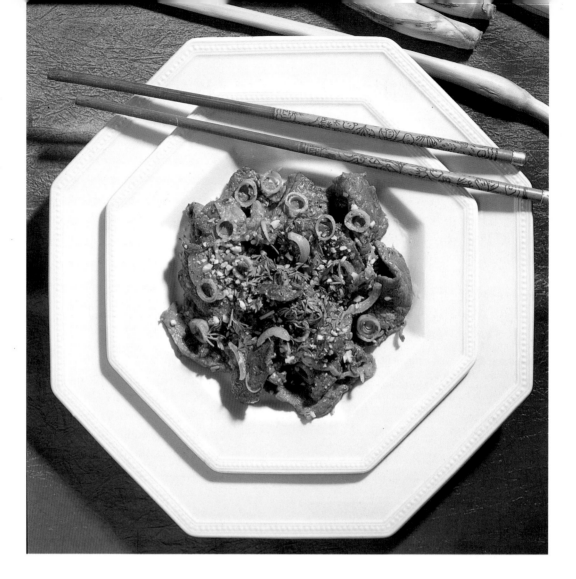

Beef in Coconut Milk

SERVES 4

2 Tbsp vegetable oil

1 clove garlic, crushed

8 oz topside of beef, thinly
  sliced

1 small onion, thinly sliced

pinch of turmeric

½ green chile pepper

½ in lemon grass, cut from the
  bottom, thinly sliced

1 Tbsp canned coconut milk

FOR THE GARNISH

1 tbsp peanuts, crushed

handful of fresh cilantro,
  chopped

● Heat the oil until very hot. Add the garlic. When
the smell is released, add everything except the
coconut milk. Stir-fry for about 3 minutes or until the
meat is cooked.

● Add the coconut milk and stir once. Serve
garnished with crushed peanuts and chopped cilantro.

Korean "Hot Meat"

SERVES 4–6

The beef is served cold with its own spicy jelly as a side dish, and is eaten in small amounts. Because the jelly is an integral part of the dish, it is important to use a gelatinous cut of beef, such as shank. Adjust the number of chiles so suit your taste for "hot" foods.

2 lb beef shank

3 Tbsp sesame oil

6 Tbsp Japanese soy sauce

about 8 fresh red or green
    chiles, halved and seeded

1 red bell pepper, seeded and
    quite thinly sliced

● Put the meat into a saucepan. Add enough water just to cover it and bring to a boil. Skim the scum from the surface, then add the remaining ingredients.

● Cover the pan and simmer very slowly for 2–3 hours until the meat is so tender it is beginning to fall apart. Keep an eye on the water level to make sure the pan does not become dry, but do not drown the meat. At the end of the cooking, it should be surrounded by a thick sauce.

● Remove from the heat and let the meat cool in the liquid. Break the meat apart with a fork and serve with the jelly, chiles, and sliced red bell pepper.

Beef with Lemon Grass and Mushrooms

SERVES 4

1 lb filet mignon, sliced very
    thinly across the grain and
    cut into 2 x 3 in pieces

2 stalks fresh lemon grass,
    sliced paper-thin and finely
    chopped

2 fresh red chile peppers,
    minced

6 cloves garlic, minced

3 Tbsp fish sauce or light soy
    sauce

1 tsp cornstarch

freshly ground black pepper

3½ Tbsp vegetable oil

2 medium onions, finely sliced

4 oz button mushrooms

1 tsp sugar

2 oz roasted peanuts, coarsely
    ground

FOR THE GARNISH

sprigs of cilantro

● Combine the beef, lemon grass, chile, half the garlic, 2 tablespoons fish sauce, cornstarch, black pepper, and 2 tablespoons oil in a bowl. Set aside for 30 minutes.

● Pour 1 tablespoon oil in the wok over a medium heat and add the onions and the remaining garlic. Stir-fry for 1–2 minutes until they are golden-brown. Remove the onions and set aside. Add ½ tablespoon more oil and, when hot, add the beef, the mushrooms, the rest of the fish sauce, and the sugar. Sauté over a high heat for 1–2 minutes or until the beef is just cooked.

● Scoop the food from the wok and arrange it on a warmed serving platter. Arrange the sautéed onions around it and sprinkle the peanuts and black pepper over everything. Garnish with cilantro sprigs.

Green Beef Curry

Definitely green, but rarely sweet, this is one of the basic Thai curry styles, and can be used with pork, chicken, or duck as a variation from beef.

5 cups thin coconut milk

11 oz beef sirloin, cut into 1 x ¾ x ¼ in slices

2 Tbsp fish sauce

½ Tbsp palm sugar

10 small white eggplants, quartered

3 fresh red chiles, quartered lengthwise

3 kaffir lime leaves, torn into small pieces

¼ cup sweet basil leaves

FOR THE CHILI PASTE

1 Tbsp shallot, sliced

1 Tbsp garlic, chopped

1 Tbsp galangal, sliced

½ stalk of lemon grass, sliced

½ Tbsp coriander seeds

2 tsp salt

1 tsp shrimp paste

½ tsp chopped kaffir lime zest

½ tsp cilantro root or stem, cilantro

6 white peppercorns, crushed

20 fresh small green chiles, chopped roughly

● Pound all the chili paste ingredients, except the green chiles, together to form a fine paste, using a mortar and pestle or blender if you have one. Stir in the green chiles.

● Heat 1 cup of the coconut milk in a pan, add the chili paste and cook for 2 minutes. Add the beef and the rest of the coconut milk, and bring to a boil.

● Add the fish sauce and palm sugar, boil for 2 more minutes, then add the eggplant and chile, and cook for 1 minute. Stir in the lime leaf, boil for 1 minute, add the basil and remove from the heat.

● Serve in bowls accompanied by rice, pickled vegetables, salted eggs, and sun-dried beef.

Stir-fried Beef with Peppers and Bamboo Shoots

SERVES 4

1 Tbsp vegetable oil

1 lb rump steak, thinly sliced

3 scallions, cut in ½ in lengths

2 cloves garlic, crushed

1 cup canned bamboo shoots, sliced

1 large green bell pepper, seeded and sliced

2 Tbsp fish sauce or 2 Tbsp light soy sauce and ½ tsp anchovy extract

⅔ cup beef broth

2 Tbsp sugar

2 tsp cornstarch mixed with a little water

● Heat the oil in a wok over a high heat, add the beef and stir-fry for 2–3 minutes, stirring all the while, to seal in the flavors of the meat. Scoop out the beef and place it in a warm oven.

● Add the scallions and garlic to the wok and stir-fry over a moderate heat for 3 minutes. Increase the heat to high, stir in the bamboo shoots and pepper, and stir-fry for 1–2 minutes.

● Stir in the fish sauce, broth, and sugar. Cover and cook for 3 minutes. Return the beef to the wok and stir for 1 minute. Add the cornstarch to the beef mixture and stir constantly until the mixture thickens. Serve immediately.

Beef in Oyster Sauce

SERVES 4

If you include this dish as part of a Chinese menu, reduce the quantities by half, or serve it with plain cooked rice or chow mein.

1 lb frying steak, cut into small, thin slices

¼ cup oyster sauce

3 Tbsp soy sauce

1 garlic clove, crushed

⅓ cup dry sherry

4 large dried Chinese mushrooms

⅓ cup oil

1 green bell pepper, seeded and cut into chunks

1 red bell pepper, seeded and cut into chunks

1 onion, cut into chunks

● Place the meat in a dish. Mix the oyster sauce, soy sauce, garlic, and sherry together, pour the mixture over the meat, and mix well. Cover and leave to marinate for 2–4 hours.

● Place the mushrooms in a small basin or mug and pour in just enough hot water to cover them. Place a saucer or the base of another mug on the mushrooms to keep them submerged, then leave to soak for 20 minutes. Drain, reserving the soaking liquid, discard tough stalks and slice the mushroom caps.

● Heat the oil, then stir-fry the peppers and onion for 3 minutes. Use a draining spoon to add the beef to the pan, then continue stir-frying until the meat is cooked and lightly browned. Add the mushrooms.

● Pour the soaking liquid into the oyster sauce marinade left from the meat and mix well, then pour the liquid into the pan. Bring to a boil and boil rapidly for a few minutes so that the meat is coated in a slightly thickened sauce. Serve at once.

Quick Beef

SERVES 2

The original concept of this recipe is that it is prepared and cooked quickly for people who are waiting to eat, but the beef can be marinated with the remaining ingredients for 1–3 hours to give it extra flavor.

8 oz round steak

2 garlic cloves, crushed and finely chopped

2 scallions, finely chopped

2 Tbsp sesame oil

1 Tbsp beef broth

salt and freshly ground black pepper

● Preheat the broiler. Cut the beef across the grain into slices about ½ inch thick. Score the slices on both sides. Put into a bowl.

● Mix the remaining ingredients together, and pour over the beef. Stir to coat in the marinade, then broil for 5–7 minutes, turning halfway through, until cooked to your liking.

Beef in Oyster Sauce

Stir-fried Beef with Garlic and Chiles

SERVES 3–4

Garlic and chiles give the character to this simple, tasty stir-fry, but the number of each can be adjusted according to personal taste.

1 lb sirloin steak, cut into strips

2 Tbsp soy sauce

1 scallion, white and green part thinly sliced

1½ tsp sesame oil

2 Tbsp rice wine or dry sherry

1½ tsp sugar

1½ Tbsp vegetable oil

3 garlic cloves, cut into slivers

4 fresh red chiles, seeded and cut into strips

FOR THE GARNISH

½ egg, beaten, fried and cut into strips

toasted sesame seeds

● Put the beef in a bowl. Add the soy sauce, scallion, sesame oil, rice wine or dry sherry, and sugar. Stir, then cool for 1 hour.

● Heat the oil in a skillet. Add the garlic and chiles, and stir-fry over a high heat until fragrant, about 1 minute. Remove with a slotted spoon and reserve.

● Lift the beef from the marinade, and add to the pan. Stir-fry for 2–3 minutes. Return the chiles and garlic to the pan. Add the marinade and cook, stirring, over a medium heat for about 2 minutes.

● Serve the beef garnished with egg strips and toasted sesame seeds.

Broiled Beef

SERVES 4

This dish, **pulgogi,** *is one of the most popular Korean dishes.* **Pulgogi** *is also the name of the domed-shape metal hotplate that is put on a table-top burner for cooking the beef. A broiler and broiler rack or a barbecue can be used instead.*

4 scallions, coarsely chopped

3 garlic cloves, crushed and finely chopped

1 Tbsp crushed toasted sesame seeds

3 Tbsp soy sauce

2 tsp rice wine or dry sherry

1 Tbsp sesame oil

2 Tbsp sugar

freshly ground black pepper

1¼ lb filet mignon, sirloin, or round steak, frozen for 1 hour

vegetable oil for brushing

● Mix together the scallions, garlic, sesame seeds, soy sauce, rice wine or sherry, sesame oil, sugar, 2 tablespoons water, and plenty of black pepper.

● Cut the beef crosswise into ¼ inch thick slices. Lay in a shallow dish. Pour over the scallion mixture, cover and let marinate for 1 hour.

● Preheat the broiler or barbecue. Lightly oil a broiler rack or table-top grill plate. Cook the beef in batches in a single layer for about 1 minute on each side until browned on the outside but still pink inside.

Steak with Garlic and Soy Sauce

SERVES 2

A combination of a Western cut of meat with a Japanese sauce that works really well. Remember that the frying times given for the steak will vary depending on the thickness of the meat and personal preference. This flexible dish can be served with Japanese side dishes or vegetables.

2 x 5–7 oz sirloin or rump
   steaks

freshly ground black pepper

1 Tbsp vegetable oil

5 garlic cloves, sliced

1 Tbsp *sake*

½ oz butter

1 Tbsp soy sauce

● Beat the meat on both sides using a steak hammer or a rolling pin, then season with the pepper.

● Heat the oil in a skillet and fry the garlic briefly. Remove and set aside.

● Fry the steaks lightly on both sides, then add the *sake* and fry for a further minute before placing the steaks on warmed serving plates.

● Return the garlic to the pan, add the butter and soy sauce and when the mixture begins to bubble pour over the steaks and serve immediately.

Coconut Beef Curry

SERVES 8

This is one of the driest of Thai curries, and it is usually quite fiery.

FOR THE CURRY PASTE

6 dried red chiles, chopped roughly

7 white peppercorns

1½ oz garlic, roughly chopped

1 oz shallots, roughly chopped

2 cilantro roots, roughly chopped

2 tsp salt

1 tsp galangal, roughly chopped

1 tsp lemon grass, roughly chopped

1 tsp kaffir lime zest, roughly chopped

1 tsp shrimp paste

¼ cup peanut or corn oil

11 oz beef sirloin, cut into 1¼ x ¾ x ¼ in pieces

3 cups thin coconut milk

1 Tbsp fish sauce

2 tsp sugar

2 fresh red chiles, sliced

2 kaffir lime leaves, sliced finely

⅓ cup sweet basil leaves

● Pound all the curry paste ingredients together with a mortar and pestle or in a blender to form a paste.

● Heat the oil in a pan or wok and fry the curry paste for 3–4 minutes. Add the beef and fry for 2 minutes, then add the coconut milk and boil until the beef is tender, about 15 minutes.

● Add the fish sauce, sugar, and chile. Remove from the heat, transfer to a serving plate and sprinkle with the lime zest and basil. Serve accompanied by rice.

● Serve in bowls accompanied by rice, pickled vegetables, salted eggs, and sun-dried beef.

Korean Meatballs

SERVES 2–3

These flavorful meatballs are served as one of the side dishes in a Korean meal. They are also good cold, so a useful item for a picnic.

2 cups lean ground beef

3 Tbsp soy sauce

2 scallions, finely chopped

2 garlic cloves, finely chopped

1 Tbsp crushed toasted sesame seeds

1½ tsp sesame oil

freshly ground black pepper

seasoned all-purpose flour for coating

2 eggs, lightly beaten

vegetable oil for frying

vinegar dipping sauce to serve

● Mix together the beef, soy sauce, scallions, garlic, sesame seeds, sesame oil, and plenty of pepper. Leave for 30 minutes.

● Form the meat mixture into flattened rounds, about 1½ inches in diameter. Toss in seasoned flour to coat evenly, then dip in beaten egg, letting excess egg drain off.

● Heat a little oil in a skillet, preferably nonstick, and fry the meatballs until brown and crisp on both sides and cooked through.

● Serve with vinegar dipping sauce.

Parties and
Special Occasions

Whether you are planning a small buffet party or an elegant
dinner, you will find recipes to suit any occasion here—from
pretty marbled eggs to whole suckling pig. Many of these
dishes are perfect for buffet or cocktail parties, and they
are sure to win the praises of your guests for innovation,
flavor, and style.

Sizzling Butterfly Shrimp

SERVES 4

Uncooked Mediterranean or jumbo shrimp are available frozen from good fish merchants and oriental supermarkets. Since they tend to be rather expensive, the portions can be small but the end result need not look mean with the right accompaniments— for example, serve a chow mein with some sliced scallops.

24 uncooked large Mediterranean shrimp, shelled with tails on

cornstarch for coating

2 in piece fresh gingerroot, peeled and grated, then chopped into small pieces

1 garlic clove, crushed

1 green chile, seeded and finely chopped (optional)

2 tsp sugar

2 tsp white wine vinegar

½ tsp tomato paste

1 Tbsp light soy sauce

1 Tbsp dry sherry

pinch of five-spice powder

1 tsp sesame oil

½ cup vegetable oil

FOR THE VEGETABLE GARNISH

6 scallions, cut into very fine strips

½ red bell pepper, seeded and cut into short, very fine strips

¼ cucumber, peeled and cut into short, fine strips

lemon wedges to serve

● To prepare the shrimp, first remove the fine black cord that runs down the back (this may have been removed). Using a small sharp knife, take a shrimp and cut it down the back, almost through in half, then press it open. Repeat with all the shellfish. Coat them generously with cornstarch and shake off excess.

● In a bowl, mix the ginger, garlic, chile, sugar, vinegar, tomato paste, soy sauce, sherry, five-spice powder, and sesame oil. Add the shrimp and mix well to coat them with the flavoring ingredients. They should be thoroughly tossed to ensure that they are all flavored with the paste.

● Heat the vegetable oil until it is shimmering hot, then stir-fry the shrimp over high heat until they are crisp and golden—this takes only a few minutes. Use a slotted spoon to transfer them to a serving plate.

● Add all the vegetables for garnish to the oil remaining in the pan and stir-fry for 2 minutes. Spoon them on the plate with the shrimp and add the lemon wedges. Serve the dish immediately.

Seaweed-wrapped Avocado

SERVES 2

Avocado is not a traditional ingredient of Japanese cooking but it is certainly popular in many Japanese homes. This popularity is said to be due to the similarity between the taste of the avocado and the taste of raw tuna as used in **sushi** *and* **sashimi**. *You can mix in* **wasabi**, *the green Japanese mustard powder, to spice up the soy sauce, which can be used as a dressing, if you wish.*

● Slice the avocado in two, remove the stone and peel. Cut in half again, then slice into ½ in widths.

● Cut the *nori* into strips and wrap the avocado slices in the *nori*.

● Pour soy sauce into a small dish. If you are using *wasabi*, mash in a small amount. Dip the avocado into the sauce before eating.

1 avocado

nori (2 sheets of dried seaweed)

2 tsp soy sauce

1 tsp *wasabi* (optional)

Oysters

SERVES 4

Instead of the traditional lemon juice, try spooning a little of this Korean sauce over oysters before sucking them, with their juices, from their shells.

12–24 oysters in the shell, opened

FOR THE SAUCE

2 Tbsp rice vinegar

1 Tbsp chile bean paste

½ in piece of gingerroot, crushed and finely chopped

1½ tsp sugar

few drops of soy sauce to taste

● Mix together all the ingredients for the sauce, adjusting the levels of flavorings to taste. Pour into a small bowl. Cover and chill until ready to serve.

● Spoon the prepared sauce over the oysters.

Oyster Fritters

SERVES 4–6

Use Pacific oysters for these fritters—not only are they the authentic ones, but they may be cheaper than those grown off the east coast such as bluepoint. Save the liquid that is in the oyster shells to strain into the batter; reduce the water by the amount of oyster liquid added and omit the salt from the recipe if you do this. Add some sesame seeds to the batter for an extra nutty, crunchy texture.

1 cup all-purpose flour

2 tsp baking powder

very small pinch of Korean chili powder, or cayenne pepper mixed with paprika

salt

1 egg, beaten

about 24 oysters, opened

vegetable oil for deep-frying

sesame or vinegar dipping sauce

● Sift the flour, baking powder, Korean chili powder, or cayenne pepper, and paprika, and salt into a bowl. Slowly pour in ⅔ cup water, stirring, to make a smooth batter. Leave for 30 minutes.

● Half fill a deep-fat fryer with vegetable oil and heat to about 350°F. Dip the oysters in the batter, then fry for about 2 minutes until the batter is crisp and golden; take care not to overcook the oysters as they will become tough.

● Drain the oysters on paper towels and serve hot with sesame or vinegar dipping sauce.

Oysters

Spicy-fried Frogs' Legs

SERVES 4

⅓ cup peanut or corn oil

2 Tbsp red chili paste

8 sets frogs' legs

2 oz green peppercorns

5 small white eggplants, quartered

3 fresh red chiles, sliced lengthwise

¼ cup galangal or gingerroot, cut into fine matchsticks

2 tsp fish sauce

½ tsp palm sugar

⅓ cup sweet basil leaves

● Heat the oil in a wok or pan, add the chili paste and fry for 2 minutes, then mix in the frogs' legs and peppercorns.

● Add the eggplant, chile, galangal or ginger, fish sauce and sugar, mix well and fry for 3 minutes.

● Stir in the basil and take off the heat. Serve accompanied by rice.

Tea Eggs

MAKES 12 EGGS

12 eggs

2 tsp salt

3 Tbsp light soy sauce

2 Tbsp dark soy sauce

1 tsp five-spice powder

1 Tbsp red tea leaves

● Cook the eggs in water for 5–10 minutes. Remove and gently tap the shell of each egg with a spoon until it is cracked finely all over.

● Place the eggs back in the pan and cover with fresh water. Add the salt, soy sauces, five-spice powder, and tea leaves (the better the quality of the tea, the better the result). Bring to a boil and simmer for 30–40 minutes. Leave the eggs to cool in the liquid.

● Peel off the shells—the eggs will have a beautiful marbled pattern. They can be served either on their own or as part of a mixed hors d'oeuvre, whole or cut into halves or quarters.

Salmon Roe Sushi

SERVES 2

Salmon roe is an expensive but popular ingredient in Japan. This dish makes a rather nice starter, although you can eat it combined with rolled **sushi** *or with fried bean curd* **sushi** *as a main dish.*

4 Tbsp cooked *sushi* rice

1½ x 5 in strips *nori*

2 slices cucumber, cut in half

4 tsp salmon roe

● Wet your palm with a little water. Take 1 tablespoon of rice and form it into a square-shaped ball. Make three other balls in the same way.

● Place each rice ball in the middle of a strip of *nori*. Roll the *nori* around it, then stand it on a plate.

● Place the sliced cucumber on top of each of the rice balls, and put 1 teaspoon of salmon roe on top of the cucumber. Serve with a dash of soy sauce.

Sukiyaki

SERVES 2

Sukiyaki *is one of the few examples of Japanese cuisine to have become popular throughout the West. In Japan, a special, heavy pan is used, however* **sukiyaki** *can be prepared with any large, deep, skillet. Like fondue,* **sukiyaki** *is always cooked at the table.*

1 Tbsp vegetable oil

5 fl oz *dashi* broth

1½ tsp sugar

2 Tbsp *mirin*

1 Tbsp *sake*

2½ Tbsp soy sauce

1 medium onion, halved and sliced

7 oz bean curd, cut in half lengthwise and sliced

10 oz *pak choi*, halved lengthwise and sliced

6 shiitake mushrooms, halved

1 short leek, sliced on a slant

10 oz beef, sliced paper thin

2 raw eggs (optional)

● Heat the oil in a frying pan and add the *dashi* broth, sugar, *mirin, sake,* and soy sauce. When this mixture begins to simmer, add half the amount of onions, bean curd, *pak choi,* and shiitake mushrooms, keeping each ingredient in its own separate group in the pan. Simmer for 7 minutes and then add half the beef, placing it in the center of the pan. Continue to simmer for several minutes until cooked.

● Break the raw eggs into 2 serving bowls and mix the yolk and white with your chopsticks. Take the cooked meat, bean curd, and vegetables a little at a time from the pan, dip them into the raw egg and eat with a bowl of rice. As the cooked ingredients are taken from the pan, replenish with the raw ingredients.

Steamed Crab with Light Wine Sauce

SERVES 4

Vietnamese people eat crabs a lot as they are plentiful and inexpensive; they are found in the lakes, rivers, mangrove swamps, and coastal waters. The freshwater crab is highly prized for its sweet-flavored meat.

1½ lb crab claws

2 stalks lemon grass, peeled and finely chopped, or grated peel of 1 lemon

1 slice fresh gingerroot, peeled and finely chopped

FOR THE SAUCE

4 Tbsp rice wine, dry sherry, or dry white wine

1 Tbsp fish sauce or 1 Tbsp light soy sauce

1 Tbsp sesame seed oil

1 Tbsp lemon grass, finely chopped

½ Tbsp scallions, finely chopped

● Break open the crab claws by placing a newspaper on top and tapping with the back of a cleaver or a steak mallet. Carefully extract the flesh and discard any shell and cartilage. Place in a bowl and flake with a fork.

● Add the lemon grass and ginger. Mix well, cover, and steam for about 15 minutes.

● Mix together the sauce ingredients and serve separately.

Sukiyaki

Ramen with Crab Omelet

SERVES 4

Typically, crab omelet is served on its own. The inspiration behind the dish is Chinese, but the Japanese have a preference for it served on a bowl of noodles. Ideally, individual omelets should be made, but if time is against you, make one large one and cut it into four portions.

1 lb *ramen* noodles or 14 oz fresh or ¾ lb dried thin egg noodles

6 cups soy sauce broth

FOR THE OMELET

6 eggs

6 oz crabmeat (canned)

4 shiitake mushrooms, sliced

2 scallions, thinly sliced

4 Tbsp canned bamboo shoots, thinly sliced

salt and white pepper

2–3 Tbsp vegetable oil

1 scallion, chopped

● To make the omelet, put the eggs, crabmeat, mushrooms, scallion, and bamboo shoots in a bowl. Season with salt and pepper, and mix.

● Heat the oil in a skillet or wok until very hot. Pour in the egg mixture, and heat for 30 seconds. Stir lightly with chopsticks or a spatula a few times. When it is nearly set, turn it over. The mixture should be soft like scrambled eggs, but be cooked just enough to be able to retain the shape of an omelet.

● Boil plenty of water in a large pan. Add the noodles and cook for 3 minutes, or according to the instructions on the package. Drain, then divide into four bowls.

● Heat the soy sauce broth. Place the crab omelet on the noodles, and pour the broth over the top. Sprinkle with the chopped scallion and serve.

Crab Stuffed with Ground Pork and Cilantro

SERVES 4

2 cooked crabs

1 cup chopped lean pork

1 onion, chopped

1 tsp black pepper

1 Tbsp sugar

1 Tbsp fish sauce (optional)

1 Tbsp cilantro root, chopped

2 eggs, separated

1 Tbsp scallions, chopped

1 Tbsp fresh cilantro leaves, chopped

1 fresh red or green chile pepper, finely sliced

● Remove the limbs from the crabs. Remove the flesh from the shells, taking care to keep them intact. Remove the flesh from the limbs as well. Flake all the flesh and set aside.

● Combine the pork, onion, pepper, sugar, fish sauce, if used, and cilantro root in a food processor or blender. Remove and place in a bowl. Add the crab meat and egg white. Add the green onions and cilantro leaves and mix by hand, using more egg white if necessary.

● Fill the crab shells with the mixture to form a generous mound. Carefully break the egg yolk and place ½ teaspoon yolk on the top of each mound. Sprinkle with chile. Be very careful when moving the crab shells or else the yolk will run. (If you think this is too difficult, brush the filling with the beaten egg yolk and sprinkle with the sliced chile and some cilantro leaves.)

● Place each crab, stuffed side up, in a large steamer and steam for 20 minutes. Serve with a generous green salad.

Tempura

SERVES 2

One of the most famous dishes in the Japanese repertoire, **Tempura** *needs no introduction. Ironically, strong evidence exists that* **Tempura** *is not originally Japanese, but was introduced into Japan by Portuguese traders in the seventeenth century. One of the great advantages of* **Tempura** *is its versatility. Virtually any seafood and vegetable can be prepared and served in this way. The ingredients suggested below are those most commonly served in Japan. Mix the dip first, so that the* **Tempura** *can be served and eaten immediately after being fried.*

½ green bell pepper, seeded and cut into four pieces lengthwise

4 shiitake mushrooms

½ lb sweet potatoes, unpeeled but sliced into ¾ in circles

¼ lb carrots, peeled and cut into 2½ in lengths, then cut into matchsticks

4 large shrimp, peeled but tails on

vegetable oil, for deep frying

small amount of all-purpose flour

1 small white radish, peeled and grated

FOR THE BATTER

¼ cup all-purpose flour

¼ cup cornstarch

1 egg, beaten

¾ cup water

FOR THE DIP

2 Tbsp *mirin*

2 Tbsp soy sauce

⅝ cup *dashi* broth

● To make the dip, put the *mirin*, soy sauce, and *dashi* broth in a pan, bring to a boil, and simmer for 1 minute. Leave to cool.

● To make the batter, place the flour, cornstarch, egg, and water into a bowl and mix lightly using chopsticks or a fork. The batter should be quite lumpy with some flour visible on top of the mixture.

● Heat the oil in a pan to 350°F. Check the temperature by dropping in some batter or a piece of bread; if it bubbles and floats to the surface, the oil is at the right temperature.

● Dip the vegetables into the batter and deep-fry until the batter has turned golden brown. Check the harder vegetables, such as sweet potatoes, are cooked by piercing with a skewer. If it runs through smoothly with no resistance, the vegetables are ready. The carrot matchsticks should be picked up in small bunches, dipped in the batter and then fried, held together by the batter.

● To deep-fry the shrimp, coat them with a little flour before dipping into the batter as this will stop them from spitting while frying.

● When all the ingredients have been fried, serve immediately. Place the dip in small bowls and into the center, add a spoonful of grated radish. Dip the pieces of *tempura* into the dip before eating.

Tempura

Steamed Crab

SERVES 6

The crab mixture can be steamed in a large crab shell. It is well worth using fresh crab meat for better flavor and texture.

2 oz bean sprouts

scant ¼ cup medium-firm bean curd

about 2 cups mixed white and brown crabmeat, finely chopped

½ in gingerroot, grated

2 scallions, very finely chopped

1 tsp sesame oil

salt and freshly ground black pepper

1 Tbsp all-purpose flour

1 egg, beaten

diagonally sliced white and green parts of scallion for garnish

● Add the bean sprouts to a saucepan of boiling water. Quickly return to a boil and boil for 1 minute. Tip into a colander and rinse under cold water. Drain well, then squeeze out as much water as possible. Chop finely.

● Wrap the bean curd in a clean cloth and squeeze firmly to express surplus liquid. Finely crumble the bean curd. Mix the crabmeat, bean sprouts, bean curd, ginger, scallions, sesame oil, and seasonings together. Divide among six individual heatproof dishes.

● Sift the flour over the tops of the dishes, then brush with beaten egg. Put in a steaming basket. Cover the dishes with baking parchment and cover the steaming basket. Put the steaming basket over a saucepan of boiling water and steam the crab for about 10 minutes. Garnish with scallions.

Stuffed Crab Shells

SERVES 4

This dish is as well-known in Thailand for its name, **poo jag,** *as for anything else—it means, literally, "dear crab," for reasons that no one has ever been able to explain convincingly.*

4 blue crab shells, well cleaned

3 eggs, beaten

5 cups peanut or corn oil for deep-frying

¼ cup cilantro leaves

2 fresh red chiles, cut into lengthwise strips

FOR THE STUFFING

1 cup cooked ground pork

½ cup ground shrimp

⅓ cup crabmeat, fresh or drained very well if canned

2 Tbsp onion, finely chopped

1 Tbsp scallion, finely sliced

1 tsp ground white pepper

1 tsp sugar

¼ tsp light soy sauce

¼ tsp salt

● Mix all the stuffing ingredients together and fill the crab shells. Heat the oil in a pan or wok to approximately 350°F.

● Dip the stuffed crabs in the beaten egg to coat them well all over, and then deep-fry until thoroughly cooked, about 10–15 minutes. Remove and drain well on paper towel. Sprinkle with the cilantro and chile before serving. Serve as an hors d'oeuvre or with rice and bottled Chinese plum sauce.

Korean Crab Cakes

SERVES 4

Although not quite authentic, these crab cakes go very well with a crisp green salad.

12 oz floury potatoes, unpeeled

1½ garlic cloves, crushed and finely chopped

1 fresh red chile, seeded and finely chopped

1 in gingerroot, grated

3 scallions, finely chopped

1½ cups white and brown crabmeat

finely grated rind of ½ lime

2 Tbsp chopped fresh cilantro

salt and freshly ground black pepper

1½ Tbsp sesame seeds

1 cup fresh bread crumbs, for coating

flour for coating

1 egg, beaten

vegetable oil for deep-frying

ginger dipping sauce to serve

● Boil the potatoes in their skins until tender. Drain and leave until cool enough to handle. Peel the potatoes and mash the flesh.

● Mix the mashed potato with the garlic, chile, ginger, scallions, crabmeat, lime zest, cilantro, and salt and pepper. Form into eight round cakes, about the size of golf balls. Chill for 30 minutes.

● Stir the sesame seeds into the bread crumbs. Coat the crab cakes in the flour, then the egg and finally coat in the bread crumbs.

● Half fill a deep-fat fryer with vegetable oil and heat to about 325°F. Fry the crab cakes in batches for about 8 minutes until golden. Transfer to paper towels to drain while frying the remaining crab cakes. Serve hot with ginger dipping sauce.

Marinated Thinly Sliced Chicken Breast

SERVES 3–4

Traditionally, vegetables, rice and pickles are served with the chicken, but this is also delicious with a crisp salad, or on firm white, crusty bread.

3 Tbsp Japanese dark soy sauce

2 Tbsp sesame oil

1 Tbsp crushed toasted sesame seeds

1 in ginger root, grated

2 garlic cloves, crushed

2 scallions, white and green parts thinly sliced into rings

2 Tbsp rice wine

salt and freshly ground black pepper

12 oz skinned, boneless chicken breast, chilled

2 Tbsp vegetable oil

2 fresh hot red chiles, thickly sliced crosswise

4 large brown mushrooms, oyster or shiitake, each cut into 4 slices

● Mix together the soy sauce, sesame oil and seeds, ginger, garlic, scallions, rice wine or sherry, salt and plenty of black pepper to taste.

● Holding the knife at a slight angle, cut across the chicken breasts to make ⅛ inch wide slices. Using a meat mallet or the flat side of a cleaver, pound each slice, at the same time dragging the mallet or cleaver across the slice. Lay the slices in a large, shallow dish, pouring some of the soy/sesame sauce over each layer. Cover and leave for 1 hour.

● Heat the vegetable oil in a large, preferably nonstick, skillet. Lift some of the chicken slices from the marinade and add to the pan so they lie flat in a single layer. Cook for 1 minute on each side until lightly browned and cooked through. Transfer to a warm plate and keep warm while frying the remaining chicken.

● When all the chicken has been cooked through, add the chiles, mushrooms, and remaining marinade to the pan. Stir continuously and cook for 1 more minute. Pour the sauce evenly over the chicken and serve immediately.

Japanese Chicken Shish Kabob

SERVES 2

The Japanese name for this dish, **yakitori,** *lends its name to the Japanese* **yakitori bar,** *a popular place to meet, eat, drink, and socialize throughout Japan. Chicken and chicken livers are the two most commonly eaten* **yakitori.**

FOR THE STUFFING

¼ cup soy sauce

¼ cup *mirin*

1 Tbsp superfine sugar

1 Tbsp honey

skin from the chicken

FOR THE *YAKITORI*

2 boneless chicken breasts (with skin) diced, making 24 pieces

1 leek, cut into 1 in lengths, making 8 pieces

½ green bell pepper, seeded and diced, making 8 pieces

8 bamboo or steel skewers

● To make the sauce, put the soy sauce, *mirin*, sugar, honey, and chicken skin into a saucepan, bring to a boil and simmer for about 10 minutes.

● Turn up the heat to medium and brush the *yakitori* with the sauce frequently, turning from time to time, for about 6–7 minutes or until the meat is cooked through. Serve with rice and a vegetable dish.

● To prepare the *yakitori*, thread onto a skewer pieces of chicken, leek, chicken, bell pepper, and chicken again, in that order.

● Pre-heat the grill to low and cook the *yakitori* until the meat has turned white, about 3 minutes.

Duck with Plums and Port

SERVES 4

Serve this rich stir-fry with rice or noodles.

3 duck breasts, skinned and thinly sliced across (into medallions)

½ cup port

grated zest and juice of 1 orange

1 bay leaf

1 parsley sprig

1 thyme sprig

1 rosemary sprig

¼ cup all-purpose flour

salt and freshly ground black pepper

3 Tbsp oil

knob of butter

½ lb plums, halved, pitted, and quartered

FOR THE GARNISH

orange slices

fresh herbs

● Place the duck in a dish. Add the port, orange zest and juice, and all the herbs. Mix well, cover, and leave to marinate overnight.

● Strain the duck well, reserving the marinade. Pick out the herbs, then pat the duck on absorbent paper towels. Toss the slices of duck in the flour, adding plenty of seasoning.

● Heat the oil and butter with the herbs. Add the duck and stir-fry the pieces until lightly browned. Sprinkle any leftover flour into the pan, then stir in the marinade and add the plums. Stir all the time until the juices boil and thicken. Reduce the heat and cook for 2 minutes, then taste for seasoning before serving. Halved orange slices and fresh herbs may be added for garnish.

Japanese Chicken Shish Kabob

Crispy Roast Duck with Pancakes and Fresh Herbs

SERVES 4

If you prefer not to make pancakes, buy 12 wheaten pancakes, which are available in good delicatessens.

1 lb of Ho Chi Minh duck (see Duck with Ginger Sauce, page 139)

FOR THE PANCAKES

2 cups all-purpose flour

¾ cup boiled water

½ Tbsp cold water

1 tsp sesame seed oil

FOR THE VEGETABLE PLATTER

1 bunch scallions, cut into 2 in lengths

1½ cups fresh cilantro

1½ cups fresh mint

1½ cups fresh basil

½ cucumber peeled in alternating strips, halved lengthwise and sliced thinly crosswise

5 cups fresh bean sprouts

sweet plum sauce to accompany (this can be obtained from large food stores and delicatessens)

● To make the pancakes sift the flour into a mixing bowl. Pour in the boiled water, stirring quickly and then stir in the cold water. When cool enough, mold with your hands and form a dough. Cover with a cloth and leave for 30 minutes.

● When ready, knead lightly on a lightly floured board. Roll the dough into a sausage shape and cut into 1 inch portions. This will make about 12 rounds. With the heel of the hand flatten into circles of about 2½ inches across.

● Using a pastry brush paint half the pieces with the sesame oil. Place the remaining pieces onto the oiled surfaces making six pairs in total. With a lightly floured rolling pin roll out each pair to about 6 inches across. Turn them to make them round.

● Fry for 1–2 minutes in a heavy un-oiled pan until they begin to turn light brown. Turn them over and repeat. They will puff up.

● Remove and separate the two thin pancakes. Repeat until all the dough is used up. Put on a plate and cover with a cloth to prevent from drying. Steam all the pancakes in a steamer for 7 minutes just before serving with the duck.

● Arrange the duck on a plate. Arrange the vegetables on a plate. Put some plum sauce into a dish. Place the pancakes on a flat plate. Guests place a teaspoon of plum sauce and some duck and vegetables on a pancake.

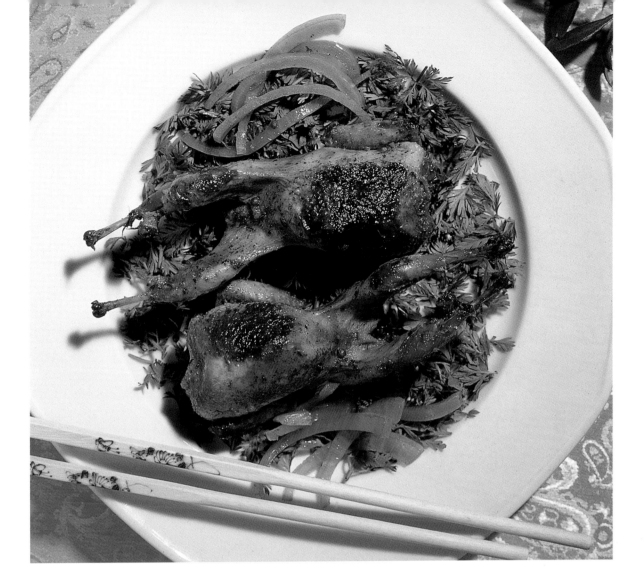

Marinated Quail in Honey

SERVES 4

1 tsp coriander seeds, lightly
  crushed

2 Tbsp clear honey

2 onions, sliced

1¼ cups dry cider

1¼ cups chile vinegar

8 quails

2 Tbsp butter

2 Tbsp vegetable oil

salt and freshly ground black
  pepper

FOR THE GARNISH

parsley, chopped

● Mix the coriander, honey, onion, cider, and vinegar in a large bowl (not a metal one). Add the quails and marinate overnight.

● Preheat the oven to 350°F. Drain and reserve the marinade. Dry the quails with paper towels. Heat the butter and oil in a large casserole. Add the quails, 4 at a time, seasoning them with salt and black pepper. Brown on both sides.

● Put all the birds in the casserole and pour the marinade over them. Cover and cook in the oven for 40–45 minutes, basting occasionally, or until tender. Garnish with chopped parsley to serve.

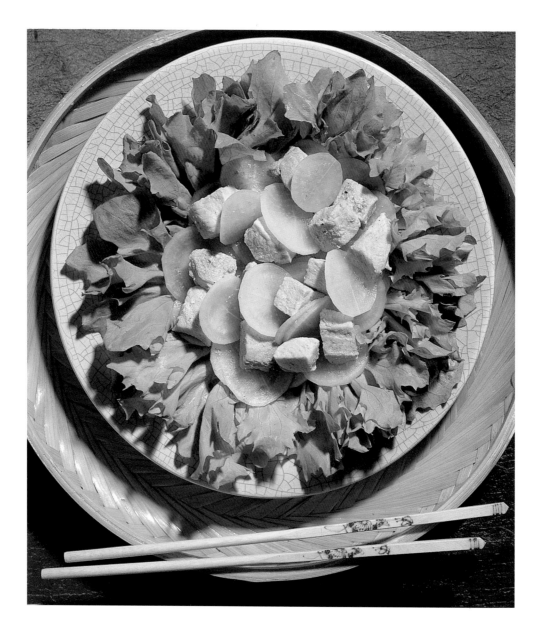

Vietnamese Pork au Caramel

SERVES 4

¼ cup sugar

2 Tbsp water

1 lb leg of pork, cut into large cubes

3 white radishes, peeled and thinly sliced

½ onion, chopped

⅓ cup fish sauce or light soy sauce

freshly ground black pepper

● Put the sugar in the wok and heat gently until it starts to smell as though it is burning. Stir in the water very carefully so that the mixture does not break up.

● Add the pork and radishes, and cover with water. Add the remaining ingredients and bring to a boil. Reduce the heat, cover, and allow to simmer for about an hour or until the pork is cooked.

Pork Meatballs in Sweet Soy Sauce

MAKES 16 MEATBALLS

*The use of ground meat is widespread in Japan, and this form, **niku-dango**, is sold ready-made in delicatessens as well as being prepared at home. Take care, as the sweet-tasting sauce makes it all too easy to gorge oneself on these little balls of pork!*

FOR THE MEATBALLS	FOR THE SAUCE
8 oz ground pork	4 Tbsp water
1 oz leek, finely chopped	1 Tbsp *sake*
1 Tbsp *sake*	1 Tbsp *mirin*
large pinch of salt	1 Tbsp superfine sugar
½ egg, beaten	1 Tbsp soy sauce
1 Tbsp cornstarch	2 tsp cornstarch
vegetable oil, for deep frying	

● To make the meatballs, mix the pork, leek, *sake*, salt, beaten egg, and cornstarch in a bowl. Knead the mixture until the beaten egg is well combined and gives a stickiness to the rest of the mixture. Then, take 1 tablespoon of the mixture in hour hand and mould it into a ball.

● Fill a pan about one-third full with cooking oil. Heat to 350°F and then deep-fry the meatballs for 5 minutes or until browned. Remove and drain off any excess oil using paper towels.

● Put the water, *sake, mirin*, sugar, soy sauce, and cornstarch together in a pan. Mix together over a low heat stirring until the sauce has thickened. Add the meatballs and continue to stir until they are all covered in the sauce. Serve with a bowl of hot, plain boiled rice and a vegetable dish.

Stuffed Roast Suckling Pig

SERVES 20

10 lb prepared suckling pig (ask your butcher to leave enough flesh and skin on the belly for sewing)

juice of 1 lime

2 Tbsp sea salt

4 cloves, ground

freshly ground black pepper

vegetable oil

FOR THE STUFFING

heart, liver, and kidneys of the pig

6 Tbsp butter

2 onions, finely chopped

4 cloves garlic, finely chopped

6 cups fresh bread crumbs

1 red chile pepper, chopped

4 Tbsp scallions, chopped

1 large sprig of parsley, finely chopped

1 Tbsp fish sauce or light soy sauce

¾ cup rice wine

½ tsp thyme, finely chopped

½ tsp allspice, crushed

juice of 1 lime

salt

FOR THE SAUCE

2½ cups chicken broth

2½ cups clear honey

½ cup light soy sauce

4 Tbsp tomato paste

4 tsp five-spice powder

½ cup rice wine or sherry

salt

2 Tbsp cornstarch mixed with a little water

● Run cold water over the suckling pig and dry thoroughly inside and out. Rub the inside of the pig with lime juice. Mix the salt, cloves, and black pepper and use half of it to rub the inside of the pig.

● Clean and wash the liver, heart, and kidney. Dry and grind. Melt the butter in a pan on a low heat, add the onions and garlic, and sauté until softened. Add the ground liver, heart, and kidney mixture and continue to sauté for a further 5 minutes. Remove from heat and allow to cool.

● Add the other ingredients, mixing well. (If the stuffing is too dry, add 1–2 tablespoons water or milk.) Fill the cavity with the stuffing and sew it up with kitchen twine. Stuff a ball of foil in the pig's mouth. Tie each pair of legs together and fold under the animal. Place belly downwards in a shallow pan. Brush the back with oil and sprinkle the remainder of the ground cloves, sea salt, and black pepper over the suckling pig. Cover the ears with foil for the first 90 minutes of cooking.

● Preheat the oven to 325°F and cook the pig for 2½ hours or until the juices run clear when pricked with a knife, basting regularly. Remove from the pan and allow to cool for 15 minutes. Replace the foil in the mouth with an orange and put the pig on a dish.

● Drain the juices from the roasting pan to a wok. Add all the sauce ingredients except the cornstarch. Bring the juices to a boil and add the cornstarch, stirring gently until it thickens.

Wild Boar Country Curry

SERVES 4

Well, wild boar is not strictly necessary (and in any case in Thailand these days is bred, not hunted). Substitute pork.

¼ cup peanut or corn oil

8 oz boar or pork loin, cut into
　1¼ x ¾ x ¼ in slices

5 cups water

7 oz bamboo shoots, diced

5 oz small white eggplants

4½ oz string beans

¼ cup krachai, sliced lengthwise

3 fresh red chiles, quartered
　lengthwise

2 Tbsp fish sauce

3 kaffir lime leaves, torn into
　small pieces

¼ cup sweet basil leaves

FOR THE CHILI PASTE

1 oz shallots, chopped

1 oz garlic cloves, chopped

½ oz dried red chiles, chopped

2 cilantro roots, chopped

1 Tbsp lemon grass, chopped

1 tsp galangal, chopped

1 tsp kaffir lime zest, chopped

1 tsp salt

½ tsp shrimp paste

● Pound all the chili paste ingredients together with a mortar and pestle or in a blender to a fine paste.

● Heat the oil in a wok or pan and fry the chili paste for 3 minutes. Add the meat and stir-fry for 2 minutes; then add the water and bamboo shoots and cook until the shoots are tender, about 3–5 minutes.

● Add the eggplants, string beans, krachai, chiles, fish sauce, and lime leaf, boil for 3 minutes more and then remove from the heat. Stir in the basil and serve.

● Serve accompanied by pickled garlic, salted eggs, and sticky rice.

One-Pan
Dishes

Braised and steamed dishes, which often constitute the main
courses in the serving sequence of a traditional Asian meal,
take a little longer to cook than stir-fried dishes, but most can
be prepared and cooked in advance. Some of these recipes
can be served cold, making them ideal buffet dishes, and most
blend well with Western food, so that they can be used
in conjunction with non-Asian food as part of your family's
regular menu.

Lion's Head Casserole

SERVES 4

"Lion's head" in Chinese cuisine means pork meatballs with cabbage. Here the "meatballs" are entirely made from vegetables.

4 cakes of bean curd

4 oz gluten

2 oz cooked carrots

4–5 dried Chinese mushrooms, soaked

2 oz bamboo shoots

1 Tbsp salt

1 tsp gingerroot, finely chopped

2–3 Tbsp ground rice or bread crumbs

1 Tbsp cornstarch

2 tsp sesame seed oil

all-purpose flour for dusting

6 cabbage or lettuce hearts

oil for deep-frying

1 tsp sugar

approx. 2½ cups water

5 large cabbage leaves

1 tsp ground white pepper

2 Tbsp rice wine or dry sherry

● Squeeze as much liquid as possible from the bean curd using a cheesegauze, then mash.

● Finely chop the gluten, carrots, mushrooms, and bamboo shoots. Place them with the mashed bean curd in a large mixing bowl. Add 1 teaspoon salt, the finely chopped ginger root, ground rice or breadcrumbs, cornstarch, and sesame seed oil and blend everything together until smooth. Make 10 "meatballs" from this mixture and place them on a plate, lightly dusted with flour.

● Trim off any hard or tough roots from the cabbage or lettuce hearts.

● Heat the oil in a wok or deep-fryer. When hot, deep-fry the "meatballs" for about 3 minutes, stirring very gently to make sure that they are not stuck together. Scoop out with a slotted spoon or strainer, and drain.

● Pour off the excess oil leaving about 2 tablespoons in the wok. Stir-fry the cabbage hearts with a little salt and sugar. Add about 2½ cups water and bring to a boil. Reduce the heat and let the mixture simmer.

● Meanwhile, line the bottom of a casserole with the cabbage leaves and place the "meatballs" on top. Pour the cabbage hearts with the soup into the casserole and add the remaining salt, ground pepper and rice wine. Cover, bring to a boil, reduce the heat, and simmer for 10 minutes.

● To serve, take off the lid and rearrange the cabbage hearts so that they appear between the "meatballs" in a star-shaped pattern.

Stewed Gluten in Sweet Bean Sauce

SERVES 4

11 oz gluten in small pieces

3 Tbsp oil

1 Tbsp dark soy sauce

1 Tbsp sugar

1 tsp five-spice powder

2 Tbsp rice wine or dry sherry

1 Tbsp sweet bean paste or
  hoisin sauce

1 slice gingerroot, peeled

2 tsp sesame seed oil

● Boil the gluten pieces in a pan of water for about 4–5 minutes or until they float to the surface. Remove and drain off as much water as possible.

● Heat the oil in a hot wok or pan. When hot, add the boiled gluten, stir for a few seconds and then add the soy sauce, sugar, five-spice powder, wine, sweet bean paste, crushed ginger root, and ½ cup water.

● Bring to a boil and cook over high heat for 20–25 minutes or until there is very little juice left, stirring now and again to make sure that each piece of gluten is well covered by the gravy.

● Add the sesame seed oil, blend well and serve hot or cold.

Chinese Cabbage and Straw Mushrooms in Cream Sauce

SERVES 4

14 oz Chinese cabbage or *pak choi*

12 oz canned straw mushrooms or 8 oz fresh straw mushrooms

4 Tbsp oil

1½ tsp salt

1 tsp sugar

1 Tbsp cornstarch mixed with 3 Tbsp cold water

½ cup milk

● Separate the cabbage leaves and cut each leaf in half lengthwise.

● Drain the straw mushrooms. If using fresh ones, do not peel them, but just wash and trim off the roots.

● Heat 3 tablespoons of the oil in a hot wok and stir-fry the cabbage leaves for about 1 minute. Add the salt and sugar and continue stirring for another minute or so. Remove the cabbage leaves and arrange them neatly on one side of a serving dish.

● Heat the remaining oil until hot, then reduce the heat and add the cornstarch and water mixture and the milk, and stir until thickened. Pour about half of the sauce into a pitcher and keep warm.

● Add the mushrooms to the remaining sauce in the wok and heat them thoroughly over high heat. Remove the mushrooms and place them next to the cabbage leaves on the plate. Pour the sauce evenly over the cabbage and mushrooms and serve hot.

Cashew Casserole

SERVES 4

Soy sauce is excellent in casseroles, its piquancy adding a hint of Asia to this cashew nut and chicken dish.

2 Tbsp sunflower oil

4 chicken pieces

8 shallots

2 cups chestnut mushrooms, quartered

1 cup baby turnips

2 celery stalks, sliced

1 carrot, diced

¼ cup all-purpose flour

2½ cups chicken broth

2 Tbsp light soy sauce

⅔ cup dry white wine

½ cup unsalted cashew nuts

1 Tbsp tomato paste

salt and ground black pepper

FOR THE DUMPLINGS

1 cup self-rising flour

½ cup shredded beef suet

1 Tbsp light soy sauce

1 tsp fresh rosemary, chopped

● Heat the oil in a large skillet. Add the chicken and cook until browned, about 10 minutes. Remove with a slotted draining spoon and place in an ovenproof casserole dish.

● Heat the oven to 350°F. Add the shallots, mushrooms, turnips, celery, and carrot to the skillet and cook for 5 minutes, stirring. Add the flour and cook 1 minute.

● Gradually add the broth, soy sauce, and wine, then bring to a boil, stirring. Add the cashew nuts and tomato paste and season well. Pour onto the chicken in the casserole dish. Cover and cook in the oven, about 45 minutes.

● Place the dumpling ingredients in a bowl. Stir in ½ cup cold water and bring together to form a dough. Divide into eight and roll into balls.

● Uncover the casserole and place the dumplings on top of the chicken mixture. Return to the oven, uncovered, until cooked through, about 15 minutes.

Casserole of Vegetables

SERVES 4

2 tbsp dried wood ears

1 cake bean curd

4 oz green beans or snow peas

4 oz cabbage or broccoli

4 oz baby corn or bamboo
   shoots

4 oz carrots

3–4 tbsp oil

1 tsp salt

1 tsp sugar

1 Tbsp light soy sauce

1 tsp cornstarch mixed with
   1 Tbsp cold water

● Soak the wood ears in water for 20–25 minutes, rinse, and discard the hard roots, if any.

● Cut the bean curd into about 12 small pieces and harden the pieces in a pot of lightly salted boiling water for 2–3 minutes. Remove and drain.

● Trim the beans or snow peas. Leave whole if small; cut in half if large.

● Cut the vegetables into thin slices or chunks.

● Heat about half of the oil in a flameproof casserole or saucepan. When hot, lightly brown the bean curd on both sides. Remove with a slotted spoon.

● Heat the remaining oil and stir-fry the rest of the vegetables for about 1½ minutes. Add the bean curd pieces, salt, sugar, and soy sauce, and continue stirring to blend everything well. Cover, reduce the heat and simmer for 2–3 minutes.

● Mix the cornstarch with water to make a smooth paste, pour it over the vegetables and stir. Increase the heat to high just long enough to thicken the gravy. Serve hot.

Chinese Cabbage Casserole

SERVES 4

1 lb Chinese cabbage or *pak choi*

2 oz deep-fried bean curd or 2 cakes fresh bean curd

4 oz carrots

3 Tbsp oil

1 tsp salt

1 tsp sugar

2 Tbsp light soy sauce

2 Tbsp rice wine or dry sherry

1 tsp sesame seed oil

● Separate the cabbage leaves, wash and cut them into small pieces. If using fresh bean curd, cut each cake into about 12 pieces and fry them in a little oil until golden.

● Peel the carrots and cut them into diamond-shaped chunks.

● Heat the oil in a hot wok and stir-fry the cabbage with the salt and sugar for a minute or so. Transfer it to a Chinese sand-pot or casserole and cover with the bean curd, carrots, soy sauce, and sherry. Put a lid on the pot and when it comes to a boil, reduce the heat and simmer for 15 minutes.

● Stir in the sesame oil. Add a little water if necessary and cook for a few more minutes. Serve hot.

Steamed Eggs

SERVES 4

5 eggs

4 Tbsp hot water

1 tsp salt

2 tsp rice wine

spinach leaves, chopped
(optional)

1 Tbsp soy sauce

● Beat the eggs in a bowl, and mix in the water, salt and rice wine.

● Place the bowl, uncovered, in a saucepan half-filled with boiling water. Cover the saucepan and steam gently for 20 minutes. If the heat is too high, the eggs will not congeal, or holes will form.

● A garnish of chopped spinach leaves may be added before steaming. Add the soy sauce before serving.

Braised Quails' Eggs with Bean Curd and Vegetables

SERVES 4

1 piece bean curd, cut into 6 pieces ½ in thick

6 Tbsp vegetable oil

10 straw mushrooms or firm button mushrooms

8 quails' eggs, hard-cooked and shelled

1 scallion, cut into 1 in lengths

2 pieces canned bamboo shoots, cut into 1 in cubes

4 tsp bottled satay sauce

1 tsp cornstarch

3 tsp fish sauce or light soy sauce

2 tsp sugar

½ cup water

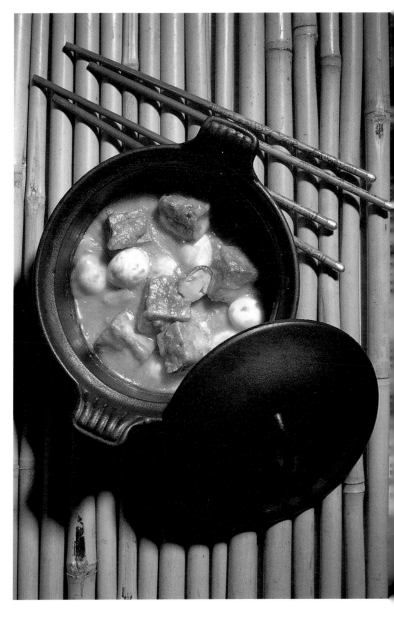

● Fry the bean curd in 4 tablespoons hot oil until brown, taking care not to let it stick. Set aside and discard the oil.

● Put the remaining oil into a small casserole dish with a tight-fitting lid. Heat over a medium heat. Add the straw mushrooms, quails' eggs, scallion, bean curd, bamboo shoots, and satay sauce.

● Mix the cornstarch, fish sauce, and sugar to form a smooth paste. Mix into the water. Stir this into the casserole pot and cover. Cook for 4 minutes.

Cod and Chinese Cabbage Pot

SERVES 2

This popular winter dish is normally cooked on the table using a portable gas or electric ring. Everyone at the table takes food from the pan, transferring it to their own individual dishes while the host takes care to keep the pan stocked up with fresh raw ingredients. You will need an 8 inch casserole dish.

3¾ cups water

3 in piece dried *konbu* (kelp)

1 small leek, sliced on a slant into ½ in widths

1 medium onion, sliced

2 10 oz cod fillets or steaks, cut into large, bite-sized pieces

7 oz Chinese or *pak choi* leaves, cut in half lengthwise and then sliced into ½ in strips

4 oz *momen* or "cotton" bean curd, cut into ½ in cubes

4 oz carrots, peeled and thinly sliced

4 shiitake mushrooms, cut into halves

6 snow peas

FOR THE *PONZU* DRESSING

3 Tbsp soy sauce

1 Tbsp lemon juice

1 Tbsp vinegar

1 Tbsp *mirin*

½ Tbsp Japanese instant broth granules

FOR THE GARNISH

1 lb white radish, peeled, grated, and lightly squeezed

pinch of seven-spice powder or chili pepper

● Put the water and *konbu* in a flameproof casserole and bring to a boil. Add half the leek, onion, cod, Chinese leaves or *pak choi, tofu,* carrots, shiitake mushrooms, and snow peas keeping groups together in the pan. Cook for 5–8 minutes, or until the vegetables are cooked.

● Meanwhile, mix the soy sauce, lemon juice, vinegar, *mirin* and broth granules in a jar and stir well.

● When roughly half of the cooked food has been taken from the casserole, replenish with the raw ingredients.

● To serve, put 2 tablespoons of radish and 1 tablespoon *ponzu* dressing into each serving bowl.

● As you take food from the casserole with your chopsticks, dip it into the dressing and eat. Add some seven-spice if you wish to add a little more fire to the meal. As you eat, add more *ponzu* dressing and radish when you need to. Serve with rice.

Cod and Chinese Cabbage Pot

Fishballs with Noodles

SERVES 4

1 lb white fish, skinned and cut in chunks

¼ cup cornstarch

1 egg white

salt and freshly ground white pepper

¾ cup Chinese egg noodles

¼ cup oil

4 thin slices fresh gingerroot

1 piece lemon grass or strip of lemon zest

1 celery stalk, cut diagonally into thin slices

1 bunch scallions, sliced

¼ lb snow peas, trimmed

¼ cup soy sauce

¼ cup dry sherry

● Pound the fish with the cornstarch until it is reduced to a paste, then work in the egg white and seasoning. Wet your hands and shape the mixture into small balls, kneading it together so that the fish binds well.

● Place the noodles in the pan and pour in enough boiling water to cover them. Bring back to a boil and cook for 2 minutes, then drain and set aside.

● Heat the oil, then stir-fry the gingerroot and lemon grass or lemon zest for 1 minute before adding the fish balls. Stir-fry the fish balls until firm and golden.

● Add the celery, scallions, and snow peas, and continue to stir-fry for 5–8 minutes, or until the vegetables are slightly tender but not soft.

● Add the noodles, soy sauce, and sherry, and stir the mixture over high heat until the noodles are hot. Serve the dish at once.

Chicken with Mustard Sauce

SERVES 4

Wholegrain mustard is used here for a strong flavor with added texture. Any strong mustard could be used in the recipe if preferred.

1 Tbsp vegetable oil

2 garlic cloves, minced

1 lb chicken breast, boned and skinned

1 fennel bulb, trimmed and sliced

2 Tbsp light soy sauce

¼ cup butter

⅔ cup heavy cream

2½ cups open cap mushrooms, peeled and sliced

2 Tbsp wholegrain mustard

3 Tbsp chopped fresh chives

salt and ground black pepper

● Heat the oil in a large skillet and cook the garlic 1 minute. Cut the chicken into 1 inch cubes, add to the pan, and cook for 2–3 minutes, stirring.

● Add the fennel, soy sauce, and butter, and stir-fry for 5 minutes. Stir in the cream, mushrooms, and mustard, and cook 5 minutes. Sprinkle with chopped chives. Season and serve.

Szechwan Noodles

¾ lb Chinese egg noodles

1 Tbsp cornstarch

3 Tbsp dry sherry

⅓ cup chicken broth

⅓ cup light soy sauce

⅓ cup oil

2 green chiles, seeded and chopped

2 garlic cloves, crushed

2 in piece fresh gingerroot, peeled and cut into fine strips

½ lb lean boneless pork, cut into fine strips

1 red bell pepper, seeded and cut into fine, short strips

1 bunch scallions, cut diagonally into fine slices

7 oz can bamboo shoots, drained and cut in strips

1 in slice Chinese cabbage head, separated into pieces

● Place the noodles in the pan and pour in enough boiling water to cover them. Bring back to a boil and cook for 2 minutes, then drain the noodles. While the noodles are cooking, blend the cornstarch with the sherry, broth, and soy sauce, then set aside.

● Wipe the pan and heat the oil. Add the noodles, spreading them out thinly, and fry over medium to high heat until they are crisp and golden underneath, patting them down slightly into a thin cake—they will set more or less in shape. Use a large slice to turn the noodles over and brown the second side. Don't worry if the noodles break up slightly—the aim is to end up with some that are crisp and others that remain soft. Transfer the noodles to a large serving dish and keep hot until needed.

● Add the chiles, garlic, ginger, and pork to the oil remaining in the pan. Stir-fry the mixture over high heat until the pork is browned. Add the pepper and scallions and stir fry for a further 2 minutes before adding the bamboo shoots. Stir fry for 1 minute to heat the bamboo shoots.

● Give the cornstarch mixture a stir and pour it into the pan. Bring to a boil, stirring, and cook over high heat for 30 seconds. Mix in the Chinese cabbage, stir for less than a minute to heat the cabbage. Spoon the pork mixture over the noodles and serve at once.

Chicken Balls with Rice Sticks

SERVES 4

3 boneless chicken breasts,
skinned and ground

⅓ cup all-purpose flour

¼ cup *sake* or dry sherry

6 tbsp soy sauce (use Japanese
sauce if possible)

1 small egg

1 bunch scallions

salt and pepper

2 tsp sugar

½ lb ribbon rice sticks

¼ cup peanut oil

2 small carrots, cut lengthwise
into very thin strips

½ lb snow peas, trimmed

½ cucumber, peeled, halved
crosswise, and thinly sliced
lengthwise

● A food processor is ideal for grinding the raw chicken, otherwise it may be done by hand using a chef's large knife and a chopping action: eventually the chicken will progress from being chopped in fine dice into a fine, almost ground, mixture.

● Mix the flour with the chicken, pounding the mixture well. Add 1 tablespoon each of the *sake* or dry sherry and soy sauce, then mix in the egg. Finely chop the white parts from 2 scallions, then add them to the mixture with the seasoning. When all the ingredients are thoroughly combined the mixture may seem a little soft, but don't worry—if it is too firm at this stage the cooked balls will be slightly tough in texture. Cover the mixture and chill it on a low shelf in the refrigerator for 30 minutes, or put it in the freezer for about 15 minutes.

● Heat the remaining *sake* and soy sauce with the sugar, stirring, then bring the mixture to a boil and boil hard for 1 minute, set aside. It is best to do this in a saucepan but you can use your stir-fry pan, then pour the mixture into a large bowl, making sure you

scrape it all out of the pan by using a plastic spatula. In a wide pan 1 minute's cooking may be too long as the liquid evaporates more speedily.

● Slice the remaining scallions diagonally. Place the rice sticks in the pan and pour in boiling water to cover them. Bring to a boil and cook for 1–2 minutes, until just soft. Drain and rinse under cold water.

● Wet your hands and shape the chicken mixture into balls, slightly smaller than walnuts—they do not have to be perfect in shape, but if you keep your hands well wetted with cold water the mixture is easier to shape.

● Heat the oil and stir-fry the chicken balls over medium to high heat, until they are golden brown all over. At first they should be coaxed and stirred around the pan gently until the mixture firms. If they are stirred smoothly and constantly they will form neat balls. Then they may be stir-fried with more vigor so that they brown evenly and cook through.

● Use a slotted spoon to remove the chicken balls from the pan, adding them to the boiled soy sauce mixture. Toss the balls in the sauce to coat them completely.

● Add the carrots, snow peas, and scallions to the oil remaining in the pan and stir-fry the vegetables for about 3 minutes before adding the cucumber. Continue stir-frying for about 2 minutes, until the vegetables are just cooked and piping hot.

● Toss in the rice sticks (you may have to rinse them quickly under cold water if they have set in a block— shake off excess water) and stir-fry them for a minute or so to heat them up. Replace the chicken balls in the pan and mix well, then serve.

Casserole of Duck with Dumplings

SERVES 4

1 duck, about 5 lb

1 tsp peeled gingerroot

salt and black pepper

2 Tbsp dry sherry

4 x 1 in slices gingerroot, peeled

1 large whole scallion

4 oz sliced cooked ham

8 oz can bamboo shoots, cut into 1 in pieces

salt

FOR THE DUMPLINGS

2 cups all-purpose flour

1 cup boiling water

1 lb ground pork

⅔ cup shrimp, peeled and deveined

1½ cups white cabbage, finely chopped

salt

2 x 1 in slices gingerroot, peeled and ground

1 scallion, finely chopped

2 Tbsp light soy sauce

2 Tbsp dry sherry

¼ tsp sugar

1 Tbsp sesame oil

1 Tbsp cornstarch dissolved in 3 Tbsp water

black pepper

all-purpose flour

● Remove the fat from the cavity of the duck, discard the tail end, and trim off any excess neck skin. Rinse and drain the duck. Mix the ginger, salt, and black pepper, and rub well into the duck, inside and out. Leave to stand for 1 hour.

● Place the duck in a large casserole, add the sherry, ginger slices, and scallion, cover and bring to a slow boil over moderate heat. Turn down the heat, skim off any scum, adding enough liquid so that the duck does not burn and adjust the heat so that it simmers at its gentlest. Cover and leave for 3 hours.

● Make the dumplings by mixing the flour and boiling water in a large bowl, a little at a time, with a wooden spoon. Do not concern yourself with what it looks like at this stage.

● Chop the pork to loosen it and put it in a second bowl. Slice the shrimp lengthwise and then cut them into ¼ inch pieces. Mix with the pork.

● Cut the white cabbage leaves lengthwise into narrow strips and then cross-cut to dice them. Grind and mix with salt and leave for 5 minutes. Squeeze dry and add to the meat mixture with the rest of the ingredients except the flour. Stir until smooth and pasty. Divide the mixture into 16 portions.

● Knead the dough for a few minutes until it is soft and smooth, dusting with flour if necessary. Roll it out into a 16 inch long sausage and cut with a sharp knife into 1 inch pieces. Dip the cut sides in flour, press into small round cakes with the palm of your hand and roll out into round wrappers 4 inches across.

● Lay a wrapper in the palm of one hand and put a portion of filling in it with the other. Spread with a table knife to within ½ inch of the edge. Gather the wrapper up and press the ends to make a little "basket." Press the back of a knife deep into the basket about 10 times to form indentations, which help to hold the filling in place. You should have 16 dumplings. Put them on a plate and steam over a medium-high heat for 20 minutes. Set aside.

● Skim off the fat from the casserole after it has been cooking for 3 hours and discard it. Scatter in the ham, bamboo shoots, and the dumplings. Cover and simmer for another 5–10 minutes. Add salt to taste.

● Serve in the casserole. Guests help themselves by tearing the bird apart with chopsticks. If they are not sufficiently proficient, you could chop it in the kitchen, put the pieces back into the casserole and bring it back to a boil before serving at the table. Ladle into individual soup bowls.

Rice with Pork and Peppers

SERVES 4

¼ cup oil

1 large onion, thinly sliced

¾ lb lean boneless pork, cut in thin strips

1 red bell pepper, seeded and thinly sliced

1 green bell pepper, seeded and thinly sliced

salt and freshly ground black pepper

a little grated nutmeg

grated zest of 1 orange

¼ lb long-grain rice, freshly cooked

¼ lb wild rice, freshly cooked

● Heat the oil and stir-fry the onion for 2 minutes before adding the pork. Stir-fry the meat and onion together until the meat is cooked through and lightly browned, keeping the heat fairly high to seal the strips of meat.

● Add the peppers, seasoning, nutmeg, and orange zest. Reduce the heat slightly and stir-fry for 3–5 minutes, or until the peppers are cooked.

● Stir in both types of rice and cook for a few minutes so that the ingredients are well combined. If the rice has been allowed to cool, it should be reheated thoroughly at this stage—the result is best if the rice is freshly cooked and piping hot when added to the pan.

Southern Chile Curry

SERVES 4

As with most of the **nam phriks** *(spiced dishes), this thick, spicy southern curry is intended to be eaten with plain rice. Don't be fooled by the simplicity: it's both tasty and satisfying.*

2½ cups water

8 oz pork loin, cut into 1¼ x ¾ x ¼ in pieces

3 Tbsp fish sauce

1 tsp curry powder

3 kaffir lime leaves, torn into quarters

FOR THE CHILI PASTE

8–10 dried small green and red chiles, chopped

6 white peppercorns

2 Tbsp shallot, sliced

1 Tbsp garlic, sliced

1 tsp galangal, sliced

1 tsp shrimp paste

¼ stalk of lemon grass, sliced

● Pound all the ingredients for the chile paste finely with a mortar and pestle or in a blender.

● Boil the water in a pan or wok, add the chile paste and boil briefly before adding the pork, fish sauce, curry powder, and lime leaf.

● Boil again for 10 minutes before transferring to bowls. Serve accompanied by rice.

Rice with Pork and Peppers

Northern Thai Pork Curry

SERVES 6

This dish originally came from across the Burmese border, as shown by the use of tamarind and turmeric. The palm sugar adds an intentional slight sweetness.

4 stalks lemon grass, chopped

1 Tbsp galangal, chopped

1 Tbsp shrimp paste

4 dried red chiles, chopped

2¼ lb pork belly, cut into small
½ in thick strips

3 cups cold water

1 Tbsp turmeric

1 tsp black soy sauce

10 shallots, sliced

¼ cup palm sugar

¼ cup ginger, chopped and
pounded

¼ cup tamarind juice

2 Tbsp garlic, chopped

½ Tbsp marinated soy beans

fish sauce, to taste (optional)

● Pound the lemon grass, galangal, shrimp paste, and chiles with a mortar and pestle or in a blender until fine, then mix with the pork.

● Put in a pan with the water, turmeric and soy sauce. Bring to a boil and cook until tender, about 15 minutes, then add the rest of the ingredients. Boil again for 5–8 minutes and remove from the heat.

● Taste and season with fish sauce if necessary.

Five-spice Pork with Noodles

SERVES 4

1 lb lean boneless pork, cut in thin slices

½ tsp five-spice powder

salt and freshly ground black pepper

2 scallions, finely chopped

1 garlic clove, crushed

½ lb Chinese egg noodles

⅓ cup peanut oil

8 oz can bamboo shoots, sliced

½ lb snow peas, trimmed

¼ cup soy sauce

3 Tbsp roasted sesame seeds

● Mix the pork with the five-spice powder, seasoning, scallions, and garlic. Cover and leave to marinate for at least an hour or as long as overnight.

● Cover the noodles with boiling water and bring back to a boil. Cook for 2 minutes, then drain and rinse under cold water.

● Heat the oil and stir-fry the pork until well browned. Add the bamboo shoots and snow peas, and continue to stir-fry for 3–4 minutes, or until the vegetables are cooked.

● Push the meat mixture to one side of the pan or make a space in the middle and add the noodles. Stir the noodles for 2 minutes to heat them through, then stir in the other ingredients, soy sauce and sesame seeds. Cook for 1 minute before serving.

Pigs' Feet Stew

SERVES 4

2 lb pigs' feet, washed, blanched and chopped into 1½–2 in pieces

5 cups chicken or pork broth

1 large onion, sliced

3 boiled potatoes, quartered

3 tomatoes, diced

½ cup green beans or similar vegetable, sliced

3 Tbsp bean sprouts

FOR THE VIETNAMESE BOUQUET GARNI

2 large celery stalks with leaves, roughly chopped

6 small cilantro plants with roots, roughly chopped

2 large stalks lemon grass, chopped

6 large cloves garlic, finely chopped

1 cinnamon stick

2 star anise

1 Tbsp black peppercorns

FOR THE GARNISH

3 Tbsp fresh cilantro, chopped

3 Tbsp scallions, chopped

● Put the pigs' feet in a large saucepan and bring to a boil. Allow to boil for about 20–30 minutes until the meat pulls away from the bones. Drain.

● Put the feet back into the washed saucepan and add the broth and, if necessary, a little extra water, to cover the meat. Bring to a boil. Wrap the bouquet garni in a piece of cloth and tie to form a little bundle. Drop this into the saucepan when it starts to boil. Simmer for 10 minutes or so until you get the right consistency, which should be slightly thickened.

● Add the onion, potatoes, and tomatoes and simmer for a little while, just long enough for them to get warmed through but not long enough for them to disintegrate. Just before serving, add the beans and cook until they are just tender.

● Remove the bouquet garni and stir in the bean sprouts. Sprinkle the garnish over the stew.

Pork Hock and Peanut Stew

SERVES 4

3 fresh pork hocks

1 smoked pork hock or ham hock

⅓ cup fresh peanuts, blanched

4 x 1 in slices peeled ginger, ½ in thick

2 large scallions

6 pt water

salt

● Put the fresh and smoked hocks, peanuts, ginger, and scallions into a large, heavy pot together with the water and bring to a boil over a high heat. Turn down the heat to a simmer and skim off any scum. Cover and simmer for 2½ hours, stirring once in a while.

● Skim off scum and season with salt to taste. Discard the ginger, scallions, and the hock bones, if so desired. The meat may be served in chunks or cut into small pieces. Serve hot with a dip of fish sauce with a sprinkling of ground Szechwan peppercorns.

Simmered Belly of Pork and White Radish

SERVES 2

Simmering is a widely used technique in Japanese cooking as it brings out the flavors of the ingredients. Its European equivalent, the white radish, contains more water than the Japanese giant radish or **daikon**, *making it easier to cook. From the point of view of taste, though, there is little different between the two.*

● Heat the oil in a saucepan and add the meat. Fry until browned.

● Add the white radish and stir well, then add the *sake* and simmer, covered, for 10 minutes.

● Add the soy sauce and continue to cook, covered for a further 5 minutes or until the white radish is cooked through. Serve hot with a bowl of boiled rice.

2 tsp vegetable oil

8 oz pork, cut into ½ in lengths

8 oz white radish, peeled and chopped into randomly-shaped, bite-sized pieces

1 Tbsp *sake*

2 Tbsp soy sauce

Braised Beef with Carrots and Onions

SERVES 4

The beef is marinated, then cooked slowly for a long time so that it can easily be removed from the bone with chopsticks.

3 lb beef short ribs

1½ Tbsp vegetable oil

2 carrots, cut into chunks

1 onion, cut into chunks

FOR THE MARINADE

2 Tbsp sesame oil

6 Tbsp soy sauce

4 scallions, white and green parts thinly sliced

4 Tbsp rice wine or dry sherry

2 Tbsp crushed toasted sesame seeds

1 in gingerroot, finely chopped

3 garlic cloves, crushed and finely chopped

black pepper, freshly ground

FOR THE GARNISH

pine nuts

sesame seeds

cilantro

● Separate the beef into individual ribs and cut each one into 2-inch lengths. Make four deep slashes in a lattice pattern on the meaty sides of each piece of rib, going right through to the bone. Put into a bowl. Add the marinade ingredients, and stir together well. Cover and leave in a cool place for 4 hours, stirring the beef occasionally.

● Remove the beef from the marinade; reserve the marinade for later.

● Heat the vegetable oil in a heavy flameproof casserole and fry the beef for 5 minutes. Add the onion and carrot chunks, and fry for 3 minutes more. Pour in the reserved marinade and add enough water just to cover the beef and vegetables. Bring to a boil, cover and simmer slowly for 1½–2 hours, turning the beef and vegetables occasionally, until the beef is very tender. Uncover the casserole about half to three-quarters of the way through the cooking so the sauce reduces.

● At the end of the cooking, boil the sauce hard to reduce it to a thickish syrup, turning the ribs to make sure they are evenly coated. Skim any fat from the surface and serve garnished with pine nuts, sesame seeds, and cilantro.

Spicy Beef Stew

SERVES 4

3 Tbsp vegetable oil

2 medium onions, finely chopped

5 cloves garlic, finely chopped

10 scallions, dead skin peeled off

1 stalk lemon grass, cut into 2 in sections and crushed

2 lb stewing beef, cut into 1 in cubes

5 cups water

6 Tbsp yellow bean sauce, chopped and crushed

1 tsp chili powder

4 star anise

1 in cinnamon stick

½ tsp whole peppercorns

sugar

● Heat 1 tablespoon oil in a wok over a medium high heat. Put in the onions, garlic, and whole scallions and stir-fry for 2 minutes. Add the lemon grass and continue to stir until the scallions become lightly brown, remove the scallions and set aside.

● Heat the remaining oil over a high heat. Stir-fry as many pieces of beef as are convenient until they are brown, turning them over from time to time. Continue until all the beef has been cooked.

● Add the water. Add the lemon grass mixture, yellow bean sauce, chili powder, star anise, cinnamon, peppercorns, and sugar and bring to a boil. Cover and lower the heat to simmer gently for 1½ hours.

● Add the reserved scallions; cover again and allow to simmer for a further 15 minutes or until the sauce has thickened a little and the meat is tender.

Spicy Beef Stew II

SERVES 4

2 lb stewing beef, cut into 2 in cubes

2 stalks lemon grass, sliced paper-thin and finely chopped

2 fresh red chile peppers, minced

2 tsp sugar

2 Tbsp gingerroot, grated

2 tsp ground cinnamon

2 tsp curry powder

3 Tbsp fish sauce or 3 Tbsp light soy sauce and ½ tsp anchovy essence

salt and freshly ground black pepper

4½ Tbsp vegetable oil

1 large onion, minced

6 cloves garlic, minced

⅓ cup tomato paste

4 star anise

5 cups water

2 medium carrots, cut into 1 in chunks

2 medium potatoes, peeled and cut into 1 in chunks

1 small white radish, peeled and cut into 1 in chunks

● Mix the beef, lemon grass, chiles, sugar, ginger, cinnamon, curry powder, fish sauce, salt, and black pepper and leave to stand for 1 hour.

● Heat 4 tablespoons of oil in the wok over a high heat. Add the beef and marinade and stir quickly to sear. This should not take much more than 2 minutes. Remove the meat to a bowl and set aside.

● Add a little more oil and, when hot, add the onion and garlic and stir-fry until fragrant. Add the tomato paste and stir for 2 minutes. Add the beef, star anise, a little salt, and the water. Bring the mixture to a boil, reduce the heat to low, cover the wok and simmer until the beef is tender, about 1½ hours.

● Add the carrots and simmer for 10 minutes. Add the potatoes and simmer for a further 10 minutes. Finally, add the white radish and cook for another 10 minutes.

Simmered Beef and Potatoes

SERVES 2

This dish is one of several described in Japan as "mother's taste dishes," and it is very much a family-style creation.

3 Tbsp water

1½ Tbsp *sake*

2 Tbsp superfine sugar

2 Tbsp soy sauce

8 oz thinly sliced beef, cut into 2 in lengths

9 oz potatoes, peeled and cut into bite-sized pieces

3 oz frozen peas

● Put the water, *sake*, sugar and soy sauce in a pan and bring to a boil.

● Add the meat and simmer for a few minutes or until the meat browns. Remove from the pan and set aside. Put the potatoes in the pan and simmer, covered, for 10 minutes or until tender. Add the peas and simmer for a further 3 minutes.

● Return the meat back to the pan and simmer for about 3 minutes. Serve hot with a bowl of rice and one or two vegetable dishes.

Simmered Beef and Potatoes

Beef and Vegetable Hotpot

SERVES 4–6

*This communal one-pot meal, known as **chongol**, allows every person to dip into the pot to select their chosen morsels. Any number of a wide variety of ingredients can be added, according to what is available or to suit the occasion. Traditionally, it is prepared over a burner at the table.*

1¼ lb sirloin or filet mignon, partly frozen

3 cups brown veal or chicken broth

6 celery stalks, cut into 2 in pieces

2 young carrots, finely sliced diagonally

8 scallions, cut diagonally into 2 in pieces

6 Chinese leaves, cut into 2 in pieces

8 crimini mushrooms

1½ 4-oz cakes of bean curd, cut into 1 in cubes

FOR THE MARINADE

2 tsp sesame seeds

3 Tbsp sugar

1 fresh red chile, seeded and finely chopped

6 Tbsp soy sauce

1 plump garlic clove, finely crushed

● For the marinade, heat a dry heavy-bottomed saucepan, add the sesame seeds and toast until pale brown. Remove and crush finely. Mix with the remaining marinade ingredients.

● Slice the beef and cut into 1 x 2 inch strips. Put into a bowl. Pour over the marinade and stir to coat. Leave for 1 hour.

● Heat a dry heavy-bottomed pan. Remove the beef from the marinade and add to the pan. Cook briefly and quickly to sear the meat. Remove. Add the stock and any remaining marinade to the pan and bring to a boil. If using a fondue pot, boil the broth in a saucepan, then pour into the fondue pot.

● Add the celery and carrots to the pot. Boil for 5 minutes, then add the mushrooms, scallions, Chinese leaves, bean curd, and beef. Simmer together for 2–3 minutes, then lower the heat so the stock simmers slowly while the *chongol* is eaten.

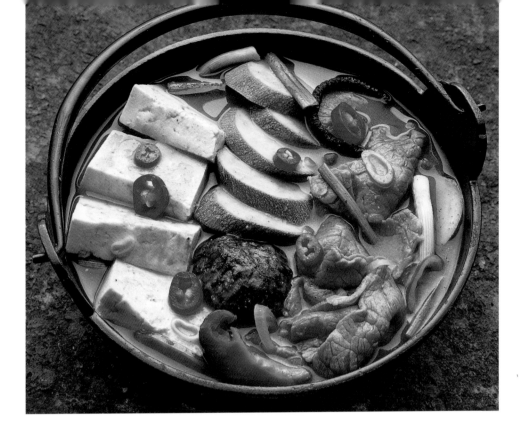

Quick-Cook Beef, Bean Curd, and Vegetable Stew

SERVES 3–4

*Richness and depth is given to the flavor of this "stew" by making the stock with **twoenjang, Korean fermented bean curd**. The beef is then cooked for just two minutes.*

8 oz sirloin or ground steak, cut into 1 x 2 in slices

2 tsp sesame oil

1½ tsp sugar

freshly ground black pepper

8 dried Chinese black mushrooms, soaked in hot water for 30 minutes, drained, and stalks removed

1 onion, thinly sliced into rings

1 zucchini, sliced

2 scallions, white and green parts sliced

1–2 fresh red chiles, seeded and thickly sliced

2 x 4 oz cakes of medium-firm bean curd, cut into 1½ in chunks

FOR THE BROTH

8 tbsp *twoenjang* (fermented bean curd) or *miso*

2 garlic cloves, lightly crushed

1 onion, cut into chunks

1 carrot, cut into chunks

3 scallions, white and green parts cut into 3 in lengths

● Put the *twoenjang* or *miso* in a strainer placed over a saucepan. Slowly pour through 4 cups of water, pushing the *twoenjang* or *miso* with the back of a wooden spoon so it is all pushed through. Add the remaining stock ingredients and bring to a boil. Cover and simmer slowly for 30 minutes.

● Meanwhile, mix the beef with the sesame oil, sugar, and plenty of black pepper. Leave for 30 minutes.

● Drain the stock, squeezing out as much liquid as possible. Pour the stock back into the pan and add the mushroom caps, onion, zucchini, scallions and chiles. Bring to a boil, then simmer for 2 minutes. Add the beef slices to the stock with the bean curd. Return to a boil, then simmer for 2 minutes.

Rice and Noodles

Rice and noodles provide the bulk in many Asian dishes, and they are served, in one form or another, from the wastes of northern China to the heart of busy Tokyo. Most of the recipes in this section can be served as a light meal or snack—they are filling and nutritious on their own—but these dishes will more often be served with one or two other dishes from this section and a meat or seafood main dish to create a satisfying meal for four or more people.

Boiled Rice

SERVES 4–6

Boiled rice not only provides a foundation for other dishes but is enjoyed on its own.

scant 2 cups short-grain rice

● Put the rice in a large bowl and add water to cover. Swish the rice around with your hand. When the water has become milky white, pour it away. Repeat the washing until the water is virtually clear.

● Put the rice into a heavy-bottomed saucepan. Add 2½ cups water and bring to a boil. Stir once, cover, and turn the heat right down. Cook the rice for 20 minutes, without removing the lid even once.

● Turn up the heat as high as it will go for 30 seconds, then turn it off, or remove the pan from the heat. Leave, without removing the lid at all, for 10–15 minutes before serving.

Vegetable Rice

SERVES 4

2 cups short-grain rice, washed and drained

2 Tbsp vegetable oil

1 lb *pak choi,* cut crosswise in 1 in pieces

salt

1–1¼ pt water

● Wash the rice several times until the water runs clear. Drain thoroughly.

● Heat a heavy saucepan over a high heat. Add the oil, swirl and heat for a further 30 seconds or so. Add the *pak choi* and stir rapidly. The leaves should now be shiny with oil. Sprinkle some salt and stir and the leaves will brighten.

● Put the rice and water in a saucepan and bring to a boil. Let it bubble for a couple of minutes, stirring occasionally. Turn the heat to medium and let it bubble for another 2 minutes, stirring occasionally.

● Turn to the lowest possible heat, cover and let the rice cook for 20 minutes. When it is cooked, leave it to rest for 10 minutes before serving.

● Lay the rice on a flat dish, placing the *pak choi* on top, and serve.

Rice with Millet

SERVES 2–4

Traditionally, this kind of rice was prepared for the same reasons as Rice with Barley (see page 238). A nuttier flavor can be obtained by toasting the millet, prior to boiling, in a dry saucepan over a moderate heat for 3 minutes.

1½ cups short-grain rice, washed and soaked (see above)

⅔ cup millet

● Put the rice and millet into a saucepan. Add 3 cups water and bring to a boil. Stir once, cover, and turn the heat right down. Cook the rice for 20 minutes, without removing the lid even once.

● Turn up the heat as high as it will go for 30 seconds, then turn it off, or remove the pan from the heat. Leave, without removing the lid at all, for 10–15 minutes before serving.

Rice with Shrimp

SERVES 4

2 Tbsp vegetable oil

1 lb shrimp, peeled

1 scallion, chopped

2 oz fresh button mushrooms

1 zucchini, thinly sliced

½ carrot, thinly sliced

2 oz fine beans, cut into 1 in lengths

1 Tbsp rice wine or dry sherry

1 tsp light soy sauce

freshly ground black pepper

salt

3 cups plain boiled rice

FOR THE GARNISH

2 scallions, neatly chopped into rounds

● Heat ½ tablespoon oil in a wok and stir-fry the shrimp for 1 minute. Remove and set aside.

● Add the remaining oil and lightly cook the scallion. Add the mushrooms and the other vegetables and stir-fry for about 2 minutes over a high heat.

● Put the shrimp back into the wok with the vegetables and add the rest of the ingredients, except the rice, continuing all the while to stir.

● Add the rice and stir-fry until the rice has changed color. Place in a large serving bowl and garnish with the chopped scallions.

Sticky Rice

SERVES 4

4 cups glutinous rice (specified on packet)

1 tsp salt

METHOD 1

● Rinse and drain the rice after soaking overnight. Spread the soaked rice mixed with the salt over a dampened cheesegauze in the top of a steamer and steam for about 40 minutes, sprinkling water over it occasionally. Taste while cooking for consistency. It should not be crunchy; Vietnamese prefer it well boiled.

METHOD 2

● Boil about 3 cups water in a thick saucepan. Add the rice and salt and bring it back to a boil. Let it boil for 1 minute or so and then cover it with a well fitting lid. Take it off the heat and hold the lid tightly on the saucepan. Turn it over and drain it fairly dry.

● Return to a very low heat and allow the rice to cook for about 20 minutes. After cooking, set it aside for 10 minutes to complete the cooking. When ready to serve, fluff it up with a ladle or chopsticks, whichever you prefer.

Rice with Shrimp

Mixed Rice

SERVES 2

Japanese-style mixed rice is easy to make and can be served either as a main course with a soup and salad or instead of plain boiled rice.

⅔ cup Japanese short-grain rice

2 oz carrot, peeled and cut into short matchsticks

3 shiitake mushrooms, cut into short matchsticks

½ sheet *abura-age*, rinsed in hot water and cut into short matchsticks

¼ in piece bean curd, soaked in water for 5 minutes, then cut into matchsticks

8½ Tbsp *dashi* broth

1 Tbsp sugar

1½ Tbsp soy sauce

3 snow peas

pinch of salt

1 egg

½ Tbsp water

vegetable oil, for frying

FOR THE GARNISH

2 red radishes, thinly sliced

nori strips

● First make *sushi* rice according to the instructions on page 242.

● Put the carrots, shiitake, *abura-age*, bean curd, *dashi* broth, sugar, and soy sauce in a pan. Bring to a boil and simmer for 15 minutes.

● Meanwhile, boil the snow peas in salted water for 3 minutes, then remove and cut finely on the slant.

● Mix the egg, water, and a pinch of salt together in a bowl. Heat the vegetable oil in an omelet pan and make two thin omelets. Let the omelets cool, then cut each one in half then slice it into thin strips.

● When the vegetables are cooked, mix the ingredients with the rice. Place the rice mixture onto a large plate. Spread the egg, then the snow peas over the top and decorate with the radish and strips of *nori*.

Egg Fried Rice

SERVES 4

2 eggs

2 Tbsp water

2 Tbsp vegetable oil

2 scallions, finely chopped

3 cups plain boiled rice

2 Tbsp soy sauce

salt

½ tsp sugar

● Beat the eggs with the water in a bowl. Heat ½ teaspoon oil in a wok and add the egg mixture. Swirl it around to make an omelet. Transfer to a plate and allow to cool. When cool, cut into strips.

● Heat the remaining oil, add the scallions, and stir-fry for 2 minutes. Add the plain boiled rice and cooled omelet strips.

● Stir in the soy sauce, salt and sugar and cook for a further 2–3 minutes, until all ingredients have been coated. Serve in a large bowl.

Perfumed Rice

SERVES 4

4 cups Thai perfumed rice

2½ cups water

1 tsp salt

● Wash the rice several times and drain; when the washing water is clear, the rice is as clean as it can possibly be. In large families rice needs washing with both hands but cooking for a small family does not require more than the rubbing between the fingers.

● Put the rice and water in a saucepan, add the salt and bring quickly to a boil. Reduce the heat immediately and cover. Allow to simmer for as long as necessary—30 minutes is about right.

● The rice should be taken off the heat and allowed to rest for about 10 minutes before serving. The result should be a rather moist, slightly sticky boiled rice that people east of the Ganges prefer.

Shrimp-fried Rice

SERVES 6

½ cup peanut or corn oil

1 Tbsp chopped garlic

7 oz raw shelled shrimp

3 eggs, beaten

⅓ cup sliced onion

1 tomato, cut into 6 pieces

4 cups cooked rice

⅛ cup scallion, chopped

½ Tbsp light soy sauce

1 tsp sugar

1 tsp salt

1 tsp ground white pepper

½ cup cucumber, peeled and sliced into circles

● Heat the oil in a wok or pan and add the garlic.

● Stir-fry and then add the shrimp and fry for 1 minute. Add the eggs and cook for another minute, stirring well, then add the onion and tomato.

● Stir-fry for 1 minute then add the rice, soy sauce, sugar, salt and pepper. Stir well over a high heat for a further 3 minutes.

● Scoop onto serving plates and arrange the cucumber pieces around.

● Serve accompanied by fish sauce with chiles, and eat with whole scallions and raw sliced cucumber.

Japanese Rice Balls

SERVES 2

*The Japanese name for this dish is **onigiri**, and it is a simply prepared and handy "eat anytime" meal, which can be packed up in a picnic or served as an accompaniment at dinner. The use of the word "ball" is slightly misleading as the shape of the finished product more closely resembles a triangle. The use of Japanese rice for making rice balls is strongly recommended as other varieties tend to lack the characteristic stickiness of the Japanese grains.*

⅔ cup Japanese short-grain rice, rinsed well

pinch of flaked *bonito*

½ Tbsp soy sauce

1 Japanese pickled plum (*ume-boshi*), seeded and halved

4 strips 2 x 6 in *nori*

● Rinse the rice until the water runs off almost clear.

● Cook the rice the same way as making *sushi* rice (see page 242) but do not add the *sushi-zu*.

● Let the rice cool down before use. Mix the *bonito* flakes with the soy sauce in a small saucer or plate to make a paste.

● Wet and then sprinkle your palms with a little salt. (You will need to repeat this process with every ball you make.) Scoop up 3 heaped tablespoons of rice and mould it lightly into a round shape.

● Once the rough ball shape is formed, make a small hole in the middle and put either half of the *bonito* paste or one half of the Japanese plum inside.

● Cover the hole while at the same time trying to form the rice into a triangular shape.

● When the four rice balls have been formed, wrap each with a strip of *nori*.

Fried Rice with Spicy Sauce

SERVES 4–6

2 Tbsp peanut or corn oil

4 cups cooked rice

3 Tbsp fish sauce with chiles

● Heat the oil in a wok or pan, add the rice and mix well, stir-frying for 1 minute.

● Add the sauce, mix well and cook for 1 more minute. Remove from the heat.

● Serve accompanied by preserved salted eggs, cucumber slices, fried eggs, and raw vegetables.

Pineapple Rice

SERVES 4–6

A "show-off" dish that is quite easy to make but always impressive to present. Although the pineapple also adds flavor to the rice, there is scarcely any point attempting it just with pineapple pieces—appearance is everything.

1 pineapple

4 Tbsp peanut or corn oil

3 cups cooked rice

½ cup ham, finely diced

½ Tbsp garlic, chopped

¼ cup raisins

2 Tbsp chicken broth

2 tsp curry powder

1 tsp sugar

1 tsp salt

¼ tsp ground white pepper

● Cut one side off the pineapple lengthwise to expose the inside. Carefully remove the inside fruit and cut into small dice. Reserve the outside of the pineapple.

● Heat the oil in a pan or wok, add the ham and garlic, stir-fry, then add ½ cup of the diced pineapple and all the rest of the ingredients. Mix well.

● Spoon into the empty pineapple, cover with the pineapple lid and bake in a preheated 275°F oven for 30 minutes.

Rice with Spinach, Bean Sprouts, and Laver

SERVES 4–6

This dish is generally eaten with a dipping sauce.

8 oz young fresh spinach, cut across into ¾-in strips

8 oz mung bean sprouts

1 garlic clove, chopped

1 carrot, cut into fine strips

2 scallions, white and green parts, sliced diagonally

1½ sheets *kim* (*nori* or laver), cut into thin strips

2 tsp sesame oil

3 Tbsp soy sauce

2 tsp crushed toasted sesame seeds

½ tsp sugar

freshly ground black pepper

scant 2 cups short-grain rice, washed and soaked

● Add the spinach and bean sprouts to a large saucepan of water. Cover and quickly return to a boil. Boil for 1 minute, then tip into a colander. Drain well, then squeeze out as much water as possible. Mix with the remaining ingredients except the rice and leave for 30 minutes.

● Drain the rice and put into a saucepan with the vegetable mixture and 2½ cups water. Stir, then cover and bring to a boil. Stir once, cover again, and turn the heat to very low. Cook for 20–30 minutes, without removing the lid even once. Turn the heat up as high as it will go for 30 seconds, then turn it off, or remove the pan from the heat. Leave, without removing the lid at all, for 10–15 minutes before serving.

Rice with Soybean Sprouts

SERVES 4–6

The bean sprouts provide a crisp contrast to the softness of the rice.

8 oz soybean sprouts

scant 2 cups short-grain rice, washed and soaked

● Add the bean sprouts to a saucepan of boiling water, cover and quickly return to a boil. Boil for 2 minutes, then drain.

● Drain the rice and put it into a saucepan. Put the bean sprouts on top and pour in 2½ cups water. Cover and bring to a boil. Stir once and cover again. Turn the heat to very low and cook for 20–30 minutes, without removing the lid. Turn the heat up high for 20 seconds, then turn it off. Leave for 10–15 minutes before serving.

Rice and Mushrooms

SERVES 3–4

Using mushrooms (of which Koreans are very fond) with a small amount of beef to flavor rice is a good way of boosting the meaty flavor and giving the illusion that there is more meat than there actually is.

5 oz lean ground beef

8 oz open-cap mushrooms, preferably brown cap, chopped

2 garlic cloves, crushed and finely chopped

2 scallions, white and some green parts, chopped

2 Tbsp soy sauce

1½ tsp sesame oil

1 Tbsp crushed toasted sesame seeds

freshly ground black pepper

2 tsp vegetable oil

1 cup short-grain white rice, washed and soaked

FOR THE GARNISH

very fine slices of red chile

● Mix together the beef, mushrooms, garlic, scallions, soy sauce, sesame oil, sesame seeds, and plenty of pepper. Leave for at least 30 minutes.

● Heat the vegetable oil in a saucepan. Add the mushroom and beef mixture, and stir until the beef just changes color. Stir in the rice and 1¼ cups water. Cover and bring to a boil. Stir once and cover again. Turn the heat to very low and cook for 20–30 minutes, without removing the lid even once. Turn up the heat as high as it will go for 30 seconds, then turn it off, or remove the pan from the heat. Leave, without removing the lid at all, for 10–15 minutes. Stir before serving garnished with very fine slices of red chile.

Rice with Beef and Bean Sprouts

SERVES 3–4

This dish is traditionally eaten by poorer people as adding plain rice and bean sprouts to beef makes the meat go further.

2 Tbsp soy sauce

2 garlic cloves, crushed and chopped

2 scallions, white and a little green part finely chopped

1½ Tbsp crushed toasted sesame seeds

1 Tbsp sesame oil

freshly ground black pepper

5 oz lean beef, chilled

1 Tbsp vegetable oil

1 cup short-grain rice, washed, soaked and drained

8 oz bean sprouts

FOR THE GARNISH

very thin strips of red chile

● Mix the soy sauce, garlic, scallions, sesame seeds, sesame oil, and pepper in a bowl.

● Slice the beef very thinly and cut into strips. Stir into the bowl with the soy mixture to coat evenly and leave for 1 hour, stirring two or three times.

● Heat the vegetable oil in a large saucepan. Add the beef and stir-fry for 2–3 minutes until darker brown. Stir in the rice and bean sprouts, then add 1½ cups water. Bring to a boil. Stir once, cover, and turn the heat to very low. Cook the rice for 20 minutes, without removing the lid even once. Turn up the heat as high as it will go for 30 seconds, then turn it off, or remove the pan from the heat. Leave, without removing the lid at all, for 10–15 minutes. Serve garnished with very thin strips of red chile.

Rice with Barley

SERVES 4

Barley used to be added to rice toward the end of summer when rice stocks were getting low, to eke it out until the next crop was harvested.

1½ cups short-grain rice, washed and soaked

⅔ cup pearl barley

● Put the rice and pearl barley into a saucepan. Add 3 cups water and bring to a boil. Stir once, cover, and turn the heat right down.

● Cook the rice for about 20 minutes, without removing the lid even once. Continue as in the recipe for Rice with Millet (see page 227).

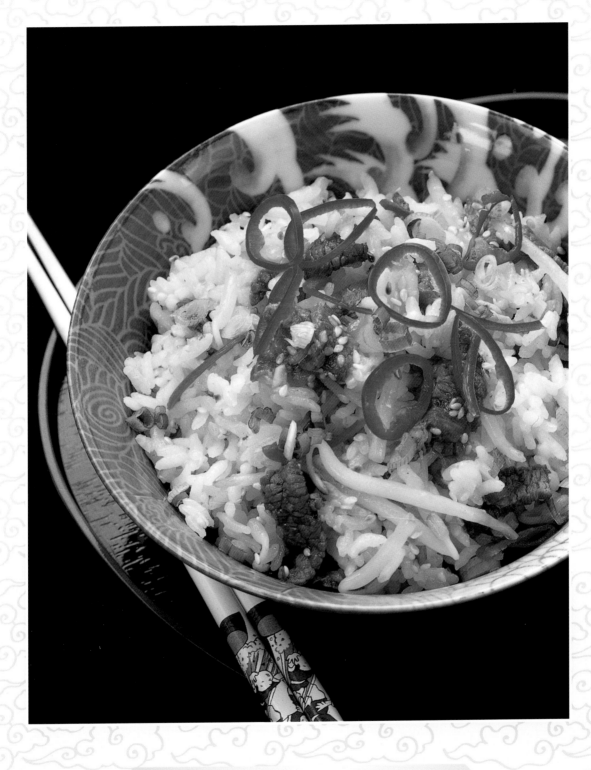

Rice with Beef and Bean Sprouts

Chicken Rice

SERVES 4

A very popular day-time dish, and Chinese in origin, the special feature of the dish is that the rice is cooked in chicken broth (ideally, capon). The chicken pieces are always arranged on top of the mound of rice.

11 oz boneless skinned capon or chicken breasts

5 cups water

1 cilantro roots

2 tsp salt

1 cup rice, rinsed

10 garlic cloves, chopped

½ oz ginger, sliced and crushed

3 tbsp peanut or corn oil

5 in piece of cucumber, cut into ¼ in slices

¼ cup cilantro leaves

FOR THE *KHAO MAN* SAUCE

5 fresh small green chiles, chopped

2 Tbsp pickled soy beans

● Boil the water in a pan, add the chicken with the cilantro root and salt, and cook until the chicken is soft, about 15 minutes. Remove the meat with a slotted spoon and put to one side. Strain the cooking liquid, put 4 cups back in the pan and add the rice, garlic, ginger, and oil. Bring back to a boil and cook, covered, until the rice is tender but not soft, about 15–18 minutes.

● Place the rice on serving plates. Slice the chicken across into ½ in pieces and place on top of the hot rice. Arrange the cucumber slices around the sides and sprinkle with the cilantro leaves.

● Mix all the ingredients for the sauce together in a bowl and serve with the chicken and rice, and with the remaining cup of chicken broth if desired.

Vegetarian Special Fried Rice

SERVES 4

Vegetarian special fried rice is one stage richer and more elaborate than egg-fried rice and almost a meal in itself.

4–6 dried Chinese mushrooms

1 green bell pepper, cored and seeded

1 red bell pepper, cored and seeded

4 oz bamboo shoots

2 eggs

2 scallions, finely chopped

2 tsp salt

4–5 Tbsp oil

6 cups cooked rice

1 Tbsp light soy sauce (optional)

● Soak the dried mushrooms in warm water for 25–30 minutes, squeeze dry, and discard the hard stalks. Cut the mushrooms into small cubes.

● Cut the green and red bell peppers and the bamboo shoots into small cubes.

● Lightly beat the egg with about half of the scallions and a pinch of the salt.

● Heat about 2 tablespoons of oil in a hot wok, add the beaten eggs and scramble until set. Remove.

● Heat the remaining oil. When hot, add the rest of the scallions followed by all the vegetables and stir-fry until each piece is covered with oil. Add the cooked rice and salt and stir to separate each grain of rice. Finally add the soy sauce, blend everything together, and serve.

Rice Crackers with Pork and Coconut Sauce

SERVES 4–6

3 cups cooked rice

3 cups peanut or corn oil for deep-frying

1 tsp cilantro root, chopped

1 tsp garlic, chopped

2 cups thin coconut milk

¾ cup cooked pork, chopped

¾ cup raw shelled small shrimp, chopped

1 tsp cilantro leaf and stem, lightly chopped

1 fresh red chile, cut into lengthwise strips

1 cup unsalted peanut, chopped small

2 Tbsp shallots, sliced

¼ tsp ground white pepper

½ Tbsp palm sugar

1 tsp salt

● Knead the rice slightly until it is sticky, then press it onto a slightly soiled nonstick baking pan in a layer ⅛ inch thick. Place in the sun for 1–2 days or in a warm (325°F) oven until very dry, 3–5 hours. Remove the rice from the pan and break it into 2 inch pieces.

● Heat the oil in a wok or pan to a temperature of 350°F. Fry the rice crackers until a light tan color, 3–5 minutes. Remove them with a slotted spoon and drain well on paper towel.

● To make the sauce, pound the cilantro root and garlic together in a pestle and mortar. Heat the coconut milk in a pan and add the coriander and garlic mixture. Bring to a boil, add the pork, shrimp, and remaining ingredients, and continue to boil until the meat is cooked, about 7–10 minutes. Remove the pan from the heat, pour into a bowl and sprinkle with the cilantro leaf and chile.

● Serve the sauce with the rice crackers.

Basic Sushi Rice

SERVES 2

This is the basic technique for producing the glutinous, vinegar-flavored rice that forms the basis of all the variants of sushi. *Japanese short-grain rice is essential for making* sushi *rice. The ratio of Japanese rice to water should be 1:1¼ parts water.*

⅔ cup Japanese short-grain rice

1 in strip dried kelp

1 cup water

FOR THE *SUSHI-ZU*

1½ Tbsp rice vinegar

1 Tbsp superfine sugar

½ tsp salt

● Put the rice in a pan and rinse several times with cold water until the water is almost clear. Leave the rice in a sieve for approximately 30 minutes so that individual grains can begin to absorb the water remaining in the sieve.

● Add the water, rice, and kelp to a pan. Bring to a boil, taking the kelp out just before boiling point. Simmer, covered, for about 10 minutes. (Simmering time depends on the amount of rice you cook.)

● Test the rice to see if it has softened. Turn off the heat and leave for 10 minutes.

● Mix the vinegar, sugar, and salt in a bowl. Put the rice in a large bowl. Wet the wooden spoon and add the *sushi-zu* a little at a time, "cutting" it into the rice with the wooden spoon (not stirring or mashing), until you have used all the liquid. The rice will now be giving off the sharp aroma of the *sushi-zu*. Leave to cool before using.

"Roll Your Own" Sushi

SERVES 2

A modern and very popular variant on the sushi *theme. This makes a great change for dinner parties.*

1 quantity basic *shushi* rice (see page 244)

5 sheets of *nori*, each cut into 4 pieces

5 diagonal slices of cucumber, cut into long matchsticks

¼ avocado, sliced

1 rollmop herring, sliced

1 bunch cress

soy sauce

FOR THE FILLING

3½ oz tuna in brine

1 Tbsp mayonnaise

FOR THE OMELET

1 egg

1 tsp superfine sugar

pinch of salt

2 tsp vegetable oil for frying

● To prepare the filling, drain the tuna and mix with the mayonnaise. Make a Japanese-style omelet (see page 320), which should be cut into strips after cooling down. Now lay all the ingredients out on a large serving platter. The rice is laid out on a separate plate as are the strips of *nori*.

● Each diner takes a piece of *nori* in one hand and scoops about a tablespoon of rice onto it, spreading it quite thinly.

● Next, a portion of one or a combination of the fillings are taken with *hashi* and laid in the center of the sheet. Last, the diner rolls the *nori* into a cornet shape, dipping it into his or her small bowl of soy sauce before eating.

Large Sushi Rolls

SERVES 2

You might think it takes real skill and experience to produce good sushi rolls or **futo-maki,** *but after a couple of practice runs, you should get the hang of it. Nevertheless well-made* **futo-maki** *will undoubtedly impress your dinner guests.*

1 quantity basic *sushi* rice (see page 242)

3 dried shiitake mushrooms, rinsed and soaked in ¼ cup water

1 tsp superfine sugar

1 tsp soy sauce

2 sheets *nori* seaweed sheets

6 seafood sticks

1 bunch cress

FOR THE OMELET

1 egg, beaten

1 tsp superfine sugar

pinch of salt

vegetable oil, for frying

● To prepare the filling, slice the mushrooms, and put in a pan with the water they were soaked in, the sugar and the soy sauce. Bring this mixture to a boil and simmer for 5 minutes. Put the sugar and salt into a bowl with the beaten egg and mix together well. Heat the oil in an omelet pan and make a Japanese-style omelet (see page 320). Let the omelet cool and then cut lengthwise into three strips.

● Place the *nori* squarely on a *sushi* mat or a chopping board covered with plastic wrap. Spread the rice onto the *nori*, leaving a 1 in strip free of rice at the far edge.

● Next, lay, in order, half the omelet, shiitake, seafood sticks, and cress in lines across the bed of rice, leaving a small strip of bare rice between each ingredient.

● Now, holding the egg in place, pull the near edge of the *nori* sheet up and over in one motion until the *nori* has enfolded all the ingredients laid on the rice. Next, use your fingers to tuck the near edge of the *nori* inside the roll. Then, rotate the mat until the join is turned to the bottom of the roll.

● Grip the far end of the *sushi* mat with your right hand and hold the roll with your left. Now, pull the roll firmly towards you to ensure that the roll becomes well-packed. Finally, line up the sides of the mat by gently patting with the palms of your hands to clean up the ends of the roll. Gently unroll the mat to reveal the finished roll inside.

● Repeat with the remaining half of the ingredients. When finished, slice the rolls into pieces the thickness of your thumb. Use a knife dipped in water mixed with vinegar so that the rice will not cling to the blade. Serve displayed on a large plate. The slices should be taken from the plate and then dipped into individual dishes of soy sauce before being eaten by your guests.

Large Sushi Rolls

Thin Rolls of Cucumber and Pickled Radish

SERVES 2

1 quantity *sushi* rice (see page 244)

2.5 sheets *nori*, cut into half

1 cucumber

2 *takuwan* sticks of ¼ x 7½ in

2½ tsp toasted sesame seeds

little *wasabi* (optional)

● Cut the cucumber into three 7½ x ¾ in pieces.

● Place the *nori* on a *sushi* mat or a chopping board, covered with plastic wrap or polythene. Spread the rice evenly on the *nori*, except for a ¾ in strip clear along the far edge. Using the tip of your finger, smooth a small amount of *wasabi* paste over the rice.

● Place the cucumber sticks on the rice and sprinkle over ½ teaspoon of toasted sesame seeds.

● Roll over the *sushi* mat and form to shape. The *nori* is sealed by the moisture from the rice. In the same way, make two more rolls with the cucumbers and make two with pickled radish. Cut each roll into five pieces using a knife wetted with a mixture of water and vinegar to give a clean cut.

Fresh Bean Curd

SERVES 4

Fresh bean curd, which is as white and soft as the white of poached eggs, is not difficult to make.

2 cups yellow soybeans, soaked overnight

juice of 2 lemons

● Drain the beans and put half of them in a blender or food processor with 2½ cups warm water. Mix to a smooth purée. Pour the contents of the blender or food processor into a fine strainer lined with a large piece of cheesecloth and placed over a large bowl.

● Repeat with the remaining beans and another 2½ cups warm water, adding the purée to the strainer. Fold the cheesegauze over the pulp in the strainer and press firmly to extract as much liquid as possible.

● Return the residue in the strainer to the blender or food processor and add another 2½ cups warm water. Mix again for a couple of minutes, then pour into the strainer to drain. Discard the residue in the strainer. The thickish white liquid is soy milk.

● Bring the soy milk to a boil in a large saucepan. As soon as it begins to rise in the pan, lower the heat and simmer the milk, uncovered, for 15–20 minutes, stirring occasionally.

● Remove from the heat and stir in the lemon juice, which should make the milk curdle. Pour the curds and liquid into a fine strainer lined with a large clean piece of cheesegauze, and leave to drain.

● To make medium-firm bean curd, fold the cheesegauze over the curds, cover the surface of the curd with a weight (a heavy saucepan will do) and let drain for 15 minutes. To make firm bean curd, let drain for 2 hours. It will keep for up to two days.

Braised Bean Curd with Sesame Seeds

SERVES 2–4

Braised bean curd is a typical dish of Korean home cooking. Serve braised bean curd as a side dish, accompanied by rice and vegetables, and meat or fish as liked.

2 Tbsp Japanese soy sauce

1 tsp sesame oil

1½ garlic cloves, crushed and chopped

2 tsp sugar

¼ tsp chili powder

2 tsp crushed toasted sesame seeds

2 scallions, white and green parts thinly sliced

7 oz medium-firm bean curd, cut into ¼-in thick rectangular slices

1½ Tbsp vegetable oil

freshly ground black pepper

● Mix together the soy sauce, sesame oil, garlic, sugar, chili powder, sesame seeds, and scallions.

● Put the bean curd in a single layer between two layers of paper towels. Cover with a plate and put a weight on the plate. Leave for 30 minutes or so.

● Heat the vegetable oil in a large skillet. Add the bean curd in a single layer and fry for about 1½ minutes on each side until browned. Using a slotted spatula, transfer to a large plate. Pour or wipe the oil from the pan.

● Return the bean curd to the pan in a single layer. Pour over the soy sauce mixture, partially cover the pan, and simmer for 6–7 minutes, turning the bean curd halfway through. Most of the sauce should be absorbed into the bean curd during this time.

● Transfer the bean curd to a warm plate and pour over the remaining sauce.

Braised Bean Curd with Pork

SERVES 4

This is a family way of braising bean curd.

2 Tbsp soy sauce

1 tsp sesame seeds

2 Tbsp sugar

1½ Tbsp chile bean paste

2 garlic cloves, crushed and
finely chopped

1-in gingerroot, grated

1½ tsp crushed toasted sesame
seeds

12 oz lean pork loin, very
thinly sliced on the diagonal

3 Tbsp vegetable oil

2 4-oz cakes of medium-firm
bean curd

FOR THE GARNISH

scallions, shredded diagonally

● Mix together the soy sauce, sesame seeds, sugar, chile bean paste, garlic, and ginger.

● Lay the pork slices in a shallow dish and pour over the soy sauce mixture. Coat the pork with the mixture and leave for 30 minutes.

● Heat half the vegetable oil in a skillet. Add the pork mixture and cook for 12–15 minutes, turning the pork halfway through, until cooked through. Add a little water, as necessary, to keep the mixture fairly liquid.

● Meanwhile, cut each bean curd cake horizontally in half, then cut across each half into three pieces. Fry in the remaining oil in another skillet for about 3 minutes on each side, until golden. Transfer to paper towels to absorb excess oil.

● Pour the oil from the second skillet, then make a layer of bean curd in the pan. Cover with some of the pork mixture. Repeat, then cover and heat through gently for 5 minutes. Serve garnished with scallions.

Fried Bean Curd

SERVES 6

A little sesame oil adds a subtle yet distinctive flavor that "lifts" simple fried bean curd.

4 x 4-oz cakes of medium-firm
    bean curd

vegetable and sesame oil for
    frying

vinegar dipping sauce to serve

● Cut the bean curd into rectangles approximately 1½ x ¾ x ¾ inches. Dry on paper towels.

● Heat a thin film of vegetable oil mixed with a little sesame oil in a nonstick skillet over a medium heat. Add half the bean curd and cook for 3 minutes on each side until golden. Using a slotted spoon, transfer to paper towels to drain while frying the remaining bean curd in the same way.

● Serve the bean curd on a warm plate with vinegar dipping sauce.

Fried Bean Curd Sushi

SERVES 2

These sweet-tasting sacks of **sushi** *rice can be eaten along with other* **sushi** *dishes or alone as a tasty and filling snack.* **Inari-zushi** *also forms a part of many a Japanese picnic as well as being a firm favorite as a lunch box filler. Refer to the instructions for making basic* **sushi** *rice while cooking the rice.*

½ quantity of basic *sushi* rice (see page 242)

2 sheets *abura-age* (thin bean curd)

½ cup *dashi* broth

1½ Tbsp superfine sugar

1 Tbsp *mirin*

2 tsp soy sauce

1 tsp toasted sesame seeds

● Gently roll the *abura-age*, using a chopstick as a rolling pin, to make it easier to handle. Place in a colander and rinse with hot water. Cut in half and gently open the "sack".

● Put the *dashi* stock, *mirin*, soy sauce and *abura-age* in a pan, bring to the boil and simmer for 20 minutes or until the *dashi* mixture has almost evaporated. Make a small lid with some aluminum foil and place on top of the *abura-age*. Continue to cook until the remaining liquid has been completely absorbed.

● Remove the *abura-age* and leave on a plate or chopping board until dry.

● Mix the *sushi* rice with the sesame and divide into four equal portions. Fill each *abura-age* with rice and fold to create a small sack.

Poached Bean Curd

SERVES 4

This plainly cooked bean curd can be eaten as it comes, or served with a dipping sauce. The role of cooking liquid in the serving dish is to keep the bean curd hot; it is not drunk. The bean curd can also be served in individual dishes with seaweed and bonito flakes.

½ oz *wakame*

3 cakes of medium-firm bean curd, each about 4 oz

vinegar dipping sauce to serve (optional)

● Bring 5½ pints water to a boil in a wide saucepan. Add the *wakame* and bean curd, and simmer gently for 5 minutes.

● Using a slotted spoon, transfer the bean curd to a warm serving dish deep enough to let the cakes be almost covered by the cooking liquid. Pour in simmering cooking liquid to come three-quarters of the way up the sides of the bean curd cakes. Serve straightaway, accompanied by vinegar dipping sauce, if liked.

Spicy Fried Noodles

SERVES 4

You can make your own chili powder by roasting 4 oz red chile peppers in the oven at 400°F until brown. Blend briefly if you want flakes. Process more for powder. Store in an airtight container.

2 Tbsp vegetable oil

2 cloves garlic, finely chopped

4 oz pork, sliced

4 large uncooked shrimp, peeled, deveined, tails intact

1 Tbsp dried shrimp

2 Tbsp pickled white radish, finely chopped

½ cup diced bean curd

3 Tbsp lemon juice

3 Tbsp fish sauce or light soy sauce and ½ tsp anchovy extract

3 Tbsp sugar

6 oz rice stick noodles (preferably the thicker ones), soaked in warm water for 15 minutes and drained well

2 eggs, beaten

1 cup bean sprouts

3 Tbsp peanuts, crushed

2 Tbsp scallions, chopped

2 Tbsp fresh cilantro, chopped

FOR THE GARNISH

½ tsp roasted chili powder or flakes

lemon wedges

● Heat the oil in a wok and gently stir-fry the garlic for 3–4 minutes until golden-brown. Increase the heat, add the pork, and fry for 6 minutes until cooked. Add the shrimp, dried shrimp, and pickled radish, and continue stir-frying for 1 minute. Add the bean curd, stir, reduce the heat and add the lemon juice, fish sauce, and sugar, stirring all the while for 3 minutes.

● Add the noodles and stir the mixture thoroughly for 1–2 minutes. Push to one side and quickly add the beaten eggs. Once they begin to set, stir them, effectively scrambling them. Push to one side.

● Place most of the bean sprouts and a handful of crushed peanuts, scallions, and cilantro over the noodles. Stir these in with the scrambled eggs and noodles. Serve on a large plate with little mounds of bean sprouts, peanuts, scallions, cilantro, chili flakes, and lemon wedges.

White Noodles with Spicy Meat Sauce

SERVES 4–6

¼ cup peanut or corn oil

11 oz ground pork

11 oz pork spare ribs, cut into 1 in pieces

4 oz chicken blood pudding, cut into 1 in pieces

6 cups chicken broth

1 Tbsp marinated black soy beans, pounded finely

1 Tbsp salt

5 oz cherry tomatoes

15 oz fresh rice vermicelli (if dried, soak for 5 minutes and boil for 2 minutes) or cooked spaghetti

FOR THE CHILI PASTE

7 dried red chiles, chopped

1 oz garlic, chopped

½ oz shallot, chopped

2 Tbsp lemon grass, chopped

1 Tbsp galangal, chopped

1 tsp cilantro root or stem, chopped

1 tsp shrimp paste

1 tsp salt

● Pound all the chili paste ingredients together with a mortar and pestle or in a blender.

● Heat the oil in a wok or pan, fry the chili paste and then add the ground pork and spare ribs. Cook for 10 minutes, mixing well, then add the blood pudding, broth, soy beans, and salt. Bring to a boil, add the tomatoes and simmer for 20 minutes or until the spare ribs are tender.

● Boil the rice noodles in water until just done, 5–8 minutes, drain and place in serving bowls. Spoon the meat mixture over the noodles.

● Serve the dish accompanied by sliced fried garlic, deep-fried dried red chiles, scallions, fresh cilantro, and lime wedges.

Curried Noodles

SERVES 4–6

A favorite lunch in Chiangmai and other towns in northern Thailand. The curry ingredients give away its Indian antecedents, but **khao soi**, *as it is known, has arrived via Burma, in particular from the Shan States. Diners add the crispy noodles at the last minute so that they do not go soggy, and the condiments allow individual choice of flavor.*

6 cups thin coconut milk

11 oz boneless skinned chicken breasts, cut lengthwise into ½ in thick slices

1 Tbsp light soy sauce

1 Tbsp dark soy sauce

2 tsp salt

15 oz dried or 7 oz fresh egg noodles

peanut or corn oil for frying

FOR THE CHILI PASTE

4 dried red chiles, chopped roughly

1 Tbsp shallot, chopped

2 tsp gingerroot, sliced

1 tsp coriander seeds

1 tsp turmeric

● Dry-roast the chili paste ingredients in a 350°F oven until fragrant, about 8–10 minutes, then pound until fine with a mortar and pestle or in a blender.

● Heat 1 cup of the coconut milk in a pan or wok, add the chili paste and fry for 2 minutes, then add the chicken and soy sauces. Stir-fry for 3 minutes, then add the rest of the coconut milk and bring to a boil for 3 minutes. Add the salt and remove from the heat.

● Fry 4 oz of the noodles in a hot oil until crisp. Remove and drain well. Boil the rest of the noodles in water until firm but tender and drain.

● Place the boiled noodles in individual serving bowls, and pour the chicken mixture on top. Garnish with the fried noodles.

● Serve accompanied by bowls of diced shallots, pickled cabbage, and chili powder.

Stir-fried Egg Noodles with Barbecued Pork

SERVES 4

Literally translated as "stir-fried noodles," **chow mein** *is an archetypical noodle fast-food, and one of the very first noodle dishes to become popularized in the West.*

1 lb fresh or 10 oz dried thin egg noodles

2 Tbsp vegetable oil

1 in gingerroot, peeled and finely chopped

2 cloves garlic, finely chopped

1 medium onion, sliced

3 medium carrots, sliced into bite-sized pieces

12 snow peas, blanched

3 cups bean sprouts, rinsed

½ lb Chinese barbecued pork sliced and cut into bite-sized squares

1 Tbsp sesame oil

4 Tbsp light soy sauce

1 Tbsp dark soy sauce

1 Tbsp sugar

salt and black pepper

● Boil plenty of water in a pan, and cook the noodles for 3 minutes. Rinse under running water, and drain.

● Heat the vegetable oil in a wok or frying pan until very hot. Stir-fry the ginger and garlic for 30 seconds. Add the onion, carrots, and snow peas, and stir-fry for 2 minutes. Add the bean sprouts and *cha siu* pork, and stir-fry for another 2 minutes.

● Add the sesame oil, noodles, soy sauce, and sugar, and stir-fry for 1 minute until the noodles are coated with sauce. Season if necessary, and stir once more. Serve immediately.

White Noodles with Sauce

SERVES 4–6

7 oz sea bass, perch, or white fish fillets, skinned

11 oz thin rice noodles soaked for 3 minutes if dried, or cooked spaghetti

6 cups thin coconut milk

20 fish balls, frozen or bottled (optional)

3 Tbsp fish sauce

4 oz bean sprouts, blanched

4 oz beans, cut into ½ in lengths

4 oz swamp cabbage, blanched

2 cups lemon basil leaves

FOR THE CHILI PASTE

4 oz shallots, chopped finely

2 oz garlic cloves, chopped

2 oz dried salted mackerel or other fish, chopped lightly

1 cup water

1 cup krachai, sliced

2 Tbsp lemon grass, sliced

4 dried red chiles, seeded

2 tsp galangal, sliced

1 tsp shrimp paste

1 tsp salt

● Mix all the chili paste ingredients together, put in a pan or wok and cook over medium heat for 1 minute. Cool and then chop in a blender or food processor. Put to one side.

● Boil fish in a small amount of water for 10 minutes. Remove, cool slightly and chop finely (or process quickly in a food processor). Boil the noodles quickly for 5 minutes, drain, cool and place in serving bowls.

● Heat the coconut milk in a pan, add the chili paste mixture, the fish and the fish balls if using, the fish sauce, and boil for 3 minutes. Remove from the heat.

● Top the noodles with the fish mixture. Arrange the bean sprouts, beans, swamp cabbage, and lemon basil around the side.

Soft Noodles with Vegetable and Peanut Sauce

SERVES 4

This is a famous Indonesian dish, comprising vegetables in a peanut sauce. Normally it is served as a salad, but it also makes a great noodle topping!

¼ lb green cabbage, sliced

2½ cups bean sprouts

1 cup green beans

4–5 small carrots, cut into matchsticks

14 oz fresh or 10 oz dried thin egg noodles

1 Tbsp sesame oil

FOR THE PEANUT SAUCE

1 Tbsp vegetable oil

1 clove garlic, finely chopped

1 shallot, finely chopped

½ tsp chili powder

2¼ cups water

1 Tbsp light brown sugar

8 Tbsp crunchy peanut butter

a pinch of salt

juice of ½ a lemon

● Heat the oil in a skillet, and stir-fry the garlic and shallot for 1 minute or until softened. Add the chili powder, water, sugar, and peanut butter, and stir well. Add the salt and lemon juice, stirring again.

● Boil water in a saucepan, and blanch the cabbage, bean sprouts, green beans, and carrots for 2–3 minutes. Drain well.

● Boil more water in the pan, then cook the egg noodles for 3 minutes. Rinse, drain, and toss with the sesame oil. Divide them onto four plates.

● Pile the vegetables on the noodles, and pour the peanut sauce over the top. Serve at once.

Spicy Rice-stick Noodles with Chicken

SERVES 4

Authentic Thai spicy noodles are very, very hot. I have altered the amount of green chile used in this recipe to cool them down and save your taste buds! However, if you feel like increasing the spices, you can add more green chile if you dare.

2 lb fresh flat rice noodles or 10 oz dried rice-stick noodles

5 Tbsp vegetable oil

2 cloves garlic, finely chopped

4–6 small green chiles, chopped

½ lb boneless chicken breasts, sliced into bite-sized pieces

1¼ cups frozen green beans, halved

¼ lb mustard greens or fresh spinach

16 canned or fresh baby corn, each cut diagonally into 3 pieces

4 Tbsp fish sauce

2 Tbsp dark soy sauce

2 Tbsp light soy sauce

1 Tbsp palm or brown sugar

2 small tomatoes, halved

● If you use fresh noodles, just rinse with warm water. Soak dried rice noodles in warm water for 2–5 minutes, or according to the instructions on the package. Rinse, and drain.

● Heat 3 tablespoons of the oils in a wok or skillet until very hot. Stir-fry the garlic and green chile for 30 seconds, then add the chicken and fry for about 3 minutes more.

● Add the green beans, mustard greens or spinach, and baby corn, stirring for 1–2 minutes. Add the remaining oil and the rice noodles, and stir. Then add the fish sauce, soy sauce, and sugar, and stir well.

● Garnish with the tomatoes, and serve at once.

Fried Flat Rice Noodles with Beef and Black Bean Sauce

SERVES 4

Black bean sauce is just one of a number of end products that result from the fermentation of soybeans. Prepared with salt and spices, the black bean forms the basis of a very distinctive sauce to complement most meats. Here it is used with beef, but you will find it is equally good with pork.

2 lb fresh flat rice noodles or 10 oz dried rice-stick noodles

1 lb rump steak, sliced at a slant into bite-sized pieces

1 egg white

3 tbsp Chinese rice wine or dry sherry

4 tbsp light soy sauce

2 tsp cornstarch

7 tbsp vegetable oil

1 in gingerroot, peeled and finely chopped

3 cloves garlic, finely chopped

2 scallions, chopped

2 medium-sized onions, cut into bite-sized squares

1 large green bell pepper, cut into bite-sized squares

6 tbsp black bean sauce

2 tsp sugar

● Rinse fresh flat rice noodles with hot water, or soak dried noodles in warm water for 2–5 minutes. Rinse, and drain.

● Marinate the beef with 1 tablespoon of the rice wine, 1 tablespoon of the soy sauce, and the cornstarch for 30 minutes.

● Heat 3 tablespoons of the oil in a wok or skillet. Fry the beef for 2–3 minutes, and set aside. Clean the wok before the next step.

● Heat 2 tablespoons of the oil in a wok, and stir-fry the ginger and garlic for 30 seconds. Add the scallions, onion, and green bell pepper, and stir until the onion becomes transparent.

● Return the beef and noodles to the wok. Add 2 tablespoons of the oil, plus the black bean sauce, soy sauce, rice wine, and sugar. Stir well, until all the ingredients are thoroughly mixed. Divide the noodles onto four plates, and serve.

Fried Rice-stick Noodles with Bean Curd and Black Bean Sauce

SERVES 4

Bean curd is prepared by cutting it into small cubes. Be careful when you do this as it is delicate stuff and prone to disintegrate if handled too roughly. Nutritious and healthy as it undoubtedly is, bean curd will never win any awards for flavor, which is why its combination with the spicy, aromatic black bean sauce makes such a good pairing.

10 oz dried rice-stick noodles

4 Tbsp vegetable oil

¾ lb bean curd, diced

1-in gingerroot, peeled and finely chopped

2 cloves garlic, finely chopped

½ green bell pepper, diced

½ red bell pepper, diced

½ yellow bell pepper, diced

5 scallions, chopped

6 Tbsp black bean sauce

3 Tbsp light soy sauce

2 Tbsp Chinese rice wine or dry sherry

2 tsp sugar

● Soak the rice-stick noodles in warm water for 2–5 minutes, depending on the instructions on the package. Rinse, and drain.

● Heat 3 tablespoons of the oil in a wok or skillet. Fry the bean curd until golden brown. Add the ginger and garlic, and stir. Add the bell peppers and scallions, and stir-fry for 1–2 minutes.

● Add the remaining oil, noodles, black bean sauce, soy sauce, rice wine, and sugar, then stir until the noodles are well coated with the sauce. Divide the noodles onto four plates, and serve at once.

Thai Fried Rice-stick Noodles

SERVES 4

The most widely eaten and best known of all the noodle dishes of Thailand. Like all the best noodle dishes, it is simply prepared and ready in minutes. The key lies in the use of salty dried shrimp and roasted peanuts. You can adjust the amount of chile used depending on your liking for spiciness.

10 oz dried rice-stick noodles

12 jumbo shrimp with tails, peeled and deveined

5 Tbsp vegetable oil

3 cloves garlic, finely chopped

4 shallots, sliced

2 eggs, beaten

2 Tbsp roast peanuts, crushed

3–4 small green chiles, chopped

2 Tbsp dried shrimp, chopped

2 scallions, chopped

2½ cups bean sprouts

2½ Tbsp palm or brown sugar

6 Tbsp fish sauce

½ cup freshly squeezed lemon juice

cilantro leaves

4 lime wedges

FOR THE MARINADE

1 tsp freshly squeezed lemon juice

1 tsp fish sauce

½ tsp palm or brown sugar

● Soak the rice-stick noodles in warm water for 2–5 minutes, or according to the instructions on the package. Rinse, and drain.

● Marinate the shrimp in the lemon juice, fish sauce, and sugar for at least 15 minutes.

● Heat 2 tablespoons of the oil in a wok or skillet, and stir-fry the garlic and shallots for 30 seconds. Make a well in the center and add the eggs, then lightly scramble.

● Add the peanuts, chiles, dried shrimp, scallions, and bean sprouts, and stir.

● Add another 2 tablespoons of oil and the noodles, and stir. Add the sugar, fish sauce, and lemon juice, then stir until the noodles are well coated.

● Quickly beat the remaining tablespoon of oil in the wok, and fry the shrimp thoroughly. Put the noodles onto four plates. Lay the shrimp on top, and garnish with cilantro and lime wedges. Serve at once.

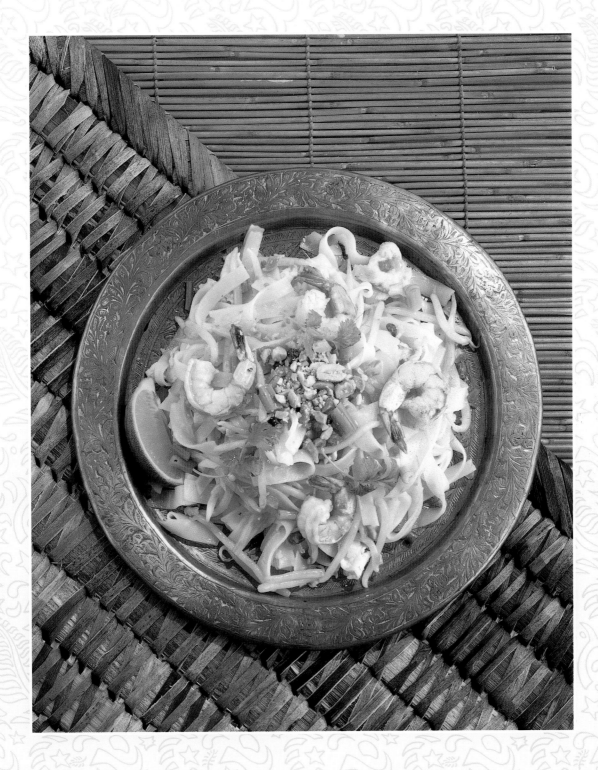

Thai Fried Rice–stick Noodles

Malaysian Flat Rice Noodles

SERVES 4

If you are ever lucky enough to visit Malaysia, you will find this dish being sold in restaurants and from roadside stalls wherever you go. The fish balls in this recipe are not available at supermarkets, but you should be able to pick them up at oriental food stores.

2 lb fresh flat rice noodles or 10 oz dried rice-stick noodles

5 Tbsp vegetable oil

2 cloves garlic, finely chopped

½-in gingerroot, peeled and minced

6 oz boneless belly of pork or chicken breasts, skinned and thinly sliced

2 small red chilies, chopped

16 large shrimp with tails, peeled and deveined

8 fish balls or portions of imitation crabmeat, sliced

3 cups bean sprouts

¼ lb fresh spinach

2 eggs, beaten

1 tsp sugar

3 Tbsp light soy sauce

3 Tbsp dark soy sauce

salt and black pepper

● Rinse the fresh flat rice noodles with warm water, or soak the dried rice-stick noodles in warm water for 2–5 minutes. Rinse, and drain.

● Heat 3 tablespoons of the oil in a wok or skillet until very hot. Stir-fry the garlic and ginger for 30 seconds. Add the pork, and fry for about 3 minutes. Add the chile and shrimp, then stir for about 1 minute. Add the sliced fish balls or crabmeat, the bean sprouts and spinach, and stir again for about 1 minute.

● Make a well in the center, then add the egg. Scramble quickly. Add the remaining oil, and the rice noodles, sugar, and soy sauce, then stir well. Taste, and add salt and black pepper as required. Put onto four plates, and serve immediately.

Fried Rice Noodles with Coconut Sauce

SERVES 4

The coconut and its parent palm have a hallowed place in the Thai psyche. The coconut itself has a wide variety of culinary uses, while the palm is employed to make furniture, toys, and musical instruments. Canned coconut milk varies in its consistency depending on the brand. A thicker product produces the richest, smoothest flavor. Remember to shake the can well before opening.

10 oz dried rice-stick noodles

3 Tbsp vegetable oil

2 cloves garlic, finely chopped

3 shallots, chopped

14 oz rump steak, thinly sliced

16 canned or fresh baby corn, cut diagonally

4 scallions, chopped

2½ cups bean sprouts

1⅔ cups canned coconut milk

2 tsp palm or brown sugar

4 Tbsp fish sauce

3 Tbsp freshly squeezed lemon juice

1 Tbsp Thai red curry paste

cilantro leaves

● Soak the rice-stick noodles in warm water for 2–5 minutes, or follow the instructions on the package. Rinse, and drain.

● Heat the oil in a wok or skillet, then stir-fry the garlic and shallots for 30 seconds. Add the beef and stir-fry for about 3 minutes, before adding the baby corn, scallions, celery, and bean sprouts.

● Add the coconut milk, sugar, fish sauce, lemon juice, and curry paste, and stir well until the sauce is absorbed into the noodles.

● Put the noodles onto four plates, sprinkle with cilantro leaves, and serve at once.

Fried Bean-thread Noodles with Bean Curd

SERVES 4

Bean curd is a favorite constituent of Thai cooking. This dish features fried bean curd. Like all other types of bean curd, it is best to use what you buy in one go as it quickly deteriorates, even if refrigerated.

½ lb bean-thread noodles

4 Tbsp vegetable oil

10 oz bean curd, diced

3 cloves garlic, finely chopped

4 shallots, finely chopped

2½ cups bean sprouts

1¼ cups frozen green beans, halved

2 scallions, chopped

2 Tbsp roast peanuts, crushed

2 Tbsp dried shrimp, chopped

3–5 small green chiles, chopped

2½ Tbsp palm or brown sugar

6 Tbsp fish sauce

½ cup freshly squeezed lemon juice

FOR THE GARNISH

2 Tbsp crispy onion

cilantro leaves

1 medium red chile, sliced

4 slices lime

● Soak the bean-thread noodles in boiling water for 5 minutes. Rinse under cold water, and drain. Heat half the oil in a wok or skillet, and fry the bean curd until golden brown. Drain on paper towels.

● Add the remaining oil to the wok, then fry the garlic and shallots for about 30 seconds. Add the bean sprouts, green beans, and scallions, and stir well.

● Add the bean-thread noodles, bean curd, crushed peanuts, dried shrimp, and green chile, then stir. Season with the sugar, fish sauce, and lemon juice, stirring again.

● Divide the noodles onto four plates. Sprinkle with the crispy onions, cilantro leaves, and red chile, and garnish with lime slices. Serve at once.

Fried Bean–thread Noodles
with Bean Curd

Wheatflour Noodles with Egg

SERVES 2

Udon is the name given by the Japanese to those noodles made from wheatflour. A great favorite in the winter months because of its warming properties, udon comes in various shapes, some flat, some round in section, some as thick as a little finger, others as thin as spaghetti.

10 oz fresh *udon*

FOR THE SOUP

2½ cups *dashi* broth (see page 62)

1 tsp salt

2 tsp superfine sugar

2 Tbsp *mirin*

2 Tbsp soy sauce

1 egg, beaten

2 tsp cornstarch

2 tsp water

2 scallions, chopped

● Bring a large pan of water to a boil. Add the *udon* and boil for 2 minutes. Drain and then place in equal portions into two bowls.

● Put the *dashi* broth, salt, sugar, *mirin*, and soy sauce in a pan and bring to a boil. Pour ⅔ of the liquid into the two bowls. Bring the remainder back to the boil and gradually add the beaten egg, mixing lightly so that when the egg rises to the surface, it is cooked in fronds.

● Mix the cornstarch and water into a paste and then add this to the soup to thicken. Pour the egg mixture into the bowls. Sprinkle with the scallion and serve immediately while still hot.

Rice-stick Noodles with Pork and Shrimp

SERVES 4

This dish contains the three foundations of Thai flavoring: garlic, shallots, and chiles. Thai garlic tends to be small compared to its western counterpart, so if the cloves you have are on the large side, use just one.

10 oz dried rice-stick noodles

5 Tbsp vegetable oil

2 cloves garlic, finely chopped

3 shallots, chopped

½ lb lean pork, sliced into small pieces

¼ lb peeled shrimp

4–6 small green chiles, chopped

2½ cups bean sprouts

8 canned or fresh baby corn, cut diagonally into bite-sized pieces

3 stalks celery, cut diagonally into bite-sized pieces

2 eggs, beaten

2½ Tbsp palm or brown sugar

3½ Tbsp tomato katsup

6 Tbsp fish sauce (*nam pla*)

½ cup freshly squeezed lemon juice

cilantro leaves

4 lime wedges

● Soak the noodles in warm water for 2–5 minutes, or according to the instructions. Rinse, then drain.

● Heat 3 tablespoons of the oil in a wok or skillet, and stir-fry the garlic and shallots for 30 seconds. Add the pork and fry for about 3 minutes. Add the shrimp and green chiles, stirring for another minute, then add the bean sprouts, baby corn, and celery, and fry for another 2 minutes.

● Make a well in the center, then pour in the egg and scramble quickly. Add the remaining oil and the rice-stick noodles, then stir. Add the sugar, tomato katsup, fish sauce, and lemon juice, and stir well.

● Divide the noodles onto four plates, and garnish with cilantro and lime wedges.

Buckwheat Noodles Topped with Deep-fried Jumbo Shrimp

SERVES 2

*Soba noodles are made from buckwheat and are distinguished by their brown color. Like **ramen** noodles, they can be bought fresh or dried. **Soba** is considered to be a very healthy food by the Japanese, and topping a dish of the noodles with a jumbo shrimp turns a nourishing meal into a gourmet experience.*

2 jumbo shrimp

all-purpose flour

4 shiitake mushrooms

5 oz dried *soba*

FOR THE BATTER

2 Tbsp all-purpose flour

½ egg, beaten

4 Tbsp water

FOR THE SOUP

2½ cups *dashi* broth

1 tsp salt

2 tsp superfine sugar

2 Tbsp *mirin*

2 Tbsp soy sauce

2 scallions, chopped

● To make the batter mix the flour, egg, and water lightly in a bowl. Coat the shrimp with flour and dip in the batter. Dip the mushrooms into the batter. Heat the oil to 350°F and deep-fry until light golden brown.

● Bring a large pan of water to a boil. Add the *soba* and cook for about 3 minutes. Briefly rinse with cold water and then drain. Divide the *soba* equally between two bowls.

● Put the *dashi* broth, salt, sugar, *mirin*, and soy sauce in a pan and bring to a boil. Add the bowls of *soba*.

● Place one shrimp and two mushrooms on the top of each bowl and sprinkle with chopped scallion. Serve immediately.

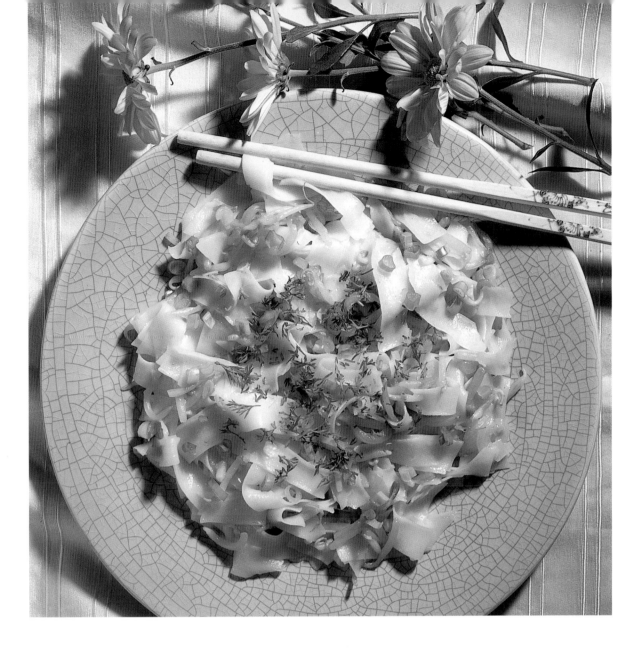

Stir-fried Noodles and Beansprouts

SERVES 4

1 Tbsp vegetable oil

2 small onions, thinly sliced

4 cloves garlic, chopped

1 cup bean sprouts

6 oz (dried weight) cellophane noodles, soaked in warm water for 30 minutes, drained and cut into 3 in lengths

½ cup chicken broth

1 Tbsp fish sauce or light soy sauce

2 scallions, thinly sliced

1 Tbsp fresh cilantro, chopped

freshly ground black pepper

● Heat the oil in a wok over high heat. Add the onions and garlic, and sauté for 2 minutes or so until the edges begin to brown.

● Add the bean sprouts and stir-fry for 30 seconds. Add the noodles and stir-fry for 1 minute. Stir in the chicken broth and fish sauce, and toss to combine. Add the scallions and remove from heat. Serve on a serving dish with cilantro and black pepper sprinkled all over.

Malaysian Egg Noodles with Chicken and Shrimp

SERVES 4

A typical feature of Malaysian and Singaporean cuisine is the frequent use of egg, as in this dish, in which strands of beaten egg are stirred into the sauce.

14 oz fresh or 10 oz dried thin egg noodles

2 Tbsp sesame oil

4 Tbsp vegetable oil

2 cloves garlic, finely chopped

¼ lb boneless chicken breasts, sliced into bite-sized pieces

¼ lb peeled shrimp

¼ lb fish balls or imitation crabmeat, sliced

3 cups bean sprouts

¼ lb mustard greens or fresh spinach

1 tsp light soy sauce

1 tsp salt

white pepper

½ tsp sugar

2½ cups chicken broth

3 Tbsp cornstarch

4 Tbsp water

2 eggs, beaten

● Boil plenty of water in a pan, and add the egg noodles. Cook for 3 minutes, then rinse under cold water and drain. Heat the sesame oil in a wok or skillet, and fry the noodles. Then divide onto four individual plates.

● Heat the vegetable oil in a wok or skillet until very hot. Fry the garlic for 30 seconds. Add the chicken and fry for 2–3 minutes. Add the shrimp and stir, then add the fish balls, bean sprouts, and spinach or greens, stirring for 2–3 minutes.

● Add the soy sauce, salt, pepper, sugar, and chicken broth; bring to a boil. Dissolve the cornstarch in water, then add to thicken the sauce. When the sauce returns to a boil, stir in the beaten egg and wait for the egg strands to float up to the surface. Pour the sauce over the noodles, and serve.

Stir-fried Egg Noodles with Shrimp and Black Bean Sauce

SERVES 4

These stir-fried noodles require cooking for only a short time. Tiger shrimp add both flavor and a certain luxury to this dish, so if you are feeling extravagant, use them in place of their smaller cousins.

1 lb fresh or 10 oz dried medium egg noodles

3 Tbsp vegetable oil

1 in gingerroot, peeled and finely chopped

3 cloves garlic, finely chopped

¼ lb peeled shrimp

12 tiger or jumbo shrimp, peeled and deveined

1 small red bell pepper, sliced

4 scallions, chopped into 1 in lengths

black pepper

1 Tbsp sesame oil

4 tsp light soy sauce

4 tsp dark soy sauce

2 Tbsp Chinese rice wine or dry sherry

3 Tbsp black bean sauce

● Cook the noodles in a pan of boiling water for 4 minutes. Rinse, and drain well.

● Heat the vegetable oil in a wok or skillet. Stir-fry the ginger and garlic for 30 seconds. Add the shrimp, bell pepper, scallions, and black pepper, and stir for 1–2 minutes or until the shrimp are heated.

● Add the sesame oil and noodles, and stir. Add the soy sauce, rice wine, and black bean sauce, then stir again until the noodles are coated well with the sauce.

● Put the noodles onto four plates, and serve at once.

Malaysian Egg Noodles
with Chicken and Shrimp

Sweet and Sour Fish on Pan-fried Egg Noodles

SERVES 4

Sweet and sour fish has never quite gained the same kind of popularity as sweet and sour pork, though it is every bit as good to eat and makes an especially good noodle topping.

vegetable oil for deep-frying

2 Tbsp cornstarch

1 egg, beaten

1 tsp water

1 lb cod or haddock steaks, cut into bite-sized pieces

10 oz dried or 14 oz fresh thin egg noodles

4 Tbsp vegetable oil

FOR THE SAUCE

1 Tbsp sesame oil

2 Tbsp vegetable oil

1 medium-sized onion, cut into bite-sized squares

1 red bell pepper, cut into bite-sized squares

½ cup frozen green peas

4 oz can bamboo shoots, cut into halves

10 shiitake mushrooms, quartered

½ tsp chili powder

2½ cups chicken broth

2½ Tbsp sugar

½ cup tomato katsup

4 tsp light soy sauce

4 Tbsp Chinese rice wine or dry sherry

4 Tbsp vinegar

salt and black pepper

3 Tbsp cornstarch

4 Tbsp water

● Heat the oil in a pan until very hot. Meanwhile, mix the cornstarch, egg, and water together, then dip the fish in the mixture. Deep-fry for about 2 minutes or until golden brown.

● Cook the egg noodles in plenty of boiling water for 3 minutes. Rinse under running water, drain well, and divide into four. Heat 1 tablespoon of oil in a wok or skillet. Add a portion of noodles, and press down lightly. Fry until lightly browned, then turn the noodles over, press down lightly, and fry until the other side turns golden-brown.

● Put the pan-fried noodles on a chopping board, make a crisscross pattern of cuts, and place on an individual plate. Repeat the process for the other three portions.

● Heat 1 tablespoon sesame oil and 2 tablespoons vegetable oil in the wok or skillet until very hot. Stir-fry the onion, red bell pepper, and peas for 2 minutes. Add the bamboo shoots and shiitake mushrooms, and sprinkle with the chili powder. Stir-fry for another 2 minutes.

● Add the chicken broth, sugar, tomato katsup, soy sauce, and rice wine, and bring to a boil. Add the vinegar, and season to taste with salt and black pepper.

● Dissolve the cornstarch in the water, and add to thicken the sauce. Add the fish, and stir gently. Pour the sweet and sour fish over the noodles. Serve immediately.

Indonesian Fried Egg Noodles with Chicken and Bean Curd

SERVES 4

Indonesian cooking has become increasingly popular over the last few years, and this, one of the most commonly eaten dishes in Indonesia, has been at the forefront of this trend.

10 oz dried medium egg noodles

4 Tbsp + 2 tsp vegetable oil

10 oz bean curd, diced

2 eggs, beaten

1-in gingerroot, peeled and finely chopped

4 shallots, finely chopped

1 tsp ground coriander seeds

1 red chile, chopped

½ lb boneless chicken breasts, diced

4–5 small carrots, sliced

3 stalks celery, sliced

4 scallions, chopped into 1-in lengths

3 Tbsp light soy sauce

salt and pepper

4 tomato wedges

sliced cucumber

● Cook the egg noodles in a pan of boiling water for 4 minutes. Rinse, and drain well.

● Heat 1 tablespoon of the oil in a wok or skillet, and fry the bean curd until lightly browned. Set aside, and clean the wok.

● To make the egg sheets, heat 1 teaspoon of the oil in an omelet pan. Add half the beaten egg and fry both sides, like a thin pancake. Repeat to make a second egg sheet. When the egg sheets are cooled, slice them thinly.

● Heat another 2 tablespoons of the oil in the wok, stir-fry the ginger, shallots, ground coriander, and red chile for 30 seconds. Add the chicken, and stir for 2–3 minutes. Add the carrots, celery, bean curd, and scallions, stirring each time you add the ingredients.

● Add 1 tablespoon of the oil, the egg noodles, and soy sauce to the wok, and stir well. Divide the noodles onto four plates, sprinkle the sliced egg sheets on top, and garnish with tomato wedges and cucumber slices. Serve at once.

Malaysian Spicy Egg Noodles

SERVES 4

This dish uses **belacan,** *the pungent shrimp-based paste commonly used in Malaysia and Thai cooking. Don't let the odor put you off when you use shrimp paste, but the aroma does tend to stick around unless you ensure your kitchen is well-ventilated!*

10 oz dried medium egg noodles

5 Tbsp vegetable oil

4–6 small dried red chiles, soaked in hot water, then ground

2 cloves garlic, finely chopped

1 tsp dried shrimp paste (optional)

10 oz rump steak, thinly sliced

1 medium-sized onion, thinly sliced

2 green chiles, chopped

2½ cups bean sprouts

¼ lb mustard greens or fresh spinach

salt and black pepper

3 Tbsp light soy sauce

FOR THE GARNISH

cilantro leaves

4 lime wedges

● Boil plenty of water in a pan, and cook the noodles for 4 minutes. Rinse under water, and drain. Set aside.

● Heat 3 tablespoons of the oil in a wok or skillet. Add the chiles, garlic, and shrimp paste, and stir. Add the beef, and fry for 2–3 minutes.

● Add the onion, green chiles, bean sprouts, and mustard greens, stirring each time you add the ingredients. Season with salt and pepper.

● Add the remaining oil and the egg noodles, sprinkle soy sauce over the mixture, and mix all the ingredients well. Put the noodles onto four plates, and garnish with cilantro leaves and lime wedges.

Stir-fried Egg Noodles with Yakisoba Sauce

SERVES 4

Maybe the most popular noodle dish eaten in Japan, this is found in noodle shops and is made and served in the street, at festivals, or cooked over a campfire during a trip out into the countryside.

¾ lb dried egg noodles or 1¼ lb Japanese steamed noodles

1 Tbsp sesame oil

2 Tbsp sunflower oil

½ lb boneless belly of pork or chicken breasts, thinly sliced

1 medium-sized onion, sliced

4–5 small carrots, cut in half lengthwise and thinly sliced

5 cabbage leaves, cut roughly

salt and black pepper

7 Tbsp *yakisoba* or Japanese brown sauce

nori seaweed flakes (optional)

red pickled ginger (optional)

● If you are using dried noodles, boil plenty of water in a pan, add the noodles, and cook for 3 minutes. Rinse with water and drain. Toss the noodles in the sesame oil. If you use Japanese steamed noodles, just rinse with very hot water.

● Heat the sunflower oil in a wok or skillet, then fry the pork or chicken for 3–4 minutes. Add the onions, carrots, and cabbage, and stir-fry for 3–4 minutes. Sprinkle with the salt and pepper, add the noodles and *yakisoba* or brown sauce, and stir well.

● Put the noodles onto four plates, and sprinkle with the *nori* flakes and pickled ginger. Serve at once.

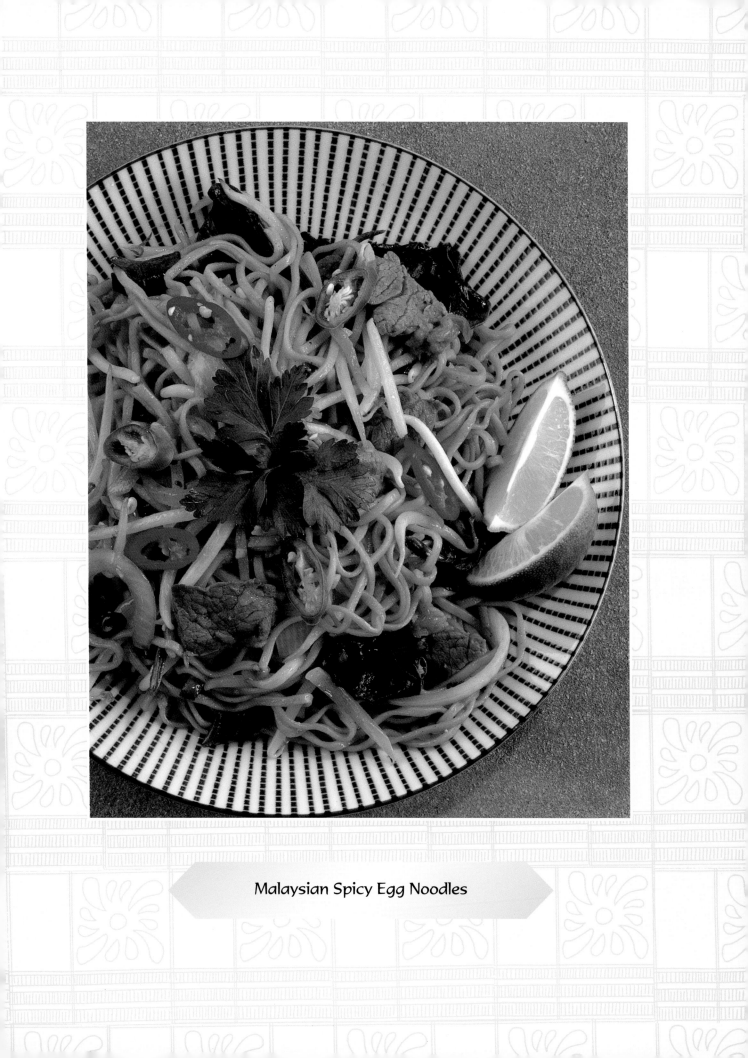

Malaysian Spicy Egg Noodles

Thai-fried Noodles

SERVES 6

The country's basic fried noodle dish. Quick and easy to prepare, it is usually eaten as a secondary rather than as a main dish.

½ cup peanut or corn oil

7 oz raw large shrimp, shelled

4 oz firm bean curd, diced

3 Tbsp preserved sweet white radish, chopped

3 Tbsp shallots, sliced

4 eggs

11 oz rice or cellophane noodles, soaked in cold water for 7–10 minutes, if dried

¼ cup chicken broth

3 Tbsp dried shrimp, chopped

⅓ cup unsalted peanuts,m chopped

4 scallions, sliced

15 oz bean sprouts

FOR THE SAUCE

1 cup water

½ cup tamarind juice

⅓ cup palm sugar

1 Tbsp light soy sauce

● Mix all the sauce ingredients together in a pan and boil until reduced to about ⅔ cup. Set aside to cool.

● Heat the oil in a wok or pan until very hot, then add the shrimps and bean curd and stir-fry lightly for 1 minute. Add the preserved radish and shallot, fry for 1 minute, and break in the eggs. Stir-fry for a minute, then add the noodles and chicken stock. When the noodles are soft (about 2 minutes), add the dried shrimp, peanuts, scallions, and bean sprouts. Add the sauce, fry for a couple of minutes and serve.

● Serve accompanied by chopped peanuts, chopped dry chiles, sugar, lime wedges, scallions, and fresh bean sprouts, all in small saucers.

Crispy Egg Noodles with Chicken and Bean Sprout Sauce

SERVES 4

Take care when preparing the noodles for this dish, as the oil may boil over if an excessive amount is used. The best and safest method is to use a wok rather than a skillet.

½ lb dried medium egg noodles

vegetable oil for deep-frying

1 egg white

2 tsp cornstarch

6 Tbsp vegetable oil

10 oz boneless chicken breasts, shredded

FOR THE SAUCE

1 Tbsp sesame oil

2 cloves garlic, finely chopped

1-in gingerroot, peeled and finely chopped

14 oz bean sprouts

15 canned straw mushrooms, halved

4 scallions, chopped

2½ cups chicken broth

2 tsp light soy sauce

2 Tbsp Chinese rice wine or dry sherry

salt and black pepper

3 Tbsp cornstarch

4 Tbsp water

● Boil plenty of water in a pan, and cook the noodles for 4 minutes. Rinse, and drain. Separate, and then spread the noodles on a tray to dry.

● Fill a saucepan or wok quarter full of oil and heat to 350°F. Deep-fry the noodles in small batches until golden and crispy. Drain on paper towels. Crush the noodles lightly to make them easier to handle, and divide onto three plates.

● Mix the egg white and 2 teaspoons of cornstarch. Heat 5 tablespoons of the vegetable oil in the wok or skillet. Coat the chicken with the cornstarch mixture, then shallow-fry until golden brown. Discard the oil, and clean the wok or skillet.

● Heat the remaining tablespoon of vegetable oil and the sesame oil in the wok until very hot. Stir-fry the garlic and ginger for 30 seconds. Add the bean sprouts, mushrooms, and scallions, then stir-fry for 2 minutes.

● Return the chicken to the wok, then add the broth, soy sauce, and rice wine. Season with salt and black pepper. Bring to a boil, and simmer for 1–2 minutes.

● Dissolve the cornstarch in the water, then add to thicken the sauce. Pour the sauce over the noodles just prior to eating.

Crispy Egg Noodles with Pork Sauce

SERVES 4

Deep-fried noodles might seem like a strange idea, but, in fact, they are very popular throughout Asia, and make a crunchy and refreshing alternative to the more traditional boiled noodles.

½ lb dried thin egg noodles

vegetable oil for deep-frying

FOR THE SAUCE

½ lb lean pork, sliced on a slant into bite-sized pieces

1 Tbsp light soy sauce

4 Tbsp cornstarch

8 large dried shiitake mushrooms, rinsed

4 Tbsp vegetable oil

1 in gingerroot, peeled and finely chopped

2 cloves garlic, finely chopped

1 medium-sized onion, cut into bite-sized squares

4–5 small carrots, thinly sliced

½ lb Chinese cabbage, cut into bite-sized squares

salt and black pepper

2½ cups chicken broth

2 Tbsp Chinese rice wine or dry sherry

2 tsp sugar

4 Tbsp water

● Boil plenty of water in a saucepan, and cook the noodles for 3 minutes. Rinse, and drain. Separate, and spread the noodles on a tray to dry.

● Heat a wok or saucepan a quarter full of oil and heat until very hot. Deep-fry the egg noodles in small batches until golden and crispy. Drain on paper towels. Set aside.

● Put the pork, soy sauce, and 1 tablespoon of the cornstarch in a bowl, mix, and leave for 15 minutes. Soak the shiitake mushrooms in a cup of hot water for 15 minutes, then remove and quarter. Retain the water. Heat 2 tablespoons of the oil in a wok or frying pan, and fry the pork for about 3 minutes. Set aside, and clean the pan.

● Heat 2 tablespoons oil in the wok or pan until very hot. Fry the ginger and garlic for 30 seconds, before adding the onion, carrots, mushrooms, and cabbage. Stir-fry for 2–3 minutes. Add in the meat, season with salt and pepper, and stir.

● Add the water used to soak the mushrooms, plus the chicken broth, rice wine, and sugar; bring to a boil, checking the saltiness.

● Dissolve the remaining 3 tablespoons cornstarch with the water, and add to thicken the sauce. Crush the crispy noodles lightly, and divide onto four plates. Pour the sauce over the noodles, and serve at once.

Crispy Egg Noodles
with Pork Sauce

Soft Egg Noodles with Ground Pork Sauce

SERVES 4

Toban djan *is a fiery Chinese chile bean sauce available from most Chinese or oriental stores, and in a growing number of supermarkets. Here, the power of the chile sauce is tempered by the addition of yellow bean sauce, leaving the dish pleasantly spicy rather than breathtakingly hot.*

10 oz dried or 14 oz fresh thin egg noodles

2 tsp sesame oil

FOR THE SAUCE

2 Tbsp vegetable oil

1 large clove garlic, finely chopped

½-in gingerroot, peeled and finely chopped

2 scallions, chopped

1 lb ground pork

3 Tbsp yellow bean sauce

1 Tbsp chile bean sauce

2 Tbsp Chinese rice wine or dry sherry

2 Tbsp dark soy sauce

scant 1 cup chicken broth, mixed to a paste with 2 Tbsp cornstarch

salt and black pepper

● Cook the egg noodles in plenty of boiling water for 3 minutes. Rinse, and drain. Toss in the sesame oil, and divide into four servings.

● Heat the vegetable oil in a pan, and stir-fry the garlic, ginger, and scallions for 30 seconds. Add the ground pork, and fry for 3–4 minutes.

● Add the yellow bean sauce, chile sauce, rice wine, and soy sauce, and stir for 1 minute.

● Add the mixture of broth and cornstarch, and stir until the sauce thickens. Season with salt and black pepper to taste.

● Pour the sauce over the noodles, and serve.

Fried Noodles with Chicken, Vegetables, and Gravy

SERVES 4

11 oz large flat rice noodles

½ cup peanut or corn oil

1 tsp dark soy sauce

2 Tbsp garlic, chopped finely

7 oz boneless skinned chicken breasts cut lengthwise into ½ in thick slices

2 Tbsp light soy sauce

2 Tbsp sugar

1 tsp ground white pepper

6 cups chicken broth

15 oz kale or broccoli, cut into ½ in pieces

1 Tbsp cornstarch, mixed with a little water

● Boil the noodles for 1 minute and drain well. Heat half the oil in a wok or pan, add the noodles and fry lightly for 1 minute. Add the black soy sauce, fry lightly for another minute. Drain off the oil and transfer the noodles to a plate.

● Heat the rest of the oil in the wok. Add the garlic and chicken, and fry lightly for 2 minutes. Stir in the white soy sauce, sugar, white pepper and then the chicken broth. Boil well for 3–5 minutes, add the kale, boil again for 1 minute and then add the cornstarch. Boil for 1 minute and pour over the noodles.

● Serve accompanied by sliced fresh red chile in vinegar, fish sauce, sugar, and chili powder, in separate bowls.

Chicken and Red Pepper in Egg Noodle Basket

SERVES 6

Noodle baskets are a Chinese innovation that appeal as much to the eyes as to the taste buds. You will need two small sieves about 5 inches across. This recipe works best with thinner noodles, and the oil needs to be hot to get nice, crisp, golden baskets. This recipe makes six baskets, which can be presented as a main dish or as a starter with less filling.

½ lb dried thin egg noodles

vegetable oil for deep-frying

FOR THE FILLING

6 Tbsp vegetable oil

1 lb boneless chicken breasts, sliced diagonally into bite-sized pieces

salt and black pepper

3 Tbsp cornstarch

4 cloves garlic, finely chopped

½ in gingerroot, peeled and finely chopped

4 oz can bamboo shoots, sliced into matchsticks

⅔ red bell pepper, diced

4 scallions, chopped

FOR THE SAUCE

⅔ cup chicken broth

1 Tbsp Chinese rice wine or dry sherry

1 Tbsp light soy sauce

2 tsp dark soy sauce

4 tsp tomato katsup

½ tsp sugar

salt and black pepper

½ Tbsp cornstarch

2 tsp water

● Boil the egg noodles for 3 minutes. Rinse with water, drain, separate, and dry on a tray lined with paper towels.

● Heat the oil in a deep pan to 350°F. Oil the sieves, one on the inside, the other on the outside. Line one sieve with egg noodles and press the other sieve down lightly to sandwich them. Carefully deep-fry the noodles with the two sieves holding them together until crispy and golden, about 3–4 minutes. Remove the noodle basket, taking care not to break it. Create five more baskets in the same way.

● Heat 4 tablespoons of oil in a wok or skillet. Sprinkle the chicken with the salt and pepper, then coat with the cornstarch. Shallow-fry the chicken for 3–4 minutes, or until golden brown. Drain on paper towels until needed.

● Heat the remaining 2 tablespoons of oil in the wok, stir-fry the garlic and ginger, then add the bamboo, bell pepper, and onion. Stir well. Add the chicken broth, rice wine, soy sauce, katsup, and sugar; bring to a boil, and season if required.

● Combine the cornstarch and water, then add to thicken the sauce. Return the chicken to the pan, and stir. Place the noodle baskets on six plates, and fill with the chicken mixture. Serve at once.

Sweet Crisp-fried Noodles

SERVES 4–6

This is a Thai embellishment of a Chinese dish, and for complete success depends on the noodles being fried just right—so that they are both crisp and puffy when served to guests.

6 cups peanut or corn oil for frying

7 oz raw medium-sized shrimp, shelled and cut into 3 pieces

5 oz pork loin, cut into cubes the same size as shrimp pieces

½ cup firm bean curd, cut into small rectangles

5 oz thin rice vermicelli noodles, soaked in cool water for 1 minute if dried and drained well

½ Tbsp garlic, chopped

½ Tbsp onion, chopped

¼ cup palm sugar

2 Tbsp white vinegar

1 Tbsp marinated soybeans

1 Tbsp fish sauce

3 cups bean sprouts

3 scallions, cut into 1½ in pieces

2 Tbsp pickled garlic, sliced

2 fresh red chiles, cut into very thin strips

● Heat the oil in a pan or wok and fry the shrimp and pork until brown and well cooked, about 10 minutes.

● Remove with a slotted spoon and drain on paper towel. Set aside.

● Add the bean curd to the hot oil and fry until brown, about 2 minutes. Remove with a slotted spoon, and drain on paper towel. Add the noodles to the hot oil and brown lightly, about 4–5 minutes. Remove and drain well.

● Remove all the oil from the pan except for 2 tablespoons. Add the garlic and onion and fry gently for a minute; then add the cooked pork, shrimps, and bean curd, the sugar, vinegar, marinated soybeans, and fish sauce. Fry until thick and sticky, about 7–10 minutes.

● Reduce the heat and add the noodles. Mix well for 1 minute, then transfer onto a large plate in a mound. Arrange the bean sprouts, scallion, pickled garlic, and chile on top.

Crabmeat Sauce on Pan-fried Egg Noodles

SERVES 4

10 oz dried or 14 oz fresh
medium egg noodles

4 Tbsp vegetable oil

**FOR THE CRABMEAT
SAUCE**

2 Tbsp vegetable oil

1 clove garlic, finely chopped

½-in gingerroot, peeled and
finely chopped

10 shiitake mushrooms, sliced

6 oz canned bamboo shoots,
sliced into matchsticks

4 scallions, chopped

¾ lb canned crabmeat

2½ cups water

4 tsp light soy sauce

salt and black pepper

3 Tbsp cornstarch

4 Tbsp water

● Cook the egg noodles in plenty of water for 4 minutes. Rinse, drain well, and divide into four. Heat 1 tablespoon of oil in a wok or skillet until very hot. Press one portion of the egg noodles down lightly into the pan and fry until lightly browned on both sides. Place on a chopping board and cut a crisscross pattern. Remove to a plate. Repeat.

● Heat 2 tablespoons of oil in the cleaned wok. Fry the garlic and ginger for 30 seconds. Add the shiitake mushrooms, bamboo shoots, and scallions, and stir-fry for 1–2 minutes. Add the crabmeat, water, and soy sauce, and season. Bring to a boil, and simmer for 1 minute more.

● Dissolve the cornstarch in the water, and add to thicken the sauce. Stir. Pour over the noodles, and serve immediately.

Fried Egg Noodles with Seafood Sauce

SERVES 4

If you have a taste for slightly richer flavors in this hearty dish, try adding eight fresh abalone to the ingredients.

10 oz dried egg noodles

4 Tbsp vegetable oil

1 Tbsp sesame oil

1 in gingerroot, peeled and
finely chopped

2 cloves garlic, finely chopped

10 oz squid, cleaned

6 oz peeled jumbo shrimp

4 fish balls or chunks of
imitation crabmeat, sliced

9 oz Chinese cabbage, cut into
bite-sized squares

salt and white pepper

2½ cups chicken or vegetable
broth

1 Tbsp Chinese rice wine or dry
sherry

3 Tbsp cornstarch

4 Tbsp water

● Cook the egg noodles in boiling water for 3 minutes. Rinse, and drain. Heat 1 tablespoon of the vegetable oil and sesame oil in a wok or skillet. Stir-fry the noodles, and put on four plates.

● Heat the remaining vegetable oil in the wok, and stir-fry the ginger and garlic for 30 seconds. Add the squid and shrimp, stirring for 1–2 minutes or until the squid is cooked thoroughly.

● Add the slices of fish ball and Chinese cabbage, sprinkle with salt and white peppere, and stir. Add the broth and rice wine, and bring to a boil. Simmer for 1–2 minutes.

● Combine the cornstarch and water, and add to thicken the sauce. Pour over the noodles, and serve.

Crabmeat Sauce on Pan-fried
Egg Noodles

Shredded Beef and Yellow Bean Sauce on Pan-fried Egg Noodles

SERVES 4

Yellow bean sauce is available in two varieties, one using whole beans, the other puréed. The texture differs, but the taste is identical. You can use either in this dish.

1 lb rump steak, shredded

1 Tbsp light soy sauce

1 Tbsp Chinese rice wine or dry sherry

1 Tbsp cornstarch

14 oz fresh or 10 oz dried thin egg noodles

4 Tbsp vegetable oil

FOR THE SAUCE

2 Tbsp vegetable oil

½ in gingerroot, peeled and finely chopped

4 in piece leek, cut in half and shredded

3 cups bean sprouts

1 small green bell pepper, sliced

salt and black pepper

1¾ cups chicken broth

6 Tbsp whole or puréed yellow bean sauce

1 Tbsp light soy sauce

2 Tbsp cornstarch

3 Tbsp water

● Marinate the beef in the soy sauce, rice wine, and cornstarch for 30 minutes.

● Meanwhile, cook the egg noodles in a pan of boiling water for 3 minutes. Rinse, drain, and divide into four. Heat 1 tablespoon of oil in a wok or frying pan. Take one quarter of the noodles and fry them like a pancake. Press the noodles to form a round, and when they have started to turn golden in color, turn to fry on the other side. Remove to a chopping board, and cut twice in a crisscross pattern to make the noodles easier to eat. Put the noodles on a plate. Repeat the process with the other three portions.

● Heat remaining 2 tablespoons of oil in the wok or skillet; stir-fry the ginger for 30 seconds. Add the leek, bean sprouts, and green bell pepper, stirring each ingredient as you add it. Season.

● Add the chicken broth, yellow bean sauce, and soy sauce; bring to a boil. Combine the cornstarch and water, then add to the sauce, stirring until it thickens. Pour the sauce over the noodles before serving.

Fried Egg Noodles with Pork and Eggplant Sauce

SERVES 4

Oyster sauce is a frequently used Chinese flavoring. The surprising thing about oyster sauce is that you would be hard put to find any trace of fishiness in its flavor. It will last for long periods if kept refrigerated, and is widely available from supermarkets.

14 oz fresh or 10 oz dried medium egg noodles

2 Tbsp sesame oil

FOR THE SAUCE

10 oz boneless belly of pork, skinned and thinly sliced

2½ Tbsp light soy sauce

2½ Tbsp Chinese rice wine or dry sherry

4 Tbsp cornstarch

4 Tbsp vegetable oil

1 in gingerroot, peeled and finely chopped

2 cloves garlic, finely chopped

¾ lb eggplant, sliced into bite-sized pieces and soaked in salted water

4–5 small carrots, sliced

16 canned straw mushrooms, halved

2 scallions, chopped into 1 in lengths

black pepper

2½ cups chicken broth

2 Tbsp oyster sauce

1 tsp sugar

4 Tbsp water

● Marinate the pork in 1 tablespoon each of soy sauce, rice wine, and cornstarch. Set aside for 30 minutes, then heat 1 tablespoon of the vegetable oil in a wok or skillet, and fry the pork for about 3 minutes until lightly browned. Clean the wok.

● Heat the rest of the vegetable oil in the wok until very hot, and stir-fry the ginger and garlic for 30 seconds. Add the drained eggplant and carrots, and stir-fry for a further 1–2 minutes. Add the pork, mushrooms, and scallions, sprinkle black pepper, and stir thoroughly.

● Add the chicken broth, rice wine, oyster sauce, soy sauce, and sugar, and bring to a boil, simmering for 1 minute. Dissolve the cornstarch in the water and add to thicken the sauce.

● Boil the egg noodles in plenty of water for 4 minutes. Rinse under running water, and drain. Heat the sesame oil in a wok, add the noodles, and quickly stir-fry for a few minutes.

● Divide the egg noodles into four plates, pour the pork and eggplant sauce over them, then serve.

Chow Mein

SERVES 4

After chop suey, chow mein (which means "fried noodles" in Chinese) must be the next most popular dish in Chinese restaurants. Try to get freshly made noodles from an Oriental food store or Italian delicatessen, as they taste much better than dried ones. As a rough guide, allow at least 2 oz dried noodles per person, and double the weight if using fresh ones.

1 oz dried bean curd skin sticks	2 scallions, thinly shredded
⅔ cup dried tiger lily buds	3–4 tbsp oil
2 oz bamboo shoots	1 tsp salt
4 oz spinach or any other greens	2 Tbsp light soy sauce
8 oz dried egg noodles	2 tsp sesame seed oil

● Soak the dried vegetables overnight in cold water or in hot water for at least an hour. When soft, thinly shred both the bean curd skins and tiger lily buds.

● Shred the bamboo shoots and spinach leaves into thin strips.

● Cook the noodles in a pan of boiling water according to the instructions on the packet. Freshly made noodles will take only about half that time.

● Heat about half the oil in a hot wok or skillet. While waiting for it to smoke, drain the noodles in a sieve. Add them with about half the scallions and the soy sauce to the wok and stir-fry. Do not overcook, or the noodles will become soggy. Remove and place them on a serving dish.

● Add the rest of the oil to the wok. When hot, add the other scallions and stir a few times. Then add all the vegetables and continue stirring. After 30 seconds or so, add the salt and the remaining soy sauce together with a little water if necessary. As soon as the gravy starts to boil, add the sesame seed oil and blend everything well. Place the mixture on top of the fried noodles as a dressing.

Stir-fried Udon with Yakisoba Sauce

SERVES 4

1½ lb parboiled fresh or 14 oz dried *udon*

3 Tbsp sunflower oil

½ lb ground pork

1 medium-sized onion, sliced

½ lb Chinese cabbage, sliced

½ red bell pepper, sliced

6 oz snow peas, cut in half

salt and black pepper

8 Tbsp *yakisoba* or Japanese brown sauce

nori seaweed flakes (optional)

red pickled ginger (optional)

● Rinse the parboiled *udon* with very hot water or, if using dried *udon*, cook according to the instructions on the package.

● Heat the oil in a wok or skillet until very hot. Add the pork and fry for 3 minutes. Add the onion, Chinese cabbage, red pepper, and snow peas, and stir-fry for about 3 minutes. Season with salt and pepper.

● Add the *udon* and *yakisoba* or Japanese brown sauce, and stir well. Divide the *udon* onto four plates. Sprinkle *nori* flakes and pickled ginger over the top, and serve.

Cellophane Noodles with Vegetables

SERVES 4

Chapchae is a colorful vegetable-packed noodle dish with a multitude of different textures. After the vegetables have been prepared, it is very quick to assemble and cook.

6 dried Chinese black mushrooms, soaked in hot water for 30 minutes

5 oz young fresh spinach leaves

2 Chinese cabbage leaves

3 shiitake or oyster mushrooms, thinly sliced

4 scallions, white and green parts thickly sliced diagonally

1 small zucchini, cut into fine strips

1 carrot, cut into fine strips

4 Tbsp vegetable oil

1 Tbsp sesame oil

3 garlic cloves, crushed and finely chopped

2 small fresh red chiles, seeded and cut into fine strips

2 oz cellophane noodles, soaked for 30 minutes and drained

1 Tbsp soy sauce

1 tsp sugar

salt

● Drain the dried mushrooms, and cut out and discard the stems and any hard parts. Thinly slice the mushroom caps.

● Add the spinach to a large saucepan of boiling water. Cover and quickly return to a boil. Boil for 2 minutes, then drain and rinse under running cold water. Drain well and squeeze out as much water as possible. Separate the leaves.

● Cut away and discard the curly outer part of the Chinese cabbage leaves, saving only the V-shaped core of the leaves. Cut this into fine strips, then mix with the spinach, dried and fresh mushrooms, scallions, zucchini, and carrot until well mixed.

● Heat the vegetable oil and sesame oil in a deep skillet. Add the garlic and chile, and stir-fry for 10 seconds. Add the mixed vegetables and stir-fry for 3–4 minutes until the vegetables are tender but still crisp. Turn the heat to low and stir in the noodles, soy sauce, sugar, and salt. Cook for 2 minutes, then serve.

Cellophane Noodles
with Vegetables

Stir-fried Egg Noodles with Vegetables

SERVES 4

1 lb fresh or 10 oz dried medium egg noodles

2 Tbsp vegetable oil

1 in gingerroot, peeled and finely chopped

2 cloves garlic, finely chopped

10 oz Chinese cabbage, chopped into bite-sized squares

2½ cups bean sprouts

1 small red bell pepper, cut into bite-sized squares

1 small green bell pepper, cut into bite-sized squares

16 straw mushrooms (canned), halved

1 Tbsp sesame oil

2 scallions, chopped

4 Tbsp light soy sauce

1 Tbsp dark soy sauce

1 Tbsp sugar

salt and black pepper

Boil plenty of water in a pan, and cook the noodles for 3–4 minutes. Rinse under cold water, and drain.

Heat the vegetable oil in a wok or skillet, then stir-fry the ginger and garlic for 30 seconds. Add the Chinese cabbage, bean sprouts, red and green bell peppers, and straw mushrooms. Stir each ingredient as you add it. Fry together for about 2 minutes.

Add the sesame oil, noodles, scallions, soy sauce, and sugar, and stir well. Check the taste, adding salt and pepper if necessary. Put the noodles onto four plates and serve immediately.

Rice Vermicelli and Egg

SERVES 4

2 oz rice vermicelli

1 tsp black jack

2 cloves garlic, crushed

2 scallions, chopped

salt and freshly ground black pepper

6 eggs, beaten

1 crisphead lettuce, shredded

½ cucumber, sliced

2 Tbsp pickled carrots or cucumbers

1 Tbsp fresh mint leaves, chopped

1 Tbsp fresh cilantro, chopped

1 Tbsp vegetable oil

FOR THE NUOC MAM GIAM SAUCE

1 clove garlic, roughly chopped

1 fresh red chile pepper, roughly chopped

1 Tbsp fish sauce

1 tsp lemon juice or vinegar

1 Tbsp sugar

To prepare the rice vermicelli, bring a large saucepan of salted water to a boil. Add the rice vermicelli and boil, stirring constantly to separate the vermicelli, for about 3 minutes. It should be tender but firm to the bite. Drain in a colander and rinse under cold running water to stop the cooking.

Make the *nuoc mam giam* sauce by grinding the garlic and chile together in a blender or, better still, pound in a mortar with a pestle. Transfer to a small bowl. Stir in the other ingredients and mix thoroughly, making sure that the sugar dissolves.

Make some black jack if you cannot find any in a food store. Heat 1 tablespoon sugar in a wok until it darkens. Remove from the heat and carefully stir in 2 tablespoons cold water. Do this extremely carefully or you will finish up with burns on your hand. Save whatever is left over in refrigerator.

Combine the garlic, scallions, and black jack in a shallow dish and add salt and black pepper, and the eggs. Mix well and set aside to marinate.

Set out the lettuce, cucumber, pickled vegetables, mint, and cilantro into four individual bowls. Top each portion of vegetables with cooked vermicelli.

Heat the oil in a wok and pour in the egg mixture. Flip it over once and let it cool for 1–2 minutes in a dish. Cut into eight pieces. Put two pieces in each bowl and top each with 2 tablespoons *nuoc mam giam* sauce. The guests mix the contents of their bowls.

Crispy Rice Vermicelli with Shredded Chicken

SERVES 4

You will be surprised at the rapid expansion of the
vermicelli the first time you try this dish. The key is to
deep-fry it in small amounts to prevent it from
overflowing from your wok or pan. The noodles are
ready when they have lost their transparency and
have turned white.

¼ lb rice vermicelli

vegetable oil for deep-frying

FOR THE SAUCE

1 lb boneless chicken breasts,
shredded

2 Tbsp light soy sauce

2 Tbsp Chinese rice wine or dry
sherry

3 Tbsp cornstarch

4 Tbsp vegetable oil

1 in gingerroot, peeled and
finely chopped

8 shiitake mushrooms,
shredded

12 water chestnuts, sliced

4 scallions, chopped into 1 in
lengths

salt and black pepper

1¾ cups chicken broth

1 tsp sesame oil

1 Tbsp tomato katsup

½ tsp sugar

3 Tbsp water

6 lettuce leaves, rinsed and
quartered

● Fill a wok or saucepan a quarter full of vegetable oil, and heat to 350°F. Deep-fry the rice vermicelli in small batches at a time. It will puff up in seconds. Drain on paper towels.

● Marinate the chicken in 1 tablespoon each of the soy sauce, rice wine, and cornstarch for 30 minutes. Heat 2 tablespoons of oil in a wok or skillet, and fry the chicken for 3–4 minutes. Set aside.

● Heat the remaining 2 tablespoons of the vegetable oil in the wok. Add the ginger and stir-fry for 30 seconds. Add the *shiitake* mushrooms, water chestnuts, scallions, and chicken, sprinkle with salt and pepper, then stir-fry for 1–2 minutes.

● Add the chicken broth, sesame oil, tomato katsup, sugar, and remaining soy sauce and rice wine, and bring to a boil. Combine the remaining cornstarch and water, then add to thicken the sauce. Stir well.

● To serve, pile the lettuce leaves onto a small plate. Put the crispy vermicelli onto four individual plates, and pour the chicken sauce over the top. When you eat, take one lettuce leaf and wrap some noodles and chicken sauce together in a bundle, then pop it into your mouth.

Thai Sweet Crispy Rice Vermicelli

SERVES 4

Although it requires a little more time than most noodle dishes, this dish is well worth the extra effort. It is essential that it is served as soon as it is ready as the vermicelli will become mushy if left for very long.

2 oz rice vermicelli, slightly crushed

vegetable oil for deep-frying

1 Tbsp vegetable oil

2 cloves garlic, finely chopped

2 shallots, finely chopped

12 tiger or jumbo shrimp with tails, peeled and deveined

4 Tbsp raw cashew nuts

FOR THE SAUCE

3 Tbsp palm or brown sugar

2 Tbsp freshly squeezed lemon juice

1 tsp vinegar

1 tsp light soy sauce

2 Tbsp tomato katsup

½ tsp chili powder

FOR THE GARNISH

2 lettuce leaves, halved

cilantro leaves

2 small tomato wedges

● Heat the oil in a wok or saucepan until very hot. Deep-fry the vermicelli for a few seconds until they puff up and become white. Drain on paper towels.

● Heat the oil in the wok or skillet. Add the garlic and shallots, and stir. Add the shrimp and cashew nuts, and stir-fry for about 2 minutes.

● Add the sugar, lemon juice, vinegar, soy sauce, katsup and chili powder, and simmer until the sauce thickens. Take out the shrimp, and set aside.

● Add the crispy vermicelli, and coat with the sauce. Put the vermicelli on a bed of lettuce on four plates. Garnish each serving with three shrimp, cilantro, and tomato wedges. Serve.

Crispy Vermicelli with Chicken and Mango

SERVES 4

A modern Chinese dish that looks set to become a great favorite. Fried vermicelli must be eaten as quickly as possible once it is ready.

5 oz rice vermicelli

vegetable oil for deep frying

1 egg white

3⅔ Tbsp cornstarch

1 lb boneless chicken breasts, sliced into bite-sized pieces

salt and black pepper

4 Tbsp vegetable oil

2 cloves garlic, finely chopped

1 in gingerroot, peeled and finely chopped

3 stalks celery, sliced diagonally

1 medium-sized onion, cubed

1 mango, cut into bite-sized pieces

2½ cups chicken broth

2 Tbsp Chinese rice wine or dry sherry

3 Tbsp light soy sauce

2½ Tbsp sugar

4 Tbsp water

● Fill a wok or saucepan a quarter full of oil, and heat to 350°F. Deep-fry the vermicelli in small batches only a few seconds until they turn white. Drain on paper towels.

● Mix the egg white and 2 teaspoons of the cornstarch in a bowl. Sprinkle the chicken with salt and black pepper, and coat thoroughly with the cornstarch mixture.

● Heat 2 tablespoons of the oil in a wok or skillet until very hot. Fry the chicken for about 2 minutes. When finished, discard the oil and clean the pan.

● Heat the remaining 2 tablespoons of oil in the wok. Stir-fry the garlic and ginger for 30 seconds before adding the celery, onion, and chicken. Stir-fry for a further 2–3 minutes.

● Add the chicken broth, rice wine, soy sauce, and sugar, then bring to a boil. Add the mango, season with salt and black pepper, and simmer for 1–2 minutes. Combine the remaining cornstarch with the water, and add to thicken the sauce.

● Divide the crispy vermicelli onto four individual plates, and lightly crush. Pour the sauce over the top just before serving.

Stir-fried Vermicelli with Vegetables

SERVES 4

1 Tbsp vegetable oil

1 clove garlic, finely chopped

1 carrot, thinly sliced

¼ cup water

2 oz pak choi or Chinese
   cabbage, shredded

½ celery stalk, shredded

3 Tbsp chicken broth

1 Tbsp oyster sauce

1 Tbsp fish sauce or 1 Tbsp light
   soy sauce and ½ tsp anchovy
   essence

1 level tsp sugar

freshly ground black pepper

4 oz rice vermicelli, soaked in
   warm water for 5 minutes
   and drained well

● Heat the oil in a wok over high heat and fry the garlic until golden-brown. Add the carrot and stir-fry for 1 minute.

● Add all the remaining ingredients, except the vermicelli, stirring gently. Cook for 2 minutes.

● Add the vermicelli and toss to combine all the ingredients. Stir for 1 minute. Serve in a large serving dish.

Sweet and Sour Pork on Crispy Vermicelli

SERVES 4

Perhaps the most popular Chinese dish in the West. It is equally at home with noodles as with rice.

5 oz rice vermicelli

vegetable oil for deep-frying

1 lb boneless belly of pork, skinned and cut into bite-sized pieces

1 Tbsp Chinese rice wine or dry sherry

1 Tbsp light soy sauce

3 Tbsp cornstarch

1 egg white

4–5 carrots, cut at random into bite-sized pieces

2 Tbsp vegetable oil

1 Tbsp sesame oil

1 medium-sized onion, cut into bite-sized pieces

1 green bell pepper, cut into bite-sized squares

FOR THE SAUCE

1¾ cups chicken broth

2⅔ Tbsp sugar

½ cup tomato katsup

1½ Tbsp light soy sauce

4 Tbsp Chinese rice wine or dry sherry

4 Tbsp vinegar

salt and black pepper

2 Tbsp cornstarch

3 Tbsp water

● Fill a wok or saucepan a quarter full of oil, and heat to 350°F. Separate the vermicelli into small portions. Deep-fry the vermicelli in several batches in the wok. They puff up in a few seconds, so be ready to take them out promptly. Drain on paper towels. Put the crispy vermicelli onto four individual plates, and lightly crush.

● Marinate the pork in the rice wine and soy sauce for 20–30 minutes. Mix 2 tablespoons of the cornstarch, the egg white, and 1 teaspoon of water together in a bowl, and coat the pork with the cornstarch mixture. Deep-fry the meat for about 4–5 minutes, or until golden brown. Drain on paper towels, then crush lightly and arrange on four plates.

● Cook the carrots in a pan of boiling water for about 15 minutes, then set aside. Heat 1 tablespoon

vegetable oil and 1 tablespoon sesame oil in the wok or skillet until very hot. Stir-fry the onion and green bell pepper for 1–2 minutes, add the carrots, and stir for a further minute.

● Add the chicken broth, sugar, tomato katsup, soy sauce, and rice wine, and bring to a boil. Add the vinegar, and season.

● Combine the cornstarch with the water, and stir well into the sauce. Add the pork. Scoop the sweet and sour pork onto the noodles, and serve immediately.

Thai Fried Vermicelli with Red Curry Paste

SERVES 4

Thai red curry paste is a result of the influence of Indian and Chinese cooking. The result is a novel and interesting combination of heat and sourness.

½ lb rice vermicelli

3 Tbsp vegetable oil

½ lb bean curd, diced

3 cloves garlic, chopped

4 oz canned bamboo shoots

3 cups bean sprouts

¼ lb mustard greens or fresh spinach

2 Tbsp Thai red curry paste

6 Tbsp fish sauce

3 Tbsp light soy sauce

1 Tbsp palm or brown sugar

FOR THE GARNISH

cilantro leaves

4 lime wedges

● Soak the rice vermicelli in warm water for 3–5 minutes. Rinse, and drain.

● Heat the oil in a wok or skillet, and fry the bean curd until golden brown. Add the garlic, bamboo shoots, bean sprouts, and mustard greens or spinach, stirring each time you add the ingredients.

● Add the red curry paste, fish sauce, soy sauce, and brown sugar; then stir well. Add the vermicelli, and stir until the noodles are well coated with sauce.

● Put the vermicelli onto four plates, and garnish with cilantro leaves and lime wedges. Serve at once.

Singapore Spicy Noodles

SERVES 4

The return home of itinerant Chinese over the years has resulted in a gradual increase in the popularity of curried dishes in China, especially in the south-western provinces. Although the origins of this dish lie in India, Singapore has been the cultural melting pot where most Chinese migrants have come into contact with Indian cuisine.

½ lb rice vermicelli

4 tbsp vegetable oil

2 cloves garlic, finely chopped

½ in gingerroot, peeled and finely chopped

1 red chili, chopped

¼ lb peeled shrimp

6 small squid, cleaned and sliced

3 cups bean sprouts

¼ lb spinach

½ lb Chinese barbecued pork, thinly sliced

2 eggs, beaten

3 scallions, roughly chopped

⅔ tsp salt

a pinch of chili powder

black pepper

2–3 tsp hot curry powder

1 Tbsp light soy sauce

2 tsp sugar

⅔ cup chicken broth

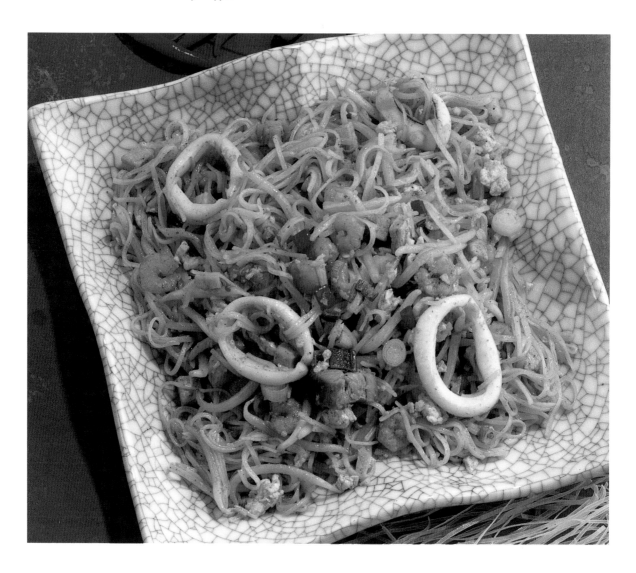

● Soak the rice vermicelli in warm water for 3 minutes, or according to the instructions on the package. Rinse with cold water, and drain.

● Heat 3 tablespoons of the oil in a wok or skillet until very hot. Add the garlic, ginger, and red chile, and stir-fry for 30 seconds.

● Add the shrimp and squid, and stir for another minute. Then add the bean sprouts, spinach, and pork, and stir-fry for 1–2 minutes.

● Make a well in the center, add the beaten egg, and scramble lightly. Quickly add the remaining tablespoon of oil and the rice vermicelli, and mix all the ingredients well.

● Add the scallions, salt, chili powder, black pepper, curry powder, soy sauce, sugar, and chicken broth. Stir until the sauce is absorbed. Put the noodles onto four plates, and serve at once.

Pork and Pineapple in Honey Sauce on Crispy Vermicelli

SERVES 4

Another dish with a sweet and sour theme. The honey and pineapple complement the pork very well.

5 oz rice vermicelli

vegetable oil for deep-frying

1 lb boneless belly of pork, skinned and cut into bite-sized pieces

salt and black pepper

1 Tbsp Chinese rice wine or dry sherry

2½ Tbsp cornstarch

2 Tbsp water

FOR THE SAUCE

2 Tbsp vegetable oil

1 in gingerroot, peeled and finely chopped

1 clove garlic, finely chopped

2 medium-sized onions, cubed

4–5 carrots, sliced

4 pineapple rings (canned), chopped

salt and black pepper

1¾ cups chicken broth

2 Tbsp honey

2 tsp brown sugar

1 tsp light soy sauce

4 Tbsp pineapple juice (from the can)

2 Tbsp cornstarch mixed with 3 Tbsp water

● Fill a wok or saucepan a quarter full of vegetable oil, and heat to 350°F. Deep-fry the rice vermicelli in small batches. They will puff up in a few seconds. Drain on paper towels.

● Sprinkle the pork with salt and black pepper, then marinate in the rice wine for 15 minutes. Combine the cornstarch and water, and coat the pork with the paste. Deep-fry the pork until lightly browned. Drain on paper towels.

● Heat the oil in the cleaned wok or skillet. Stir-fry the ginger and garlic for 30 seconds. Add the onions and carrots, and stir-fry for about 2 minutes. Add the pineapple, lightly sprinkle with salt and pepper, and stir.

● Add chicken broth, honey, sugar, soy sauce, and pineapple juice. When the sauce is boiling, add the combined cornstarch and water to thicken the sauce. Add the pork, and mix.

● Put the crispy vermicelli onto four plates, then lightly crush. Pour on sauce, and serve immediately.

Indonesian Fried Vermicelli with Squid

SERVES 4

Squid is a great favorite throughout Asia, and nowhere more so than in Indonesia. The flavorings used here are distinct, but without being so powerful as to cloak the taste of the seafood.

½ lb rice vermicelli

3 Tbsp vegetable oil

1 in gingerroot, peeled and finely chopped

4 shallots, chopped finely

8 small squid, cleaned and sliced

4–5 small carrots, cut into matchsticks

2½ cups bean sprouts

¼ lb fresh spinach, chopped

1 small red chile, chopped

1 tsp ground paprika

3 Tbsp light soy sauce

salt and black pepper

4 tomato wedges

sliced cucumber

● Soak the rice vermicelli in warm water for 3 minutes, or according to the instructions on the package. Rinse, and drain. Heat 2 tablespoons of the oil in a wok or skillet, and stir-fry the ginger and shallots for 30 seconds. Add the squid, and stir until the squid turns white.

● Add the carrots, bean sprouts, spinach, and chile, and stir for 1–2 minutes. Add the remaining tablespoon of oil, the vermicelli, paprika, and soy sauce, and stir well.

● Taste, and add the salt and black pepper if required. Put the vermicelli onto four plates, and garnish with the tomato wedges and sliced cucumber. Serve at once while still hot.

Stir-fried Udon with Seafood

SERVES 4

*Stir-frying coaxes maximum flavor out of the seafood ingredients, and gives the **udon** noodles a smooth, slippery texture in this filling dish.*

14 oz dried or 1¼ lb parboiled fresh *udon*

3 Tbsp sunflower oil

6 oz squid, cleaned and sliced

6 oz peeled shrimp

4 scallions, chopped roughly

3 cups bean sprouts

10 oz *shimeji* mushrooms, roots cut off and separated, or 15 *shiitake* mushrooms, sliced

4 tsp dried *wakame* seaweed, soaked in hot water

4 Tbsp bonito flakes

4 Tbsp Japanese soy sauce

salt and black pepper

● Boil plenty of water in a large pan, and add the *udon*. Cook for 7–15 minutes for dried, or 3 minutes for parboiled fresh *udon*. Rinse with cold water, and drain well.

● Heat the oil in a wok or skillet until very hot. Stir-fry the squid and shrimp for 2 minutes. Add the scallions, bean sprouts, mushrooms, and *wakame*, and stir-fry for about 2 minutes.

● Add the *udon, bonito* flakes, and soy sauce, and stir. Season with salt and pepper. Stir for another minute, and serve at once.

Chilled Udon with Fermented Soybeans

SERVES 4

Fermented soybeans, or **natto,** *are not to everyone's taste. Even in Japan, where it originated,* **natto** *is very much a "love it or hate it" food, despite it being a nutritious source of protein.*

14 oz dried or 1¼ lb parboiled
  fresh *udon*

2¼ cups dipping broth, chilled

FOR THE TOPPING

6 okra

salt

½ lb Japanese fermented
  soybeans (*natto*)

scant ⅓ cup *bonito* flakes

1 scallion, chopped

1 tsp hot prepared mustard

4 tsp Japanese soy sauce

½ sheet *nori* seaweed, shredded

● Remove the tiny hairs on the okra; the easiest way to do this is to first sprinkle the salt over the okra, and then roll them over on a chopping board. Blanch in the boiling water for 1 minute, then drain and chop.

● Mix the okra, *natto, bonito* flakes, scallion, mustard, and soy sauce together in a bowl.

● Bring plenty of water to a boil in a large pan, and add the *udon.* Cook according to the instructions on the package. Rinse and drain. Divide the *udon* into four bowls.

● Pile the *natto* mixture on top of the *udon.* Gently pour the dipping broth into each bowl, sprinkle with *nori,* then serve immediately.

Stir-fried Udon with Miso Sauce

SERVES 4

This is another nouveau *stir-fried* udon *dish. The* **udon** *are coated in a salty sauce, making a very appetizing fast meal.*

14 oz dried or 1¼ lb parboiled fresh *udon*

½ lb green cabbage

½ lb fresh green beans

3 Tbsp sunflower oil

½ lb rump steak, sliced on a slant into bite-sized pieces

1 small red bell pepper, chopped into bite-sized pieces

10 shiitake mushrooms, quartered

a pinch of salt and chili powder

2 Tbsp red *miso* paste

2 Tbsp Japanese soy sauce

2 Tbsp *mirin*

1 scallion, chopped

● Boil plenty of water in a large pan, and cook dried *udon* for 7–15 minutes or parboiled fresh *udon* for 3 minutes. Rinse, and drain.

● Blanch the cabbage leaves and green beans for 2 minutes. Rinse under cold water. Cut the cabbage leaves into bite-sized pieces, and halve the fresh green beans.

● Heat the oil in a wok or skillet until very hot. Add the beef, and fry for 2–3 minutes. Add the cabbage, green beans, and shiitake mushrooms, and sprinkle on salt and chili powder. Stir-fry for another 2–3 minutes.

● Mix the *miso*, soy sauce, and *mirin* together in a bowl. Add the *udon* and *miso* mixture to the pan, and stir-fry for about 1 minute. Put the *udon* onto four plates. Sprinkle with chopped scallions, and serve.

Chilled Soba with Deep-fried Mackerel

SERVES 4

Mackerel is one of the great mainstays of the Japanese diet. It is not only eaten raw as **sushi** *and* **sashimi**, *but is incorporated in many Japanese cooked dishes, as here.*

14 oz dried *soba*

2¼ cups dipping broth

FOR THE TOPPING

vegetable oil for deep frying

8 Tbsp flour

½ cup water

1 lb mackerel, gutted, filleted, and cut into 4 pieces per person

¾ lb white radish, peeled and grated

2 scallions, chopped

alfalfa sprouts to garnish

● Heat the vegetable oil in a saucepan to 350°F. Mix the flour and water lightly in a bowl to a lumpy consistency to make a batter, then dip the mackerel pieces in. Deep fry for about 3 minutes, or until golden brown.

● Bring plenty of water to a boil in a large saucepan. Add the *soba*, and cook for 5–6 minutes. Drain, and rinse well under cold running water. Drain again, and then divide into four portions.

● Place four pieces of deep-fried mackerel in each bowl. Place the grated white radish in the center and garnish with the scallions and sprouts. Pour the dipping broth over the top, and serve immediately.

Stir-fried Udon with Miso Sauce

Cold Noodles with Vegetables

SERVES 4

This is a vegetarian version of **kuksu**, *a popular noodle dish, which is served surrounded by small bowls of condiments, relishes and side dishes, the most important of which are soy sauce, Korean chili powder, and spicy pickles. If you are unable to buy* **son myon** *noodles, which are available from Korean food stores, use vermicelli and cook according to the directions on the package.*

3 Tbsp soy sauce

1 Tbsp sugar

1 Tbsp sesame oil

5 dried Chinese black mushrooms, soaked for 30 minutes in hot water

4 oz bean sprouts

1 lb young fresh spinach leaves, stalks removed

scant 2 cups vegetable broth

8 oz *son myon* noodles or vermicelli

green part of 1 scallion, diagonally sliced

1 Tbsp crushed toasted sesame seeds

very small pinch of Korean chili powder, or cayenne pepper mixed with paprika

● Mix together 2 tablespoons of the soy sauce, 2 teaspoons of the sugar, and the sesame oil.

● Drain the mushrooms, and cut out and discard the stalks and any woody parts. Thinly slice the caps.

● Bring 3 cups water to a boil in a saucepan and add the remaining sugar. Put the bean sprouts into a strainer and lower the strainer into the water. Return the water to a boil and cook the bean sprouts for 20 seconds. Remove the strainer of bean sprouts from the water and rinse them under running cold water. Leave to drain completely.

● Add the spinach to the saucepan and boil for 2 minutes or until wilted. Drain, rinse under running cold water and drain again.

● Pour the broth into a saucepan. Add the remaining soy sauce and bring to a boil. Add the noodles and boil for about 3 minutes until just tender. Quickly remove the noodles from the water using a slotted spoon and put into a warm serving dish. Add the spinach and mushrooms to the liquid, and heat through, then quickly remove. Season with the soy sauce mixture and pile onto the noodles. Keep warm.

● Heat the bean sprouts in the broth, then remove and quickly season with the remaining soy sauce mixture. Place on top of the spinach and mushrooms. Pour the remaining broth around the noodles and sprinkle with the scallion, sesame seeds, and a little chili powder or cayenne mixed with paprika. Serve immediately while still hot.

Chilled Udon with Five Toppings

SERVES 4

Dried, medium-sized udon is preferable for this dish if you can obtain them. A nonstick omelet pan will help you to prepare the egg sheets, which should resemble thin pancakes.

14 oz dried or 1¼ lb parboiled
  fresh *udon*

2¼ cups dipping broth, chilled

FOR THE TOPPINGS

2 eggs

2 tsp sugar

1 Tbsp vegetable oil

8 okra

salt

4 tsp dried *wakame* seaweed,
  soaked in warm water and
  drained

8 chunks imitation crabmeat,
  torn into shreds

handful alfalfa sprouts

● Boil plenty of water in a pan. Add the *udon* and cook 8–15 minutes for dried or 3 minutes for fresh noodles. Rinse, and put the *udon* into four shallow bowls. Set aside.

● Mix the eggs and sugar together in a bowl. Heat the oil in a skillet, and pour in a third of the egg mixture. When the egg starts bubbling, turn it over. (The method is the same as for making thin pancakes.) Repeat this and make two more egg sheets. Let them cool, and then cut in half and then into shreds.

● Sprinkle the salt over the okra on a chopping board, then roll the okra with salt to remove the fine down. Boil some water in a pan, and blanch the okra for just a minute before chopping finely.

● Arrange the shredded egg, okra, *wakame*, crabmeat shreds, and sprouts in separate groups on top of the *udon* portions.

● Just before eating, pour the chilled dipping broth over the noodles.

Chilled Udon with Eggplant and Miso Sauce

SERVES 4

Miso *sauce is a versatile ingredient, which can be paired with almost any vegetable you care to mention. Here it is combined with eggplant, which should be soaked in salted water to remove any bitterness.*

2¼ cups *dashi* broth

4 Tbsp vinegar

14 oz dried or 1¼ lb parboiled fresh *udon*

FOR THE TOPPING

1 Tbsp sunflower oil

2 cloves garlic, finely chopped

½ in ginger root, peeled and finely chopped

8 scallions, chopped

½ lb eggplant, cut into matchstick-sized pieces and soaked in salted water

1 small green bell pepper, cut into matchstick-sized pieces

a pinch of salt

4 Tbsp *miso* paste

1 Tbsp Japanese soy sauce

2 tsp sugar

3 Tbsp Japanese rice wine

● Mix the *dashi* broth and vinegar, then refrigerate. Heat the oil in a skillet. Add the garlic, ginger, and scallion, and fry for 1 minute.

● Add the eggplant, green bell pepper, and salt, and stir-fry for 4–5 minutes, or until the eggplant is softened. Add the *miso* paste, soy sauce, sugar, and wine, and stir well. Set aside.

● Boil plenty of water in a pan, and add the *udon*. Cook for 4–5 minutes for fresh or 8–15 minutes for dried *udon*, or according to the instructions on the package. Rinse with cold water. Drain and divide into four bowls.

● Place the eggplant mixture on the *udon*, and pour the broth over the top. Serve immediately.

Chilled Soba with Shredded White Radish

SERVES 4

*Japanese **daikon** is the ideal ingredient for this dish, but is hard to come by unless there happens to be a Japanese food store nearby. The European white radish, known as **mooli**, makes an acceptable stand-in, or, failing that, try ordinary radishes.*

14 oz dried *soba*

¾ lb white radish, peeled and shredded

handful alfalfa sprouts

1 sheet *nori* seaweed, shredded

3 cups dipping broth

FOR THE GARNISH

2 scallions, chopped

1 in gingerroot, grated

2 *myoga* (optional), shredded

● Bring plenty of water to a boil in a large saucepan. Add the *soba*, and cook for 5–6 minutes. Rinse and cool in cold water. Drain.

● Mix the *soba, daikon*, and sprouts well in a bowl. Divide into individual serving bowls, and sprinkle with the *nori*.

● Serve with the chilled dipping broth and garnishes on a separate small dish.

Chilled Soba with Nameko Mushrooms

SERVES 4

A light, refreshing lunch or part of a dinner that is quickly prepared and easily digested.

14 oz dried *soba*

approx 14 oz canned *nameko* mushrooms

¾ lb white radish, peeled and grated

½ sheet *nori* seaweed, shredded

2¼ cups dipping broth, chilled

● Boil plenty of water in a large pan and add the *soba*. Cook for 5–6 minutes, or according to the instructions on the package. Rinse with plenty of cold water, and drain well. Divide the *soba* into four bowls.

● Mix the mushrooms and white radish together in a bowl. Pile them onto the *soba*, and sprinkle with the *nori*. Gently pour the chilled dipping broth over the top just before serving.

Chilled Soba with Soured Plum Sauce

SERVES 4

The bite of the soured plums in the dipping broth gives an extra zest to this cold noodle dish.

4 scallions, sliced

3 boneless chicken breasts

12 okra

salt

14 oz dried *soba*

FOR THE SOUR PLUM SAUCE

4 large soured plums, seeded and chopped finely

2¼ cups dipping broth

● Soak the sliced scallions in cold water until ready for use. Cook the chicken in boiling water for about 15 minutes, or until cooked. When cooled, pull the meat into small strips with your fingers.

● Sprinkle the okra with salt, then roll each on a chopping board to remove the fine hairs. Cook for around 1 minute in boiling water, then cut into ½-inch slices.

● Put the soured plums into a mortar. Add a little broth and grind roughly into a thin paste. Return the mixture to the dipping broth, and then chill in the refrigerator until needed.

● Bring plenty of water to a boil in a large saucepan. Add the *soba*, and cook for 5–6 minutes. Drain, and rinse well under cold running water. Drain again. Mix the *soba* with the scallions in a bowl, and then divide into four portions.

● Add the chicken and okra. Pour the soured plum dipping broth over the top, and serve at once.

Chilled Soba
with Nameko Mushrooms

Chilled Egg Noodles with Chicken and Peanut Sauce

SERVES 4

A well-loved Chinese noodle dish. It can be prepared with any type of peanut butter, depending on your preference for smooth or crunchy.

1 lb boneless chicken breasts

1 lb fresh thin egg noodles

2 tsp sesame oil

1- in piece cucumber, thinly sliced diagonally, then cut into long matchsticks

FOR THE PEANUT SAUCE

8 Tbsp peanut butter

6 Tbsp sugar

4 Tbsp vinegar

5 Tbsp chicken broth

3 Tbsp light soy sauce

1 Tbsp dark soy sauce

4 tsp sesame oil

3–4 tsp chili oil

● Put the chicken in a large pan of water. Bring to a boil and simmer for 20 minutes, skimming off the scum from time to time. The poaching water can be put toward making broth. When the chicken is cooled, shred with your fingers or with a knife.

● Mix the peanut butter, sugar, vinegar, chicken broth, soy sauce, sesame oil, and chili oil together in a bowl.

● Bring a large pan of water to a boil, and add the noodles. Cook for 3 minutes, rinse, and drain. Toss the noodles in the sesame oil, then arrange them on four individual plates.

● Place a quarter of the shredded chicken and cucumber onto each serving of noodles. Pour the sesame sauce over the top of the shredded chicken, and serve immediately.

Chilled Egg Noodles with Chicken and Pepper Salami

SERVES 4

Pepper salami is not an authentic topping, but it really goes well with chilled noodles.

1 lb fresh or ¾ lb dried thin egg noodles

1 Tbsp sesame oil

FOR THE SAUCE

generous 1 cup chicken broth

½ cup light soy sauce

4 Tbsp sugar

½ cup vinegar

4 tsp sesame oil

2 Tbsp squeezed ginger juice

FOR THE TOPPING

2 boneless chicken breasts

2 eggs, beaten

2 tsp sugar

1 Tbsp vegetable oil

5 in piece cucumber, thinly sliced diagonally and cut into long matchsticks

8 slices pepper salami, cut into long matchsticks

4 tsp red pickled ginger (optional)

4 tsp toasted sesame seeds

● Boil plenty of water in a pan, and add the noodles. Cook for 3 minutes, and rinse with cold water. Drain, then toss the noodles in 1 tablespoon sesame oil. Arrange on four shallow dishes.

● To prepare the sauce, heat the broth, soy sauce, and sugar in a pan, and simmer for 3 minutes. Turn off the heat and add the vinegar, 4 teaspoons sesame oil, and the ginger juice. Mix well before refrigerating.

● Boil the chicken in a pan for about 15–20 minutes. Let it cool, then pull into shreds with your fingers or a knife. Set aside. Keep the water in the pan as stock for another use.

● Mix the beaten egg and sugar together in a bowl. Heat 1 teaspoon of oil in an omelet pan, and pour a third of the egg mixture into it. When the egg is half set, turn it over. Repeat this to make two more thin omelets, using fresh oil each time. When the omelets are cooled, cut them in half and shred.

● Arrange the chicken, egg, cucumber, and pepper salami on the noodles. Put the red pickled ginger (if using) on top, and sprinkle with the sesame seeds. Pour the chilled sauce over prior to eating.

Chilled Somen with Pork

SERVES 4

An invigorating combination of chilled noodles with pork and broccoli stir-fried in a hot sauce.

14 oz *somen*

2¼ cups dipping broth

FOR THE TOPPING

1½ Tbsp vegetable oil

4 cloves garlic, sliced

¾ lb lean pork, sliced on a slant
  into bite-sized pieces

1 Tbsp *mirin*

2½ Tbsp soy sauce

2 tsp chile bean sauce

8 small broccoli florets

1 pinch of salt

● Heat the oil in a pan, then add the garlic and fry for about 1 minute. Add the meat, and fry for a further 2–3 minutes. Then add the *mirin*, soy sauce, and chile bean sauce, and stir-fry for 2 minutes.

● Bring plenty of water to a boil in a large saucepan. Add the *somen*, and cook for 1–2 minutes. Drain, and rinse well under cold running water. Drain again, and then divide into four portions.

● Meanwhile, bring a pan of water to a boil, add a pinch of salt, and boil the broccoli for 1–2 minutes. Drain and rinse.

● Place the meat and broccoli in the four bowls. Serve immediately after pouring in the dipping broth.

Chilled Somen with Sesame Dipping Broth

SERVES 4

Fried vegetables make the chilled **somen** *more nutritious and filling, while the combinaton of the sesame sauce and dipping broth imparts a rich and delicate flavor. It is a good idea to make the dipping broth in advance; it will keep in the refrigerator for a few days.*

14 oz *somen*

**FOR THE SESAME
DIPPING BROTH**

2¼ cups dipping broth

½ in gingerroot, peeled and
  squeezed for the juice

5 Tbsp sesame sauce

2 scallions, finely chopped

FOR THE TOPPING

sunflower oil for frying

¾ lb eggplant, thinly sliced and
  soaked in salted water

4 large shiitake mushrooms

1 small green bell pepper

4 *myoga* (optional), finely
  chopped

● Heat the dipping broth, and add the ginger juice and sesame sauce. When it comes to a boil, add the scallions and turn off the heat. Refrigerate.

● Bring plenty of water to a boil in a pan, and add the *somen*. When the water returns to a boil, add half a cup of cold water. The second time the water comes back to a boil, the *somen* will be ready. Rinse with the cold water, and drain. Put the *somen* onto four plates.

● Heat 2 tablespoons of oil in a wok or skillet. Fry the eggplant slices first, then the mushrooms and bell pepper. If you need more oil, add another 2 tablespoons.

● Place the eggplant, mushrooms, and bell pepper beside the *somen*, and, if using, put the sliced *myoga* on top. Serve immediately with small bowls of the sesame dipping broth.

Chilled Somen with Pork

Side dishes

Use these recipes to create a wide range of side dishes. Allow the flavor of fresh ingredients to dominate the dish by combining one or two vegetables with herbs or seasoning, but taking care not to let the flavor become too overpowering. The dishes include satisfying rice, grain, and bean ensembles, as well as light vegetable mixtures. The secret to successful Asian dishes is that the ingredients should be perfectly fresh and only lightly cooked, and all the recipes include tips on cooking times and presentation.

Five-spice Bean Curd

SERVES 4

4 cakes bean curd

3 Tbsp light soy sauce

2 Tbsp dark soy sauce

1 tsp salt

1 Tbsp white or brown sugar

3 Tbsp rice wine or dry sherry

2–3 scallions

2–3 slices gingerroot

2 tsp five-spice powder

● Place the bean curd in a saucepan and cover with cold water. Bring to a boil, cover and cook over a high heat for 10 minutes. By then the bean curd will resemble a beehive in texture.

● Reduce the heat and add the soy sauces, salt, sugar, wine, scallions, ginger root, and five-spice powder. Bring to the boil gently under a cover and simmer for 30 minutes. Turn off the heat and leave to cool.

● Remove the bean curd and cut it into small slices or strips. Serve them either on their own or as part of a mixed hors d'oeuvre.

Szechwan Bean Curd

SERVES 4

¼ oz dried wood ears or dried Chinese mushrooms

3 cakes bean curd

1–2 leeks or 2–3 scallions

3 Tbsp oil

1 tsp salted black beans

1 Tbsp chile bean paste

2 Tbsp rice wine or dry sherry

1 Tbsp light soy sauce

1 tsp cornstarch mixed with 1 Tbsp cold water

Szechwan pepper, freshly ground to garnish

● Soak the wood ears in water for 20–25 minutes, rinse them clean, discard any hard roots and then drain. If you use dried mushrooms, they should be soaked in hot or warm water for at least 30–35 minutes. Squeeze them dry, throw out the hard stalks and cut into small pieces, retaining the water for later.

● Cut the bean curd into ½ in square cubes. Blanch them in a pan of boiling water for 2–3 minutes, remove and drain.

● Cut the leeks or scallions into short lengths.

● Heat the oil in a hot wok until it smokes and stir-fry the leeks or scallions and the wood ears or mushrooms for about 1 minute. Add the salted black beans, crush them with the scooper or spatula and blend well. Now add the bean curd, the chile bean paste, rice wine or sherry and soy sauce and continue stirring to blend. Add a little water and cook for 3–4 minutes more.

● Finally add the cornflour and water mixture to thicken the gravy. Serve hot with freshly ground Szechwan pepper as garnish.

Fu-yung Bean Curd

SERVES 4

In most Chinese restaurants, fu yung *means "omelet", but strictly speaking, it should mean scrambled egg whites with a creamy texture.*

1 cake bean curd

4 egg whites

1 romaine lettuce heart

2 oz green peas

1 scallion, finely chopped

½ tsp gingerroot, finely chopped

1 tsp salt

1 Tbsp cornstarch mixed with 2 Tbsp water

4 Tbsp milk

oil for deep-frying

1 tsp sesame seed oil

● Cut the bean curd into long, thin strips and blanch in a pan of salted boiling water to harden. Remove and drain.

● Lightly beat the egg whites. Add the cornstarch mixture and milk.

● Wash and separate the lettuce heart. If you use frozen peas, make sure they are thoroughly defrosted.

● Wait for the bean curd to cook and then coat with the egg whites, cornstarch, and milk mixture.

● Heat the oil in a wok or deep-fryer until it is very hot. Turn off the heat and let the oil cool a bit before adding the bean curd coated with the egg whites and cornstarch mixture. Cook for about 1–1½ minutes and then scoop out with a slotted spoon and drain.

● Pour off the excess oil leaving about one tablespoon in the wok. Increase the heat and stir-fry the lettuce heart with a pinch of salt. Remove and set aside on a serving dish.

● Heat another tablespoon of oil in the wok and add the finely chopped scallion, and gingerroot followed by the peas, salt, and a little water. When the mixture starts to boil, add the bean curd strips. Blend well, add the sesame seed oil, and serve on the bed of lettuce.

Green Peppers and Deep-fried Bean Curd

SERVES 4

1 Tbsp ground nut or corn oil

2 thin slices gingerroot, peeled

4 large leaves Chinese celery cabbage, cut into 1 in lengths

1 large green bell pepper, seeded and sliced

salt

oil for deep-frying

4 x 1 in square cakes bean curd, drained and cut into rectangles, 3 per cake (use paper towel to drain)

FOR THE SAUCE

1 tsp potato flour

5 Tbsp mushroom water

2 Tbsp oyster sauce

2 tsp thick soy sauce

2 Tbsp vegetable oil

1 clove garlic, finely chopped

2 scallions, cut into 1 in sections, white and green parts separated

4 large dried Chinese mushrooms, soaked, squeezed, and cut into thin strips (water to be reserved)

● Prepare the sauce by mixing together the potato flour, mushroom water, oyster saucer and soy sauce. Heat a wok and add 2 tablespoons oil and swirl around. Add the garlic, letting it sizzle and then add the white scallion and then the Chinese mushrooms. Stir for about 30 seconds and pour in the potato flour mixture. Lower the heat and continue to stir until the sauce thickens. Remove from heat.

● Heat 1 tablespoon oil in a wok over a high heat until it starts to smoke. Add the ginger and when it starts to sizzle, add the cabbage and green bell pepper. Toss for about 30 seconds. Season with a little salt, lower the heat and continue to cook, covered for a further 2 minutes. Remove and put into an earthenware pot or saucepan.

● Now half fill the wok with oil, heat to 200°F and lower the bean curd into the oil, one piece at a time, and deep-fry for 4 minutes or until golden-brown, turning over from time to time. Remove with a large strainer and drain on kitchen paper.

● Lay the bean curd on the cabbage in the pot and add the green spring onion. Heat the sauce and pour this over the bean curd. Heat the pot for 2 minutes and serve.

Japanese-style Omelet

SERVES 2

Often served for breakfast in Japan, this dish requires a little more skill and patience than a Western omelet, but the delicious result is well worth the extra effort. It is essential to use a nonstick skillet.

2 eggs	½ Tbsp *dashi*
½ Tbsp superfine sugar	pinch of salt
½ Tbsp soy sauce	vegetable oil, for frying

● Break the eggs into a bowl, add the sugar, soy sauce, *dashi* broth, and salt and mix well. Heat the oil in a nonstick skillet over a low heat. Pour one-quarter of the egg mixture into the skillet.

● Just before the surface of the egg starts to get firm, carefully flip over the edge and roll up. Store on one side of the pan.

● Holding up the rolled omelet with a fish slice or chopstick, add a second quarter of the egg mixture, making sure that it spreads beneath the already cooked roll.

● Again, just before the egg begins to firm, roll around the completed roll and store on the other side of the pan. Repeat this process with the two remaining quarters of egg mixture. Cool before cutting into 1 in lengths. When serve as a side dish, sprinkle with soy sauce.

Stuffed Omelet

SERVES 4

This is a rapidly made lunchtime dish, more easily available in markets than in restaurants.

¼ cup peanut or corn oil

½ cup ground pork

3 Tbsp tomatoes, finely diced

3 Tbsp peas

2 Tbsp green bell pepper, finely diced

2 Tbsp onion, finely diced

½ Tbsp sugar

1 tsp fish sauce

¼ tsp ground white pepper

¼ tsp black soy sauce

3 eggs, beaten

FOR THE GARNISH

3 Tbsp cilantro leaves

finely sliced red chile

● Heat half the oil in a skillet or wok over high heat and fry the pork lightly for about 2 minutes. Add all the remaining ingredients, except for the eggs, and the rest of oil. Fry until fairly thick, about 5–8 minutes, then set aside.

● Heat a shallow nonstick or good omelet pan, add a drop of the remaining oil and pour in enough egg to thinly cover the base. Brown the omelet lightly on both sides, flipping over half-way through cooking. Place a spoon of pork mixture in the center, fold two opposite sides toward the center and then fold in the remaining two sides so that it resembles a square.

● Flip onto a serving plate and repeat until all the egg and pork mixture is used up. Garnish with cilantro leaves and finely sliced red chile. Serve accompanied by rice.

Hot and Sour Cabbage

SERVES 4

1½ lb white cabbage

10 Szechwan peppercorns

5 small dried red chile peppers

3 Tbsp oil

2 Tbsp soy sauce

1½ Tbsp vinegar

1½ Tbsp sugar

1½ tsp salt

1 tsp sesame seed oil

● Choose a round, pale green cabbage with a firm heart—never use loose-leafed cabbage. Wash in cold water and cut the leaves into small pieces the size of a matchbox. Cut the chiles into small bits. Mix the soy sauce, vinegar, sugar, and salt to make the sauce.

● Heat the oil in a preheated wok until it starts to smoke. Add the peppercorns and the red chiles and a few seconds later the cabbage. Stir for about 1½ minutes until it starts to go limp.

● Pour in the prepared sauce and continue stirring for a short while to allow the sauce to blend in. Add the sesame seed oil just before serving. This dish is delicious both hot and cold.

Simmered Cabbage

SERVES 2

Japanese cabbage has a soft texture, and it is best to discard, or use for another recipe, the tougher, outer leaves of the cabbage and use only the inner leaves for this dish. Try not to overcook the cabbage or it will become limp. The leaves should be cooked but still have some crunch left in them.

6½ oz cabbage leaves, cut into
   1 in squares

2 rashers of unsmoked bacon,
   cut into 1 in lengths

1¼ cups *dashi* broth

2 tsp soy sauce

2 tsp vegetable oil

● Heat the oil in a pan and fry the bacon over a low heat until cooked.

● Add the cabbage and fry, stirring, for 2 minutes.

● Add the *dashi* broth and soy sauce. Simmer, covered for 10 minutes, or until the cabbage has softened. Stir occasionally. Serve as a side dish.

Chinese Cabbage and Mushrooms

SERVES 4

6–8 dried Chinese mushrooms

1 lb Chinese cabbage leaves

3 Tbsp oil

1 tsp salt

1 tsp sugar

1 Tbsp soy sauce

1 tsp sesame seed oil

● Soak the mushrooms in warm water for about 20 minutes. Squeeze them dry and discard the stalks. Keep the water. Cut each mushroom in half or into quarters depending on the size. Cut the cabbage leaves into pieces about the size of a large postage stamp.

● Heat the oil in a wok, add the cabbage and the mushrooms, and stir-fry until soft. Add the salt, sugar, and soy sauce, and cook for a further 1½ minutes. Mix in some of the water in which the mushrooms were cooked and the sesame seed oil.

Spicy Cabbage—Szechwan Style

SERVES 4

1 lb white cabbage

2 tsp salt

3–4 dried hot chile peppers, soaked, and finely chopped

3 scallions, finely chopped

2 tsp gingerroot, finely chopped

2 Tbsp sesame seed oil

2 Tbsp sugar

4 Tbsp water

2 Tbsp vinegar

● Discard the outer tough leaves of the cabbage and cut the tender heart into thin slices. Sprinkle with salt and let stand for 3–4 hours. Pour off the excess water and dry the cabbage thoroughly. Place it in a bowl or a deep dish.

● Heat the sesame seed oil in a pan until very hot. Add the finely chopped chiles, scallions and ginger root. Stir for a few seconds and then add the sugar and water. Continue stirring to dissolve the sugar. Add the vinegar and bring the mixture to a boil.

● Remove the pan from the heat and allow the sauce to cool slightly before pouring it over the cabbage. Cover the bowl or plate and leave to stand for 3–4 hours before serving.

Salted Cabbage and Cucumber

SERVES 2

This quickly prepared side dish makes a superb partner to fresh cooked white rice. A sharp knife will help you with the cucumber.

4 oz green cabbage (preferably the softer, inner leaves)

1½ in cucumber, halved lengthwise

1 tsp salt

1 small red chile, seeded and finely chopped

● Cut the stalks out of the cabbage leaves, then slice the leaves lengthwise, before cutting into ½ in widths. Slice the two halves of the cucumber finely.

● Put the cabbage and cucumber in a bowl and sprinkle with the salt. Leave for 30 minutes, then squeeze out any excess liquid from the vegetables with your hands.

● Add the chile and mix well. Leave for 5 minutes.

● Sprinkle with soy sauce just before serving.

Carrot Fritters

SERVES 2–4

Any of the dipping sauces in this book can be served to accompany these carrot slices.

2 carrots, thinly sliced diagonally

4 Tbsp all-purpose flour

1 large egg, beaten

vegetable oil for frying

sesame dipping sauce

● Coat the carrot slices lightly and evenly in the flour, then dip in beaten egg.

● Heat a ¼-inch layer of oil in a skillet. Add the carrot slices and fry in a single layer until golden brown on both sides. Using a slotted spoon, transfer the carrot slices to paper towels to drain. Serve hot with a dipping sauce.

Stir-fried Broccoli

SERVES 4

9 oz broccoli

3 Tbsp oil

1 tsp salt

1 tsp sugar

2 Tbsp water

● Cut the broccoli into small pieces and remove the rough skin from the stalks.

● Heat the oil in a wok until hot and stir-fry the broccoli for about 1–1½ minutes.

● Add the salt, sugar, and water and cook for a further 2 minutes. Serve hot.

Chinese Leaves and Cockles in Mustard and Soy Sauce

SERVES 2

Cockles are not very common in Japan, and clams are usually used for this dish, but cockles go so well with the other ingredients that they make an excellent and economical substitute. You can use fresh cockles or those sold in jars or tins.

5 oz Chinese leaves or *pak choi*	1 tsp mustard
4 scallions	1 tsp *mirin*
½ Tbsp soy sauce	3½ oz cockles, drained

● Bring a saucepan of water to a boil, add the Chinese leaves, and cook for 3 minutes. Then, add the scallions and boil for a further 2 minutes. Drain and rinse lightly with cold water, then squeeze out any excess water. Cut into 1 in lengths.

● Mix the soy sauce, mustard and *mirin* in a large bowl. Add the Chinese leaves or *pak choi*, scallions, and cockles and mix.

Stir-fried Greens

SERVES 4–6

Possibly the fastest dish to cook in Thailand, this is properly made with the water plant variously known as swamp cabbage or water convolvulus.

3 Tbsp peanut or corn oil

11 oz swamp cabbage leaves and stems, cut into 4 in lengths

½ cup chicken broth

2 Tbsp marinated soy beans

1 Tbsp garlic, chopped

● Heat the oil in a wok or pan until very hot. Add all the ingredients at once (watch for splattering), and stir-fry for about 2 minutes.

● Serve accompanied by Boiled Rice Soup with Chicken (page 74) or steamed rice.

Spinach with Bonito Flakes and Soy Sauce

SERVES 2

Fresh spinach is vital to make this delicious, nutritious dish. Take care not to overcook the spinach or you will destroy its vitamins.

8 oz spinach leaves, rinsed and drained

pinch of salt

Large pinch of *bonito* fish flakes

2–3 Tbsp soy sauce

● Boil the spinach in salted water for about 2 minutes or until lightly cooked.

● Drain and quickly rinse with cold water. Holding the leaves in a bunch at the stem, squeeze out any excess water.

● Cut the bunch into 1 in lengths. Place in a small bowl or dish and sprinkle with the *bonito* flakes, followed by a drizzle of soy sauce.

Crispy "Seaweed"

SERVES 4

You might be surprised to learn that the very popular "seaweed" served in Chinese restaurants is, in fact, green cabbage! Choose fresh, young spring greens with pointed heads. Even the deep green outer leaves are quite tender. This recipe makes an ideal garnish for a number of dishes, particularly cold appetizers and buffet dishes.

1½–1¾ lb young cabbage	1 tsp salt
2½ cups oil for deep-frying	1 tsp sugar

● Wash and dry the cabbage leaves and shred them with a sharp knife into the thinnest possible shavings. Spread them out on paper towel or put in a large colander to dry thoroughly.

● Heat the oil in a wok or deep-fryer. Before the oil gets too hot, turn off the heat for 30 seconds. Add the cabbage shavings in several batches and turn the heat up to medium high. Stir with a pair of cooking chopsticks. When the shavings start to float to the surface, scoop them out gently with a slotted spoon and drain on paper towel to remove as much of the oil as possible. Sprinkle the salt and sugar evenly on top and mix gently. Serve cold.

Green Beans with Crushed Garlic

SERVES 4

1 Tbsp vegetable oil

1 onion, finely chopped

4 cloves garlic, finely chopped

3 large green chiles, seeded and sliced thinly diagonally

1 tsp ground coriander

½ tsp ground cumin

2 ripe tomatoes, blanched, skinned, seeded, and chopped roughly

1 lb green beans, washed, trimmed, and halved

½ tsp sugar

pinch of salt

2 Tbsp fresh cilantro, chopped

● Heat the oil in a wok and stir-fry the onion, garlic, and green chiles, stirring constantly for 2 minutes.

● Add the coriander and cumin, stir vigorously and add the chopped tomatoes and beans. Stir and cover the wok for 5 minutes. Remove the cover, add the sugar and a little salt, and stir again for 1 minute. Add the cilantro, stir for 30 seconds and transfer to a warm serving dish.

Green Beans in a Sesame Dressing

SERVES 2

Sesame enjoys a reputation for being a healthy food in Japan, and both black and white sesame are common ingredients in Japanese cuisine. To toast the seeds for this recipe, simply put them in a skillet without oil then heat while stirring until the seeds have puffed up and you can smell the distinctive aroma of sesame.

6 oz frozen whole green beans

pinch of salt

FOR THE DRESSING

1 Tbsp toasted sesame seeds

1 Tbsp superfine sugar

⅔ Tbsp *dashi* broth

½ Tbsp *miso* paste

1 Tbsp soy sauce

● Boil the beans in a pan of boiling water for 5 minutes or until tender.

● Finely grind the sesame seeds in a pestle and mortar or in a coffee grinder. Add the sugar, *dashi, miso* paste and soy sauce and mix together well.

● Toss the green beans in the sesame dressing and serve as a side dish.

Fried Flat Beans with Pork

SERVES 4

You can use fresh beans as a substitute for the sator beans, but really the basis for this quintessentially southern dish is the strange flavor of the latter. The recipe is included here for authenticity and just in case you are able to find the real sator beans in a Thai delicatessen or greengrocer.

3 fresh yellow or green chiles, chopped

1 Tbsp garlic, chopped

½ tsp shrimp paste

2 Tbsp peanut or corn oil

5 oz pork loin (or chicken or shrimp), cut into thin strips

2 cups fresh sator or lima beans

½ tsp fish sauce

½ tsp sugar

½ tsp lime or lemon juice

● Pound the chiles and garlic together with a pestle and mortar or in a blender to a fine paste. Mix with the shrimp paste.

● Heat the oil in a pan or wok. Add the chile-garlic mixture, then add the pork and stir-fry for 3 minutes. Add the beans and all the remaining ingredients, plus 3 tablespoons of water if using lima beans, then fry until the beans are cooked, about 10 minutes—they should be quite firm.

● Serve accompanied by rice.

Beans with Mixed Grains

SERVES 4

The combination of red and black beans and three different grains makes this a colorful dish with many different tastes and textures.

⅓ cup kidney beans, soaked overnight

⅓ cup black kidney beans, soaked overnight

1 cup short-grain rice, washed and soaked

2 Tbsp millet

2 Tbsp pearl barley

● Drain the beans, and add to a saucepan of boiling water. Cover and bring to a boil. Boil for 10 minutes, then simmer for 1–1½ hours until just tender; the time will depend on the beans. Drain them, reserving the water.

● Drain the rice. Put all the ingredients in a saucepan. Add 1¾ cups of the bean cooking water and bring to a boil. Stir once, then cover and turn the heat to very low. Cook for 20–30 minutes, without removing the lid even once. Turn the heat up as high as it will go for 30 seconds, then turn it off, or remove the pan from the heat. Leave, without removing the lid at all, for 10–15 minutes before serving.

Spicy Eggplant and Tomatoes

SERVES 4

1 eggplant

2 cloves garlic, thinly sliced

2 red bell peppers

1 medium tomato, thinly sliced

1 Tbsp fish sauce

2 Tbsp rice wine

1 Tbsp olive oil

● Preheat the oven to 400°F.

● Cut slits all over the eggplant and push a slice of garlic into each slit. Place the eggplant and the whole bell peppers in a baking dish and bake, turning regularly to brown evenly, for 45 minutes or until all are very soft. Set aside to cool.

● Cut the stem off the eggplant and, with your fingers or a paring knife, peel off the skin. Shred the flesh, discarding any big lumps of seeds. Place the eggplant in a bowl with the garlic slices.

● Peel the skin off the bell peppers and discard the stems, cores and seeds. Cut into long, thin strips and add to the eggplant. Add the tomato, fish sauce, rice wine, and olive oil, and toss to mix well.

Deep-fried Eggplants

SERVES 4

These deep-fried eggplant pieces can be served as a first course, or to eat with drinks; in which case, supply toothpicks for spearing the eggplant slices.

2 eggplants, thinly sliced on the
  diagonal

salt

all-purpose flour for coating

Korean chili powder, or cayenne
  pepper mixed with paprika

1–1½ Tbsp fresh cilantro,
  chopped

1 large egg, beaten

oil for deep-frying

sesame dipping sauce to serve

● Put the eggplant slices into a colander. Toss with salt and leave for 30 minutes. Rinse the eggplant slices, drain and dry thoroughly on paper towels.

● Season some all-purpose flour with salt and chili powder, or cayenne and paprika, to taste, and add the cilantro. Toss the eggplant slices in the flour to coat evenly, then dip in the beaten egg. Let the excess egg drain off.

● Heat a deep-fat fryer half-filled with oil to 350°F. Add the eggplant slices in batches so the pan is not crowded and fry until golden brown. Drain on paper towels. Serve hot with sesame dipping sauce.

Spicy Eggplant and Tomatoes

Eggplant with Szechwan "Fish Sauce"

SERVES 4

Szechwan "fish sauce" is commonly served with fish, but it does not have any fish in it.

1 lb eggplant	1 tsp sugar
4–5 dried red chile peppers	1 Tbsp soy sauce
oil for deep frying	1 Tbsp vinegar
3–4 scallions, finely chopped	1 Tbsp chile bean paste
1 slice gingerroot, peeled and finely chopped	2 tsp cornstarch, mixed with 2 Tbsp water
1 clove garlic, finely chopped	1 tsp sesame seed oil

● Soak the dried red chiles for 5–10 minutes, cut them into small pieces and discard the stalks.

● Peel the eggplant, discard the stalks and cut them into diamond-shaped chunks.

● Heat the oil in a wok and deep-fry the eggplant for 3½–4 minutes or until soft. Remove with a slotted spoon and drain.

● Pour off the oil and return the eggplant to the wok with the red chiles, scallions, ginger root, and garlic. Stir a few times and add the sugar, soy sauce, vinegar, and chile bean paste. Continue stirring for 1 minute.

● Finally add the cornstarch and water mixture, blend well and garnish with the sesame seed oil. Serve either hot or cold.

Fried Eggplant and Green Pepper in Sweet Miso Sauce

SERVES 2

Fall is the season for eggplants in Japan, when greengrocers stock their shelves with the numerous varieties available. Japanese eggplant vary greatly in length, though none possess the girth of those typically produced in the United States.

2 Tbsp sesame oil

1 medium onion, peeled and cut into bite-sized pieces

8 oz eggplant, cut into bite-sized pieces and soaked in water

½ green bell pepper, cut into bite-sized pieces

FOR THE SWEET *MISO* SAUCE

3 Tbsp *miso* paste

2 Tbsp superfine sugar

2 Tbsp water

2 Tbsp *mirin*

● Heat 1 tablespoon of sesame oil in a pan and fry the onion for 3–4 minutes. Add the rest of the oil and the eggplant and continue to fry for 3–4 minutes. Add the green bell pepper and fry until the eggplant has softened.

● Mix together the *miso* paste, sugar, water, and *mirin* in a bowl, then add to the pan, stirring for 1–2 minutes. Serve hot as a side dish.

Fried Zucchini with Sesame Seeds

SERVES 4

A coating of sesame seeds gives zucchini an interesting nutty flavor and a crisp texture. This picture also shows Deep-fried Eggplant (page 338), Carrot Fritters (page 326).

1¼ lb small zucchini, cut
    diagonally into ¼ in thick
    slices

salt

seasoned all-purpose flour

1 large egg, beaten

sesame seeds

vegetable oil for frying

sesame dipping sauce or
    vinegar dipping sauce

● Put the zucchini into a colander. Toss generously with salt and leave for 30 minutes.

● Rinse the zucchini well and dry thoroughly with paper towels. Toss the zucchini in seasoned all-purpose flour to coat evenly, then dip in beaten egg. Finally, coat in sesame seeds.

● Heat a thin layer of oil in a wide skillet. Add the zucchini slices in a single layer and fry for 3–4 minutes on each side until golden on the outside.

● Using a slotted spoon, transfer to paper towels to drain. Serve hot with dipping sauce.

Stir-fried Zucchini

SERVES 4

1 lb zucchini

3 Tbsp oil

2 tsp salt

1 tsp sugar

2 Tbsp water

● Do not peel the zucchini; just trim off the ends. Split the zucchini in half lengthwise and cut each length diagonally into diamond-shaped chunks.

● Heat the oil in a wok. When the oil starts to smoke, put the zucchini in and stir-fry for about 30 seconds. Add the salt and sugar and cook for a further 1–1½ minutes, adding a little water if necessary. Serve hot.

Zucchini with Beef

SERVES 2-4

*This is a simple but very tasty dish that can be served in traditional Korean manner with **kimchis**, rice, salads and vegetables, or Western-style with a green vegetable or salad.*

4 small zucchini, cut diagonally into ¼ in thick slices

salt

1 cup lean beef, freshly ground

2 Tbsp vegetable oil

2 scallions, white and green parts very thinly sliced

1 Tbsp sugar

1 Tbsp soy sauce

½–1 tsp chili powder

FOR THE MARINADE

1 scallion, white and green part very thinly sliced

2 garlic cloves, crushed and finely chopped

1½ Tbsp soy sauce

1 Tbsp sesame oil

1 in piece of fresh ginger, finely chopped

1 Tbsp toasted sesame seeds

freshly ground black pepper

FOR THE GARNISH

toasted sesame seeds

● Put the zucchini in a colander, and sprinkle generously with salt. Toss together and leave for 30 minutes. Meanwhile, mix all the marinade ingredients together. Add the ground beef, and leave for about 30 minutes.

● Rinse the zucchini well and dry thoroughly with paper towels: Heat the vegetable oil in a large skillet over a fairly high heat. Add the beef and marinade, and fry, stirring to break up the lumps, for about 1 minute or until the beef changes color.

● Lightly stir in the zucchini, then add the remaining ingredients. Cook for 2 minutes, stirring lightly. Lower the heat and continue to stir for another minute until the zucchini are tender but still retain some bite.

● Serve sprinkled with toasted sesame seeds.

Zucchini with Beef

Stir-fried Snow Peas and Corn Beef

SERVES 2

It has been said many times that the Japanese are a nation of innovators, and this dish illustrates the Japanese habit of absorbing a foreign influence into their culture and then enhancing it with a distinctive Japanese flavor. The snow peas should be firm, so be careful not to overcook them.

5 oz snow peas, rinsed and trimmed

1 Tbsp vegetable oil

4 oz canned corn beef, chopped

1 tsp soy sauce

salt and freshly ground black pepper

● Boil the snow peas in salted boiling water for 3 minutes, then drain.

● Heat the oil in a skillet. Add the corn beef and stir-fry for 5 minutes over a medium heat.

● Add the snow peas, sprinkle with salt and pepper and stir-fry for another 5 minutes. Sprinkle with the soy sauce. Serve hot as a side dish.

Stir-fried Bean Sprouts with Green Peppers

SERVES 4

1 lb fresh bean sprouts

1 small green bell pepper, cored and seeded

1–2 scallions

3 Tbsp oil

1 tsp salt

1 tsp sugar

● Wash and rinse the bean sprouts in cold water, discarding the husks and other bits and pieces that float to the surface.

● Cut the green bell pepper into thin shreds. Cut the scallions into short lengths.

● Heat the oil in a hot wok until smoking. Add the scallions and green bell pepper, stir a few times, and then add the bean sprouts. Continue stirring.

● After about 30 seconds, add salt and sugar, and stir a few times more. Do not overcook, or the sprouts will become soggy. Serve hot or cold.

Stir-fried Green Peppers, Tomatoes, and Onions

SERVES 4

1 large or 2 small green bell peppers

1 large or 2 small firm tomatoes

1 large or 2 small onions

3 Tbsp oil

1 tsp salt

1 tsp sugar

● Core and seed the green bell peppers and peel the onions. Cut all the vegetables into uniform slices.

● Heat the oil in a wok and wait for it to smoke. Add the onions and stir-fry for 30 seconds. Add the green bell peppers and continue cooking for 1 minute. Add the tomatoes, salt and sugar and cook for 1 minute more. Serve hot or cold.

Stir-fried Lettuce

SERVES 4

1 large Romaine lettuce	1 tsp salt
3 Tbsp oil	1 tsp sugar

● Discard the tough outer leaves of the lettuce. Wash the remaining leaves well and shake off the excess water. Tear the larger leaves into two or three pieces.

● Heat the oil in a wok or large saucepan. Add the salt followed by the lettuce leaves and stir vigorously as though tossing a salad. Add the sugar and continue stirring. As soon as the leaves become slightly limp, transfer them to a serving dish and serve.

Shredded Cabbage with Red and Green Peppers

SERVES 4

1 lb white cabbage

1 green bell pepper

1 red bell pepper

3 Tbsp oil

1 tsp salt

1 tsp sesame seed oil

● Thinly shred the cabbage. Core and seed the green and red bell peppers and thinly shred them.

● Heat the oil in a wok until hot. Add the cabbage and the peppers and stir-fry for 1–1½ minutes. Add the salt and stir a few more times. Add the sesame seed oil to garnish and serve either hot or cold.

Stir-fried Green and Red Peppers

SERVES 4

1 large or 2 small green bell
    peppers, cored and seeded

1 large or 2 small red bell
    peppers, cored and seeded

3 Tbsp oil

1 tsp salt

1 tsp sugar

● Cut the peppers into small, diamond-shaped pieces; if you use one or two orange peppers, the dish will be even more colorful.

● Heat the oil in a hot wok or skillet until it smokes. Spread the oil with a spatula so that the cooking surface is well greased. Add the bell peppers and stir-fry until each piece is coated with oil. Add the salt and sugar.

● Continue stirring for about 1 minute and serve if you like your vegetables crunchy and crisp. If not, you can cook them for another minute or so until the skin of the peppers becomes slightly wrinkled. Add a little water if necessary during the last stage of cooking.

Stuffed Chiles

SERVES 4

Touching chiles can make your hands, particularly any cuts or bruises, sting, so it is a good idea to wear fine rubber gloves when preparing this dish.

2 cups lean pork, freshly ground

1 garlic clove, finely chopped

½ in piece of fresh ginger, finely chopped

4 scallions, finely chopped

2 tsp crushed toasted sesame seeds

2–3 tsp soy sauce

16–20 large fresh red chiles

seasoned all-purpose flour for coating

1 large egg, beaten

vegetable oil for frying

vinegar dipping sauce to serve

● Mix the pork, garlic, ginger, scallions, sesame seeds, and soy sauce together very well.

● Cut the chiles in half lengthwise and remove the seeds. Break off small pieces of the meat mixture to fill the chiles. Form into torpedo shapes and use to stuff the chiles, packing the meat stuffing in firmly.

● Roll the stuffed chiles in seasoned flour to give an even coating, then dip in beaten egg.

● Heat 1½ inch layer of oil in a skillet. Add the chiles in batches and fry for 4–5 minutes on each side until golden brown and cooked through. Remove from the oil with a slotted spoon and drain on paper towels. Serve hot with vinegar dipping sauce.

Spiced Sweet Potato Slices

SERVES 4

Traditionally, these potato slices are served with a dipping sauce but they can also be served as a vegetable accompaniment.

2 sweet potatoes, cut diagonally into ¼ in thick slices

salt

all-purpose flour for coating

chili powder

1 large egg, beaten

vegetable oil for frying

vinegar dipping sauce to serve

● Add the sweet potato slices to a saucepan of boiling salted water and cook for about 5 minutes. Drain well and dry on paper towels.

● Season the flour with chili powder, then coat the sweet potato slices evenly in the seasoned flour. Dip in beaten egg.

● Heat a thin layer of vegetable oil in a wide skillet. Add a layer of sweet potato slices, and fry for about 4 minutes on each side.

● Transfer to paper towels to drain. Serve hot with vinegar dipping sauce.

Stuffed Chiles

Braised Bamboo Shoots

SERVES 4

If possible, use the "Evergreen" brand slender bamboo shoots, a specialty from Kiangsi province in southeast China; they need only be drained and they are ready to cook. The next best are "maling" bamboo shoots from Shanghai. If you can get winter bamboo shoots, so much the better.

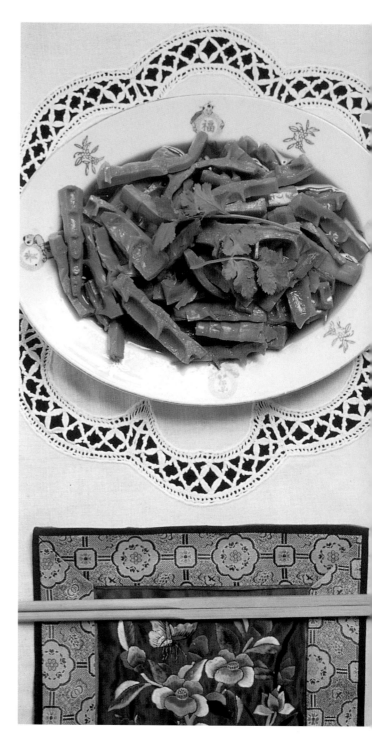

1 lb slender bamboo shoots

3 Tbsp oil

2 Tbsp rice wine or dry sherry

1 Tbsp sugar

2 Tbsp light soy sauce

1 Tbsp dark soy sauce

2 tsp sesame seed oil

● Drain the water from the bamboo shoots and slice each shoot lengthwise into thin strips.

● Heat the oil in a hot wok or skillet, add the bamboo shoots and stir-fry until well covered with oil. Add the wine, sugar, and both soy sauces and stir.

● Braise for about 3–4 minutes or until almost all the liquid has evaporated. Add the sesame seed oil and serve either hot or cold.

Stir-fried "Four Treasures"

SERVES 4

Like stir-fried mixed vegetables, the ingredients are specially selected to achieve a harmonious balance of colors, textures, and flavors.

3–4 tbsp wood ears, dried	3–4 Tbsp oil
8 oz broccoli	1½ tsp salt
6 oz bamboo shoots	1 tsp sugar
4 oz oyster mushrooms	1 tsp sesame seed oil

● Soak the wood ears in water for 15–20 minutes. Rinse until clean. Discard the hard roots if any and cut the extra large ones into smaller pieces.

● Wash the broccoli and cut into whole florets. Do not discard the stalks; peel off the tough outer skin and cut them into small pieces.

● Cut the bamboo shoots into slices, or, if using winter bamboo shoots, cut them into roughly the same size pieces as the broccoli stalks.

● Wash and trim the mushrooms. Do not peel if using fresh ones. Canned oyster mushrooms are ready to cook; just drain off the water.

● Heat a wok or large skillet over high heat until really hot. Add the oil and wait for it to smoke. Then stir the oil with a spatula so that most of the surface of the wok is well greased.

● Add the broccoli first, and stir until well coated with oil. Then add the bamboo shoots and mushrooms and continue stirring for about 1 minute. Add the wood ears, salt, and sugar and stir for another minute or so. The vegetables should produce enough natural juices to form a thick gravy. If the contents in the wok are too dry, add a little water and bring to a boil before serving. The sesame seed oil should not be added until the very last minute.

Stir-fried Leeks with Wood Ears

SERVES 4

The mild, subtle flavor of the wood ears is a great accompaniment to leek. Do not overcook the leeks—they should stay crunchy.

3–4 Tbsp wood ears

1 lb leeks

3 Tbsp oil

1 tsp salt

1 tsp sugar

1 tsp sesame seed oil

● Soak the wood ears in water for 20–25 minutes, rinse well, and discard the hard roots if any. Drain.

● Wash the leeks and cut them diagonally into 2-inch chunks.

● Heat the oil in a hot wok or skillet. Use your spatula to spread the oil so that most of the surface is well greased. When the oil starts to smoke, add the leeks and wood ears, and stir-fry for about 1 minute. Add the salt and sugar and continue stirring. Wet with a little water if necessary. Add the sesame seed oil to garnish and serve hot.

Mushrooms with Chicken and Vegetables

SERVES 3–4

Mushrooms of many different types are very popular in Korea. The most widely available of these in the West are both fresh and dried shiitake (when dried they are more commonly known as dried Chinese black mushrooms), dried wood ear, which have little flavor but a pleasing texture and attractive appearance, and stone mushrooms.

6 oz chicken breast, cut into strips

3 garlic cloves, crushed and finely chopped

4 Tbsp soy sauce

2 tsp sesame oil

freshly ground black pepper

vegetable oil for frying

1 lb shiitake or oyster mushrooms, thinly sliced

1 red bell pepper, cut into thin strips

1 zucchini, thinly sliced diagonally

4 scallions, white and some green parts thinly sliced diagonally

FOR THE GARNISH

fresh cilantro leaves

● Mix the chicken with the garlic, soy sauce, sesame oil, and plenty of black pepper. Leave for 30 minutes.

● Heat a little vegetable oil in a large skillet. Lift the chicken from the marinade (reserve the marinade) and stir-fry for 2 minutes or so.

● Stir in all the vegetables and cook, stirring, for about 5 minutes until the vegetables are tender but still crisp. Stir in the reserved marinade about 1 minute before the end of cooking. Serve garnished with cilantro leaves.

Stir-fried Leeks with Wood Ears

"Buddha's Delight"

SERVES 4-6

The original recipe calls for 18 different ingredients to represent the 18 Buddhas. Later, this was reduced to eight ingredients, usually consisting half of dried and half of fresh vegetables.

½ oz dried bean curd skin sticks

⅓ cup dried tiger lily buds

3–4 tbsp dried tree ears

¼ oz dried black moss

2 oz bamboo shoots

2 oz lotus root

2 oz straw mushrooms

2 oz white nuts

4 Tbsp oil

1½ tsp salt

1 tsp sugar

1 Tbsp light soy sauce

1 tsp cornstarch mixed with 1 Tbsp cold water

2 tsp sesame seed oil

● Soak the dried vegetables separately in cold water overnight or in warm water for at least 1 hour. Cut the bean curd sticks into short lengths.

● Cut the bamboo shoots and lotus root into small slices. The straw mushrooms and white nuts can be left whole.

● Heat a wok or large skillet. When it is hot, put in about half of the oil and wait until it smokes. Stir-fry all the dried vegetables together with a little salt for about 1 minute. Remove and set aside.

● Add and heat the remaining oil and stir-fry the rest of the vegetables and the salt for about 1 minute. Add the partly cooked dried vegetables, the sugar, and soy sauce stirring constantly. If the contents start to dry out, pour in a little water. When the vegetables are cooked, add the cornstarch and water mixture to thicken the gravy. Garnish with the sesame seed oil just before serving. This dish can be served either hot or cold.

Stir-fried Celery with Mushrooms

SERVES 4

1 small head of celery

4 oz white mushrooms

3 Tbsp oil

1½ tsp salt

1 tsp sugar

● Wash the celery and thinly slice the stalks diagonally.

● Wash the mushrooms and cut them into thin slices. Do not peel.

● Heat the oil in a hot wok or skillet until it smokes, swirling it so that it covers most of the surface.

● Add the celery and mushrooms and stir-fry for about 1 minute or until each piece is coated with oil. Add the salt and sugar and continue stirring. Add a little water if the contents get too dry. Do not overcook because the celery will lose its crunchy texture. This dish can be served either hot or cold.

The "Two Winters"

SERVES 2–4

The "Two Winters" are winter bamboo shoots and winter mushrooms.

1 oz dried Chinese mushrooms

8 oz winter bamboo shoots

2 Tbsp oil sauce

3 Tbsp soy

1 tsp sugar

4 Tbsp mushroom broth

1 tsp cornstarch mixed with 2 tsp water

1 tsp sesame seed oil

● Select mushrooms of a uniform, small size. Soak them in warm water for about half an hour, squeeze dry, and keep the water as mushroom stock.

● Cut the bamboo shoots into thin slices not much bigger than the mushrooms.

● Heat the oil until it smokes. Stir-fry the mushrooms and bamboo shoots for about 1 minute. Add the soy sauce and sugar and stir a few more times. Add the mushroom broth, bring to a boil and cook for about 2 minutes. Add the cornstarch and water mixture and blend well. Add the sesame oil and serve.

Mushrooms Baked in Foil

SERVES 2–4

Cooking mushrooms in foil so that the aroma, flavor and juices are trapped inside is a specialty of many of Korea's older, traditional restaurants. The unseasoned mushrooms are either eaten plain, with a dipping sauce, or as a contrast to hot and garlicky dishes.

6 oz large white mushrooms, caps and stalks cut into ¼ in slices

vinegar dipping sauce (optional)

● Cut a large piece of foil—about 20 x 12 inches. Put the mushrooms in the center of the foil. Fold over the long sides of the foil, then the short sides to make a neat, secure package.

● Preheat a broiler. Cook the mushroom packages about 4 inches from the heat for 5–7 minutes.

● Serve the mushrooms straightaway, accompanied by a dipping sauce if liked.

Bean Curd with Mushrooms

SERVES 4

4 cakes bean curd

3–4 medium-sized dried
   Chinese mushrooms

1 Tbsp sherry

4 Tbsp oil

½ tsp salt

½ tsp sugar

1 tsp cornstarch

1 Tbsp soy sauce

1 tsp sesame seed oil

● Soak the dried mushrooms in warm water for about 30 minutes. Squeeze them dry and discard the stalks. Keep the water for use as stock.

● Slice each square of bean curd into ¼ inch thick slices and then cut each slice into six or eight pieces.

● Heat the oil in a wok and stir-fry the mushrooms for a short time. Add about ½ cup of the water in which the mushrooms have been soaking. Bring to the boil and add the bean curd with the salt and sugar. Let it bubble for a while and then add the sherry and the sesame seed oil.

● Mix the cornstarch with the soy sauce and a little water in a bowl and pour it over the bean curd in the wok so that it forms a clear, light glaze.

Soy-glazed Pumpkin

SERVES 4

The mixture of pumpkin with ginger and soy sauce gives an attractive color, taste, and texture.

8 oz pumpkin, cut into 1 in
    cubes

½ cup sugar

2 in piece of fresh ginger,
    grated

6 Tbsp soy sauce

freshly ground black pepper

FOR THE GARNISH

toasted sesame seeds

garlic chives

● Cook the pumpkin in boiling water for 2 minutes. Drain well, then put into a skillet. Add 6 tablespoons of water, the sugar, ginger, soy sauce, and pepper. Heat slowly, stirring, until the sugar dissolves.

● Partially cover and simmer slowly for about 15 minutes, stirring occasionally, until the pumpkin is tender and glazed with soy syrup.

● Garnish with sesame seeds and garlic chives.

Braised Sweet Potatoes

SERVES 2

A traditional favorite, sweet potatoes are eaten throughout the year in Japan.

12 oz sweet potatoes, cut into
    ½ in pieces

1 scant cup water

pinch of salt

1 Tbsp superfine sugar

1 tsp soy sauce

● With a knife, bevel off the edges of the sweet potato. This will help prevent them breaking up while they are cooking.

● Put the potatoes, water, salt, sugar, and soy sauce into a large pan, making sure that the pieces of potato are laid flat on the bottom. Bring to a boil, then simmer, covered, for 10–15 minutes, until the potatoes have softened, removing the lid for the last 5 minutes.

Soy-glazed Pumpkin

Salted Turnip with Lemon

SERVES 2

This dish is one of many Japanese **tsukemono** *or pickles. The freshness of the turnip is essential for the success of this dish.*

4 oz turnips peeled, halved and
   thinly sliced

1 tsp salt

3 lemon slices, cut into quarters

1 tsp soy sauce

● Place the sliced turnip in a bowl, sprinkle with the salt, and leave for 20–30 minutes.

● Rub the turnip until it is soft, then squeeze out any excess liquid.

● Add the lemon quarters, then drizzle with soy sauce. Serve as a side dish.

Simmered Mixed Vegetables

SERVES 2

The potato is not a staple part of the Japanese diet, but it is nevertheless much used in Japanese cookery. It is usually diced and cooked with other vegetables as in this dish.

1 scant cup *dashi* broth

4 oz carrots, peeled and chopped at random into bite-sized pieces

8 oz potatoes, peeled and cut into bite-sized pieces

1 medium onion, sliced

2 tsp superfine sugar

½ Tbsp *mirin*

pinch of salt

1 Tbsp soy sauce

2 oz frozen, whole string beans, halved

● Put the *dashi*, carrots, and potatoes in a pan. Bring to a boil and simmer, covered, for 5 minutes.

● Add the onion, sugar, *mirin*, salt, and soy sauce and continue to simmer, covered, for a further 5 minutes.

● Finally, add the beans and simmer as before for 4 minutes. Serve hot as a side dish.

Fried "Pocketed Eggs"

SERVES 4

Eggs are frequently cooked this way in China. The only preparation you will need to do is to chop the scallion very finely. Taking a bite of the egg and finding the yolk inside the white is rather like finding something in a pocket—hence the name of this dish.

4 eggs

2–3 Tbsp oil

1 Tbsp light soy sauce

1 scallion, finely chopped

● Heat the oil in a hot wok or skillet and fry the eggs on both sides. Add the soy sauce and a little water and braise for 1–2 minutes. Garnish with scallion and serve hot.

Eggs with Tomatoes

SERVES 4

Other vegetables such as cucumber, green bell peppers, or green peas can be substituted for the tomatoes.

9 oz firm tomatoes

5 eggs

1½ tsp salt

2 scallions, finely chopped

4 Tbsp oil

1 tsp gingerroot, finely chopped (optional)

● Scald the tomatoes in a bowl of boiling water and peel off the skins. Cut each tomato in half lengthwise and then crosscut each half into wedges.

● Beat the eggs with a pinch of salt and about one-third of the finely chopped scallions.

● Heat about half the oil in a hot wok or skillet and lightly scramble the eggs over a moderate heat until set. Remove the eggs from the wok.

● Heat the wok again over high heat and add the remaining oil. When the oil is hot, add the rest of the finely chopped scallions, the gingerroot (if used), and the tomatoes. Stir a few times and then add the scrambled eggs with the remaining salt. Continue stirring for about 1 minute and serve hot.

Braised Soybeans

SERVES 2

The humble soybean is the most widely used
ingredient in Japanese cuisine, forming the basis for
soy sauce, bean curd, and **miso**. Soybeans are rich in
nutrients and fiber and are regarded in Japan as
"meat from the earth."

3 dried shiitake mushrooms

3 in dried kelp, wiped with a
damp cloth

15 oz canned soybeans, drained

2 oz carrots, peeled and diced

2 Tbsp superfine sugar

1½ Tbsp soy sauce

● Soak the shiitake mushrooms and kelp in a cup of
water for 30 minutes. Reserve the water. Dice the
shiitake mushrooms and kelp into small pieces.

● Put the kelp, mushrooms, and reserved water into
a pan. Add the soybeans, carrot, an extra ½ cup of
fresh water, and the sugar. Bring to a boil and cook,
uncovered, for 15 minutes.

● Add the soy sauce and simmer for a further 10
minutes. Serve as a side dish. Any leftovers can be
stored in a refrigerator for up to a week.

Sesame-grilled Seaweed

SERVES ABOUT 4

Crisp, smoky, nutty-tasting, paper-thin sheets of
grilled **kim** or laver are an extremely moreish
"nibble" to serve with drinks.

8–10 sheets *kim*

sesame oil for brushing

salt

toasted sesame seeds to serve

● Brush both sides of each sheet of *kim* with sesame
oil and sprinkle with salt.

● Hold each sheet in turn in tongs and pass backward
and forward over a fairly low gas flame until crisp.

● Sprinkle the *kim* sheets with toasted sesame seeds.
Let people break off pieces as they like, or cut the
sheets into strips or squares.

Cucumber and Wakame

SERVES 2

Although this is a cold dish, it is not regarded as a salad in Japan. If you cannot get hold of rice vinegar, ordinary malt vinegar will do as a substitute.

7 oz cucumber, cut in half lengthwise and then very thinly sliced

1 tsp salt

½ Tbsp dried *wakame*, soaked in hot water for a few minutes until swollen

FOR THE SWEET AND SOUR DRESSING

5 tsp rice vinegar

½ Tbsp superfine sugar

½ tsp soy sauce

● Put the cucumber in a bowl, sprinkle with the salt, and leave for 15 minutes.

● Taking the cucumber in your hands, squeeze out as much liquid as you can. Do the same with the soaked *wakame*.

● Mix together the sugar, vinegar, and soy sauce in a small bowl.

● Just before eating, mix the dressing together with the cucumber and *wakame*. Serve as a side dish.

Stir-fried Mixed Vegetables in a Fish Sauce

SERVES 4

2 carrots, finely sliced

4 oz bamboo shoots, thinly sliced

1 *pak choi*, stems only, diced

4 oz string beans, halved

1 oz wood ear, soaked in warm water for 15 minutes and roughly chopped

½ tsp vegetable oil

2 cloves garlic, crushed

3 slices gingerroot, peeled and finely sliced

4 oz bean sprouts

salt

freshly ground black pepper

½ Tbsp cornstarch

1 Tbsp fish sauce or 1 Tbsp light soy sauce

● In a large saucepan half full of water boil the carrots for 10 minutes. Add the bamboo shoots, *pak choi*, string beans, and wood ear and cook for a further 5 minutes. Drain and reserve.

● Heat the oil in a wok and stir-fry the garlic and ginger for 2 minutes. Add the bean sprouts and stir-fry for 30 seconds. Stir in all the reserved vegetables and season with salt and black pepper. Stir-fry for a further 2 minutes.

● Mix the cornstarch and fish sauce with a little water and fold into the vegetables to bind them.

Hot and Sour Cucumber—Szechwan Style

SERVES 4

1 cucumber

1 tsp salt

2 Tbsp sugar

2 Tbsp vinegar

1 Tbsp chile oil

● Split the cucumber in two lengthwise and then cut each piece into strips, rather like French fries. Sprinkle with the salt and leave for about 10 minutes to extract the bitter juices.

● Remove each cucumber strip. Place it on a firm surface and soften it by gently tapping it with the blade of a cleaver or knife.

● Place the cucumber strips on a plate. Sprinkle the sugar evenly over them and then add the vinegar and chile oil just before serving.

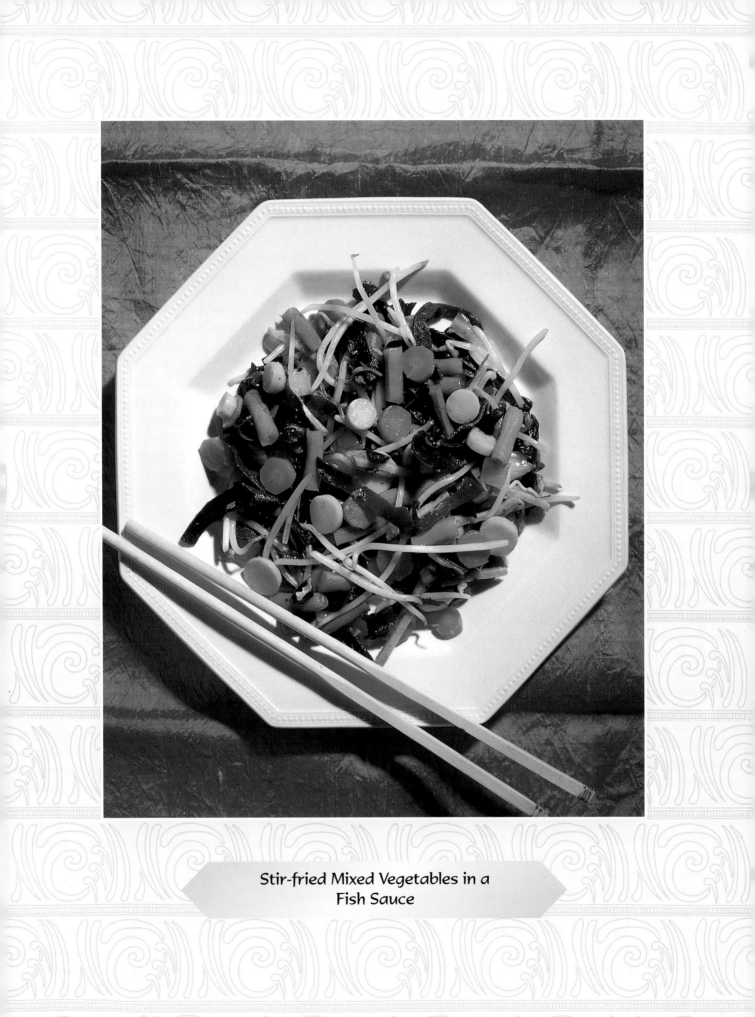

Stir-fried Mixed Vegetables in a
Fish Sauce

Simmered Hijiki Seaweed

SERVES 2

Hijiki *is one of the many types of seaweed used in Japanese cookery.* **Hijiki** *is a source of several minerals, including calcium and iodine.*

¼ oz dried *hijiki*

½ sheet *abura-age*

2 oz carrots, peeled, and cut into short matchsticks

2 tsp vegetable oil

1 cup *dashi* broth

1½ Tbsp superfine sugar

1½ Tbsp soy sauce

1 Tbsp *mirin*

● Rinse the *hijiki* then soak in a bowlful of water for 20–30 minutes. Rinse then drain again. The *hijiki* should swell to six or seven times its original size.

● Rinse the *abura-age* with hot water, then cut into small slices, about the same size as the carrot.

● Heat the oil in a saucepan and fry the *hijiki*, *abura-age* and carrots for 1 minute.

● Add the *dashi* broth, sugar, soy sauce, and *mirin*, then simmer, uncovered for about 25 minutes or until the liquid has almost evaporated. Serve as a side dish. Any leftovers can be kept refrigerated for 3–4 days.

Vegetarian Chop Suey

SERVES 4

Many of us know that chop suey is a creation of the West, but the Chinese have a dish called tsa-sui, which literally means "miscellaneous fragments" or "mixed bits and pieces." The genuine article should have all the ingredients specially selected in order to achieve the desired harmonious balance of colors, textures, and flavors. It should never be the soggy mess one often finds in a cheap take-away.

2 cakes of bean curd

¼ oz wood ears, dried

6 oz broccoli or snow peas

6 oz bamboo shoots

4 oz mushrooms

4–5 Tbsp oil

1½ tsp salt

1 tsp sugar

1–2 scallions, finely chopped

1 Tbsp light soy sauce

2 Tbsp rice wine or dry sherry

1 tsp cornstarch mixed with
1 Tbsp cold water

● Cut the bean curd into about 24 small pieces. Soak the wood ears in water for about 20–25 minutes, rinse them clean, and discard any hard roots.

● Cut the broccoli or snow peas, bamboo shoots, and mushrooms into uniformly small pieces.

● Heat a wok over a high heat, add about half of the oil and wait for it to smoke. Swirl the pan so that its surface is well greased. Add the bean curd pieces and shallow-fry them on both sides until golden, then scoop them out with a slotted spoon and set them aside until needed.

● Heat the remaining oil and add the broccoli or snow peas. Stir for about 30 seconds and then add the wood ears, bamboo shoots, mushrooms, and the partly cooked bean curd. Continue stirring for 1 minute and then add the salt, sugar, scallions, soy sauce, and wine. Blend well and when the gravy starts to boil, thicken it with the cornstarch and water mixture. Serve hot.

Salads

Salads, which are as often made with lightly steamed or fried
vegetables as raw ingredients, are served simply and lightly dressed
with fragrant, mouth-watering sauces. In the East, dishes such as those
in this section are traditionally served as accompaniments to main
dishes, but Western cooks will find here suggestions for salads and cold
dishes that will win a regular place in their culinary repertoire.

Chinese Vegetable and Omelet Salad

SERVES 4

Resembling a raw stir-fry, this colorful salad makes use of Chinese vegetables. Top with shredded omelet for a special finishing touch.

1 lb young cabbage

oil for deep frying

1 tsp salt

½ tsp ground cinnamon

2 cups bean sprouts

4 scallions, halved lengthwise

½ cup canned water chestnuts, drained and chopped

1 red bell pepper, sliced

1 yellow bell pepper, sliced

½ cup salted cashew nuts

FOR THE OMELET

2 eggs

½ tsp Chinese five-spice powder

FOR THE DRESSING

2 Tbsp light soy sauce

1 Tbsp lime juice

1 Tbsp sesame oil

½ tsp ground ginger

● Shred the young cabbage. Heat the oil in a wok and deep-fry the greens, 4–5 minutes. Drain well on paper towels and sprinkle with salt and cinnamon. Place in a large serving bowl. Top with the bean sprouts, scallions, water chestnuts, peppers, and cashew nuts.

● Beat the eggs for the omelet with the Chinese five-spice powder. Heat a 6 inch omelet skillet and pour in the eggs, tilting the pan to coat the base with egg. Cook for 2 minutes until the top is set. Flip over and cook for 2 minutes. Remove and cut into strips. Sprinkle over the vegetables. Mix the dressing, pour on, and serve.

Hot Egg and Shredded Vegetable Salad

SERVES 4

2 oz bean thread vermicelli

4 dried Chinese mushrooms

1 Tbsp sesame seeds

2 cloves garlic, crushed

salt

2 Tbsp rice vinegar

1½ tsp sugar

2 Tbsp soy sauce

2 Tbsp sesame oil

4 oz snow peas, thinly sliced

2 oz bamboo shoots, thinly sliced

1 small carrot, peeled and thinly sliced

1 small white radish, peeled and thinly sliced

1 small cucumber, peeled, seeded, and sliced thinly

1 small green bell pepper, thinly sliced

1 small red bell pepper, thinly sliced

2 celery stalks, thinly sliced

1 small red onion, thinly sliced

salt

1 Tbsp roasted peanuts, ground

fresh ground black pepper

sprigs of cilantro

FOR THE EGG PANCAKES

2 eggs

¼ tsp fish sauce or light soy sauce

freshly ground black pepper

½ tsp water

1 Tbsp vegetable oil

● Soak the vermicelli in warm water for 30 minutes, drain and cut into 2 inch lengths. Soak the dried Chinese mushrooms in warm water for 30 minutes, squeeze, discard the stems, and slice thinly.

● Make the egg pancakes by beating together the eggs, fish sauce, black pepper, and about ½ teaspoon water in a bowl. Heat the oil in a wok over a moderate heat. Pour in half of the egg mixture and immediately tilt the wok to spread the egg evenly over the bottom. The egg pancake should be crêpe-thin. Cook for about 30 seconds. Turn and cook on the other side for 15 seconds. Repeat with the rest of the mixture. Cool and cut into thin strips.

● Toss the sesame seeds in a dry wok over a moderate heat. Stir constantly until golden-brown. This should take about 3 minutes. Set aside.

● Combine the garlic, salt, vinegar, sugar, soy sauce, and sesame oil in a small bowl by stirring. Set this sauce aside.

● Bring a saucepan of salted water to a boil and put in the noodles, snow peas, bamboo shoots, and mushrooms and cook for 30 seconds. Drain into a colander immediately and run under a cold tap for a few seconds. Dry with a paper towel and set aside.

● Mix the carrot, white radish, cucumber, bell peppers, celery, and red onion in a bowl and sprinkle on some salt. Toss well and let stand for 30 minutes. Rinse the salt off and squeeze the vegetables dry by hand to remove all excess liquid, and dry with kitchen paper to ensure the vegetables remain firm.

● Combine all the shredded vegetables with the blanched vegetables in a large salad bowl. Sprinkle the sauce over the mixture. Toss well. Transfer the salad to a serving platter. Sprinkle the ground nuts and black pepper over the top and garnish with the egg pancake strips and cilantro sprigs.

Simple Salad

SERVES 4

1 lettuce, finely shredded

1 cucumber, peeled and cut lengthwise into thin strips

2 carrots, peeled and cut lengthwise into thin strips

1 large handful of bean sprouts, washed and drained thoroughly

3 Tbsp fresh cilantro, chopped

3 Tbsp fresh mint, chopped

FOR THE GARNISH

2 hard-cooked eggs, quartered

FOR THE SALAD DRESSING

4 Tbsp fish sauce

4 Tbsp lemon juice

1 Tbsp wine vinegar

3 cloves garlic, finely chopped and crushed

1 tsp sugar

1 red chile pepper, finely chopped

3 Tbsp roasted peanuts, crushed

● Combine the lettuce, cucumber, carrots, and bean sprouts. Mix lightly.

● Mix the fish sauce, lemon juice, and vinegar. Add the garlic and sugar and stir thoroughly, then add the chile and peanuts, and stir again.

● Toss the dressing into the salad and scatter the cilantro and mint over the top. Garnish with the egg quarters before serving.

Cucumber Salad

SERVES 2–4

Mixing the cucumber with salt and leaving it for 1 hour draws out moisture, so preventing the sauce from being too watery.

1 long cucumber, very thinly sliced

salt

pinch of Korean chili powder, or cayenne pepper mixed with paprika

1 Tbsp sugar

2 Tbsp rice vinegar

sesame oil for sprinkling

● Put the cucumber slices in a bowl. Toss with salt, then add cold water to cover. Leave for 1 hour. Drain the cucumber. If the cucumber tastes very salty, rinse it under running cold water and dry thoroughly on paper towels. Put the cucumber into a bowl.

● Mix the Korean chili powder, or cayenne pepper and paprika, with the sugar and vinegar, and pour over the cucumber. Sprinkle with sesame oil and toss to mix. Cover and chill. Toss again before serving.

Simple Salad

Vietnamese Salad

SERVES 6

Most meals in Vietnam are accompanied by a salad or salad ingredients. Salads are also eaten as first courses or a side dish. A Vietnamese salad is never plain—Vietnamese are adventurous in their mixing of textures and tastes.

2 stalks fresh lemon grass (discard outer leaves), thinly sliced

2 oz each leftover roast beef, pork, lamb, or chicken, finely shredded

1 bunch scallions, washed and finely chopped

2 carrots, finely grated

1 red chile pepper, finely sliced

2 cloves garlic, finely sliced and crushed

3 Tbsp fish sauce

9 Tbsp lime or lemon juice

2 Tbsp fresh basil, chopped

2 Tbsp cilantro, finely chopped

● Lightly hit the sliced lemon grass with the back of a cleaver or heavy knife to release the flavor and smell. Mix the lemon grass with the leftover meat, then add the green onions and toss well. Mix in the carrot.

● Mix together the chile, garlic, fish sauce, and lime juice, and stir well. Add to the salad and toss well. Throw in the basil and cilantro, and toss again. If you think you need more salad dressing, add equal parts of fish sauce and lime juice.

Chinese Cilantro Salad

SERVES 4

This is a variation on a classic salad, made extra special by the cheese dressing, which is poured over the salad ingredients.

8 oz head Chinese leaves or *pak choi*

1 ripe avocado, seeded

1 yellow bell pepper, diced

½ bunch cilantro (about ½ oz), chopped

2 tomatoes, seeded and diced

4 slices bacon, broiled and chopped

1 tsp sesame seeds

FOR THE DRESSING

¼ cp shredded Parmesan cheese

1 Tbsp sesame oil

4 Tbsp salad oil

1 garlic clove, minced

1 Tbsp honey

2 Tbsp garlic wine vinegar

¼ tsp Chinese five-spice powder

2 tsp light soy sauce

● Wash the Chinese leaves well and cut into bite-size pieces. Chop the avocado and add to the leaves with the pepper, cilantro, scallions, tomatoes, bacon, and sesame seeds.

● Mix together the dressing ingredients and pour over the salad. Toss and serve.

Shan Lee Salad

SERVES 4

3 Tbsp sesame seed oil

3 Tbsp orange juice, freshly squeezed

1 butterhead lettuce, the leaves washed and separated

4 Tbsp bamboo shoots

● Mix the sesame oil and orange juice together, and toss into the salad leaves and bamboo shoots.

● Serve as a simple accompaniment to a satay dish or Stuffed Chicken Wings (page 130).

Spinach Noodle Salad

SERVES 4

Young spinach leaves should be used for this recipe. The small leaves taste and look terrific with the spicy sauce and noodles.

8 oz flat rice noodles

2 Tbsp groundnut oil

8 scallions, sliced

2 garlic cloves, minced

½ tsp star anise, ground

2 tsp chopped fresh gingerroot

2 Tbsp dark soy sauce

3 oz young spinach leaves, washed

1 Tbsp sesame oil

FOR THE GARNISH

2 Tbsp fresh cilantro, chopped

● Cook the noodles in boiling water, 4–5 minutes. Drain and cool in cold water.

● Heat the groundnut oil in a wok and cook half of the scallions, the garlic, star anise, ginger, and soy sauce for 2 minutes. Cool completely.

● Arrange the spinach in a serving bowl. Drain the noodles and toss into the vegetables. Sprinkle over the sesame oil and place on top of the spinach. Sprinkle with remaining scallions and serve garnished with fresh cilantro.

Lotus Root Salad

SERVES 2–4

Lotus roots have a firm, crunchy texture, a taste similar to artichoke hearts, and the slices display an attractive flower-like pattern.

4 oz young lotus roots, thinly sliced

2 Tbsp soy sauce

1 Tbsp rice vinegar

2 tsp sesame oil

2 tsp toasted sesame seeds

1 tsp sugar

● Arrange the lotus roots in a steaming basket. Cover and put over a saucepan of boiling water. Steam for about 1 hour—the time will depend on the age and therefore toughness of the roots.

● Transfer the lotus roots to a bowl. Add the remaining ingredients and stir together. Serve warm or chilled.

Spinach Salad

SERVES 4

This salad can be served with almost any other dish and is equally good served warm or chilled.

1 lb young fresh spinach leaves

2 garlic cloves, crushed and
    finely chopped

1 Tbsp sesame oil

2 Tbsp soy sauce

2 tsp sesame seeds

freshly ground black pepper

● Add the spinach to a large saucepan of boiling water. Cover and quickly return to a boil. Boil for 1 minute, then tip the spinach into a colander and refresh under running cold water. Drain, then dry on paper towels.

● Coarsely shred the spinach, then toss with the remaining ingredients. Serve warm, or leave until cold, then cover and chill. Toss again before serving.

Bean Sprout Salad

SERVES 4–6

This is a much loved, crunchy, nutritious salad or side dish. In restaurants it may be served with your pre-prandial drinks, so you have something to nibble while you are waiting for your meal to arrive.

1½ lb soybean sprouts or mung
    bean sprouts

2 garlic cloves, very finely
    chopped

5 scallions, white and green
    parts thinly sliced into rings

1 fresh hot red chile, seeded
    and thinly sliced into rings

1 Tbsp crushed toasted sesame
    seeds

salt

● Remove the roots from the bean sprouts. Add the bean sprouts to a pan of boiling water. Return to a boil, then tip into a colander and rinse under running cold water. Squeeze as much water as possible from the bean sprouts.

● Toss the bean sprouts with the remaining ingredients. Serve either at room temperature or slightly chilled.

Spinach Salad
and Bean Sprout Salad

Carrot and White Radish Salad

SERVES 4

Both the colors and flavors of white radish and carrot complement each other in this attractive salad.

1 carrot, thinly sliced on the diagonal

8 oz white radish, cut into fine strips

salt

1 Tbsp sesame oil

1 tsp soy sauce

1 tsp sugar

very small pinch of Korean chili powder, or cayenne pepper mixed with paprika

● Cut the carrot slices into very fine strips and put into a bowl with the white radish strips. Sprinkle lightly with salt, and toss together well; then leave for 1 hour. Drain, then rinse and drain thoroughly, pressing out as much liquid as possible. Dry on absorbent paper towels.

● Mix the vegetables with the remaining ingredients and serve.

White Radish Salad

SERVES 3–4

In Korea, they use long, pointed white radishes, which are known in the West by the Japanese name of **daikon** *or the Indian name of* **mooli**. *They are available in some markets as well as ethnic stores.*

1 white radish, coarsely grated or cut lengthwise into fine strips

salt

½–1 tsp Korean chili powder, or cayenne pepper mixed with paprika

2 tsp sugar

1 Tbsp sesame oil

4 Tbsp rice vinegar

½ in gingerroot, finely chopped

FOR THE GARNISH

sesame seeds

● Put the white radish into a colander. Mix with salt and leave for 10–15 minutes.

● Rinse the radish well, then drain and dry thoroughly on paper towels.

● Toss the radish with the remaining ingredients, except the sesame seeds. Cover and chill. Garnish with sesame seeds to serve.

Spiced White Radish Salad

SERVES 4

White radishes have a milder flavor than Western red radishes, so respond well to being mixed with typical Korean flavorings.

1 large white radish, sliced

salt

1 Tbsp soy sauce

2 tsp rice vinegar

½ in gingerroot, finely chopped

1 tsp sugar

2 tsp crushed toasted sesame seeds

1½ tsp chile bean paste

1 garlic clove, finely chopped

1 scallion, white and green part thinly sliced diagonally

● Put the white radish into a colander, mix with salt and leave for 10–15 minutes.

● Rinse the radish well, then drain and dry thoroughly on paper towels.

● Mix together the remaining ingredients, except the scallions, and toss with the white radish. Scatter over the scallions, cover and chill. Toss the salad lightly before serving.

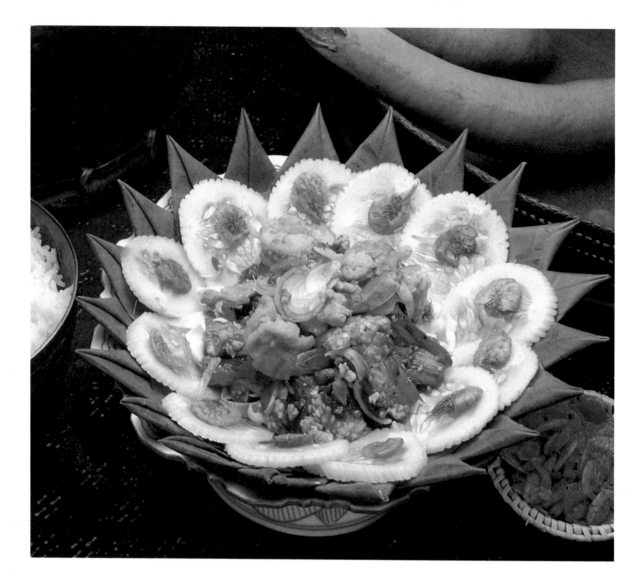

Roasted Eggplant Salad

SERVES 6

3 long green eggplants, combined weight approx 11 oz

⅛ cup ground pork

3 Tbsp peanut or corn oil

2 oz dried shrimp, rinsed in hot water and drained

2 oz shallots, sliced

5 fresh small green chiles, chopped roughly

2 Tbsp lime juice

1 tsp fish sauce

¼ tsp sugar

● Dry-roast the eggplants in a 350°F oven for about 15–20 minutes until soft, then cool, remove the skin and slice into 1 inch pieces.

● Sauté the pork in a skillet or wok in a little oil over high heat until done, about 10 minutes. Mix the eggplant, pork, shrimp, and all the remaining ingredients together well in a bowl. Serve accompanied by rice.

Eggplant Salad with Sesame Seeds

SERVES 4–6

This dish doubles as a salad and as a first course; it is usually served at the beginning of a meal, then left on the table until the end.

1¼ lb oriental eggplants, or small, slim eggplants

1 scallion, white and green part sliced into rings

1 Tbsp sugar

1 Tbsp sesame oil

3 Tbsp Japanese soy sauce

2 garlic cloves, finely chopped

2 Tbsp rice vinegar

2 Tbsp crushed toasted sesame seeds

salt

● If you are using oriental eggplants, cut them lengthwise into quarters, then slice across the middle of each piece. If using ordinary eggplants, cut them into long pieces about 1 inch thick and 1 inch wide.

● Steam the pieces of eggplant in a covered container until tender and soft.

● Mix together the remaining ingredients.

● Leave the eggplants until cool enough to handle, then tear into long, thin strips. Put into a bowl. Pour over the dressing mixture and stir together. Serve at room temperature, or chill before serving.

Green Bean and Red Pepper Salad

SERVES 4

8 oz green beans

1 medium or 2 small red bell peppers, cored and seeded

2 slices fresh gingerroot, thinly shredded

1½ tsp salt

1 tsp sugar

1 Tbsp sesame seed oil

● Wash the beans, snip off the ends and cut into 2 inch lengths. Cut the red bell peppers into thin shreds. Blanch them both in boiling water and drain.

● Put the beans, peppers, and ginger into a bowl. Add the salt, sugar, and sesame seed oil. Toss well to coat the vegetables, and serve.

Cooked Watercress Salad

SERVES 4

Steaming the watercress rather than boiling it keeps it drier and saves having to drain it.

2 large bunches watercress

3 Tbsp soy sauce

1 Tbsp sesame oil

2 tsp toasted sesame seeds

salt and freshly ground black
   pepper

● Cut off and discard the coarse parts of the watercress stalks, then spread it out in a shallow layer in a steaming basket; you may have to cook the watercress in two batches if the steaming basket is not very large. Cover the basket and put over a saucepan of boiling water. Steam for 1–2 minutes. Remove the watercress from the steaming basket and coarsely chop it.

● Toss the watercress with the soy sauce, sesame oil and seeds, salt, and pepper. Leave until cold, then cover and chill. Toss again before serving.

Tomato Salad with Scallion and Oil Dressing

SERVES 4

Other vegetables such as cucumber, celery, and green bell peppers can be served in the same way.

10 oz firm tomatoes

1 tsp salt

1 tsp sugar

3–4 scallions, finely chopped

3 Tbsp salad oil

● Wash and dry the tomatoes. Cut them into thick slices. Sprinkle with salt and sugar. Leave to marinate for 10–15 minutes.

● Place the finely chopped scallions in a heat-resistant bowl. In a pan, heat the oil until quite hot and pour over the scallions. Add the tomatoes, toss well, and serve.

Green Mango Salad

SERVES 4

If this is too sour for some people, you can add more sugar if you like.

2 cups green unripe mango flesh, cut into long matchsticks

¼ cup unsweetened grated coconut, dry-fried until light brown

¼ cup dried shrimp

3 Tbsp shallots, sliced

5 fresh small green chiles, chopped

1 Tbsp palm sugar, or to taste

fish sauce, to taste (optional)

lime juice, to taste (optional)

● Mix all of the ingredients together. If not salty enough add a little of the fish sauce; if not sour enough, add the lime juice.

Green Papaya Salad

Although unripe papaya is not easy to buy in the West, this famous northeastern Thai dish is well worth the trouble. Much of the popularity of this dish, traditionally eaten with sticky rice, is its combination of sweet and sour flavors.

11 oz green papaya, peeled and cut into long matchsticks

7 fresh small whole green chiles

6 garlic cloves, chopped roughly

½ cup string beans, cut into 1 in pieces

¼ cup unsalted roasted peanuts

¼ cup dried small shrimp

6 cherry tomatoes, quartered

¼ cup lime or lemon juice

1 Tbsp palm sugar

1 Tbsp fish sauce

● Take a little of the papaya, the chile, and garlic, and pound together lightly with a mortar and pestle or in a blender. Put in a bowl and stir in the beans, peanuts, shrimp, tomato, and the rest of the papaya. Mix well, then stir in the lemon juice, sugar and fish sauce.

● Serve accompanied by raw vegetables chopped into bite-sized pieces—perhaps swamp cabbage and string beans—sticky rice and roasted chicken.

Rice Salad

SERVES 4–6

This is another "leftover" dish made with rice from a previous occasion.

2 cups cooked rice

2 cups unsweetened grated coconut, browned in a 350°F oven for 5–8 minutes

1 small pomelo or grapefruit, shredded

½ cup dried shrimp, chopped

½ cup bean sprouts

½ cup lemon grass, finely sliced

¼ cup string beans, sliced

2 dried red chiles, pounded

1 Tbsp kaffir lime leaf, finely shredded

FOR THE SAUCE

1 cup water

2 Tbsp anchovies, chopped

1 Tbsp palm sugar

2 kaffir lime leaves, torn into small pieces

¼ tsp lemon grass, sliced

● Put all the sauce ingredients in a pan, boil for 5 minutes, remove from the heat, and strain.

● Place the rice in half-cup molds or large ramekins, press and invert onto a large serving platter. Arrange the rest of the raw ingredients around the edge of the rice in separate piles. To eat, spoon some rice onto individual plates and take a little of each ingredient to mix with the rice according to taste. Spoon the sauce over the top.

Sweet and Sour Cucumber Salad

SERVES 4

1 cucumber

2 tsp fresh gingerroot, finely chopped

1 tsp sesame seed oil

2 Tbsp sugar

2 Tbsp rice vinegar

● Select a dark green and slender cucumber; the fat pale green ones contain too much water and have far less flavor. Cut it in half lengthwise, then cut each piece into slices. Marinate with the ginger and sesame seed oil for about 10–15 minutes.

● Make the dressing with the sugar and vinegar in a bowl, stirring well to dissolve the sugar.

● Place the cucumber slices on a plate. Just before serving, pour the sugar and vinegar dressing evenly over them and toss well.

Chinese Cabbage Salad

SERVES 4

Green or red bell peppers can be added to the cabbage.

1 small Chinese cabbage

2 Tbsp light soy sauce

1 tsp salt

1 tsp sugar

1 Tbsp sesame seed oil

● Wash the cabbage thoroughly, cut into thick slices and place in a bowl.

● Add the soy sauce, salt, sugar and sesame seed oil to the cabbage. Toss well and serve.

Celery Salad

SERVES 4

1 celery

1 tsp salt

7½ cups water

2 Tbsp light soy sauce

1 Tbsp vinegar

1 Tbsp sesame seed oil

2 slices fresh gingerroot, finely shredded

● Remove the leaves and outer tough stalks of the celery. Thinly slice the tender parts diagonally. Blanch them in a pan of boiling, salted water. Then pour them into a colander and rinse in cold water until cool. Drain.

● Mix together the soy sauce, vinegar, and sesame seed oil. Add to the celery and toss well.

● Garnish the salad with finely shredded ginger root and serve.

Seafood Salad with Ponzu Dressing

SERVES 2

Ponzu *can be used as a dip sauce or as a tangy, non-oily salad dressing. It is equally good used in both ways.*

2 celery stalks

3 in piece cucumber

3½ oz carrot, peeled

2 oz frozen whole string beans

5 seafood sticks

pinch of salt

1 quantity of *ponzu* dressing (see page 206)

● Slice the celery, cucumber, and carrot on a slant then cut into matchsticks.

● Cook the beans in salted boiling water for 4–5 minutes, then rinse with cold water and cut in half.

● Mix the vegetables together on a plate or in a bowl. Then pull the seafood sticks into strands with your fingers and use to garnish the top of the salad. Drizzle with the *ponzu* dressing on serving.

Spicy Seafood Salad

SERVES 6

The Thai versions of salad, of which this is one, are flavorful assemblies of different ingredients quite unlike those we are accustomed to in the West. Most are extremely spicy. This dish combines three of the basic five flavors: spicy, sour, and salty.

5 oz sea bass or perch, cleaned, gutted, and sliced thinly into strips

5 oz large shrimp, shelled

5 oz squid, body and tentacles, cleaned, gutted, and sliced into ¾ in strips

7 fresh small green chiles

5 garlic cloves

2 cilantro roots

2 Tbsp fish sauce

½ tsp sugar

2 Tbsp lime or lemon juice

4 scallions, sliced into ¼ in pieces

4 oz onions, sliced thinly

2 oz celery leaves and stalks, sliced

● Cook the fish, shrimp, and squid separately in salted water until cooked, about 2–3 minutes each, and drain.

● Pound the chiles, garlic, cilantro root, fish sauce, and sugar together with a pestle and mortar or in a blender until fine.

● Place in a bowl and mix in the lemon juice, scallion, onion, and celery. Stir in the fish and seafood and mix well. Serve immediately.

Spicy Mussel Salad

SERVES 4

15 oz cooked mussel meat (steam approx 3½ lb mussels in their shells and remove meat)

10 fresh small green chiles, finely chopped

¼ cup mint leaves

3 Tbsp lime or lemon juice, or to taste

2½ Tbsp fish sauce, or to taste

2 Tbsp shallots, sliced

2 Tbsp ginger, cut into matchsticks

2 Tbsp lemon grass, finely sliced

½ Tbsp kaffir lime leaf, shredded

1 small head of white Chinese cabbage, cut into wedges

½ small head of green cabbage, cut into wedges

● Mix together all the ingredients, except the cabbage, in a bowl. Taste for seasoning, adding extra lime juice or fish sauce if you like. Serve on a platter, with the cabbage leaves around the edge to be eaten with the salad.

Jellyfish, Chicken, and Cucumber Salad

SERVES 4

4 oz dried jellyfish

2 cooked chicken breasts, cut into strips

½ cucumber, cut into thin strips

1 Tbsp fresh mint, chopped

1 Tbsp fresh cilantro, chopped

FOR THE NUOC CHAM SAUCE

2 dried hot red chile, cut into pieces

1 clove garlic, chopped

2 tsp sugar

½ fresh lime

2 Tbsp fish sauce or 2 Tbsp light soy sauce and 1 tsp anchovy extract

3 Tbsp water

FOR THE GARNISH

roasted peanuts, crushed

● Make the *nuoc cham* sauce by mixing the chiles, garlic, and sugar, and pounding. Squeeze the lime over the mixture. Add the fish sauce and water and stir thoroughly. Set aside.

● Soak the jellyfish in hot water for about 30 minutes. Remove and soak in cold water for 2 hours, squeezing constantly to remove the salt.

● Mix together the jellyfish, chicken, and cucumber. Add the mint and cilantro. Add the dressing and toss. Sprinkle with the crushed peanuts.

Ground Meat, Crab, and Grapefruit Salad

SERVES 4

¾ cup ground pork or beef

3 Tbsp water

2 Tbsp lime or lemon juice

2 Tbsp fish sauce

1 green chile pepper, finely sliced

1 small Spanish onion, finely diced

½ in fresh gingerroot, finely chopped

1 Tbsp fresh cilantro, finely chopped

1 small can crabmeat, thoroughly drained

1 Pomelo or pink grapefruit, segmented then halved

FOR THE GARNISH

lettuce leaves

grated carrot

● Place the ground meat in the water and slowly cook over a medium heat until the meat turns color and is just cooked but still tender. Remove from the heat and leave to cool slightly.

● Add the lime juice, fish sauce, and chile to the meat. When thoroughly cooled, add the onion, ginger, cilantro, and crabmeat and stir thoroughly. Toss the grapefruit into the salad.

● Place the lettuce leaves on a flat dish. Arrange the grated carrot on the lettuce to form a ring. Spoon the salad into the center of the carrot.

Fresh Chicken Salad with Grapefruit, Mint, and Lemon Grass

SERVES 6

vegetable oil for deep frying

about 40 shrimp chips

1 Tbsp unsalted peanuts

1 Tbsp sesame seeds

1 oz dried shrimp, soaked in hot water for 30 minutes

2 oz fresh pork sides

2 oz uncooked shrimp in the shell

salt

1 medium cucumber, unpeeled, halved lengthwise, seeded, and sliced thinly

1 large carrot, shredded

1 cup fresh bean sprouts

1 oz cooked chicken meat, cut into thin strips

1 Tbsp mint, chopped

½ Tbsp lemon grass, chopped

salt

1 large grapefruit, peeled, sectioned and cut crosswise into 1 in pieces

FOR THE EGG PANCAKES

2 eggs

¼ tsp fish sauce

freshly ground black pepper

vegetable oil

FOR THE DRESSING

1 clove garlic, minced

1 fresh red chile pepper, seeded and minced

½ Tbsp sugar

½ Tbsp fresh lime juice

½ Tbsp rice vinegar

1½ Tbsp fish sauce

FOR THE GARNISH

sprigs of cilantro

● Heat about 2 inches oil to 350°F in a wok. Add the chips 2–3 at a time and keep them immersed in the oil with a pair of chopsticks or perforated spoon until puffy. This should take about 10 seconds. Turn and cook for the same length of time. Set aside.

● Rub down the wok, return it to a moderate heat and cook the peanuts. Stir constantly until the peanuts are golden brown—about 5 minutes. Grind with a grinder or put between a couple of sheets of clean strong paper and grind with a rolling pin or milk bottle. Toast the sesame seeds in the same way for only 3 minutes. Grind lightly to a grainy texture.

● To make the pancakes, beat the eggs, fish sauce, and pepper together with ½ teaspoon water in a bowl. Brush the bottom of a nonstick omelet pan with some oil and place over moderate heat until hot. Pour in half of the egg mixture and tilt the pan immediately to spread the mixture evenly over the bottom—the pancake should be paper-thin. Cook until the egg is set—this should not take more than 30 seconds. Turn and cook on the other side for about 15 seconds. Set aside. Repeat, using up the rest of the mixture.

● Combine the garlic, chile, sugar, lime juice, vinegar, and fish sauce in a bowl. Stir to blend thoroughly.

● Drain the dried shrimp and pound or blend in a blender or processor until very fine. Set aside.

● Cover the pork with water and bring to a boil over a high heat. Lower and boil for about 30 minutes. Run cold water over the pork and set aside.

● Cook the raw shrimp in boiling water until just pink—about 2 minutes. Run cold water over them, drain, peel, devein, and cut lengthwise in halves. Shred the shrimp and set aside.

● Sprinkle salt over the cucumber and carrot, and leave to stand for 15 minutes. Run cold water over them and squeeze dry with your hands. It is imperative that the vegetables are bone dry to ensure their crunchiness.

● Dip the bean sprouts in salted boiling water for 30 seconds. Run cold water over them and drain.

● Cut the egg pancakes into strips. Combine the egg pancake strips, dried shrimp, shredded shrimp, chicken, cucumber, carrot, bean sprouts, mint, lemon grass, grapefruit, and sesame seeds. Mix well with your hands and pour over the dressing mixture.

● Transfer to a serving dish or serve separately, and sprinkle the ground peanuts over it. Garnish with cilantro. Serve with shrimp chips on which guests place bite-sized portions of the salad.

Fresh Chicken Salad with Grapefruit,
Mint, and Lemon Grass

Ground Pork, Shrimp, and Pineapple Salad with a Fish Sauce Dressing

SERVES 2

1 lb fresh lean pork, ground or, preferably, finely chopped

2 Tbsp water

8 oz cooked shrimp

2 Tbsp lemon juice

2 Tbsp fish sauce

½ tsp dried powdered chili

1 tsp fresh red chile pepper, finely sliced

2 Tbsp onion, finely sliced

2 Tbsp scallions, cut into ½ in sections

2 Tbsp roasted peanuts

2 slices pineapple, roughly chopped

2 Tbsp gingerroot, finely sliced

1 Tbsp fresh mint leaves, chopped

2 Tbsp fresh cilantro leaves and stem, chopped

6 large lettuce leaves

FOR THE GARNISH

roasted peanuts

1 Tbsp gingerroot, finely sliced

pinch of dried powdered chili

fresh red chile pepper, sliced

sprigs of mint

sprigs of cilantro

scallion curls

chile flowers

● Cook the pork in a wok over medium heat with the water until the pork is cooked thoroughly but still tender and juicy. Remove from the heat.

● Add the shrimps, lemon juice, fish sauce, and dried and fresh chile and stir. Add the onion, scallion, peanuts, pineapple, ginger, mint, and cilantro leaves. Toss lightly.

● Serve on a bed of lettuce leaves. Garnish with peanuts, ginger, chile, sprigs of mint and cilantro, scallion curls, and chili flowers.

Bean-thread Noodle Salad with Barbecued Pork

SERVES 4

The secret of success with this dish is to have good quality pork well marinated in cha siu *sauce, and then roast it long enough to be edible, but not so long as to overcook the center of the meat.*

½ lb bean-thread noodles

4–5 small carrots, cut into matchsticks

½ lb cucumber, cut into matchsticks

½ lb Chinese barbecued pork, shredded

2 dried wood ear, soaked and shredded, or 2–3 shiitake mushrooms (optional)

4 tsp toasted sesame seeds

FOR THE DRESSING

4 Tbsp light soy sauce

2½ Tbsp dark soy sauce

2½ Tbsp sugar

5 Tbsp vinegar

4 Tbsp sesame oil

● Soak the bean-thread noodles in warm water for 5 minutes, or according to the instructions on the package. Rinse under water, and drain.

● Mix the soy sauce, sugar, vinegar, and sesame oil together in a bowl. Add the carrots, cucumber, *cha siu* pork, wood ear, or mushrooms, if using, and noodles, and mix well.

● Serve the noodles either on a large dish or in four individual dishes, and sprinkle with toasted sesame seeds before eating.

Cold Crispy Roast Lamb, Beansprout, and Bean Salad

SERVES 4

4 oz crispy roast leg of lamb, thinly sliced and cut into ½ x 1 in strips

2 cups bean sprouts, washed and dried

1 cup green beans, tossed in boiling water for 5 minutes

1 cup broccoli florets, blanched

6 lettuce leaves, preferably Chinese

3 large tomatoes, cut into wedges

1 large cucumber, peeled and sliced

½ medium bell pepper, cut in strips

2 medium-sized onions, finely sliced into rings

6 scallion curls

3 hard-cooked eggs, peeled and halved

FOR THE DRESSING

½ cup unsalted roasted peanuts

½ cup lemon juice

3 Tbsp vinegar

4 cloves garlic

3 Tbsp fresh cilantro, chopped

3 Tbsp sugar

1 Tbsp fish sauce

FOR THE GARNISH

1 hard-cooked egg, sliced

fresh cilantro, chopped

chile flowers

● Blend all the dressing ingredients in a blender using a little water to give you the consistency you want. Adjust by increasing vinegar, sugar, or fish sauce.

● Arrange the salad ingredients on a large dish. Start off with a bed of lettuce and from there, you are on your own.

Bean-thread Noodle Salad with Shrimp

SERVES 4

This is a hot Thai salad. The fish sauce, an essential ingredient in Thai cuisine, enhances the flavor of the dish. It is a good idea to prepare this salad at least 30 minutes before you serve it to allow the full sweet, hot flavor to mature.

½ lb bean-thread noodles

16 tiger shrimp, peeled and deveined

1 tsp fish sauce

2 tsp freshly squeezed lemon juice

1 tsp palm or brown sugar

1 Tbsp sunflower oil

1 small red bell pepper, finely chopped

2 stalks celery, thinly sliced

4–5 small carrots, cut into matchsticks

2 scallions, chopped

4–5 lettuce leaves

cilantro leaves to garnish

FOR THE DRESSING

2 shallots, finely chopped

1 dry red chile, crushed

3 small green chile, chopped

4 Tbsp fish sauce

½ cup freshly squeezed lemon juice (about 2 lemons)

4½ Tbsp palm or brown sugar

1 Tbsp sunflower oil

● Soak the bean-thread noodles in warm water for 5 minutes, or according to the instructions on the package. Rinse under cold running water, and drain.

● Marinate the shrimp in a mixture of 1 teaspoon fish sauce, 2 teaspoons of lemon juice, and 1 teaspoon sugar for 15 minutes.

● Meanwhile, mix together the dressing ingredients.

● Heat 1 tablespoon oil in a frying pan, and stir-fry the shrimp thoroughly.

● Put the red bell pepper, celery, carrot, scallions, and noodles in a bowl, and mix together. Place a lettuce leaf on each plate, and pile the noodle mixture onto it. Put the shrimp on the noodles, and sprinkle with the cilantro leaves.

Spicy Catfish Salad

SERVES 4

11 oz whole catfish, cleaned and gutted

1 Tbsp peanut or corn oil

¼ cup mint leaves, sliced

3 Tbsp lime juice, or to taste

3 Tbsp shallots, sliced

2½ Tbsp fish sauce, or to taste

1½ Tbsp sticky rice, dry-fried for a few minutes and pounded finely

1 tsp chili powder

1 tsp kaffir lime leaf, finely shredded

● Rub the catfish with the oil and roast in the oven at 350°F for 40 minutes until firm but tender. When cooked, remove the skin and bones and chop the fish meat finely. Place in a bowl and stir in the rest of the ingredients—mix well. Check the seasoning, and add more fish sauce or lime juice if you like.

● Serve accompanied by raw string beans, cabbage, sweet basil, and scallions.

Bean-thread Noodle Salad
with Shrimp

Fried Catfish Spicy Salad

SERVES 4–6

This crispy dish is often served as a snack to accompany drinks (an important and distinct category of dish in Thailand, where drinking tends to be separated from eating main meals).

2 whole catfish (1 lb 2 oz each), cleaned and gutted

5 cups peanut or corn oil for deep-frying

1 green unripe mango, cut into matchsticks

¼ cup unsalted roasted peanuts

7 fresh small green chiles, chopped

3 Tbsp shallots, sliced

3 Tbsp fish sauce

2 Tbsp cilantro leaves and stems, cut into 1 in pieces

● Steam the catfish for 15 minutes until well cooked. Remove all the skin and bones and chop finely.

● Heat the oil in a wok or pan until hot, about 350°F, sprinkle in the chopped fish and fry until light brown and crispy, 3–5 minutes. Remove with a slotted spoon or strainer and drain well.

● Mix all the remaining ingredients except the cilantro with the fish. Place the salad on plates, and garnish with cilantro, and serve accompanied by rice.

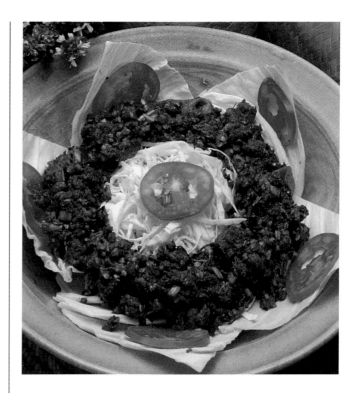

Raw Beef Salad

SERVES 6

This salad from the north of Thailand differs from the better known southern version chiefly in that it does not include the roasted ground rice. Northerners also have a special liking for raw meat dishes. The origin for this and our more familiar steak tartare may well be the same.

7 oz very fresh lean beef sirloin, chopped finely at the last minute

2 oz beef liver, sliced thinly

½ cup very fresh beef blood

¼ cup mint leaves

3 Tbsp scallion, finely sliced

3 Tbsp lime or lemon juice

½ Tbsp fish sauce

1½ tsp chili powder

● Simply mix all the ingredients together well and place on serving plates.

● Serve accompanied by raw swamp cabbage, raw cabbage wedges, fresh basil, and sticky rice.

Stir-fry Pork and Vegetable Salad

SERVES 4

The vegetables can be altered according to taste or availability.

vegetable oil for frying

4 oz piece of pork loin, cut into fine strips

1 small turnip, cut into 2 in long strips

1 small carrot, cut into 2 in long strips

1 small onion, cut into 2 in long strips

2–3 celery stalks, cut into 2 in long strips

2 oz mushroom caps, cut into 2 in long strips

1 small garlic clove, crushed and finely chopped

1 tsp grated fresh ginger

2 scallions, white and some green parts finely chopped

3 Tbsp soy sauce

1½ tsp sesame oil

1 Tbsp sugar

1 tsp rice vinegar

freshly ground black pepper

sesame seeds for garnish

● Heat about 2 tablespoons of oil in a skillet. Add the pork and stir-fry for 3–4 minutes until cooked through. Using a slotted spoon, transfer it to a bowl.

● Add the turnip and carrot strips to the pan and fry for 5–7 minutes until just beginning to soften.

● Add the onion and celery to a saucepan of boiling water and simmer for 2–3 minutes. Drain and refresh under running cold water. Add to the pork with the mushrooms, garlic, ginger, and scallions.

● Using a slotted spoon, transfer the turnips and carrots to paper towels to drain.

● Whisk together the soy sauce, sesame oil, sugar, and rice vinegar. Add the turnips and carrots to the pork. Pour over the dressing and toss. Leave until cold. Serve sprinkled with sesame seeds.

Sauces, Pickles, and Dips

Many of the dishes described in earlier sections can be served with
a variety of accompaniments, and some of the best known dips and
sauces are included here. In addition, Asian cuisine features many
preserved foodstuffs, which were developed in the days before
refrigerators were available. Pickled, salted, fermented, and
sun-dried vegetables, meat, and fish are flavorsome and economical
accompaniments to plain noodles or rice.

Cabbage Pickle

FILLS ABOUT 2 2-QUART JARS

*This is a standard cabbage **kimchi**. Some of the cabbage can be replaced by thinly sliced white radish, if liked.*

2 lb Chinese cabbage

salt

6 scallions, white and green parts thinly sliced

4 garlic cloves, crushed and finely chopped

2 Tbsp gingerroot, finely chopped

1 Tbsp Korean chili powder, or cayenne pepper mixed with paprika

1 tsp sugar

● Quarter the Chinese cabbage lengthways, then cut each quarter widthways into 2 inch pieces.

● Pour 6¼ cups water into a large bowl and stir in 3 tablespoons salt until dissolved. Add the cabbage and weight down with a plate.

● Cover and leave for 12 hours, stirring the cabbage occasionally. Using a slotted spoon, remove the cabbage from the bowl, and reserve the salted water.

● Mix the cabbage with the remaining ingredients and 1 teaspoon salt. Pack into clean, dry jars. Pour in enough of the reserved salted water to cover the cabbage; leave a space of 1 inch at the top of the jar.

● Cover the jar loosely with a non-metallic lid and leave for 3–6 days until the pickle has become sour enough for your taste. Cover tightly and keep in a cold, dark place. It will keep in these conditions for up to 1 year.

Stuffed Cucumber Pickle

FILLS ABOUT 3 1-PINT JARS

Use a potato peeler or the slicing disk of a food processor to slice the white radish. To serve, slice through the cucumbers completely and arrange on a plate.

1½ lb pickling cucumbers

12 oz white radish

1 in gingerroot

2 Tbsp garlic, very finely chopped

6 scallions, white and some green parts very thinly sliced

2½ tsp Korean chili powder, or cayenne pepper mixed with paprika

1½ tsp sugar

2 tsp salt

● Cut the cucumbers crosswise, slightly diagonally, at ½ inch intervals but not going quite all the way—the slices should remain attached at the bottom.

● Pour 4½ cups water into a bowl and stir in 4 tablespoons of salt until dissolved. Add the cucumbers and weight down with a plate to keep them submerged. Leave for 3–4 hours.

● Just before the cucumbers are ready, cut the ginger into very fine strips. Cut the white radish into very fine strips. Mix with the remaining ingredients.

● Lift the cucumbers from the liquid; reserve the liquid. Dry the cucumbers with paper towels. Fill the gaps between the cucumber slices with as much of the white radish stuffing as they will hold easily. Put into a bowl. Add any remaining white radish stuffing and liquid from it. Cover and leave for 8 hours.

● Carefully pack the cucumbers fairly tightly into clean, dry 1-pint jars. Push any loose stuffing between the cucumbers and pour in all the juices from the bowl. Push the cucumbers down; if the liquid does not cover them by ½ inch, add some of the reserved cucumber soaking water.

● Cover loosely and leave for 3–6 days until the pickle has soured to your taste. Seal tightly and keep until required. It will keep for up to a year.

Spiced Turnip Pickle

FILLS A 1½-CUP JAR

Turnip is a very popular root vegetable in Korea, used in many everyday recipes as well as in pickles.

2 turnips, each weighing about 5 oz, peeled, halved lengthways and thinly sliced

1½ tsp salt

3 garlic cloves, finely chopped

1 scallion, white and green part finely chopped

1 dried red chile, seeded and coarsely crushed

● Rub 1 teaspoon of the salt into the turnip slices, then put into a bowl. Leave for 3 hours, stirring the slices every 30 minutes.

● Drain the turnips and rinse under running cold water, then mix with the remaining ingredients.

● Pack into a clean, dry jar, then cover with cold water. Put a saucer on the jar and leave for 6–8 days until the pickle turns sour.

● Cover the jar with a vinegar-proof lid and store in a cool, dry place for up to a year.

Instant Cucumber Pickle

SERVES 6–8

*This is a very convenient version of **kimchi** as it can be eaten as soon as it has been chilled (see page 413).*

1 lb cucumbers

2¼ tsp salt

1 garlic clove, crushed and finely chopped

3½ in piece of white radish, cut into fine strips

2 scallions, white and green parts thinly sliced

1 in piece of fresh ginger, crushed to a pulp

1½ tsp Korean chili powder, or cayenne pepper mixed with paprika

2 tsp crushed toasted sesame seeds

1 Tbsp sesame oil

● Cut the cucumber into 2 inch lengths, then cut each piece lengthways in half. Place each half skin-side up and slice across. Put the slices in a colander, and toss with 2 teaspoons of the salt. Leave for at least 3 hours.

● Drain the cucumber gently, squeezing out as much water as possible.

● Mix the cucumber with the remaining salt, garlic, white radish, scallions, ginger and chili powder, or cayenne and paprika. Cover and chill. Drain off the liquid from the vegetables, then toss them with the sesame seeds and sesame oil. This will keep for a day or two in the refrigerator.

Pickled Garlic

FILLS A 1-CUP JAR

Green garlic is used in Korea for this recipe, but it works very well with ordinary garlic if the heads are made up of large, plump cloves. After pickling, the cut garlic heads are cut crossways to make attractive slices.

2 heads of garlic with plump cloves

½ cup rice vinegar

½ cup soy sauce

2 Tbsp sugar

1 tsp salt

● Put the garlic in a clean, dry 1-cup jar. Bring the remaining ingredients to a boil in a small saucepan, then simmer gently until reduced by half. Pour over the garlic.

● Cover tightly and leave for 2 months. It will keep for up to a year in a cool, dry place.

Stuffed Cabbage Pickle

FILLS A 1-CUP JAR

*Salted fish, especially anchovies, are a popular addition to **kimchis**; the fish dissolve during the fermentation and storage, enriching the flavor of the **kimchi**, not giving it a fishy taste. This recipe uses fish sauce instead of salted anchovies.*

6 Tbsp salt

½ Chinese cabbage, about 8 oz

6 oz piece of white radish, halved crosswise

4 scallions, coarsely chopped

4 garlic cloves, crushed and finely chopped

1 in piece of gingerroot, crushed and finely chopped

1 Tbsp Korean chili powder, or cayenne pepper mixed with paprika

1 tsp sugar

2 Tbsp fish sauce

● Pour 4½ cups water into a large bowl and stir in all but ¼ teaspoon of the salt until dissolved. Add the cabbage and put a plate on top to keep it submerged. Leave for 8–10 hours.

● Cut the white radish into thin strips, then mix well with the remaining ingredients, including the remaining salt. Drain the cabbage well, then squeeze hard to remove as much water as possible.

● Place the cabbage cut-side up. Beginning with the outer leaves, pack the white radish mixture between each leaf.

● Fold the cabbage leaves and pack them into a clean, dry jar. Add any remaining white radish mixture. Cover loosely with vinegar-proof lids and leave for at least 3 days until sour enough for your taste. Push the cabbage down so it remains beneath the liquid that is produced. Cover tightly and keep in a cold place. It will keep for up to a year.

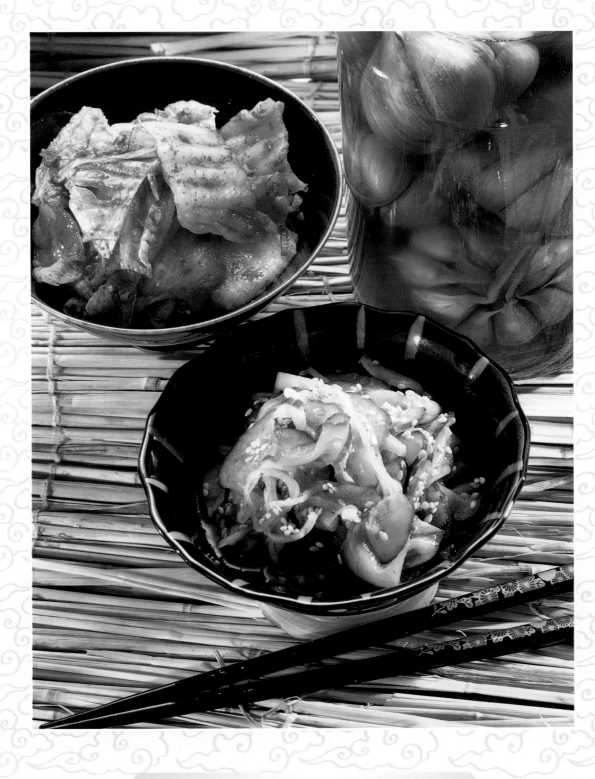

Stuffed Cabbage Pickle, Pickled
Garlic, and Instant Cucumber Pickle

Northeastern Spicy Dip

SERVES 4–6

This dip is not very spicy, but has an interesting combination of flavors.

6 garlic cloves

1 Tbsp shallot, sliced

1 tsp galangal, chopped

2 Tbsp anchovies, finely chopped

1 Tbsp lemon juice

1 dried red chile, pounded finely

1 kaffir lime leaf, torn into small pieces

½ stalk of lemon grass, sliced finely

● Dry-fry the garlic, shallot, and galangal for 3 minutes over medium heat, then chop finely. Pound with the rest of the ingredients with a mortar and pestle or in a blender.

● Serve accompanied by cabbage, string beans, fresh basil, and sticky rice.

Fermented Dip for Vegetables and Rice

SERVES 6–8

Northeasterners have their own special version of fish sauce, a much more substantial affair containing fish pieces, vegetables and flavorings. Quite pungent!

2½ cups thin coconut milk

3 oz dried salted mackerel (the smellier the better) or anchovies

1½ oz galangal, sliced

1½ oz lemon grass, sliced

5 oz catfish fillets, skinned and cut into pieces

6 fresh small whole red chiles

1 Tbsp kaffir lime leaves, finely sliced

1½ oz *krachai,* cut into lengthwise matchsticks

4 oz string beans, cut into 1 in pieces

2 oz shallots, halved

2 oz bamboo shoots, cut into ¼ in pieces

4 baby white eggplants, the size of large grapes

fish sauce, to taste (optional)

● Heat the coconut milk in a pan, add the salted fish, boil for 1 minute, add the galangal and lemon grass, boil again, then add the catfish, chiles and lime leaf and cook for another minute.

● Add the krachai—don't stir it in—and bring back to a boil. Simmer for 3 minutes, add the rest of the ingredients and cook for another 2 minutes. Taste for saltiness and add fish sauce as necessary. Serve hot or cold—this dish can be refrigerated for 2–3 days to enhance the flavors.

● Serve accompanied by raw vegetables and rice.

Spicy Dip with Mackerel

SERVES 6

3 x 4 oz baby mackerel, cleaned and gutted, or 11 oz boneless mackerel fillets

1½ tsp salt

½ Tbsp shrimp paste

2 Tbsp dried shrimp, pounded fine

1 Tbsp sliced garlic

2 small green eggplants, peeled

15 fresh small whole green or red chiles

6 pea-sized eggplants or fresh green peas

2 Tbsp lemon juice

1 Tbsp fish sauce

½ Tbsp palm sugar

1 fresh large red chile, sliced into small circles

¼ cup peanut or corn oil

● Rub the mackerel inside and out with the salt and leave in a cool place for 1 hour.

● Dry-fry the shrimp paste in foil over high heat for 5 minutes (or roast in a 350°F oven for 8 minutes), then remove and unwrap.

● Pound the shrimp paste, dried shrimp, garlic, and eggplant together with a mortar and pestle or in a blender. Add the small chiles, pound lightly, then thoroughly mix in the rest of the ingredients, except the red chile slices, which are used for garnish.

● Heat the oil in a skillet over medium heat and fry the fish for 6–8 minutes on each side—the flesh should be tender but firm and white at the center.

● Serve accompanied by fresh vegetables, such as lightly boiled cabbage and string beans.

Pickled Radishes

SERVES 4

24 radishes	1 tsp salt
2 tsp sugar	

● Choose fairly large radishes that are roughly equal in size, if possible, and cut off and discard the stalks and tails. Wash the radishes in cold water and dry them thoroughly. Using a sharp knife, make several cuts from the top about two-thirds of the way down the sides of each radish.

● Put the radishes in a large jar. Add the sugar and salt. Cover the jar and shake well so that each radish is coated with the sugar and salt mixture. Leave to marinate for several hours or overnight.

● Just before serving, pour off the liquid and spread out each radish like a fan. Serve them on a plate on their own or as a garnish with other cold dishes.

White Radish Pickle

FILLS 1 JAR

Some people find that chiles and chili powder irritate their skin; if this happens to you, wear fine rubber gloves when rubbing the chili powder into the radish.

2 Tbsp Korean chili powder or cayenne pepper mixed with paprika	1 in piece of fresh gingerroot, finely chopped
1¾ lb white radish, cut into 1 in cubes	1 small garlic clove, finely chopped
4 scallions, white and green parts thinly sliced	2 tsp sugar
	4 tsp salt

● Rub the chili powder or cayenne and paprika into the white radish. Put in a bowl and leave for at least 30 minutes.

● Mix the remaining ingredients with the white radish, and cover with plastic wrap. Put a plate that just fits inside the bowl, on top of the plastic wrap, and put a heavy weight on top. Leave for about 48 hours until the liquid rises above the white radish.

● Remove the weight and leave the pickle for a further 3–7 days, depending on the temperature, until it turns sour.

● Transfer the pickle to a dry, clean jar. Cover with a vinegar-proof lid and keep in a cold, dark place. It will keep for up to a year in these conditions.

Pickled Vegetables

SERVES 4

Use 4–6 of the following vegetables or more: cucumber, carrot, radish or turnip, cauliflower, broccoli, green cabbage, white cabbage, celery, onion, fresh gingerroot, leek, scallion, red bell pepper, green bell pepper, green beans, and garlic

9½ pints cold boiled water

¾ cup salt

2 oz chile peppers

3 tsp Szechwan peppercorns

4 Tbsp Chinese distilled spirit (or white rum, gin, or vodka)

4 oz gingerroot

4 oz brown sugar

● Put the cold boiled water into a large, clean earthenware or glass jar. Add the salt, chiles, peppercorns, spirit, ginger, and sugar.

● Wash and trim the vegetables, peel if necessary and drain well. Put them into the jar and seal it making sure it is airtight. Place the jar in a cool place and leave the vegetables to pickle for at least five days before serving.

● Use a pair of clean chopsticks or tongs to pick the vegetables out of the jar. Do not allow any grease to enter the jar. You can replenish the vegetables, adding a little salt each time. If any white scum appears on the surface of the brine, add a little sugar and spirit. The longer the pickling lasts, the better.

Fried Egg Strip Garnish

SERVES 1

A common garnish for Korean savory dishes. Lightly beaten eggs are fried one at a time to keep the mixture thin. Sometimes, the eggs are separated and the yolks and whites cooked separately.

1 egg, lightly beaten   vegetable oil for frying

● Heat a very thin film of vegetable oil in a large nonstick skillet. Pour in the egg, and tilt and swirl the pan to spread the egg out in a thin even layer.

● Fry for 1–2 minutes until set underneath, then turn the "omelet" over and fry until set. Transfer the "omelet" to a wooden board, or a work surface, and roll it up. Cut into ¼ inch strips.

Southern Vegetable Dip

SERVES 4

½ cup raw large shrimp, shelled and cut into 3 pieces

2 Tbsp fish sauce

2 Tbsp lemon or lime juice

1 Tbsp fresh small green chile, chopped

1 Tbsp shallot, sliced

1½ tsp shrimp paste

● Boil the shrimps in a small amount of water for 2 minutes and drain. Place in a bowl and mix well with the rest of the ingredients except the shrimp paste.

● Wrap the shrimp paste in foil, and roast in a 350°F oven for 5 minutes, or dry-fry in a hot wok for 3 minutes. Remove and stir into the shrimp mixture.

● Serve accompanied by string beans, lima beans, raw cabbage, and rice.

Green Chile Dip

SERVES 6

This is high on the scale of chile "heat," but green and fresh-tasting. It is intended to be eaten with sticky rice and assorted raw vegetables, and as part of a larger meal. Traditionally, everyone eats from one bowl.

1 Tbsp dried salted mackerel or anchovy, chopped

4 Tbsp peanut or corn oil

10 fresh 2 in green chiles, chopped roughly

10 garlic cloves, chopped roughly

6 shallots, chopped roughly

3 cherry tomatoes

2 Tbsp hot water

1 Tbsp scallion, chopped

1 Tbsp cilantro leaves, chopped

fish sauce, to taste (optional)

● Fry the dried fish in the oil over medium heat for about 7–10 minutes and drain. Dry-fry the chiles, garlic, shallots, and tomatoes until fragrant, about 8–10 minutes. Place in a bowl.

● Pound them lightly with the dry fish. Add the water, scallion and cilantro, and mix well. Taste to check—it should be of a saucy consistency and a touch salty; if not, add more water or fish sauce.

● Serve accompanied by a selection of raw cabbage wedges, sliced cucumbers, raw string beans, and/or fried or roasted fish.

Spicy Meat and Tomato Dip

SERVES 4–6

This is a relatively mild dip, and in northern Thai fashion, guests eat from the bowl in which it is served, scooping with the pork rind, vegetables or sticky rice.

6 dried red chiles, chopped	½ cup raw ground pork
3 Tbsp shallots, chopped	8 cherry tomatoes, diced
1 Tbsp lemon grass, sliced	½ cup water
1 Tbsp garlic, chopped	lemon juice, to taste
2 tsp shrimp paste	fish sauce, to taste
2 tsp salt	sugar, to taste
2 Tbsp peanut or corn oil	1 oz cilantro leaves

● Pound the chiles, onion, lemon grass, garlic, shrimp paste, and salt together with a mortar and pestle or in a blender until fine.

● Heat the oil in a wok or pan and add the chile mixture and the pork, and tomatoes. Cook until thick, about 15 minutes, then add the water and cook again for 10 minutes until thick.

● Adjust the seasoning to taste with lemon juice, fish sauce, and/or sugar. Garnish with the cilantro leaves.

● Serve accompanied by raw or slightly cooked vegetables, sticky rice, and if you can buy it, crispy pork rind.

Crushed Toasted Sesame Seeds

MAKES ABOUT 1/3 CUP

Prepare the quantity of these that is appropriate to the amount of Korean cooking you are going to do (it is easy to increase or halve the recipe), and store them in a screw-top jar in a cool, dark place.

⅓ cup sesame seeds

2 tsp salt

● Heat a small, heavy skillet over a medium-low heat. Add the sesame seeds and stir until they darken a shade and give off a toasted, nutty aroma.

● Crush the seeds with the salt in a pestle and mortar. Keep in a screw-top jar.

Vinegar Dipping Sauce

MAKES 10 TABLESPOONS

This can serve as a basic Korean dipping sauce.

7 Tbsp soy sauce

2 Tbsp rice vinegar

½ in gingerroot, grated

2 tsp crushed toasted sesame seeds

about ½ tsp Korean chili powder

pinch of sugar

● Combine the soy sauce and vinegar in a small bowl, and add remaining ingredients. If you do not have the chili powder, use cayenne pepper mixed with paprika.

Ginger Dipping Sauce

MAKES ABOUT 10 TABLESPOONS

There are no chiles in this sauce but ginger provides some "hotness." Also the predominance of soy sauce and rice vinegar are reversed.

6 Tbsp rice vinegar

1 in piece of gingerroot, grated

2 scallions, white part only, finely chopped

2 Tbsp dark soy sauce

2 tsp sugar

● Pour the vinegar into a small bowl. Add the remaining ingredients and mix together well.

Sesame Dipping Sauce

MAKES 6 TABLESPOONS

Sesame oil and toasted sesame seeds make a more richly flavored dipping sauce.

3 Tbsp soy sauce

1 tsp sesame oil

1½ Tbsp rice vinegar

1 tsp toasted sesame seeds

pinch of sugar

1 small scallion, finely chopped

● Combine the soy sauce, sesame oil, and rice vinegar in a small bowl. Add the remaining ingredients and mix well.

Seasoned Dipping Sauce

MAKES 7 TABLESPOONS

4 Tbsp soy sauce

2 tsp sesame oil

1 Tbsp rice vinegar

about ¼–½ fresh red or green chile

2 tsp toasted sesame seeds

pinch of sugar

½–1 small garlic clove, finely chopped

● Combine the soy sauce, sesame oil, and rice vinegar in a small bowl. Deseed the chile and chop finely. Add to the bowl with remaining ingredients and mix well.

Yakisoba Sauce

5–6 SERVINGS

5 Tbsp brown sauce

4 Tbsp light soy sauce

4 tsp tomato katsup

4 tsp oyster sauce

4 Tbsp sugar

● Mix all the ingredients together.

Fish Sauce with Chiles

MAKES ABOUT 1/3 CUP

This spicy sauce is found on all Thai tables and is used to add both spiciness and saltiness to dishes.

¼ cup fish sauce

10 fresh small green chiles, sliced into small circles

1 tsp sliced shallot

¼ tsp palm sugar

1 Tbsp lime or lemon juice

● Mix all the ingredients together well. This is good for accompanying almost all Thai food, especially rice. Just sprinkle a little on your food to liven it up.

Homemade Red Pepper Paste

MAKES ABOUT 7 TABLESPOONS

This is an important seasoning and flavoring in Korean cuisine. It used to be made at home, from home-fermented soybeans, but even in Korea it is often bought ready-made nowadays. In the West it can only be purchased from Korean stores, but an approximation can be made at home quite easily using fairly readily available ingredients.

4 Tbsp brown or red *miso*

1½ Tbsp paprika

1 tsp cayenne pepper

1 Tbsp sugar

● Mix all the ingredients together in a small bowl. Keep in a screw-top jar in a cool, dark place. It will keep for up to 6 months in these conditions.

Desserts

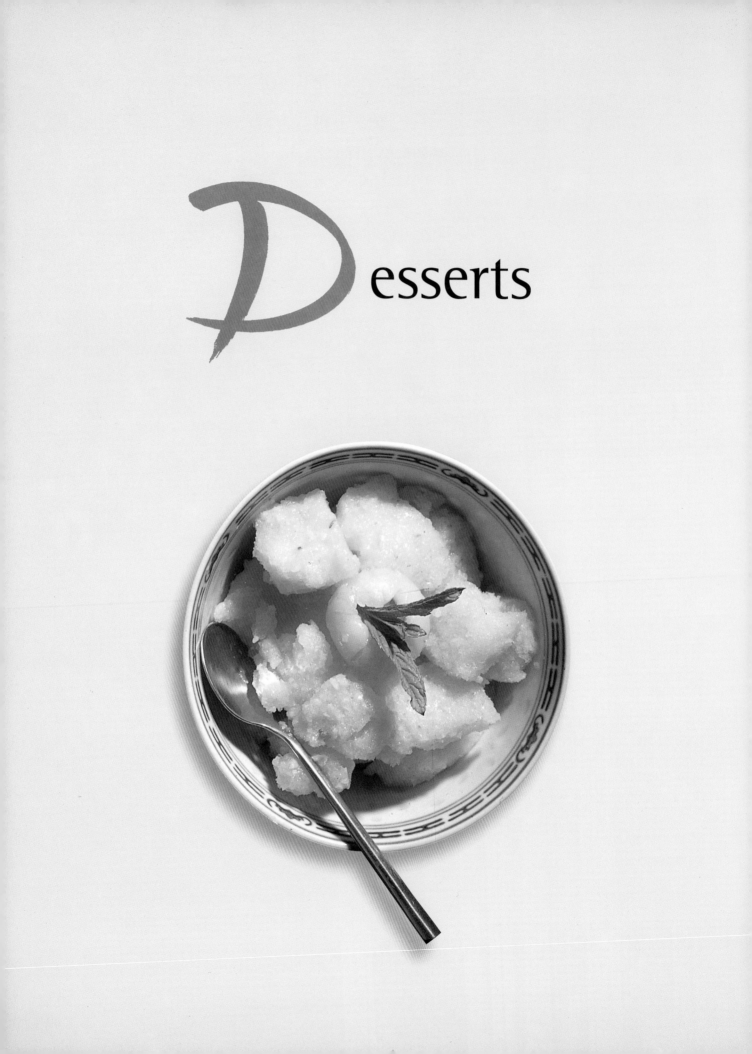

Asian meals do not usually conclude with a dessert, but these delicious treats are the perfect way to end a meal. Cakes and sweetmeats are popular throughout the Far East, and they are often served on special occasions such as birthdays and New Year celebrations. The section ends with a number of recipes for tea, the traditional accompaniment to many Asian meals.

Golden Balls

SERVES 6

20 egg yolks, duck if available

4 cups rice flour

8 cups water

6 cups sugar

4 egg shells

1 tsp jasmine water or vanilla
essence

● Mix the egg yolks well with the flour in a bowl and put to one side until needed. Boil the water and sugar in a pan with the egg shells until reduced to about half, then strain through muslin, put back in the pan and bring back to simmer. Add the jasmine or vanilla essence at this point.

● Take pieces of the egg mixture and form balls the size of large round grapes. Place them in the simmering sugar syrup; cook the balls until they float to the surface, then remove with a slotted spoon and drain on paper towel. Strain the syrup, again through cloth, into a large bowl and set aside to cool until needed.

● Soak the cooked balls in the strained syrup for 30 minutes, then remove them with a slotted spoon and refrigerate. Serve when cool.

Gold Threads

SERVES 6

4 egg shells

6 cups sugar

8 cups water

1 tsp vanilla essence or
  jasmine water

15 egg yolks, duck if available,
  whisked lightly

● Punch about 25 small holes into the base of a can. Wash well.

● Put the egg shells, sugar, and water in a pan, bring to a boil and simmer until reduced by about half. Strain the liquid through cheesegauze.

● Bring the strained syrup back to a simmer, and add the essence. Then, pour the whisked egg yolks through the "strainer" over the simmering sugar syrup. Let cook for 1 minute and remove with a slotted spoon or strainer. Repeat the process until all the egg is used, packing the threads on a rack to drain.

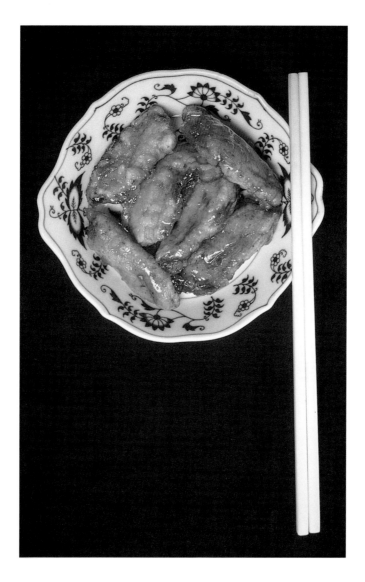

Toffee Bananas

SERVES 4

4 bananas, peeled

1 egg

2 Tbsp all-purpose flour

oil for deep-frying

4 Tbsp sugar

1 Tbsp cold water

● Cut the bananas in half lengthwise and then cut each half into two crosswise.

● Beat the egg, add the flour and mix well to make a smooth batter.

● Heat the oil in a wok or deep-fryer. Coat each piece of banana with batter and deep-fry until golden. Remove and drain.

● Pour off the excess oil, leaving about 1 tablespoon of oil in the wok. Add the sugar and water and stir over a medium heat to dissolve the sugar. Continue stirring and when the sugar has caramelized, add the hot banana pieces. Coat well and remove. Dip the hot bananas in cold water to harden the toffee and serve immediately while still hot.

Banana and Pineapple Fritters

SERVES 4

vegetable oil for deep-frying

4 bananas, peeled and halved
lengthwise

4 pineapple rings, fresh or
canned, dried on paper
towels

confectioner's sugar, sieved

FOR THE BATTER

½ cup self-rising flour

1¼ cups all-purpose flour

½ tsp baking powder

2 Tbsp vegetable oil

salt

1 egg white, beaten until stiff

● Make the batter first. Mix the flours, baking powder, salt, and oil in a large bowl. Stir in just enough water to make a smooth paste. Fold in the egg white a little at a time.

● Heat some oil in a wok for deep-frying. Dip the fruit in the batter and cook in small batches (do not put more than can comfortably float on the oil) until puffy and golden. This should not take much longer than 2 minutes.

● Drain the cooked fritters on paper towels and sprinkle with the sieved confectioner's sugar. Serve while hot.

Banana Cooked in Coconut Milk

SERVES 4

The addition of a little salt gives a refreshing and slightly unusual flavor. This dessert goes very well with ice cream.

2–3 small, slightly green
bananas

4 cups thin coconut milk

1 cup sugar

¼ tsp salt

● Slice the bananas lengthwise, then in half. Pour the coconut milk into a pan, add the sugar and salt. Bring to a boil, add the bananas, bring back to a boil for 2 minutes and then remove from the heat.

● Serve, hot or cold, with the coconut milk.

Bananas in a Rich Coconut Sauce

SERVES 4

1½ cups coconut milk

1½ Tbsp sugar

salt

6 large bananas, peeled and
sliced diagonally about ¾ in
thick

ice cream or whipped cream to
serve

● Heat the coconut milk in a small saucepan and add the sugar and salt. Bring to a boil. Lower the heat and simmer for 2 minutes.

● Remove from the heat and stir in the banana slices. Bring back to a boil for a few seconds to coat the bananas. Serve with ice cream or whipped cream.

Imitation Fruits

SERVES 6–8

This refined dessert was invented for the court and originally was served only at the Thai Royal Palace. Even today it is hardly common, because of the time and skill needed to fashion these perfect miniatures of fruits and vegetables. They are spectacular to serve to guests, but only attempt them on a day when you have plenty of time to spare!

2 cups dried mung beans	edible food colorings
2 cups water	1 cup water
1 cup thin coconut milk	2 Tbsp agar agar or gelatin
1 cup + 1 Tbsp sugar	

● Place the mung beans in a container with the water and steam until soft, about 15 minutes, then pound them into a fine paste with a mortar and pestle or in a blender. Put in a pan with the coconut milk and 1 cup of the sugar, and heat slowly, stirring constantly, until very thick—about 15 minutes. Remove and allow to cool before using.

● When cool, shape the paste into small fingertip-sized fruit and vegetable shapes—oranges, bananas—it's up to your imagination. Stick them on cocktail sticks and stand them in a sheet of polystyrene or styrofoam. Using a small paint brush and food colorings in appropriate shades, paint the fruits.

● Heat the water, 1 tablespoon of the sugar and the agar agar in a pan until dissolved. Cool slightly and then dip in the painted fruits. Place them back on the foam and allow to dry for 15 minutes; then dip once more in the liquid, spinning the fruit slowly after removing them so that the syrup coats evenly. Leave to harden on the foam, then remove the toothpicks and decorate the fruits with any (non-poisonous) leaves of your choice, trimmed down to a small size. Serve as a special dessert.

Lychee and Ginger Ice

SERVES 4

4 oz lychees in heavy syrup

½ oz gingerroot, peeled and grated

⅔ cup water

FOR THE GARNISH

fresh mint leaves

lychees

sponge ginger cookies (optional)

● Put the lychees in a blender or food processor together with the ginger and water, and process to a fine purée. Pour the mixture into a 9 inch square baking pan and put into the freezer for 3 hours.

● Break the iced mixture into chunks and process again until slushy. Return to the baking pan and freeze once more until solid.

● Allow the mixture to soften slightly (about 5 minutes) and scoop into four champagne glasses or rice bowls. Garnish with mint leaves, lychees, and a cookie, if desired.

Lychee Sorbet

SERVES 4

This is a really simple and refreshing sorbet, which is quick and easy to make.

1 lb fresh lychees or 4 oz can lychees

1 egg white

● Peel the lychees and pit them. Purée the flesh, adding some sugared water if necessary. Pour into a container and freeze until nearly set.

● Whip up the egg white. Mix this into the nearly set lychee mixture. Put back into the freezer until solid.

Lychee and Ginger Ice

Lychee Slap

SERVES 4

1 medium jar Chinese stem
  ginger, drained

4 oz can lychees

1 Tbsp ginger wine

● Insert a piece of the drained stem ginger into the center of each lychee.

● Mix the liquid from the stem ginger and the lychee syrup, and add the ginger wine. Pour the sauce over the stuffed lychees.

Sticky Rice with Mangoes

SERVES 4–6

A simple dessert but always successful. It works because of contrasts: in flavor between the sweetness of the coconut milk and the yellow Thai mango, and in texture between the rice and the mango.

2 cups sticky rice

3½ cups thin coconut milk

⅓ cup sugar

½ tsp salt

½ tsp cornstarch

2 ripe mangoes, peeled and sliced

● Soak the rice in water for 4 hours, rinse well three times in lukewarm water and drain very well. Line a strainer with cheesegauze, add the rice and place over a pan of boiling water—do not let the water touch the bottom of the rice. Cover and steam for about 30 minutes until fairly soft.

● Mix 3 cups of the coconut milk with the sugar and ¼ teaspoon of the salt. Stir in the rice and mix well.

● Mix the remaining ½ cup of coconut milk with the ¼ teaspoon salt and the cornstarch together in a small pan, bring to a boil, simmer for 2 minutes and cool.

● Place the sticky rice onto serving plates, spoon the cornstarch sauce over the top, and arrange the mango slices around the edges.

Mango and Banana Slices

SERVES 4

4 slices plain cake

⅓ cup sherry

4 Tbsp unsalted butter

1 ripe, but firm, mango peeled, pitted and sliced

¼ cup redcurrant jelly

3 bananas, sliced

3 Tbsp orange juice

● Divide the cake slices among four plates and sprinkle a spoonful of sherry over each portion.

● Melt half the butter and stir-fry the mango slices for 1–2 minutes, until they are hot. Add the redcurrant jelly and continue stir frying for a minute or so until the jelly melts and coats the mango. Divide the mango slices among the four plates, arranging them on top of the cake. Scrape all the juices from the pan over the mango.

● Melt the remaining butter and briskly stir fry the banana slices until hot. Sprinkle the orange juice over the banana, then stir for a few seconds to heat the juices. Spoon the bananas over the mango slices and serve at once.

Coconut Ice Cream

SERVES 4

1¼ cups thick coconut milk

1½ cups fresh cream

2 eggs

2 egg yolks

1 tsp vanilla extract

½ cup sugar

salt

FOR THE GARNISH

⅔ cup shredded coconut, dry-fried until golden-brown

sprigs of mint

● Heat the coconut milk and cream cook for 5 minutes without boiling over. Beat together the eggs, egg yolks, vanilla, sugar, and salt.

● Place a deep bowl in a saucepan with boiling water up to the halfway mark of the bowl. Pour in the egg mixture and beat in the warm coconut milk mixture, a little at a time. Stir until the mixture thickens enough to coat a spoon. Remove from the heat, stirring occasionally as it cools.

● Pour into a bowl when it is cool enough to be put into the freezer. Freeze for 1 hour. Scoop out into a blender or food processor and process until smooth. Pour back into the bowl and freeze until solid.

● Serve in scoops, garnished with shredded coconut and sprigs of mint.

Mango and Banana Slices

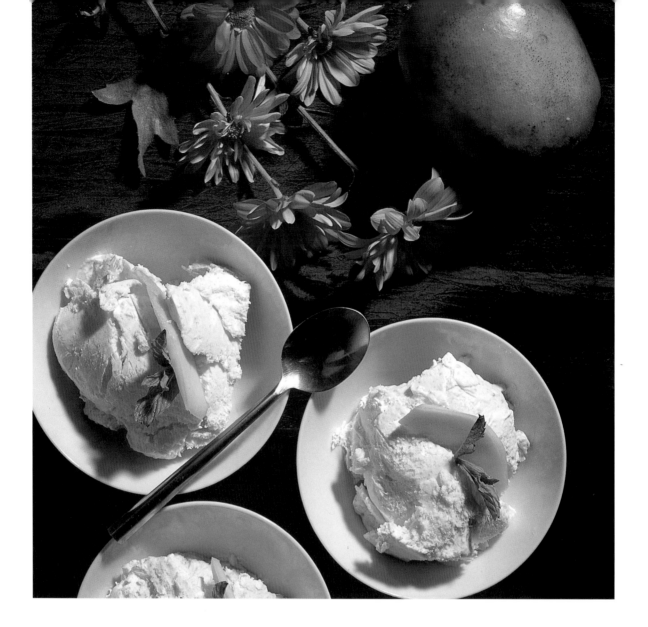

Mango Ice Cream

SERVES 4

4 ripe mangoes or 4 oz can
sliced mango

1 cup sugar or ½ cup if using
canned mango

1 Tbsp lemon juice

1 Tbsp gelatin, dissolved in
3 Tbsp water

1½ cups heavy cream, whipped
until stiff

FOR THE GARNISH

extra mango slices

sprigs of fresh mint

● Peel and cut the mangoes, discarding the pits. Place in a bowl and add the sugar, lemon juice, and dissolved gelatin. Mix thoroughly, making sure that the sugar is dissolved.

● Fold the whipped cream into the mango mixture. Spoon into a tray and put into the freezer until half-frozen. Put in a blender or food processor and process until smooth. Return to freezer and freeze until solid.

● Serve in scoops garnished with freshly sliced mango and sprigs of fresh mint.

Coconut Custard

SERVES 4

1 cup thick coconut cream

4 eggs, beaten

½ cup sugar

● Beat the coconut cream, eggs, and sugar together until the sugar dissolves and the mixture is thoroughly blended. Sieve the mixture through cheesegauze. The result should be perfectly smooth.

● Place a serving bowl on top of a wooden trivet in a wok and test it for firmness. Pour the mixture into the serving bowl. Pour some water into the wok and bring to a boil. Place the serving bowl on the wooden trivet and allow to steam until the mixture is firm, about 10–15 minutes.

● Alternatively, pour the mixture into four individual bowls and steam in a large bamboo steamer.

Coconut Custard in Young Pumpkin

SERVES 4 – 6

This is a special version of one of the best known and best loved Thai desserts. Although more usually served in a coconut shell, a hollowed pumpkin not only looks more attractive, but its flesh gives a pleasing contrast to the sweet custard.

1 small pumpkin	1½ cups palm sugar
9 duck or chicken eggs	2 cups thin coconut milk

● Slice off and remove the top of the pumpkin carefully and clean out the seeds thoroughly.

● Whisk the eggs, sugar, and coconut milk together in a bowl until frothy, and allow to stand for 10 minutes. Then, strain through muslin into the pumpkin.

● Steam for 30 minutes in a covered wok or steamer with the pumpkin lid steamed on the side: the custard is cooked when a skewer comes out clean.

● Cool overnight in the refrigerator. Replace the pumpkin lid before serving, then cut into wedges at the table.

Ginger Surprise

SERVES 4

1 oz gingerroot, crushed

1 cup sugar

1½ cups hot water

FOR THE FILLING

⅓ cup dried yellow mung beans, soaked in warm water for 30 minutes and drained

1½ Tbsp sugar

4 Tbsp sesame seeds

FOR THE DOUGH

2 cups glutinous rice flour or all-purpose flour

1 cup boiling water

● Make the ginger syrup by swirling the ginger and sugar constantly in a small saucepan over low heat, until the sugar browns. When it starts to smoke, stir in the hot water (be careful: you could give yourself a nasty burn with the spluttering) and allow to boil for about 3 minutes until the sugar is dissolved. Set aside in a cool place. Discard the ginger when cooled.

● Make the filling by steaming the mung beans over high heat for 20 minutes. Transfer to a blender or food processor, add the sugar and process to a fine paste. Put in the refrigerator for 20 minutes to firm up.

● Toast the sesame seeds by dry-frying in a wok for 2 minutes. Reserve 2 tablespoons for garnishing, put the remainder in a blender and process to a paste.

Combine with the mung bean paste and blend well. Roll 16 marble-sized balls of the mixture (1 teaspoon each). Set aside.

● Place the glutinous rice flour in a mixing bowl and quickly mix with the hot water to make a sticky dough. Cover and leave to stand for 5 minutes. Dust a work surface with flour and knead the dough for 3 minutes until soft and smooth. Divide into two equal parts. Roll each into a rope about 10 inches long and 1 inch in diameter. Cut each into 10 equal portions and roll each one into a ball. Cover with a damp cloth until ready to proceed.

● Flatten the dough balls, one at a time, into 2½ inch discs. Place a mung bean ball in the center, gather the edges around the pinch to seal. Roll the dumplings between the palms to form perfect balls.

● Divide each of the remaining four dough balls into four, cover and set aside.

● Bring a large pot of water to a boil. Boil the filled dumplings for 2 minutes over a moderate heat. Add the smaller dumplings and cook for a further 3 minutes or until they rise to the surface. Drain.

● Reheat the ginger syrup over low heat in a large saucepan. Add the dumplings and allow to simmer for 2 minutes. Set aside to cool.

● Serve four large dumplings and four small ones to each person in individual dessert cups or rice bowls. Sprinkle with the reserved toasted sesame seeds.

Fried Bananas

SERVES 4–6

If at all possible, buy small, fragrant bananas for this (and other) banana desserts.

3 cups rice flour

1 cup water

½ cup unsweetened grated coconut

3 Tbsp all-purpose flour

3 Tbsp sugar

2 Tbsp sesame seeds

2 tsp baking powder

1 tsp salt

approx 6 cups peanut or corn oil for deep-frying

1 lb small, slightly green bananas, quartered

● Mix together well in a bowl all the ingredients except the oil and bananas. Heat the oil in a wok or deep pan to about 350°F.

● Dip the banana pieces into the coconut batter and then deep-fry until brown but not dark, about 3 minutes. Turn over and cook for 2 more minutes. Take out with a slotted spoon and drain on paper towel. Serve immediately.

Almond Junket

SERVES 4

*This junket can be made from **agar-agar**, isinglass or gelatin. When chilled and served with a variety of fresh and canned fruit, it is a most refreshing dessert.*

⅓ oz *agar-agar* or isinglass (or
   1 oz gelatin powder)

4 Tbsp sugar

⅔ cup evaporated milk

2½ cups water

1 tsp almond extract

1 can cherries or mixed fruit
   salad with syrup to garnish

● Dissolve the *agar-agar* or isinglass and the sugar with water in two separate pans over gentle heat. (If you are using gelatin powder, just follow the instructons on the packets.)

● Add milk and almond essence and pour the mixture into a large serving bowl. Allow to cool for at least 30 minutes and then place in the refrigerator for 2–3 hours to set.

● To serve, cut the junket into small cubes and pour the canned fruit and syrup over it.

Sweet Blackened Jelly

SERVES 6–8

This unusual dessert must be one of the few dishes anywhere in the world that makes use of the outside of a mature coconut—something that, fortunately, is usually readily available in the West.

½ cup coconut hair (hairy brown coating from outside of coconuts)

6 cups water

3 cups rice flour

½ Tbsp tapioca flour

2½ cups palm sugar

2½ cups unsweetened grated coconut

¼ tsp salt

● Take the coconut hair and roast it in a 375°F oven for about 20 minutes until black, stirring occasionally, then chop well. Mix it with 1 cup of the water and then strain twice through cheesecloth.

● Put both the flours in a large bowl, mix well, then stir in the remaining water and the sugar. Stir in the cup of black water mixture and strain again through cheesecloth.

● Place the liquid in a stainless steel pan and slowly bring to a boil, stirring constantly, for about 20 minutes, until very thick—don't burn the bottom. When thick, pour into ungreased shallow cake pans and leave to cool for 1 hour. Refrigerate for at least 1 hour or overnight.

● To remove the jelly, warm the pans by dipping them in warm water and then inverting onto a plate. Cut the jelly into bite-sized pieces. Mix the coconut with the salt and sprinkle over the top.

Jackfruit Seeds

SERVES 6–8

These candies are one of a range of Thai sweetmeats made with egg yolks. Kanoon, or jackfruit, is not used in the recipe—they are only called after the fruit because of the similar shape.

2 cups dried yellow mung beans	5 cups water
5 cups sugar	10 egg yolks, duck if possible, whisked lightly
4 cups thin coconut milk	

● Soak the mung beans in water for 1 hour, then drain and steam them for 20 minutes or until soft. Mash or purée in a food processor.

● Put the beans in a pan with 2 cups of the sugar and the coconut milk. Bring to a boil and then simmer, stirring, until reduced to a paste, about 15 minutes—be careful not to burn the mixture. Remove from the heat and leave to cool.

● Meanwhile, make the syrup. Boil the water with the remaining sugar until reduced by half. Remove 1 cup of the syrup and put to one side. Keep the remaining syrup simmering slowly.

● Take pieces of the bean paste and shape them into small fingertip-sized ovals. Cook them in batches of eight to ten at a time. Dip first into the egg yolk and then into the pan of syrup. Wait until they float to the top, then remove with a slotted spoon and drain on paper towel. Place them in the reserved cup of syrup for 30 minutes, remove, set aside and allow to dry for 5 minutes.

● Serve immediately or cover and refrigerate; serve at room temperature.

Rolled Sesame Slices

SERVES 4

These uncooked cookies are rolled up like a jelly roll, then cut across into slices; this is easiest to do if you use a hot sharp knife.

⅓ cup white sesame seeds	about ⅓ cup light brown sugar
⅓ cup black sesame seeds	8 Tbsp light corn syrup

● Heat the white and black sesame seeds in separate dry heavy skillets until they just begin to pop.

● Gently heat the sugar in the corn syrup, stirring until the sugar has dissolved. Mix half with the white sesame seeds and half with the black sesame seeds.

● Spread each mixture out on a sheet of waxed paper. Put another sheet of waxed paper on each and roll out. Remove the top sheets of waxed paper and invert the black sesame seed mixture onto the white sesame seed mixture.

● Remove the waxed paper now on top. Roll up the sesame seed mixtures firmly, enclosing the black in the white and using the underneath sheet of paper to help you. Leave until cold, then cut into slices.

Cookie Bows

These crisp cookies are very moreish, but if you can resist eating them all soon after they are made, they will keep in an airtight container for several days.

1 cup all-purpose flour	vegetable oil for deep-frying
1½ Tbsp superfine sugar	about ⅓ cup clear honey
3 Tbsp rice wine or dry sherry	chopped pine nuts for coating

● Stir together the flour and sugar, and slowly pour in the rice wine or dry sherry to make a smooth dough; add a little water if necessary. Knead lightly on a floured surface, then roll out lightly to a thin rectangle. Cut into 2 x 1 inch pieces. Cut a lengthwise slit about 1 inch long in the center of each piece. Pull one end of each piece through the slit so the piece resembles a small bow shape.

● Heat the oil in a deep-fat fryer to 330°F. Add the bows and fry for 4–5 minutes until rich golden brown. Remove and drain briefly on a pad of paper towels.

● Meanwhile, slowly heat the honey (dilute with a little water if the honey is too thick). Dip the bows in the honey to coat, then sprinkle with chopped pine nuts.

Spiced Honey Cakes

SERVES 4

In Korea, there are special molds for shaping these deep-fried cakes. To get the juice from fresh ginger, squeeze a piece of peeled fresh ginger in a taint-free garlic press.

1 cup self-rising flour

1 tsp ground cinnamon

grated zest of ½ lemon

2 Tbsp rice wine or dry sherry

2 Tbsp clear honey

1 tsp fresh ginger juice

2 Ybsp sesame oil

vegetable oil for deep-frying

sesame seeds for coating

● Sift the flour and cinnamon into a bowl. Stir in the lemon zest, then add the rice wine or sherry, honey, ginger juice and sesame oil and enough water to make a smooth dough.

● Knead the dough, then roll out on a lightly floured surface to about ¼ inch. Using a 1½ inch cookie cutter, cut into rounds.

● Heat the vegetable oil in a deep-fat fryer. Add the cakes in batches so they are not crowded, and fry until they rise to the surface and are light golden brown, about 3–5 minutes.

● Transfer to paper towels to drain. Sprinkle with sesame seeds.

Southern Flat Breads

MAKES 7–8

These are derived from Thailand's Indian connections, as the name suggests. Bread is uncharacteristic of Thai cooking, and roti are used mainly in this way, as a dessert snack.

1½ cups all-purpose flour

¼ cup water

1 Tbsp butter, softened

1 egg

¼ tsp salt

1 cup peanut or corn oil for frying

● Mix all the ingredients except the oil together well in a bowl; if the mixture is too wet to shape, add a little more flour. Shape the dough in bite-sized balls and flatten them into 4 inch circles by throwing them onto a lightly floured table surface—be careful to throw them quite horizontal.

● Heat enough oil to just cover the bottom of a skillet over medium heat. Place the flattened dough balls in the pan and brown lightly, about 3–4 minutes, on each side. Drain on paper towel and repeat.

● Three delicious ways of serving the flat breads are: to place an egg on top of each browned roti, flipping it over to cook the egg and rolling it up to eat (perhaps with coffee); to sprinkle them with sugar and condensed milk; or to spread them with butter.

Spiced Honey Cakes

Red Bean Paste Pancakes

SERVES 4

2 cups all-purpose flour

½ cup boiling water

1 egg

3 Tbsp oil

4–5 Tbsp sweetened red bean paste or chestnut purée

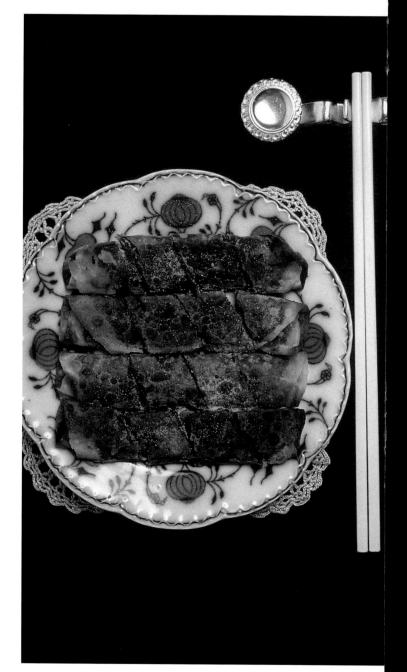

● Sift the flour into a mixing bowl and very gently pour in the boiling water. Add about 1 teaspoon oil and the beaten egg.

● Knead the mixture into a firm dough and then divide it into two equal portions. Roll out each portion into a long "sausage" on a lightly floured surface and cut it into four to six pieces. Using the palm of your hand, press each piece into a flat pancake.

● On a lightly floured surface, flatten each pancake into a 6 inch circle with a rolling pin and roll gently.

● Place an ungreased skillet on a high heat. When hot, reduce the heat to low and place one pancake at a time in the pan. Turn it over when little brown spots appear on the underside. Remove and keep under a damp cloth until you have finished making the rest of the pancakes.

● Spread about 2 tablespoons red bean paste or chestnut purée over about 80 percent of the pancake surface and roll it over three or four times to form a flattened roll.

● Heat the oil in a skillet and shallow-fry the pancakes until golden-brown, turning over once.

● Cut each pancake into three or four pieces and serve hot or cold.

Barley Tea

MAKES 3¾ CUPS

Poricha is ubiquitous throughout Korea. In winter it is served hot, in summer it is served cold, sweetened with honey or sugar. Poricha has a distinctive, smoky taste, and is quite free of caffeine. Roast barley is available from Korean and Japanese food shops.

2 Tbsp roast barley

3¾ cups water

● Put the roast barley and water into a saucepan and bring to a boil. Lower the heat and simmer the tea until it is as strong as you like it. Strain.

Ginseng Tea

MAKES 3¾ PINTS

Korean ginseng is believed to be the best, and in Korea (and elsewhere) ginseng is purported to cure all manner of ills, from insomnia to impotence. A favorite way of taking ginseng is in the form of a tea.

3 slices of red ginseng

½ in piece of fresh ginger, sliced

3 jujubes (Chinese dates), cut into pieces

● Put all the ingredients into a saucepan. Add 3¾ cups water and bring to a boil. Lower the heat, cover and simmer for 1 hour.

● Strain into cups. Add pieces of jujube, ginseng, and ginger to each cup if liked.

Rice Tea

MAKES 3¾ CUPS

When rice is cooked in the traditional way in large pots (although now electric rice cookers are often used) some grain invariably sticks to the bottom of the pot and burns. After all the non-burned rice is served, hot water is poured into the pot and boiled. This is then served as a digestive rice tea at the end of the meal. There are many versions of rice tea, and one can be made without first cooking and burning a pot of rice.

2 Tbsp uncooked long-grain rice

3¾ cups boiling water

● Put the rice into a small heavy skillet and cook over a medium-low heat, stirring, until the rice becomes flecked with dark patches and has a rich nutty aroma.

● Tip the rice into a saucepan, and add the boiling water. Return to a boil, then simmer for 1½ minutes. Cover and remove from the heat. Leave for 5 minutes, then strain and serve the tea while still hot.

Ginger Tea

MAKES 4 ½ CUPS

In addition to being a digestive, Saenggangcha is meant to be good for coughs and colds.

3 1 inch pieces of fresh ginger, coarsely chopped

strip of orange peel

4–5 tsp clear honey

ground cinnamon for sprinkling

pine nuts for decorating

● Put the ginger, orange peel and honey in a saucepan and add 4½ cups water. Bring to a boil, then simmer slowly for 15–20 minutes.

● Strain the tea and sprinkle a little cinnamon on top. Serve hot or cold with a few pine nuts floating on the surface.

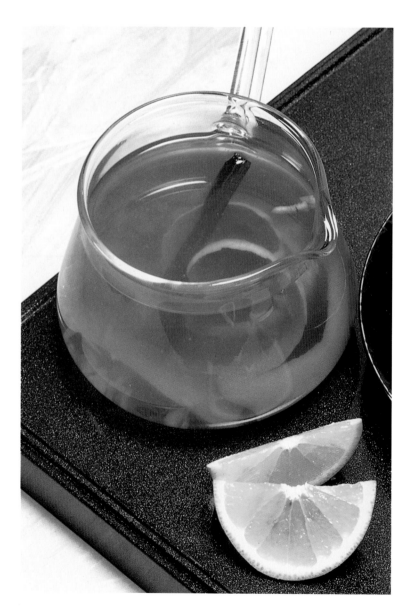

Glossary of Ingredients

A clear, concise guide to the ingredients used in the recipes in this
book, explaining how they are prepared and used. Many are illustrated.
These ingredients can be found not only in specialist stores and
delicatessens but also in many supermarkets. Wherever appropriate,
however, more easily obtainable alternatives are suggested.

Rice

RICE AND NOODLES

RICE Korean rice is a medium- to short-grain variety that becomes sticky when cooked. If you cannot find Korean rice, use Japanese rice instead.

NOODLES One of the mainstays of the Asian diet, noodles were the inspiration for spaghetti. They are used extensively throughout the area. Dried noodles should be kept in an airtight container, where they will last for several months. They are usually cooked by boiling in salted water, like pasta. *See also* CELLOPHANE NOODLES' BUCKWHEAT NOODLES.

RICE STICK NOODLES These vary in thickness and shape. They are made from rice flour, starch, and water.

BANH PHO The short, flat, white Vietnamese rice stick noodles are about ⅛ inch wide. They cook in minutes in boiling water or soup, and they should not be overdone. They are used in soup-noodle dishes, especially the Vietnamese soup known as *pho*.

BANH TRANG The Vietnamese equivalent of ravioli skins, *banh trang* is round, semi-transparent, thin, hard and dry rice paper. It is used as the wrapping of Vietnamese spring rolls and grilled meats, with salad and herbs. It is made from a dough of finely ground rice, water, and salt, with tapioca (cassava) flour as the binding agent. The dough is passed through rollers and then cut into circles 7–14 inches in diameter. These

are put on bamboo mats to dry in the sun. Once dry they will keep almost indefinitely. To use, they must be moistened by covering with a damp cloth until soft or by dipping quickly into warm water. To get a crisp, golden-brown color, the wrappers can be brushed lightly with a sugar-water solution before frying.

RICE VERMICELLI A fine, extruded, creamy-colored noodle, made from a dough of finely ground rice and water. It cooks almost instantly, needing only to be dipped in very hot water and drained thoroughly. Rice vermicelli can be stir-fried and served as soft noodles. It should be softened first and drained before stir-frying. To deep-fry, the dried noodles are added directly to the oil.

BEAN THREAD NOODLES or VERMICELLI *see* CELLOPHANE NOODLES

CELLOPHANE NOODLES These noodles are also known as bean-thread noodles, glass noodles, or transparent noodles. They are made from ground mung beans and are clear white, fine, dried strands that are so tough they are almost impossible to cut. They are sold in bundles and need to be soaked for 10–15 minutes before cooking. After cooking, cellophane noodles become soft, slippery, and gelatinous. In Szechwan and neighboring Tibet they are first softened in water and then stir-fried with vegetables. In Indonesia, Malaysia, and Singapore, the boiled noodles are added to sweet drinks and desserts, together with palm sugar, syrup, coconut milk, and diced vegetables such as yam or sweet potato or sweet corn kernels.

BUCKWHEAT NOODLES Known in Korea as *son myon*. These are thin dried noodles. Japanese *soba* noodles are also made from buckwheat, but they are fatter. Japanese *somen* noodles or Italian vermicelli or capellini are nearer in size to Korean buckwheat noodles, but they are made from wheat flour.

Cellophane Noodles

SOBA These noodles, made from buckwheat and all-purpose flour, are very nutritious, rich in protein and lecithin. Soba is sold fresh, parboiled, or dried, and it is used in hot noodle soups or as a cold dish.

SON MYON see BUCKWHEAT NOODLES

SOMEN Made from wheat flour and water, these noodles are sold dried. Take care when you handle them, because they are very fragile. They are often used in cold summer dishes as well as in hot noodle soups.

UDON Mainly eaten in Japan and Korea, these noodles are made from wheat flour and water. They come in various thicknesses, both round and flat, and are suitable for hot noodle soups, cold dishes, and stir-fries.

EGG NOODLES Made from wheat flour, egg, and water, these are eaten widely over southeast Asia in both soups and stir-fried dishes. They generally come in thin or medium thicknesses. Fresh and steamed egg noodles should be eaten within two or three days. Dried noodles can be kept almost indefinitely as an airtight container.

RAMEN Fresh egg noodles or fresh Japanese ramen noodles are best in hot noodle soups.

FRUIT AND NUTS

CANDLE NUT Round candle nuts are the fruit of the candleberry tree. They are used, crushed or ground, as thickening agents. Macadamia nuts can be used as a substitute.

WATER CHESTNUTS The water chestnut is actually a bulb, very similar in shape to the chestnut but unrelated. Water chestnuts have a crunchy texture and are used in Chinese dishes. Peeled, white water chestnuts are available in cans.

COCONUT MILK There are a number of excellent brands of canned coconut milk available, but it should be remembered that it will keep for only a few hours at room temperature or two days in a refrigerator. If there is a great deal left over, it should be frozen. Desiccated coconut can be soaked in hot water or milk, and then squeezed through cheesecloth. The first squeeze is very rich and tends to curdle during cooking. To avoid this, continual stirring is recommended.

POMELO This large Chinese fruit resembles a grapefruit. It tapers slightly at the stem end and has a thick, sweet, slightly rough-textured skin and a dry, semi-sweet flesh. Like many other fruits, it is sometimes eaten in southeast Asia with salt.

SOURED PLUMS (umeboshi) Green plums are salted with red shiso leaves to form a traditional Japanese preserved food. They taste quite sour, so a little goes a long way.

VEGETABLES

ABURA-AGE see BEAN CURD SHEET

BEAN CURD (tofu) This thick, custard-like ingredient is made from dried soybeans, soaked, puréed, and boiled with water. The resulting milky liquid is strained and then mixed with a coagulant or natural solidifier, which causes it to form curds. Fresh bean curd is inexpensive and easily available. Although it is bland, it absorbs the flavors in which it is cooked. It is available in three textures—soft, medium, and firm—and is best eaten on the day it is bought. It is served on its own after being sautéed, deep-fried, or braised, and it is added soups, casseroles, and braised dishes.

BEAN CURD SHEET Known as *abura-age* in Japan. Deep-fried thin bean curd, usually sliced and used as a garnish, or slit to make a pocket and stuffed with rice. The bean curd sheet can be frozen, but does not keep longer than 48 hours in the refrigerator. Do not confuse bean curd sheet with dried bean curd.

GOBO This is a narrow, long, edible root akin to burdock. When using fresh, scrape with a knife and soak in vinegared water to prevent discoloration. It is full of fiber and used in Japanese cooking.

KOYA DOFU Japanese freeze-dried bean curd, which will keep for up to 6 months in its dried form. To prepare for use, soak in water until the bean curd has swollen and become spongy.

BEAN SPROUTS Sprouted mung beans are eaten raw or steamed, and used in stir-fries, soups, and salads.

Bean Curd (tofu)

SCALLIONS A much wider variety of shape and size of scallion is available throughout the East than in the West. Use the plumpest you can find.

BAMBOO SHOOTS Sold in cans, bamboo shoots should be eaten as soon as possible after the can has been opened. They will, however, last for up to 6 days in a refrigerator if the water in which they are stored is changed every day. Cooked dried bamboo shoots, *shinachiku*, originated in China but are now frequently used as a garnish for ramen dishes in Japan.

DAIKON *see* WHITE RADISH

MOOLI *see* WHITE RADISH

WHITE RADISH Daikon is a long, white radish, which is also known as mooli in the West. It is eaten raw, grated and added to stir-fries, pickled, or cooked in stews.

MUSTARD GREENS Mustard greens are used for Chinese dishes. Spinach can be used as a substitute.

BLACK BEANS When black beans are listed in ingredients, the fermented black bean is meant—that is, the original *shih* or darkened, salted soybeans of China. Dried soybeans are cooked, salted, and fermented until they become almost black and soft. They can be kept almost indefinitely in airtight jars. They should be washed and dried before use and may be cooked whole, finely chopped, or mashed.

FERMENTED SOYBEANS (natto) The end produce of fermenting soybeans, this is a sticky substance and has a smell that many people find off-putting. It is high in fiber and protein and is used in Japanese dishes.

Chinese Mushrooms

CHINESE MUSHROOMS These are black or brown dried mushrooms. Long ago the Chinese discovered that drying mushrooms intensifies the flavor. They should be soaked in water for about 20 minutes, then squeezed to get rid of the salt. The stalks should be cut off, because they are too tough to eat.

ENOKI or ENOKITAKI MUSHROOMS These mushrooms are slender, creamy in color, with tiny caps. They grow from a dense set of roots, which must be cut off before use. They are used in both Japanese and Chinese dishes, and have a sweet, almost fruity flavor.

NAMEKO MUSHROOMS The small mushrooms, with light brown caps, have a slippery outer coating.

SHIITAKE MUSHROOMS Dried shiitake mushrooms are widely used in Asian cookery. They have a characteristic, smoky smell. When bought dried, they should be soaked in water for at least 30 minutes before use. The water can be reserved for later use in *dashi* stock.

SHIMEJI MUSHROOMS These mushrooms grow in short stumpy clusters from a simple root. The stalks are creamy at the base, gradually becoming grayish-brown toward the cap. They have a mild, subtle flavor and are a favorite ingredient in Japanese cooking. Cut off the root before use.

STRAW MUSHROOMS The distinctly earthy taste derives from the paddy-straw on which these mushrooms are grown. They are available in cans. They are globe shaped, about the size of a quail's egg, and buff-colored, growing gray-black as they become older. They have no stems, but a cross-section reveals an internal stem.

WOOD EAR Known also as black fungus, cloud ear and tree ear mushroom. This type of dried mushroom is valued for its subtle, delicate flavor, and slightly crunchy "bite." When soaked, tree ear expands to five times its dried size.

Wood Ear

BLACK FUNGUS *see* WOOD EAR

TREE EAR *see* WOOD EAR

HERBS AND SPICES

CHINESE STEM GINGER Probably better known as ginger preserve, this is traditionally preserved with cucumber, fruits, and spices. It is used as a relish and in sweet and sour sauces.

GALANGAL (ka) A member of the ginger family and in many countries used as a substitute for ginger. It has a hot, peppery taste and is used mainly as a flavoring. In Thailand, greater galangal is ground with chiles and other herbs and spices to make a refreshing drink. Lesser galangal is eaten as vegetable, both raw and cooked. In Indonesia, lesser galangal is used as a spice. *See also* KRACHAI.

KRACHAI There is no generally accepted English word for this small, yellow-brown rhizome, which is related to ginger and galangal. It is sometimes called lesser galangal or finger root.

GINGER ROOT Ginger is a popular addition to many Asian dishes. Choose plump fresh ginger so that there is a high proportion of flesh to skin, and make sure it feels firm and has a shiny skin.

WASABI Sometimes translated as "horseradish," wasabi is ground from the Japanese riverside plant, *Wasabia japonica*. Like mustard, wasabi can be bought ready made or in powder form, which is then mixed with a little water. Powdered wasabi is generally better than the ready-made kind, which loses its "bite" fairly quickly.

CUMIN Although it is Mediterranean in origin, it is widely used in Asian cuisine. It is both pungent and aromatic. The seeds should be roasted in a dry pan or in a very hot oven before using, either whole or ground.

The temperature should be high enough to make them pop.

TURMERIC A native of southeast Asia, turmeric belongs to the same family as ginger and galangal. It has a bright orange-yellow flesh, with a strong, earthy smell and a slightly bitter taste. The flesh is responsible for the yellow color associated with curry.

STAR ANISE The seedpod of one of the magnolia species, the tan-colored, eight-pointed pods resemble stars. It has a pronounced licorice flavor, and the ground spice is one of the essential ingredients in the Chinese five-spice powder. In Vietnam it is used primarily in simmered dishes and for making stock.

GROUND CORIANDER One of the essential ingredients in curry powder, it is made from the seed spice and it is best to buy the spice whole and grind it when needed. To get the best out of coriander seeds, it is advisable to toast them first in an oven and then grind them finely.

SESAME SEEDS These seeds are widely used in Japanese, Chinese, and Korean cooking. Small quantities of sesame seed are roasted in a heavy, dry pan, then lightly crushed with salt before being added to sauces, marinades, dips and salads, and to braised dishes. Black sesame seeds have a more pronounced, and slightly more bitter taste than white sesame seeds.

FIVE-SPICE POWDER This aromatic Chinese spice powder is made according to an ancient formula using three native spices—star anise, cassia bark, and Szechwan peppercorns—with the seeds of wild fennel and cloves from the nearby Moluccas or Spice Islands. The five spices in their whole form can be used as an Asian bouquet garni, tied up in a small cheesecloth bag and put into stews and the like and retrieved before serving. Five-spice powder can also be made into a dip by adding five-spice powder to heated salt.

You can make your own five-spice powder by placing 40 Szechwan peppercorns, 2 cinnamon sticks (2 inches long), 1½ teaspoons fennel seeds, 12 whole cloves and 2 whole star anise in a mortar and spice grinder and grind to a fine powder. This should produce about 1 ounce of powder. Store in a tightly closed jar.

SEVEN-FLAVORS CHILI POWDER (shichimi) A Japanese chili powder, ground and blended with a mixture of red chile pepper, black pepper, sesame seeds, poppy seeds, *nori*, hemp seeds, and *sansho* pepper. It is used as a seasoning over udon or soba noodle soup and other Japanese dishes.

PAPRIKA Also known as capsicum or bell peppers, paprika can be used as both a vegetable and a spice.

Sesame Seeds

CHILE There are many different varieties of chile, and each variety has its own flavor and hotness. Size is not an infalliable guide to hotness, but, in general, the larger chile, the less intense the heat. Chopping a chile increases the amount of "fire" in a dish, as does including the seeds. Chiles add flavor as well as hotness, and for a milder dish, instead of reducing the number of chiles, leave the chiles whole if possible and discard the seeds. In Korean cooking, chiles are painstakingly cut into fine shreds to use as a garnish.
NOTE: Chiles should always be handled carefully because they contain a substance that can irritate the skin. If you have a cut, bruise, or scratch on your hands or if your skin is sensitive, wear thin rubber gloves when you are preparing chiles.

CHILI POWDER The chili powder from Korea is among the best in the world. It is relatively mild, a glowing carmine color, and coarsely pounded. It tastes somewhat like a cross between paprika and cayenne pepper (which can be used as a substitute if necessary). It is added to dishes in generous quantities, imparting not only flavoring and adding "heat," but giving a characteristic vibrant color.

GROUND CHILES Made from dried pods, which are also used whole, broken or desiccated, the pods are best dried by roasting in a hot oven or in a dry pan. They are then ground to a coarse powder, which can be added to ground rice. This mixture is used as a strongly flavored thickener or coating for fried foods. It may also be sprinkled over foods as a condiment.

CILANTRO (Chinese parsley) These leaves are used extensively in southeast Asian cooking, although they are hardly used in Japan. The flavor is fresh, strong, and earthy.

CORIANDER ROOTS In Thai cooking, the roots are ground together with the stems for curry pastes and sauces. The leaves, cilantro, are used in salads and as a garnish.

KAFFIR LIME LEAVES These leaves are widely used as a flavoring in Thai cuisine and in some Malaysian and Indonesian dishes. They are sold fresh or dried.

LEMON GRASS Also known as citronella, this herb is named for its distinctive lemon flavor. It is best used fresh, but can be kept, loosely wrapped, in the refrigerator for about 10 days. To store, the bulb end should be rinsed and dried, then finely sliced or chopped. When ready for use, it should be slit open lengthwise to release the flavor.

SZECHWAN PEPPERCORNS The aromatic, small, red-brown seeds from the prickly ash tree are known as *fagara*. The whole "peppercorns" can be kept for years without loss of flavor if they are sealed in a tightly sealed jar away from light, heat, and moisture. In China, they are mixed into heated fine salt to produce pepper-salt, a fragrant, salty dip for grilled and fried foods and often used in marinades.

PALM SUGAR Made from the sap of the coconut palm, palm sugar is used throughout southeast Asia. It is light brown in color and has got a distinguishing sweet toffee smell.

SUGAR CANE This is reasonably easy to obtain from large greengrocers. It is cultivated exclusively for its sweet sap that is made into sugar. The sugar cane bought for cooking consists of the stem, the leaves being chopped off in the cane field. The cane should be carefully peeled with a strong, sharp knife.

SEAFOOD

BONITO FLAKES (katuso-bushi) Bonito is a member of the tuna family. When dried and grated into flakes, it is an essential ingredient in Japanese cuisine. It is mainly used for making *dashi* stock, but is also an ingredient in other dishes and as a garnish.

DRIED JELLYFISH Although it has little taste, it is valued for its crunchy texture. It is the salted and sun-dried skin of the mantle of the jellyfish. It should be soaked in warm water for several hours and does not require cooking, which only serves to toughen it. It is usually shredded finely and marinated in vinegar to be served in a salad. Add a little sesame oil to transform it into a delicious and crunchy salad.

DRIED SHRIMP These salty, hard, whole shrimps are used to add extra flavor. They are sometimes soaked in water before use. Dried shrimps used in Chinese and Thai recipes are very different from those sold for inclusion in Japanese cooking.

KELP Known as *tasima* in Korea; *kombu* or *konbu* in Japan. One of the

Kelp

best sources of iodine, calcium, and other valuable minerals, it resembles large, long leaves. It is available either folded or cut into small pieces. Care should be taken not to over-boil kelp, as it very quickly becomes bitter. To prepare for cooking, wipe the kelp with a damp cloth but do not rinse, because this will wash away many of the nutrients.

DRIED LAVER Known as *nori* in Japan; *kim* in Korea. The most widely used seaweed in Japanese cooking. It is vitamin- and mineral-packed, and there are many varieties and qualities, from dark green to purplish-black. Price is usually a good guide to quality. It is sold in paper-thin sheets. Before use, it is cooked quickly under a broiler or over a gas flame until it becomes crisp. It may then be eaten as it is or crumbled over noodle or rice dishes. Some pre-cooked laver is available in the West, so check which kind you have bought before use.

KOMBU or KONBU *see* KELP

NORI *see* DRIED LAVER

TASIMA *see* KELP

WAKAME This type of dried seaweed is widely used in Japanese and Korean soups and stews, and in salads, when it is dressed with a vinegar dressing. It should never be cooked for long and can, in fact, be used after simply being dipped into boiling water. When it is bought dried, it should be soaked in cold water before being used in any recipe. It is thinner than kelp (*konbu*).

SALTFISH First imported from Newfoundland in Canada as a survival food for British colonies, saltfish somehow found its way to Vietnam, where it has become something of a delicacy.

Wakame

OILS/VINEGARS/PICKLES

CHILE OIL The red-colored oil is made from ground chiles. It is used for cooking, as a spice, and can be added to some dips.

SESAME OIL This is used as a flavoring as well as for cooking in many Asian cuisines. In Korea, the sesame oil is made from toasted sesame seeds, so has an amber color and a nutty, sesame flavor. As it therefore provides both a distinctive flavor and color, pale sesame oil does not result in authentic-looking and -tasting dishes. Store sesame oil in a cool, dark place.

SU *see* RICE VINEGAR

RICE WINE This is a light, slightly sweet wine used in many Asian dishes. Use dry sherry if it is not available. *See also* SAKE.

MIRIN Japanese cooking wine, a mixture of a variant of *sake* with sugar. It contains only a trace of alcohol but imparts a distinctive sweet flavor to any dish in which it is used.

SAKE Japanese rice wine, which is widely available outside Japan, is made by introducing a yeast mould to steamed rice. It is used only sparingly in Japanese cooking. If you cannot get genuine *sake*, use dry sherry instead.

RICE VINEGAR Known as *su* in Japan. Made from naturally fermented rice, clear *su* is widely available and suitable for *sushi* rice. Brown *su*, which is the unrefined basis for white *su*, can be used in any recipe when the color of the vinegar is not important to the appearance of the finished dish. The Japanese rice vinegar is lighter and milder than Chinese versions. White wine vinegar can be used instead; alternatively, dilute three parts white distilled vinegar with one part water; if the recipe does not include sugar, add a small pinch.

Sesame Oil

Rice Vinegar

BLACK VINEGAR This dark, mild, almost sweet vinegar has only one equivalent: balsamic vinegar. It is usually made from glutionous rice or sorghum, which gives it its distinctive taste. The better varieties have a range of flavors, from smoky to wine-yeasty. In central China and parts of the north, black vinegar is used like tomato ketchup and is added to almost every dish.

KIMCHI The spicy pickle is a vital part of almost every Korean meal, including breakfast. It is also added to soups, stews, stir-fries, and pancakes. Although you can make your own, bottles of ready-made *kimchi* are available. Among the more than 160 types that are produced, there are white radish, cucumber, stuffed cucumber, garlic, Chinese turnip, and onion *kimchi*.

RED PICKLED GINGER (beni-shouga) Slivered ginger is pickled with a little sugar and vinegar and used as a garnish in Japanese dishes.

MYOGA This relation of the ginger plant is eaten, raw, pickled or as a garnish, in Japanese dishes.

Soybean Paste

PASTES/SAUCES/STOCKS

CHILE BEAN PASTE (toban djan) This thick, dark reddish sauce, made from chile, soy beans, and soy sauce, is used for spicing up Chinese dishes. Chile bean sauce or paste is available from large supermarkets. *See also* KOCHUJANG.

DRIED SHRIMP PASTE (belacan) This fermented shrimp paste has a very characteristic, strong smell. Before it is used, the paste has to be fried.

SOYBEAN PASTE Soybean paste is made from fermented soybean cakes, pepper, and salt. The thick, brown paste has a pungent, characteristic flavor. Japanese *miso* can be used instead.

FERMENTED SOYBEAN PASTE Known as *twoenjang* in Korea.

OYSTER SAUCE One of the most popular sauces in southeast Asia, oyster sauce is made from dried oysters. It is thick and richly flavored. The cheaper brands tend to be more salty. The original sauce was thinner and contained fragments of dried, fermented oysters. Many people use it as a superior version of soy sauce, but Asian cooks use it as an accompaniment for stir-fried vegetables and to flavor and color braised and stir-fried dishes.

BLACK BEAN SAUCE Black beans are salted and fermented with spices to produce the sauce. It has a strong salty taste, and is used widely in Asian cooking.

CHA SIU SAUCE This is the marinade sauce used for making Chinese barbecue pork. It is a blend of many ingredients, including Chinese five-spice powder, honey, sugar, soy sauce, rice wine, and garlic.

SOY SAUCE Known as *kanjang* in Korea. This is an essential flavoring and seasoning in many Asian dishes. Light, medium, and dark soy sauces are available; light versions tend to be the thinnest and most salty. The Japanese version (medium) of this combination of fermented soy beans, wheat and salt is lighter and sweeter than the Chinese equivalent. Japanese brands such as Kikkoman are now widely available in the West.

CHILE SAUCE (sambal celek) This Indonesian chil- paste is made from crushed red chiles. It is used for cooking as well as a condiment.

YELLOW BEAN SAUCE Made according to the ancient recipe for *jiang* or pickled yellow soybeans in a salty liquid. It is normally bought in cans and jars, but if bought in a can it is best transferred to a jar in which it can be stored in a refrigerator.

YAKISOBA SAUCE A dark brown sauce, this is used in Japanese stir-fried noodle dishes. Japanese brown sauce is a good substitute, or blend your own *yakisoba* sauce.

FISH SAUCE Known as *nam plaa* in Thailand; *nuoc mam* in Vietnam. This powerfully flavored, pungent seasoning sauce is used extensively in southeast Asia, especially Burma, Cambodia, Thailand, and Vietnam. It is made by layering fish and salt into large barrels and allowing the fish to ferment for three or more months before the accumulated liquid is siphoned off, filtered, and bottled. It is made into different dipping sauces by adding chiles, ground, roast peanuts, sugar, and other ingredients. It is something of an acquired taste, and soy sauce can be used instead. As an alternative, use Maggi liquid seasoning.

HOISIN SAUCE This reddish-brown sauce is best used as a condiment for roast pork and poultry. It is made from fermented soybean paste, sugar, garlic, and spices (usually five-spice). Hoisin sauce should not be confused with Chinese barbecue sauce, *sha cha jiang*.

MISO A fermented, protein-rich soybean paste used in Japanese cooking. The cooked soybeans are fermented with a type of yeast known as *koji*. *Miso* is unique for Japanese cooking, in which it is used widely both as a flavoring and as the basis for many dressings. It will keep for several months in the refrigerator. White *miso* is made from a rice-based yeast, and it is commonly used in soups; red *miso* is made from a barley yeast and is used as a general-purpose flavoring and for dishes requiring a rich flavor.

KANJANG *see* SOY SAUCE.

KOCHUJANG This is the Korean version of chile bean paste. It is an essential seasoning and is used as a relish and as a spice. It is added to meats that are to be stir-fired, stews, and dips and is served in small bowls as a sweet, spicy, hot relish. Every Korean household has a tall earthenware jar of thick, red *kochujang*—its preparation is lengthy and elaborate, using glutinous rice powder or barley mixed with malt, which is then cooked slowly to a smooth, thick paste. This is mixed with fermented chili powder, soybean powder, and salt. If you cannot obtain Korean *kochujang*, use Chinese chile bean paste, which is widely available in the West.

NUOC MAM *see* FISH SAUCE

NAM PLAA *see* FISH SAUCE

DASHI A stock, used in Japanese cooking, made from dried *bonito* flakes (*katsuo-bushi*) or dried kelp (*konbu*) or a mixture of the two, depending on the flavor desired. Premier *dashi* stock is used in Japanese consommé, *chawan mushi*, and *miso* soup; normal *dashi* is suitable for simmered dishes and noodles or for use as a supplement to premier *dashi*. Freeze-dried *dashi* stock granules are available.

Soy Sauce

Miso

Index